Before the Luddites

00100241

Before the Luddites

Custom, community and machinery in the English woollen industry, 1776–1809

ADRIAN RANDALL

Senior Lecturer in Social History
Department of Economic and Social History, The University of Birmingham

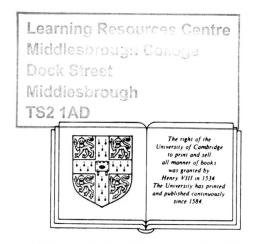

The right of the
University of Cambridge
to print and sell
all manner of books
was granted by
Henry VIII in 1534.
The University has printed
and published continuously
since 1584.

CAMBRIDGE UNIVERSITY PRESS

Cambridge
New York   Port Chester
Melbourne   Sydney

PUBLISHED BY THE PRESS SYNDICATE OF THE UNIVERSITY OF CAMBRIDGE
The Pitt Building, Trumpington Street, Cambridge, United Kingdom

CAMBRIDGE UNIVERSITY PRESS
The Edinburgh Building, Cambridge CB2 2RU, UK
40 West 20th Street, New York NY 10011–4211, USA
477 Williamstown Road, Port Melbourne, VIC 3207, Australia
Ruiz de Alarcón 13, 28014 Madrid, Spain
Dock House, The Waterfront, Cape Town 8001, South Africa

http://www.cambridge.org

First published 1991
First paperback edition 2004

A catalogue record for this book is available from the British Library

Library of Congress cataloguing in publication data
Randall, Adrian J.
Before the Luddites: custom, community and machinery in the
English woollen industry, 1776–1809 / Adrian Randall.
p.   cm.
Includes bibliographical references.
ISBN 0 521 39042 7 hardback
1. Wool trade and industry – England – History.   2. Wool trade and
industry – England – Employees – History.   I. Title.
HD9901.5.R35   1990
338.4′767731′094209033 – dc2o   89–77365 CIP

ISBN 0 521 39042 7 hardback
ISBN 0 521 89334 8 paperback

Transferred to digital printing 2004

To
Frederick, Marjory, Thea
and Thomas

Men make their own history, but they do not make it just as they please; they do not make it under circumstances chosen by themselves, but under circumstances directly encountered, given and transmitted from the past.

Karl Marx, *The Eighteenth Brumaire of Louis Bonaparte*, cited in J. Elster, *Karl Marx: A Reader* (Cambridge, 1986), p. 277.

CONTENTS

ILLUSTRATIONS

TABLES

ACKNOWLEDGEMENTS

This book developed, slowly, out of part of my Ph.D. thesis presented at the University of Birmingham in 1979. But its origins date back to a walk around the graveyard of Trowbridge parish church in the summer of 1971 and to the University of Sheffield in 1972. Any volume which has been so long in gestation will have been subject to a great variety of influences, many of which will be readily apparent from the following pages. Some, however, deserve special thanks. Dorothy Thompson, Professor Sidney Pollard and Professor John Harris guided and helped shape my work in its early days and have continued to offer their support. Maxine Berg, Andrew Charlesworth and Pat Hudson have variously provided me with valuable advice, friendly criticism and encouragement to persist with a subject and an approach which at times has seemed dangerously unfashionable in the 1980s. Richard Fisher has proved an unfailingly supportive and patient editor. Anonymous readers for *Social History, Technology and Culture* and for the Cambridge University Press have all offered trenchant and constructive criticism of my earlier thoughts on this subject. The editors of these two journals have also been kind enough to allow me to draw upon articles of mine published by them in 1982 and 1986 respectively. To all of them I owe a debt of gratitude. Above all, however, I must acknowledge the enormous influence of Edward Thompson. I can still recall the excitement of reading *The Making of the English Working Class* sitting in Victoria Park, Bath, in the summer of 1970 and realising for the first time both the rich potential of social history and that historical scholarship could not only inform but also delight. Since coming to know him, I have found him to be as generous with his time, advice and encouragement as he is prolific with his pen. Like many of my contemporaries, I continue to strive, if in vain, to achieve the standards of scholarship, intellectual athleticism, imagination and quality of prose he has set.

I would like to thank all the archivists and librarians who have been helpful to me at the various repositories where I have researched this book. In particular I have very fond memories of working at Devizes Museum and of the help given to me by the late R. E. Sandell. I am grateful likewise to Col. A. B. Lloyd-Baker of Hardwicke Court for his kindness in allowing me to consult his family papers.

Others have had an influence no less profound but in less purely academic ways. My parents' indefatigable pride in my modest achievements has continued to be a source of encouragement to me. Dandelion and Huffkin have frequently been my sternest critics, at times even being known to shred what they deemed to be sub-standard drafts of this work, but they have also contrived to keep me smiling. Suzy Kennedy has performed the miracle of converting my worst joined-up into tidy typescript. And, above all, Thea, my friend and spouse, has endured all my moans, groans and misdemeanours with a grace that I do not deserve. I owe her more than I can repay. To all of you I offer my grateful thanks.

ABBREVIATIONS

B.C.	*Bath Chronicle*
B.J.	*Bath Journal*
B.P.P.	*British Parliamentary Papers*
B.R.L.	Birmingham Reference Library
G.C.L.	Gloucester City Library, Gloucestershire Collection (now in Gloucestershire Record Office)
G.J.	*Gloucester Journal*
J.H.C.	*Journal of the House of Commons*
J.H.L.	*Journal of the House of Lords*
L.M.	*Leeds Mercury*
P.R.O.	Public Record Office
	ASSI. Assizes
	B.T. Board of Trade
	H.O. Home Office
	K.B. King's Bench
	P.C. Privy Council
	S.P. State Papers
	T.S. Treasury Solicitor
	W.O. War Office
S.W.J.	*Salisbury and Winchester Journal*
T.B.G.A.S.	*Transactions of the Bristol and Gloucestershire Archaeological Society*
V.C.H.	*Victoria County History*
W.A.S.L	Wiltshire Archaeological and Natural History Society Library, Devizes
W.R.O.	Wiltshire Record Office
W.W.M.	Wentworth Woodhouse Manuscripts (Fitzwilliam Collection), Sheffield Reference Library

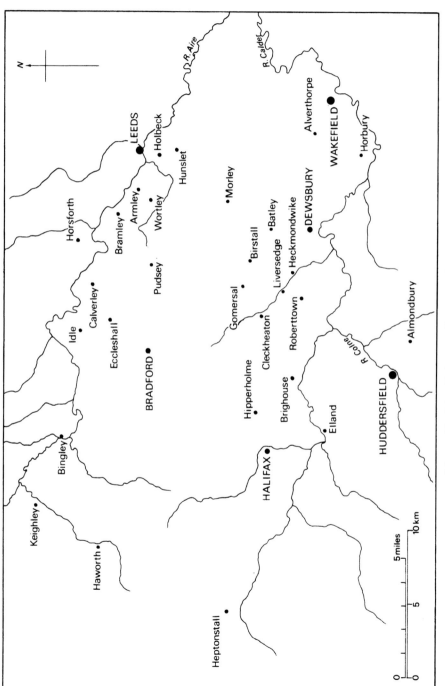

Map 1   The West Riding woollen textile district

Before the Luddites

Map 2   The Gloucestershire woollen textile district

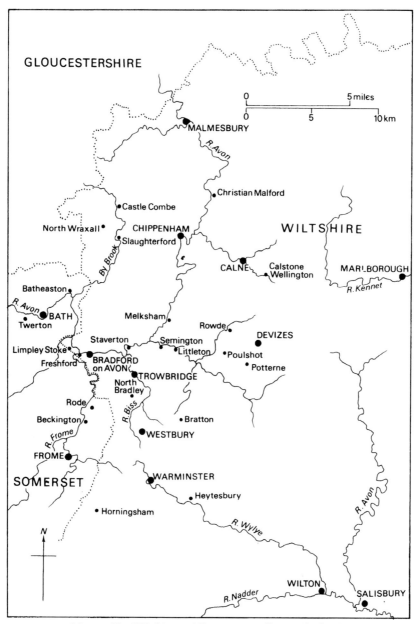

Map 3 The Wiltshire and Somerset woollen textile district

INTRODUCTION

We are experiencing, so we are frequently assured, a second Industrial Revolution. New technologies are radically restructuring both the character and organisation of work across a broad sector of the economy. The process of adjustment to this, often rapid, pattern of change frequently proves painful. Jobs, once seen as secure, are lost and with them not just their earnings but also the status and place in society with which they imbued their possessors. Other jobs survive but work patterns and modes have to be substantially altered, old customs and expectations abandoned.

In facing up to the challenge of change, we are often exhorted to learn the lessons of the past, lessons taught by the history of the first Industrial Revolution in this, the world's first, industrial nation. These lessons are, apparently, straightforward. First, since it was the dynamic of entrepreneurial ambition, seizing upon new technological innovations and scorning time-honoured but irrelevant traditions and methods in favour of new systems of production, which dragged the British economy from its pre-industrial roots into the modern age, it is obvious that such ambition must be encouraged and facilitated in every way possible. Second, it follows that attempts to obstruct the dynamic of entrepreneurial progress must be prevented, since, should they succeed in retarding change, this must prove economically disastrous as failure to adapt is deemed terminal. So obvious is this second lesson that we require only one pejorative adjective to describe the ill-considered and ignorant attempt to resist progress: that adjective is 'Luddite'.

The men of the East Midlands, Yorkshire and Lancashire who in 1811 and 1812 resorted to industrial violence in an attempt to oppose the detrimental impact of technological and organisational innovation upon their trades could little have imagined the linguistic legacy they were to bequeath to posterity. After all, their actions were not unique. Other groups before and since have resisted technological change. Yet

1

'Luddite' and its noun, 'Luddism', have entered into the language as synonymous with blinkered reaction, mindless obstructionism and pointless physical resistance to 'progress'. Thus, to take some recent examples, opposition to new type-setting technology in the printing industry, hostility to P.W.R. nuclear power stations, resistance to new work structures in the motor and furniture industries, to new motor-ways and the Channel tunnel, even the Foreign Secretary's mild criti-cism of the utility of a space-borne missile 'shield', can all be castigated in the popular press as 'Luddite'. This is a remarkable survival. In English history only the Puritans can lay claim to a similar linguistic heritage. And they, unlike the Luddites, were emphatic victors and could impose their image upon society and upon history from a pos-ition of strength. Alone of those social protest groups who fell to ignominious defeat, the Luddites can still be invoked in everyday conversation without need for footnotes.

The remarkable endurance of the image of Luddism can be ac-counted for only in part by human sympathy for the universality of the plight of men confronted by an overwhelming technological impera-tive. The story of the Luddites from *Shirley* onwards has also been deliberately popularised as part of a mythology of the Industrial Revol-ution. Millocrats, safe in the calmer waters of mid-Victorian pros-perity, wished to view the triumph of industrialism, *their* triumph, as an heroic one, not one based merely upon the power of economies of scale. The Luddites nicely fitted this propagandist scenario. As a dangerous amalgam of stupidity, inertia and criminal violence they could be deemed worthy metal on which, metaphorically, to have tested the sword of the nascent industrialist, cast in the role of conquis-tador. Luddites encapsulated all the attributes necessary to highlight the moral lessons of the Industrial Revolution. Resistance was danger-ous, resistance was foolish, resistance was useless. Their defeat was not merely their just deserts: it was a lesson to posterity. The Luddites then are remembered, but they are remembered as caricatures. On few other groups does 'the enormous condescension of posterity', Edward Thompson's ringing phrase, sit more heavily.[1]

The history of the Luddites, however, should point up another 'lesson' of the Industrial Revolution, a lesson frequently ignored or forgotten. They remind us that the process of industrial transformation has rarely been smooth and has frequently engendered bitter conflict. This continues to be the case since changes which threaten to destroy

[1] E. P. Thompson, *The Making of the English Working Class* (1963; Harmondsworth, 1968 edn), p. 13.

established patterns of work threaten more than just sources of income. They jeopardise status, security, customary social structures and concepts and feelings of community identity. Work, today as in the early Industrial Revolution, remains a vitally important element in conferring self-respect and in defining social, economic and political relations. Indeed, psychologists tell us that the loss of one's job or career is, after bereavement, the most shattering blow to the individual's equanimity. The march of progress, then as now, carries with it the promise of enhanced prosperity. But it also leaves in its wake many casualties. Not all lie down quietly to die.

The historiography of resistance to mechanical innovation in the early Industrial Revolution has been a curious one. Machine breaking plays little part in most economic history textbooks, labour's reaction to technological displacement, when noted at all, being seen as an irritating minor impediment to the inevitable with little or no account of its effect upon industrial development.[2] Political and social historians have found machine breaking to be rather more diverting but it is usually viewed as symptomatic of some other problem, economic depression or high food prices and hunger, rather than as direct hostility to technological or organisational change. Were it not for the 'unfortunate timing' of its introduction, the story often runs, machinery would not have occasioned such protest.[3] Luddism's place in labour history too is an awkward one. While labour historians have always shown sympathy for the problem faced, Luddism does not readily fit into the labour history pantheon, itself frequently too Whiggish a view of the past.[4] The violence of machine breaking does not point towards orderly trade unionism and indeed is often seen as indicative of an inability to organise effectively.[5] Even Eric Hobsbawm's pioneering essay on the Luddites did not avoid this trap entirely. While Hobsbawm's concept of 'collective bargaining by riot'

[2] For example, P. Mathias, *The First Industrial Nation: An Economic History of Britain, 1700–1914* (Methuen, 1969), pp. 363–4, notes that 'it is clear that the future lay with those that sought to accept the fundamentals of the emergent industrial society' whereas Luddism, an 'attempt to destroy it', was 'the survival of a reaction characteristic of the pre-industrial world – the peasants' revolt – a negative response'.

[3] For example, A. Briggs, *The Age of Improvement, 1783–1867* (Longman, 1959), p. 182, sees the Luddites as 'helpless victims of distress'.

[4] See, for example, J. L. and B. Hammond, *The Skilled Labourer* (1919; Longman, 1979 edn), introduction by John Rule, pp. xx–xxi; G. D. H. Cole and R. Postgate, *The Common People, 1746–1946* (Methuen, 1938; 1949 edn), pp. 184–5.

[5] M. I. Thomis, *The Luddites: Machine Breaking in Regency England* (David and Charles, 1970), p. 134; E. H. Hunt, *British Labour History, 1815–1914* (Weidenfeld and Nicolson, 1981), p. 195.

shifted attention towards the role of machine breaking as a weapon of labour in eighteenth-century industrial struggles, he still saw industrial violence of this sort as essentially a precursor to modern industrial relations and already something of an anachronism by the early nineteenth century.[6]

It was not until Edward Thompson's monumental *The Making of the English Working Class* appeared in 1963 that any really sustained attempt to understand Luddism from within its own context and community was made. Thompson's insistence on the importance of the agency of working people themselves in shaping their own social and political development shifted the focus towards seeing protest as a product of the specific culture and community values from which it sprang. In consequence a generation of social historians has been inspired to investigate 'the blind alleys, the lost causes and the losers',[7] not with the smug complacency of visitors to a heritage museum but, as far as is possible, from within an understanding of their subjects' own history and context. It is certainly this approach which is the inspiration of this book.

Since Thompson, debate on the Luddite disturbances of 1811–12, as on much else about which he wrote, has grown apace. A great deal of attention has been paid to the economic background of Luddism, to its organisation, its relationship to trade unionism, to radical politics and to class development. Only limited attention, however, has been paid to the longer term context of Luddism or to its place within the history of machine breaking. Even less interest has been shown in pursuing the issues of why some regions, places and industries saw resistance while others did not and why resistance was physical in some places, constitutional in others. Nor have historians been much concerned to examine the values, concepts and attitudes which informed machine breaking or their origins.[8]

It is these issues which form the focus of this book. It is not concerned with the events of 1811–12, at least not directly, but with the period before the Luddites, in particular the years from the 1770s to 1809, years which witnessed the earliest infancy of the Industrial Revolution. And whereas Luddism affected three industries, this book is concerned with only one, the woollen cloth industry in England.

---

[6] E. J. Hobsbawm, *Labouring Men: Studies in the History of Labour* (Weidenfeld and Nicolson, 1964; 1968 edn), pp. 5–22.

[7] Thompson, *The Making* , p. 13.

[8] M. Berg, *The Age of Manufactures, 1700–1820* (Fontana, 1985), is an honourable exception.

The woollen industry offers a fascinating model for such a study. It was the oldest, most deep-rooted and in many ways most 'traditional' of all the textile industries, its vital place in the national economy protected by statutory controls and regulations dating back to the Tudor period. It was the industry which saw the most sustained and determined resistance to machinery. It was also an industry concentrated in two regions, in the West Riding of Yorkshire and in the counties of Gloucestershire, Somerset and Wiltshire, collectively always referred to as the West of England cloth making region. The West Riding and the West of England both produced woollen cloth using the same techniques and methods but production in each was organised in very different ways. This gave rise to two very different economic and social structures and in turn produced very different histories of mechanisation and economic development. The West Riding woollen industry, the minor party in the early eighteenth century, was already developing rapidly before mechanisation enabled it to expand even more prodigiously in the decades after 1780, establishing itself as the paramount national centre of the industry by the second quarter of the nineteenth century. The West of England, predominant in 1700, experienced much slower growth, found the Industrial Revolution a far less congenial experience and was in terminal if protracted decline by 1830. The woollen industry, therefore, offers an excellent opportunity to conduct a comparative study of the impact of and response to machinery in the same industry over the same period of time.

The regional history of the Industrial Revolution is currently undergoing a long-overdue resuscitation. Economic and social historians are beginning to re-examine the origins of industrialism and in the process are rediscovering a rich regional diversity of experience and development. Inevitably, perhaps, these studies have tended to concentrate upon regions of dynamic industrial growth such as the Midlands, Lancashire and Yorkshire rather than upon those which failed to respond to the challenge of change. Thus, for example, the histories of the wool textile industries of East Anglia and Devon, which followed the same pattern of decay as the West of England, remain underresearched for this period. Equally, relatively few recent regional studies have been concerned with the social as opposed to the economic histories of their subjects. In consequence, the social context within which change occurred, or failed to occur, remains for many regions only partially charted. The student of the English woollen industry is blessed with three outstanding monographs, one on the West of England by the late Julia Mann and two on Yorkshire by R. G. Wilson and Pat Hudson, each in their own fields pioneering and definitive works.[9] None, however, are really concerned with 'history from below', concerning themselves, as was their remit, principally with the economic history of their region. Derek Gregory's ambitious attempt to fuse the disciplines of geography, economic history and sociology provides an interesting examination of the economic and social context of the West Riding during this period of transformation but his conclusions have been received with scepticism, perhaps because of this multi-disciplinary approach.[10] Nor, for the most part, have these regional historians attempted comparative accounts of the process of and the reaction to change. One has, in fact, to go back to the Hammonds to find a book which deals with the responses to industrialism within a broadly comparative perspective. Their Fabian preoccupations, however, meant that their approach to the problem of industrial violence was at best ambiguous. In recent years only John Bohstedt has essayed so wide a comparative canvas but he is less concerned with the industrial bases of protest at change than with consumer protests and radicalism.[11] The justification for this book, therefore, is as an attempt to fill these particular lacunae for the English woollen industry and perhaps in so doing to offer a new perspective on the reaction to industrial change generally.

This book is focussed upon the issues of custom, community and machinery. It is the last which justifies the starting point of the study since 1776 witnessed the introduction into both the West of England and the West Riding of the spinning jenny, the first mechanical innovation to begin the process of industrial transformation. While machines were tangible and their effects assessable, custom and community present greater difficulties of definition. While both are in essence conservative forces, as conceptual systems they may appear to lack precision or substance. It is the contention of this book that both did in fact have specific as well as general meaning within the context of the economy and the society of the two regions of which they were

---

[9] J. de L. Mann, *The Cloth Industry in the West of England from 1640 to 1880* (Oxford, 1971); R. G. Wilson, *Gentlemen Merchants: The Merchant Community in Leeds, 1700–1830* (Manchester, 1971); P. Hudson, *The Genesis of Industrial Capital: A Study of the West Riding Wool Textile Industry c. 1750–1850* (Cambridge, 1986).

[10] D. Gregory, *Regional Transformation and Industrial Revolution: A Geography of the Yorkshire Woollen Industry* (Macmillan, 1982).

[11] J. Bohstedt, *Riots and Community Politics in England and Wales, 1790–1810* (Harvard, 1983). For an outstanding and ambitious comparative study of the French textile industry, see W. M. Reddy, *The Rise of Market Culture: The Textile Trade and French Society, 1750–1900* (Cambridge, 1984).

both products and shapers. It was the structure and customs of the woollen industry which shaped community as a dynamic force for social cohesion and resistance to change. And custom was elevated above mere habit and tradition by the existence of the corpus of old regulatory legislation which in theory controlled many aspects of the manufacture. The bitterly resisted repeal of this legislation in 1809 marks the terminal point of this study since it commenced the process of the destruction and deconstruction of old concepts of custom and ultimately of community.

Reaction to the advent of a machine economy varied from region to region and from place to place. To understand why, it is necessary to examine two critical determinants: first, the organisation of work and the character of the community within which work took place; and secondly, the impact of machinery upon work itself. Chapter 1 examines the effect of the organisation of production in shaping community attitudes and craft consciousness in the two regions. The different work structures in the West of England and the West Riding generated very different capital–labour relationships and these had major repercussions for the way innovation was viewed. Such differences in economic structure have recently been engaging economic historians within the debate on proto-industrialisation, developing models to explain the successes and failures of regions in transforming from pre-industrial to industrial economies. Comparison of the West of England and West Riding woollen industries, apparently archetypal examples of the two models advanced by the proto-industrialisation thesis, demonstrates that economic structure alone cannot account for the pattern of change. Crucially it was the value systems generated by these structures which determined the response to innovation.

Chapter 2 examines the impact of technology upon work itself. Workers did not view machinery in abstract but in the way it affected their jobs. Where machinery augmented or facilitated employment within the existing work structure, it was rarely resisted. It was when machinery threatened employment or relocated it into a new factory-based system that it generally encountered hostility. Historians have been inclined to disparage hostility to the factory system, arguing that factory work was no worse than and rather better paid than outwork. Nonetheless, fear of the factory was a powerful force in the woollen industry. Historians have also tended to side with those apologists for mechanical innovation who claimed that machinery had only minor consequences for employment. Chapter 2 investigates the fear of factory work and the impact of machinery upon employment.

While the first two chapters investigate the cultural and economic context into which mechanical innovation was introduced, Chapters 3, 4 and 5 look at the response to the rise of a machine economy. Some places witnessed no resistance to machinery. Hostility to machinery in others did not necessarily lead to acts of violence and resistance did not always lead to much beyond initial protests. Yet in other places resistance was both fierce and sustained. Why was this the case? Chapter 3 examines the community reaction to the early mechanisation of the preparatory processes in the industry and argues that resistance was located within a community consensus which felt threatened by machinery. In some places this community culture had a rich tradition of protest which pre-dated mechanisation and it was here that resistance proved most sustained and implacable.

Community resistance could prove an obdurate obstacle in the path of progress but it was rarely possible to maintain opposition over lengthy periods of time or when faced with determined innovators. Sustained resistance required not just numbers but the organisational capacity of a trade union. This was found in the woollen industry in the cloth dressers of the West of England and the West Riding who found themselves threatened by technological redundancy. In 1812 the Yorkshire cloth dressers or croppers were to prove the most determined and successful of the Luddites. Their battle, however, had its origins in the 1790s. The case of the cloth dressers raises issues concerning the relationship between trade unionism and industrial violence. Much labour history has been written with the premise that the two were clearly separate, that violence was indicative of a failure to organise effectively and was conducted quite independently from 'orthodox' trade union action. Chapters 4 and 5 challenge this compartmentalist approach. Chapter 4 examines the organisation of the cloth dressers' trade, their history of combination and their response to the early introduction of finishing machinery. These demonstrate that while the cloth dressers in fact made effective use of 'orthodox' trade union sanctions, they were also willing and able to resort to more physical resistance to supplement or take the place of the strike or boycott. This inter-relationship is shown clearly in Chapter 5, which examines industrial violence and machine breaking in some detail by a study of the Wiltshire Outrages of 1802, a forerunner of the Luddite disturbances in Yorkshire ten years later. Violence is shown not to have been a product of weakness nor of an inability to organise. It was in fact part of a calculated, deliberate and graduated response to the threat posed by machinery.

Historians examining pre-industrial communities through the matrix of the riot always run the risk of being accused of accentuating the atypical. Certainly disturbances were not the everyday activity of the majority who normally simply got on with their daily tasks of producing cloth and earning a living. However, if we are seeking to understand the values, attitudes and *mentalité* of that working community, riots often provide historians with our only point of access. Since that community did not, except in exceptional cases, leave us a direct record of their opinions, we must seek them in their actions. This can be done by recognising disturbances not as unrelated, random events but as carrying purposeful statements of values which may only be decoded through a careful contextual understanding of that community. Our sources of information on these events are, of course, rarely neutral reporters. Letters to the Home and War Offices reflected the views of the propertied and newspapers reported from the perspective of and for the respectable, not the rioting, classes. Again, it is to the actions of the crowd we must turn and seek to make sense of them from within the context and culture of their own community.

The woollen workers' response to the threat of machinery was not, however, confined to violence and industrial action. They also made use of the law to appeal to the authorities for protection against structural change. The woollen industry, the ancient staple, was hedged around with legislation regulating and controlling production methods, marketing and labour relations. There proved to be over seventy such statutes still extant in 1802. Archaic and often ignored or observed only in spirit though not in detail, this body of legislation provided the woollen workers with a powerful weapon with which to resist change. The collision between the forces of innovation and tradition in the woollen industry, therefore, was more than a physical one. It was also fought out before the courts and, more importantly, before two Select Committees of the House of Commons in 1803 and 1806. In this the cloth dressers were not alone. The weavers of the West of England and the master clothiers and journeymen of the West Riding were likewise overshadowed by the threat of structural change in the form of the factory system. Chapter 6 investigates their campaign to uphold and strengthen the old acts in order to resist the rise of the weaving factory and loomshop, a campaign which helped precipitate the final battles at Westminster.

Chapter 7 examines the workers' case before Parliament. The Report of the 1806 Select Committee is deservedly well known, as is the evidence they compiled, though that of the 1803 Committee is less well used.[12] Both, however, have been used mainly to describe the economic structures and changes taking place in the industry. Yet the Parliamentary investigation of the woollen industry provided the woollen workers and master clothiers with a unique platform from which they could expound their wider values and attitudes to industrial relations and to the role of regulation in the industry. Chapter 7 argues that this evidence, together with the debate it generated in the press and in pamphlets, reveal that the woollen workers shared a coherent political economy which had no place for the *laissez-faire* values of the innovators. The debate over the old laws was not simply a question of removing obsolete impediments to economic growth. It revealed a powerful ideological struggle between an old political economy based on order, stability, regulation and control supplemented by custom and the new political economy based on a faith in free market forces and the power of capital. Taken together with the community and craft values and attitudes examined in earlier chapters, the campaign over legislative control reveals an holistic moral economy which informed woollen cloth producers' views in both the West of England and the West Riding and which repudiated the values of the new industrial society. Here we can see the real issues which the Industrial Revolution raised. It was not just a question of more and more machines. It involved a complete re-orientation of perceptions of economic and social relationships.

Chapter 8 examines the implications of these findings in relation to the issue of class consciousness. Historians have long debated how far the rise of the Industrial Revolution generated new class attitudes. Luddism in particular has been placed in a central position in this transformation for here the battle with the new industrialism seems most bitter, here the state could clearly be seen siding with the forces of innovation against labour. Chapter 8 discusses the evidence for the economic and political alienation of workers and petty capitalists both from nascent industrial capitalism and from the state in the years before 1812 in the light of the themes which run through the book, namely custom and community. The conclusions indicate that the causal relationship is far less clear than some historians have suggested since the economic and political reactions to change did not necessarily point in the same direction. Those forces which informed and shaped resistance were products of a traditional culture which could not

[12] *B.P.P., Minutes of Evidence Taken before the Select Committee on the Woollen Clothiers' Petition* (H.C. 95), 1802/3, Vol. 7; *Report of and Minutes of Evidence Taken before the Select Committee to Consider the State of the Woollen Manufacture* (H.C. 268), 1806, Vol. 3.

readily be adapted to a new age. The legacy of custom thus proved both a strength and an encumbrance to the woollen workers. The values of the past provided them with a strong sense of community with which to oppose change but they also delayed their adaptation to the newer, harsher climate which would follow their defeat.

Chapter 1

Industrial organisation and culture

From the most remote period of the woollen manufacture until about the year 1780 very few if any mechanical improvements had been introduced into it . . . In an art which had seen so many centuries roll on without any change, it did not appear possible to the manufacturer that any improvement could be effected; and had not the genius of Hargreaves and Arkwright changed entirely the modes of carding and spinning cotton, the woollen manufacture would probably have remained at this day what it was in the earliest ages.

That it would have been better for general society if it had so remained, we readily admit; but after the improved modes of working cotton were discovered, this was impossible.

A. Rees, *The Cyclopaedia*, Vol. xxxviii (London, 1819)

'The wool textile trade held a unique place in the eighteenth century economy.'[1] 'Throughout the eighteenth century wool was the major English manufacturing industry.' During that century the wool textile industry as a whole grew by some 150%[2] and, agriculture apart, constituted the largest employer of labour. Even a conservative observer like John Smith in 1757 believed that around 800,000 people were employed in the industry, while others claimed there were as many as $1^1/_2$ million. In the early eighteenth century cloth exports accounted for around 70% of English domestic exports while in 1770 the proportion was still around 50%.[3] The rapid expansion of the cotton industry and the broadening of the base of the British economy thereafter saw wool's primacy undermined. Nonetheless, even at the end of the Napoleonic Wars the industry as a whole still produced some 20% of

[1] R. G. Wilson, 'The supremacy of the Yorkshire cloth industry in the eighteenth century', in N. B. Harte and K. G. Ponting, eds., *Textile History and Economic History* (Manchester, 1973), p. 225.
[2] P. Deane, 'The output of the British woollen industry in the eighteenth century', *Journal of Economic History*, 17 (1957), pp. 207, 220.
[3] Wilson, 'The supremacy of Yorkshire', p. 225.

the value of all domestic exports.[4] It was, therefore, with good reason that a commentator in 1740 could claim, 'The Consequences of the Woollen Trade are more beneficial than any other, even than all our other Branches of Trade.'[5]

The wool textile industry was made up of three distinct parts: the woollen or cloth industry; worsted; and serge. It is with the former that this book will be concerned. While all three branches used sheep's wool, woollen cloth was manufactured from the short stapled curly wool of the hardier upland sheep, increasingly in the later eighteenth century from the merino sheep, whereas worsted cloth was made from the long stapled silkier wool of lowland sheep. The textural differences in the wool made for different processing and a different product. The long stapled wool used in worsted needed merely to be combed through before it could be spun into yarn since it was relatively easy to set all the fibres running in the same direction. Further, as thread such wool had a good tensile strength when drafted and spun, giving the woven cloth a robust and resistant texture. While such cloth was then fulled or 'felted' to help 'fill out' the ground by knitting fibres together, the cloth retained the strength and the distinctive character of the weave. The short stapled wool used in woollen cloth, however, required very much more labour in the preparatory and finishing stages. Such wool had to be carded for some time to align the staples and when drafted in yarn lacked the strength of worsted yarn. Thus woollen cloth, once woven, had to be heavily fulled to knit the fibres together across and through the weave to provide it with its strength. In this process the pattern of the weave was lost and a rough shaggy surface produced. The cloth, therefore, had to be finished, a process which involved raising a nap and then shearing it off to produce a smooth, skin-like surface. Woollen cloth could be dyed much more evenly and brilliantly than worsted, wore longer and had a much softer 'feel'. Because the raw materials were more expensive and because it required more labour and more skilled labour than either worsted or serge, a hybrid which used a worsted warp and woollen weft, woollen cloth was always more expensive than its rivals. It was, as Mann notes, 'the aristocrat of the woollen textile industries'.[6] Successive governments had for centuries viewed the woollen industry as the great national staple and, as such, too vital to the country to be allowed to

---

[4] P. Deane and W. A. Cole, *British Economic Growth, 1688-1959* (Cambridge, 1967), pp. 30–1.
[5] A Draper of London, *The Consequences of Trade* (1740), reprinted in part in *The Gentleman's Magazine*, Vol. 10, p. 500.   [6] Mann, *Cloth Industry*, p. xi.

develop without governmental control. Thus they had passed legislation intended to regulate production techniques, quality, marketing
and labour relations in the industry. By 1802 there were still some
seventy such statutes in force.[7]

In the sixteenth and seventeenth centuries woollen cloth was produced almost everywhere but by the mid-eighteenth century production had become concentrated in two main regions, in the counties of
Gloucestershire, Wiltshire and Somerset, always referred to as the
West of England, and in the West Riding of Yorkshire. In general, the
West of England specialised in the finer quality end of the market, a
specialisation which became more marked as the century progressed.
Yorkshire for the most part produced coarser varieties which competed with worsted and serge. While in 1700 the West of England was
predominant, by 1800 the positions had been reversed and Yorkshire
was firmly established as the major woollen manufacturing region.

While the cloth produced in both regions underwent the same
processes of manufacture, the structure and organisation of the woollen industry differed greatly between the West of England and the
West Riding. These differences were to have major consequences for
the way in which machinery was greeted by the woollen workers in
each region and indeed for the course of economic development in
each.

The wollen industry in the West of England was organised on an
outworking basis, the predominant mode of industrial production in
the eighteenth century. Indeed, here this system may be seen to have
reached its apogee, here capital accumulation, industrial organisation
and division of labour were more advanced than in almost any other
outworking area and very much more so than in rival Yorkshire. The
industry in the West was controlled by merchant capitalists known as
clothiers or gentlemen clothiers. Josiah Tucker noted in 1757:

One Person, with a great Stock and large Credit, buys the Wool, pays for the
Spinning, Weaving, Milling, Dying, Shearing, Dressing, etc. That is, he is the
Master of the whole Manufacture from first to last and perhaps imploys a
thousand Persons under him. This is the Clothier, whom all the Rest are to look
upon as their Paymaster.[8]

Wilson suggests, for example, that the Gloucestershire trade was
dominated by no more than 400 such clothiers.[9] Some of these gentlemen clothiers were very wealthy. Daniel Defoe was informed in 1724

---

[7] They are listed in *J.H.C.*, Vol. 61, p. 697.
[8] J. Tucker, *Instructions for Travellers* (printed privately, Gloucester, 1757), pp. 24–5.
[9] Wilson, 'The supremacy of Yorkshire', p. 239.

'that it was no extraordinary thing to have clothiers in that country worth from £10,000 to £40,000 a man, and many of the great families who now pass for gentry in those counties have been originally raised from and built up by this truly noble manufacture'.[10] The clothiers' control, however, was for the most part indirect. Of the four major productive processes, namely preparation, spinning, weaving and finishing, the clothier exercised direct control only over the first. A brief examination of these processes will make this point clear.

The clothier bought the raw wool and carefully supervised the sorting. This was, and remains, a highly skilled task. It was the financial ability of the West of England clothiers to buy large quantities of fine wool and to sort it into a large number of categories – from seven to twelve were common as against two or three in the West Riding – which enabled them to maintain careful quality control over their production and thus to manufacture such fine cloth. The wool might then be dyed. Dyeing 'in the wool' made for less problems but 'piece dyeing', after the cloth had been woven, enabled the production of much more brilliantly coloured cloths and was a speciality of many Gloucestershire clothiers. Dyeing was usually undertaken by dyers directly employed in the clothiers' premises but there were also public dyers who worked on commission. The wool was then scoured and picked to remove larger impurities and finally oil was added to make it less brittle. These processes did not require significant numbers of workers.

The wool was then scribbled, a process of carding the wool on an upright frame to disentangle the fibres and set them running roughly parallel. This task was performed in the West of England by adult male scribblers who constituted the third largest adult male trade in the industry there before mechanisation. They worked in shops, usually adjacent to the clothier's mill, and under his immediate supervision. Thereafter, however, the wool was worked up into cloth away from the clothier's control.

Scribbled wool was put out to very large numbers of women to be spun into yarn and spinning provided a major by-employment for the wives of textile workers and agricultural labourers alike. The problems of obtaining sufficient numbers of spinners and the irregularity of their production led West Country clothiers to put out spinning over a very wide geographical area. Several set up 'spinning stations' to act as secondary organisational focal points to co-ordinate spinners at a

[10] D. Defoe, *A Tour through England and Wales* (1724–6; Everyman, 1928 edn), Vol. 1, p. 281

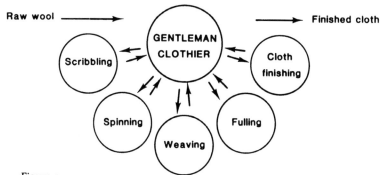

Figure 1
The organisational structure of the West of England woollen industry
Source: P. Hudson, ed., *Regions and Industries: A Perspective on the Industrial Revolution in Britain* (Cambridge, 1989), p. 180.

distance, some being over 20 miles from the clothier's own mill. Yarn was collected back by the clothier's agent and the spinners paid according to production and the fineness of their yarn.

The next process was weaving. Weavers had to collect their yarn from the clothier's mill, usually on a particular day of the week, 'bearing home day', when finished cloth was returned and new work given out. Warp yarn was measured out by winding it around two pegs set in a wall and then handed over to the weavers together with skeins of weft yarn, referred to in the West as 'abb', to be carried back to the weaver's cottage to be woven into cloth. Weavers often referred to this as collecting a new 'chain' but technically chain was the name given to warp yarn. The principal production of the West of England throughout the period under review was broadcloth which was woven in the double loom and needed two weavers to throw the shuttle from side to side until the flying shuttle loom made one redundant. A child was also needed to quill, that is, to wind the weft onto the bobbin of the shuttle. Narrow cloth, of growing importance from 1766, was woven by a single weaver in a narrow loom. There were two sorts of weaver in the West of England, those who owned their own loom and those journeymen who worked a loom for a master weaver. It was very rare, and very much resented, for a clothier to own looms and rent them to weavers. There is little evidence of the number of master weavers. The term was often used indiscriminately to describe not only employers of journeymen but also men who owned their own loom and employed merely their wives and children to help them. Indeed, this latter was the characteristic unit of production in the West of England and the family economy was much prized by the weavers.

Weavers were by far the most numerous of all the adult males employed in the industry. When completed, the cloth was carried back to the clothier's mill and the agreed price paid, less deductions for 'damages'.

The cloth then had to be fulled. Many West of England clothiers owned fulling mills but there were also many public fullers. When sufficiently shrunk, the cloth was handed over to female burlers to remove knots, etc., embedded in the fabric.

Finally the cloth had to be finished by raising a nap and then shearing it. This was performed by cloth dressers or shearmen, as they were called in the West, employed in workshops usually owned by independent master dressers who took work on commission. Before the Industrial Revolution some West Country clothiers established their own finishing shops but the great majority were reluctant to incur the expense and to take on the problem of managing the notoriously unruly shearmen. The cloth dressers were the second largest adult male trade.

Finished cloth was returned to the clothier and fine drawn, a process performed by women of repairing any damages incurred during finishing, and then marketed. Some West of England clothiers marketed their own cloth but the majority used factors.

The gentleman clothier's role, therefore, was an amalgamation of merchant and industrialist, owning the raw material throughout the manufacture and some of the plant necessary for production but having direct control over only a limited part of the process. Above all his role was that of organiser and, as Tucker claimed, 'Paymaster'. The advanced division of labour created by this highly organised putting out operation ensured the existence of a highly skilled and specialised workforce, a major factor in the West's preponderance in fine quality cloths. However, the structure of the industry, divided between the 'Paymasters' and craft-conscious workers, created a pattern of aggressive and sometimes very bitter industrial relations.

The woollen industry of Yorkshire took on a very different form. The Select Committee of 1806 drew the distinction thus: 'in the system of the West of England and in the factory system, the work is done by persons who have no property in the goods they manufacture, [and] in this consists the essential distinction between the two former systems and the Domestic'. In the Domestic System,

the Manufacture is conducted by a multitude of Master Manufacturers, generally possessing a small and scarcely ever any great extent of capital. They buy the Wool of the Dealer; and, in their own houses, assisted by their wives and children, and from two or three to six or seven Journeymen, they dye it (when dying is necessary) and through all the different stages work it up into undressed Cloth.[11]

As Pat Hudson has shown,[12] these master clothiers were generally small-scale landowners and, until the last decade of the eighteenth century, their economy was to some degree a dual one, mixing subsistence agriculture and cloth production. Their land provided them with vegetables and pasture for cows, space to tenter cloths and to keep a horse and also with a security for credit. Further, it allowed them to erect larger workshops as trade prospered and also sometimes small cottages with workshops of their own for journeymen. Possession of land made for some seasonality of production. It was normal, for example, for cloth making to be suspended during the hay and grain harvests as the diaries of Joseph Rogerson and Cornelius Ashworth show.[13] However, agriculture was in few cases a primary source of income by the later eighteenth century. 'We have not a farmer who gets his living by farming without trade besides', claimed a master clothier in 1806.[14] The author of the Board of Agriculture Report on the West Riding in 1799 believed their land was 'solely farmed as a matter of convenience or amusement' for they 'have little if any pretensions to the character of farmers. The speculations and interruptions, inseparable from trade, call for all his capital.'[15] The master clothiers were numerous. Wilson states that in the later eighteenth century there were at least 3,500 broadcloth manufacturers alone in the county, in addition to master clothiers who produced narrow cloth, blankets, white cloths and some fancy cloths.[16]

---

[11] *J.H.C.*, Vol. 61, p. 698.

[12] P. Hudson, 'Proto-industrialisation: the case of the West Riding wool textile industry in the eighteenth and early nineteenth centuries', *History Workshop Journal*, 12 (1981); 'From manor to mill: the West Riding in transition', in M. Berg, P. Hudson and M. Sonenscher, eds., *Manufacture in Town and Country before the Factory* (Cambridge, 1983); and her outstanding study, *Genesis of Industrial Capital*, pp. 30–7.

[13] 'The diary of Joseph Rogerson, scribbling miller of Bramley, 1808–1814', in W. B. Crump, *The Leeds Woollen Industry, 1780–1820* (Thoresby Society, 1931); 'The diary of Cornelius Ashworth, weaver', in F. Atkinson, *Some Aspects of the Eighteenth-Century Woollen and Worsted Trade in Halifax* (Halifax Museums, 1956).

[14] *B.P.P.*, 1806, Vol. 3, p. 10.

[15] R. Brown, *A General View of the Agriculture of the West Riding of Yorkshire* (Edinburgh, 1799), p. 229.

[16] Wilson, 'The supremacy of Yorkshire', p. 239. Aikin claimed that in 1795 some 3,240 clothiers used the Leeds halls while James Ellis in 1806 stated there were some 3,500. There were other large cloth halls, however, at Bradford, Halifax, Huddersfield and

The master clothier bought his wool either at weekly markets or from travelling dealers or foggers. Generally only sufficient wool was purchased to last till the end of the week or fortnight to avoid tying up large sums of money. This meant that, as noted above, sorting tended to be fairly rudimentary, rarely exceeding two or at most three categories. The wool was also predominantly English-grown and of a much lower quality than that generally used in the West of England. In the workshops alongside his house the master clothier and his family and journeymen would scour and pick the wool and then scribble and card it. Spinning was traditionally carried out by the clothier's womenfolk and by the wives of those journeymen who did not live in. However, it seems clear that as woollen cloth production grew steadily throughout the century, the need to find additional hands for spinning grew pressing for many clothiers. As in the West of England, therefore, but on a much smaller scale, the master clothiers had to put out spinning beyond the work unit until the advent of the jenny solved this problem.

The main labour for the master clothier and his journeymen lay in the loom. In the double loom the clothier and his journeymen wove side by side, the journeymen receiving a wage which reflected their production but which also took account of board and lodgings or cottage rent. Few clothiers employed many more than three or four journeymen. Some were little more than journeymen themselves 'who make a piece now and then are journeymen again'.[17] At the other extreme a few master clothiers employed as many as ten or twelve journeymen in their shops and were beginning to put out weaving for journeymen to work up in their own cottages.[18] Such men were to be responsible for the advent of the factory system in the West Riding woollen industry and were greatly distrusted by the many small master clothiers and journeymen weavers. William Child complained in 1806 that the trade 'has gone more into lumps'[19] but the small masters and their journeymen were to survive, if under growing pressure, into the 1830s.

Wakefield which had their own local producers, many of whom produced broadcloth. J. Aikin, *A Description of the Country from Thirty to Forty Miles round Manchester* (1795), p. 573; *B.P.P.*, 1806, Vol. 3, p. 9.

[17] *B.P.P.*, 1806, Vol. 3, p. 9.
[18] *Ibid.*, evidence of James Walker, p. 175. See also Gregory, *Regional Transformation and Industrial Revolution*, pp. 90–2.
[19] *B.P.P.*, 1806, Vol. 3, p. 107.

Once woven the master clothier would take the cloth to a public miller to be fulled. Then he took the cloth in its unfinished state to one of the many cloth halls for sale. Defoe's description of the cloth hall in Leeds in 1726 is well known.[20] The same organisation was still intact in 1806.

> Several thousands of these small Master Manufacturers attend the Market of Leeds, where there are three Halls for the exposure and sale of their Cloths: and there are other similar Halls, where the same system of selling in public Market prevails, at Bradford, Halifax and Huddersfield. The Halls consist of long walks or galleries throughout the whole length of which the Master Manufacturers stand in a double row, each behind his own little division or stand on which his goods are exposed to sale. In the interval between these rows the Merchants pass along, and make their purchases. At the end of an hour, or the ringing of a bell, the Market closes, and such Cloths as have been purchased are carried home to the Merchants' houses: such Goods as remain unsold continuing in the Halls till they find a purchaser at some ensuing Market.[21]

Not all cloth was sold in the cloth halls. Increasingly some master clothiers were working directly to orders from the merchants. This was particularly the case when trade was booming. Such trends alarmed many smaller clothiers who believed that the cloth halls and their independence might thereby be jeopardised. The 1806 Committee recognised such fears but argued that they were exaggerated, noting that cloths produced on commission, 'no less than the others, are manufactured by [the clothier] in his own family'.[22]

The Domestic System of the master clothier produced the unfinished cloth. Once bought by the merchant, however, the cloth was finished in much the same way and under the same form of organisation in Yorkshire as in the West of England, by cloth dressers known there as croppers working in workshops generally owned by independent master dressers. There were some differences in finishing practices which reflected the generally coarser cloth produced in Yorkshire but the character of the work was identical. As in the West Country there were some Yorkshire merchants who from the last quarter of the eighteenth century were beginning to set up their own finishing or cropping shops to speed up through-put, cut finishing costs and obtain a tighter control over quality. However, Yorkshire croppers enjoyed a reputation for unruliness which quite equalled that of the

---

[20] Defoe, *Tour*, Vol. II, pp. 204–6.   [21] *J.H.C.*, Vol. 61, p. 698.   [22] *Ibid.*

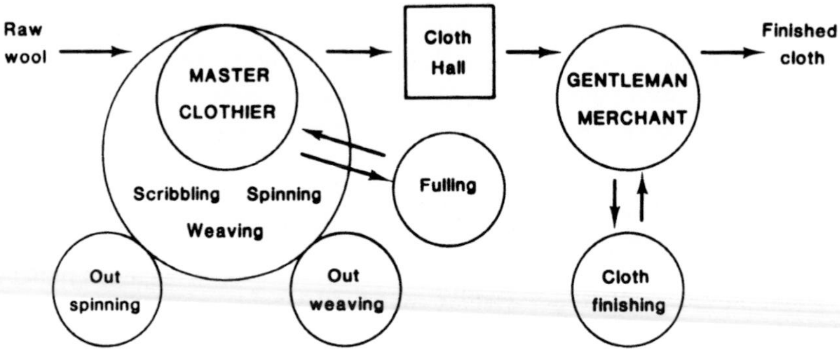

Figure 2
The organisational structure of the Yorkshire woollen industry
Source: P. Hudson, ed., *Regions and Industries: A Perspective on the Industrial Revolution in Britain* (Cambridge, 1989), p. 181.

West Country shearmen and the majority of merchants preferred to put out finishing on commission in the old way.

The finished cloth was returned to the merchant for final inspection and sale. Here the structure of the Yorkshire industry produced a major advantage for the West Riding merchants generally marketed their own cloth directly, not through factors as was the norm in the West of England.[23] By specialising only in the purchase and finishing of cloth, the Yorkshire merchants were able to direct time and entrepreneurial energy into finding and developing outlets for their product in a way which was not practicable for the West of England clothier beset with all the problems of managing the entire industry. By selling their cloths directly, the Yorkshire merchants avoided the cost of factors' profit margins and saw a return on their money much more quickly. Again, this benefited the entire industry for it ensured that the merchants could always pay on the nail for the cloths they bought in the cloth halls. Thus, the master clothier saw a quick return on his investment in wool and labour and was able to continue production requiring much lower levels of credit than a minor producer in the West of England would have needed. This rapid circulation of capital was without doubt a major reason for the vitality of the West Riding woollen industry.

The very different industrial structures of the West of England and

[23] Wilson, 'The supremacy of Yorkshire', identifies this method of marketing as being the principal reason for the West Riding's remarkable growth record in comparison to that of the West of England.

the West Riding were of major importance for the development of industrial and social relations and for the take up of machinery in both regions. Why the industrial structures were so different lies outside the parameters of this study and need not long detain us. However, it is worth noting briefly the implications of these differences in the light of the recent and on-going debate on the concept of proto-industrial-isation. The primary concern of the theory of proto-industrialisation, namely the study of the agricultural origins of industry, has for long been a source of interest for historians and many of the ideas advanced by advocates of proto-industrialisation have been anticipated by Jones and Thirsk among others if in a somewhat different form.[24] However, since 1972 much interest has been generated by the model advanced by Mendels and developed by Medick and others[25] which posits a linear development from rural industrial production with its linkages with agrarian developments to the factory system, a model based upon neo-classical economic theory and upon the theory of comparative advantage. This linear view suggests a development of two distinct and progressional systems of industrial organisation, the *Kaufsystem*, characterised by artisan domestic production in by-employment with agricultural activities, and the *Verlagsystem*, in which capitalist control has been extended into a putting out system where workers, divorced from agriculture, depend entirely on wages from industrial production. The *Verlagsystem* with its greater concentration of control and capital accumulation in the hands of the few is therefore deemed to be the launching pad for further transition into the factory-based economy.

Superficially at least the English woollen industry shows the two perfect examples of these distinct models. The West Riding Domestic System offers an excellent example of a *Kaufsystem*, although the merchants' control over finishing and ultimate marketing might be deemed to invalidate this model to some minor degree. And the West of England putting out system offers a clear example of a *Verlagsystem* in which again only the lack of direct control over finishing mars the fit. Why the same industry might develop so differently region by region

---

[24] E. L. Jones, 'The agricultural origins of industry', *Past and Present*, 40 (1968); J. Thirsk, 'Industries in the countryside', in F. J. Fisher, ed., *Essays in the Economic and Social History of Tudor and Stuart England* (Cambridge, 1961).

[25] F. F. Mendels, 'Proto-industrialisation: the first phase of the industrialisation process', *Journal of Economic History*, 32, 1 (1972); H. Medick, 'The proto-industrial family economy: the structural function of household and family during the transition from peasant society to industrial capitalism', *Social History*, 3 (1976); P. Kriedte, H. Medick and J. Schlumbohm, *Industrialisation before Industrialisation* (Cambridge, 1982).

remains a source of debate. Some historians have sought to explain the organisational differences as a consequence of the product.[26] Certainly the production of fine quality cloth required specialised skills which a sub-divided workforce such as that of the West of England provided. It is, however, a chicken and egg argument whether skills produced by sub-division led to the production of fine cloth or vice versa. Nor did the Domestic System preclude the manufacture of fine cloth. By 1800 some Yorkshire producers were able at least to match the West of England in quality and this did not entail major organisational change.[27] The most persuasive arguments explaining the origins of industrial organisation in Yorkshire are to be found in the pioneering work of Pat Hudson. Her detailed studies reveal a very clear correlation between the agrarian economy and landholding patterns of various parishes and their industrial structures. She finds that broadly the woollen manufacturing *Kaufsystem* districts tended to be those with relatively good soils, freehold land tenure and strong manorial control whereas areas of poor soils, partible inheritance and weak manorial control tended towards the production of worsted cloth on a *Verlagsystem* very similar to the putting out structure of the West of England.[28] The situation in the West of England was not, however, so clear-cut. The textile communities of Gloucestershire, Wiltshire and Somerset existed cheek by jowl with prosperous, fertile and settled agrarian economies but there was little inter-relationship. The scarp slopes of the Cotswolds and the valley bottoms into which the Gloucestershire industry was concentrated were situated on the boundary of the old-enclosed pastoral Vale and the arable Wold but the dual farming–weaving economy still to be found there in the early seventeenth century had all but disappeared by 1760. Some clothiers owned the same small plots of land held in the family for generations. Many successful clothiers bought landed estates but few weavers owned land. 'There is not one family in twenty who have as much land as this room', a Gloucestershire weaver told the 1806 Select Committee. Here the decline of the farmer clothier was more marked. The 'Cheese' country which surrounded the Wiltshire and Somerset

---

[26] For an interesting discussion of the importance of the quality of cloth as a determinant of industrial organisation, see J. K. J. Thomson, 'Variations in industrial structure in pre-industrial Languedoc', in Berg, Hudson and Sonenscher, eds., *Manufacture in Town and Country*, pp. 77–84. See also Thomson's excellent study, *Clermont-de-Lodeve, 1633–1789: Fluctuations in the Prosperity of a Languedocian Cloth-Making Town* (Cambridge, 1982).

[27] Crump, *Leeds Woollen Industry*, pp. 51–6.

[28] Hudson, 'From manor to mill', pp. 125–33.

woollen communities was old-enclosed and dominated by small owner–occupiers whose labour demands were usually met within their families. The surviving commons around the towns were packed with industrial workers and industrial housing on an extensive scale to accommodate them dated from the seventeenth century. Thus, while both the Wiltshire and Gloucestershire industries were adjacent to agrarian economies of good soils and freehold tenure, it is clear that by the mid-eighteenth century the links between agriculture and industry were almost extinguished there. This may have been because both agriculture and industry each proved more profitable in these counties than in the West Riding woollen districts, encouraging specialisation from an early date. Common land was more plentiful on the Gloucestershire Wold and on the Wiltshire 'Chalk' or downland. These areas' arable economies provided demand for labour in harvest time which gave woollen workers the chance of some alternative employment.[29] That apart, these workers depended for their livelihood upon loom, scribbling horse and shears.

While the West of England woollen districts shared points in common with the Yorkshire woollen area, it is clear that the industrial structure there had much more in common with the Yorkshire worsted *Verlagsystem*. However, in neither region can the case for developmental inevitability from *Kaufsystem* to *Verlagsystem* be sustained. The West of England industry, which had contained dominant elements of a *Verlagsystem* since the early seventeenth century, may be caricatured as ossified by its antiquity by the mid-eighteenth century when contrasted to the youthful industry of the West Riding. However, the West Riding woollen industry, though rising to national prominence only from the second half of the eighteenth century, was in no way young. As Heaton has shown,[30] the basic organisation of the industry dated back well into the sixteenth century. The rising prosperity of the eighteenth century, as Hudson's work makes clear, offers no indication that organisation was shifting from *Kaufsystem* towards *Verlagsystem*. In fact, as previously suggested, the Domestic System offered positive advantages for growth. Indeed, it can be argued that whatever form of industrial organisation developed according to local circumstances, there is as much reason to expect that this form would survive

[29] *V.C.H., Gloucestershire*, Vol. II (Archibald Constable, 1907), pp. 164–71, 239–41; *Wiltshire*, Vol. IV (Oxford, 1959), pp. 43–64; *B.P.P.*, 1806, Vol. 3, p. 350; Mann, *Cloth Industry*, pp. 92, 95–6, 102, 32–3.

[30] H. Heaton, *The Yorkshire Woollen and Worsted Industries from the Earliest Times up to the Industrial Revolution* (Oxford, 1920), pp. 89–123.

and grow as to assume it must inevitably be transformed. Work structures developed social systems which had a stronger vested interest in preserving them than in changing them.

This leads on to a second and, for this study, a more pertinent area. The theory of proto-industrialisation assumes that *Verlagsystems* were more adaptable to transition to the factory than were the more 'backward' *Kaufsystems*. The English woollen industry does not bear this out. In fact, the opposite is correct. Just as the Domestic System had proved itself adaptable to rapid growth in the eighteenth century, with the onset of mechanisation it was able to absorb much of the new technology within the existing structure and to advance still faster. Preparatory and spinning machinery which might have threatened master clothiers' control over these productive processes were in fact integrated into the industry in such a way as to bolster their independence. While pressures for a fully fledged factory system grew steadily from the foundation of Benjamin Gott's factory at Bean Ing in 1792,[31] the master clothiers proved both innovative and resilient in their efforts to defend their autonomy and style of life. The *Verlagsystem* of the West of England, on the other hand, proved to be much less adaptable to change. Here, indeed, was the requisite capital for factory building, here was a large and proletarianised workforce with specialist knowledge of cloth making. Yet these assets of the putting out system proved liabilities when the time came to move into the machine age. The wealthy gentlemen clothiers in few cases showed much inclination to involve themselves in the factory system. The fixed capital investment might have put off some, but a major reason was undoubtedly the social disdain for the necessity of managing a factory workforce. Much as many gentlemen clothiers throughout the eighteenth century may have condemned the idleness and dissipation of their workers, it is clear that few had the stomach for taking on the direct role of changing these unfortunate predispositions into a new time thrift discipline. They might be prepared to build new factories but these were frequently leased to others to actually run.[32] Likewise, the workforce in the West of England saw no reason to welcome the advent of machinery, seeing it only as a direct threat to their jobs, lifestyles and status. Their craft consciousness and solidarity proved to be one of the major stumbling blocks to the mechanisation of the industry in the West Country.

---

[31] Crump, *Leeds Woollen Industry*, pp. 255–6.
[32] J. Tann, *Gloucestershire Woollen Mills* (David and Charles, 1967); E. Moir, 'The gentlemen clothiers', in H. P. R. Finberg, ed., *Gloucestershire Studies* (Leicester, 1957).

Thus we must note the strength and vitality of the social systems to which industrial organisation gave rise. Values, attitudes and customs reinforced by generations of experience proved far more tenacious and made organisational change far more problematic than those historians who see industries only as economic systems may suggest. The West of England clothiers with their social pretensions as 'gentlemen' and merchants; the master clothiers with their corporate pride in their cloth halls which by 1800 were no longer 'necessary' as a marketing system for cloths; the West of England workers with their deep craft consciousness: all were products of social systems which were created by industrial organisation and which found wholesale change unpalatable and unacceptable.[33]

The economic and social consequences of the differing organisational structures of the English textile industries were frequently commented upon by eighteenth-century observers. Tucker in particular believed that the rapid expansion of the West Riding woollen industry and the stagnation of the West of England were entirely attributable to industrial organisational differences. He was highly impressed by the Domestic System where cloth making was in the hands of small producers and the journeymen were 'so little removed from the Degree and condition of their Masters, and likely to set up for themselves by the Industry and Frugality of a few years . . . Thus it is that the working People are generally Moral, Sober and Industrious; that Goods are well made and exceedingly cheap.' This situation he contrasted with the West of England where the Master was 'placed so high above the condition of the Journeymen [that] their conditions approach much nearer to that of a Planter and Slave in our American colonies'. This gulf between journeymen and clothiers was so great that none could hope to make the transition from worker to master and consequently the workers could have no ambitions. 'The Motives to Industry, Frugality and Sobriety are all subverted by this one consideration, viz. That they shall always be chained to the same Oar and never be but Journeymen. Therefore their only Happiness is to get Drunk, and to make Life pass away with as little Thought as possible.' 'Is it little wonder', he asked, 'that the Trade in Yorkshire should flourish, or the Trade in Somersetshire, Wiltshire and Gloucestershire be found declining every Day?'[34]

---

[33] Cf. W. Reddy, 'The spinning jenny in France: popular complaints and elite misconceptions on the eve of the Revolution', in *The Consortium on Revolutionary Europe, 1750–1850: Proceedings*, 1981 (Athens, Georgia, U.S.A., 1981), p. 52.

[34] Tucker, *Instructions for Travellers*, p. 25.

Tucker was writing in the 1750s but his characterisation of the opportunities for upward social mobility in Yorkshire was still broadly true in 1800. The Select Committee Report of 1806 noted favourably how in the West Riding 'a young man of good character can always obtain Credit for as much Wool as will enable him to set up as a little Master Manufacturer . . . thus instances not infrequently occur wherein men rise from low beginnings, if not to excessive wealth, yet to a situation of comfort and independence'.[35] The evidence given by the master clothiers in 1803 and 1806 bore this out. While there was an increasing number of clothiers who were extending their business by hiring outworking weavers and by investing in small mills, the gap between journeyman and master was still not wide.

Tucker's description of the West of England industry dominated by the great 'Paymasters' has been criticised by Mann and Wilson who stress that while the wealthy gentlemen clothiers controlled a large slice of production, there were many 'inferior' clothiers employing only a few weavers at a time.[36] This was certainly true, as was clearly demonstrated by the division within the West of England clothiers' ranks occasioned by the attempt of the leading capitalists to persuade Parliament to repeal the whole code of regulatory legislation in 1802.[37] However, it is important that in criticising the hyperbole of Tucker we do not lose sight of the capital needed to establish oneself as a clothier. Estimates in the middle seventeenth century claimed this figure was around £300. By the mid-eighteenth century it had risen to £500. It is true that credit for part of this sum was available from factors, though this could prove a very mixed blessing.[38] Nonetheless, even allowing for this, a capital requirement of between £200 and £300 was not the sort of sum easily amassed by eighteenth-century journeymen. The examples of weavers and small clothiers existing side by side with the larger producers, of clothiers going poaching with weavers and shearmen and of dual-function clothiers which Mann notes of the seventeenth century[39] are not to be found after the middle of the next century. The gap between capital and labour, always wide, had grown appreciably wider. It is true to say that the usual route from journeyman to clothier in the West of England was in any case not a direct one but more usually through the intermediary ranks of the master worker. Master shearmen or cloth dressers probably spawned the most

[35] *J.H.C.*, Vol. 61, pp. 698–9.
[36] Mann, *Cloth Industry*, pp. 96–8; Wilson, 'The supremacy of Yorkshire', p. 239.
[37] *B.P.P.*, 1802/3, Vol. 7, pp. 133, 194, 201, 205, 339–40.
[38] Mann, *Cloth Industry*, pp. 98–9, 81–2.   [39] *Ibid.*, p. 97.

successful aspirants for they were already possessed of some capital. Estimates from the seventeenth century suggested £100[40] was the minimum requirement for setting up as a master dresser and this would have certainly risen by 1800. Master weavers and master spinners might also be able to find the capital over time but their ranks were not large for their role was a usurpation of the customary direct employment by the clothier of his workforce. They did, however, exist and occasionally were able to make the transition into full-time clothier activities. It must also be noted, however, that such master workers were, by the nature of the industry's organisation, specialists and they did not necessarily have as wide a knowledge of cloth making as a Yorkshire journeyman might acquire in the Domestic System. Overall, then, it seems clear that while some West Country journeymen did escape the 'Oar', the vast majority had no hope of becoming an employer.

Did these opportunities for social mobility matter? Historians have tended to agree with Tucker in arguing that they did. Perkin, for example, places great emphasis on social mobility in the eighteenth century as a means of maintaining social stability and of reducing 'latent' class hostilities.[41] J. K. J. Thompson has suggested that the declining opportunities for mobility in older-established putting out systems led to alienation, disillusionment and mounting discontent. Like Perkin, he argues that 'It was the fact, or the prospect, of this enjoyment of independence, and hopes for social mobility ... which were the major contributors to the maintenance of social harmony.'[42] Wilson challenges this sort of assertion, believing that the varieties of opportunities in each area and the success of some West Country nascent entrepreneurs invalidates such claims.[43] However, it is clear that the different industrial structures did produce different social attitudes. In the West Riding mobility from journeyman to master was unexceptional. Indeed, as with the Birmingham trades it may well have been the hope if not the expectation of most journeymen. It was growing fears of the monopolistic ambitions of the new manufacturers around 1800 which prompted journeymen weavers to join with master clothiers in their efforts to defend the Domestic System for they believed their future prospects of advancement would be threatened if the innovators had their way. The rise from journeyman to master

[40] *Ibid.*, p. 97.
[41] H. Perkin, *The Origins of Modern English Society* (Routledge and Kegan Paul, 1969), pp. 32–3, 61–2.
[42] Thomson, 'Variations', p. 81.
[43] Wilson, 'The supremacy of Yorkshire', p. 239.

clothier was in any case not a very big step socially or economically and did not involve any serious financial risk. More important, while a master clothier might employ a few others besides his immediate family, he remained essentially a worker, continuing to prepare and weave a cloth alongside them. The jump from journeyman to clothier in the West of England was very much greater, for even the humblest clothier there was a much more substantial capitalist than the average master clothier in Yorkshire. Further, the West Country clothier's role was not as a worker but as an organiser of labour. His relationship with his workforce was both more clearly exploitative and more remote. And just as the jump was bigger, so too were the risks of failure.

The atmosphere for entrepreneurial ambition was therefore more positive in Yorkshire than in the West of England, though such ambition was limited. The industrial structure meant that there was little perception of the master clothier as a capitalist whose economic interests were inimicable to those of labour. This was not the case in the West of England where disputes evince a growing hostility on both sides between clothiers and workers in the century before 1800. In Yorkshire if a clear social division was perceived it was the gap between master clothiers and merchants who in terms of wealth and lifestyle most closely approximated to the condition of the West Country gentlemen clothiers. Here again, however, the structure of the Domestic System meant that there was no clear-cut area of conflict until the rise of machinery began to threaten the future of the cloth halls. This perception of a socially graduated but essentially holistic society comes over clearly in the oral tradition of the West Riding gleaned in the mid-nineteenth century by men such as Peel, Sykes and Waller.[44]

How far was the opposite true of the West of England? Thomson cites David Hume's assessment of the reputation for debauchery and irresponsibility evinced by such workers, that it was 'an attempt to compensate through pleasure for want of liveliness resulting from a thwarting of the design of interesting action'.[45] Certainly the history of the West of England textile industry in the eighteenth century is not lacking in commentators eager to condemn the profligacy and idleness of the workers. William Temple, a Trowbridge clothier, claimed:

If a labourer can procure by his high wages or plenty all the necessaries of life and have afterwards a residuum, he would expend the same in gin, rum,

---

[44] F. Peel, *The Risings of the Luddites, Chartists and Plug Drawers* (1880; Frank Cass, 1968 edn); D. F. E. Sykes and G. H. Waller, *Ben o'Bills, the Luddite* (1898).

[45] Thomson, 'Variations', p. 82.

brandy or strong beer: luxurize on great heaps of fat beef or bacon, and eat perhaps until he spewed; and having gorged and gotten dead drunk, lie down like a pig and snore till he was fresh.[46]

Tucker had the same view. 'The lower class of the population . . . are given up to drunkenness and debauchery: the streets swarm with prostitutes . . . The men are as bad as can be described: who become more vitious, more indigent and idle in proportion to the advance of wages and cheapness of provisions.'[47] And the Earl of Berkeley noted in 1800 that the Gloucestershire woollen workers 'want to work but five days in a week and remain idle at the alehouse the other two, which the present dearness of wheat will not allow of'.[48] Such opinions were hardly unbiassed. Circumstances did not always allow for weekly debauches. Weavers' wages in particular were frequently under attack and the clothiers were just as adept as their workers in perpetrating frauds. Complaints and protests at such treatment continued throughout the century, a major statement of their problems being published in 1739 called, appropriately enough for Thomson's case, *The Miseries of the Miserable*, which lends support to his claim of a 'gradual impoverishment and disillusionment of its labour force'.[49]

However, it would be as erroneous to accept a picture of the West of England woollen workers' lives as one of unrelieved misery, tempered only by an alcoholic-induced escapism, as to believe in totality Temple's picture of hedonistic Bacchanalia. More to the point, these workers did not see their own lives in this way. They would not have recognised Tucker's comparison of their lot with that of slaves for they believed themselves to be free men of real social status. While the economic historian is struck by their dependent relationship upon capital, the leitmotif of the West of England woollen workers' culture was their insistence upon and determination to uphold what they saw as their economic and social *independence*. Their need for work manifested dependence. But the character of that work manifested independence and status since its control remained firmly in the hands of the worker. 'Independence' was one of the most prized of the weavers' 'rights and privileges': the right to work in their own time, in their own home, for whomsoever they chose. In reality this independence and choice was limited by the availability of work and of employers and by

[46] W. Temple, *A Vindication of Commerce and the Arts* (1758), p. 35.
[47] J. Tucker, *A Brief Essay on the advantages and disadvantages which attend France and Great Britain with regard to Trade* (1753), p. 31.
[48] H.O. 42/51, Berkeley to Portland, 25 Sept. 1800.
[49] Thomson, 'Variations', p. 83.

the need to earn a subsistence but the fact that work took place outside of direct employer control was seen as a real sign of superior status. And the notorious worship of St Monday, so aggravating to the clothier, emphasised the weavers' autonomy and set them above those labourers whose employers regulated their every task. The scribblers and shearmen, though working in shops and not at home, held similarly strong views on their independence and were just as assiduous in their enjoyment of St Monday. While workshops had notionally fixed working hours, custom dictated that these were at very least flexible. Certainly any attempt to enforce a more rigorous regime and to rationalise work was most fiercely and generally successfully resisted.[50] Thus, while the organisation of the industry and the need for income dictated the structure of work, work practice was to a very great extent dictated by custom. As John Rule has shown, in the eighteenth century the concept of custom was crucial 'in determining the expectations of work from men; in conditioning their attitudes and practices in performing it and in defining their relationships with their employers'.[51] Attempts to pin down the components of custom in a precise way are fruitless since custom was not static but evolutionary, encompassing both long-standing practices and recent gains or compromises. At one level custom was merely the defence of autonomy at work, the consequence of previous struggle between capital and labour, between the imperatives of capitalist control and labour independence. However, in the woollen industry custom also had a firm backbone provided by the law. The weavers' cherished right of working at home was buttressed by the laws restricting the numbers of looms which might be owned by any artisan and by that which forbad clothiers from establishing loomshops. Likewise, weavers, scribblers and shearmen alike well recognised the significance of the apprenticeship legislation in protecting their trades, even if no one observed the law to the letter. Custom was thus a potent and conservative force, a framework which sought to provide and safeguard stability and security in an unstable, insecure and unpredictable world. The common recognition of the importance of defending custom meant that attempts by the clothiers to challenge any of its aspects touched all

[50] For example, the attempt to impose a standard twelve-hour day with only two, not the customary five, breaks for meals was one of the reasons behind the strike of Bradford on Avon shearmen in 1802. See A. J. Randall, 'The shearmen and the Wiltshire Outrages of 1802: trade unionism and industrial violence', *Social History*, 7, 3 (1982), p. 291.

[51] J. Rule, *The Experience of Labour in Eighteenth-Century Industry* (Croom Helm, 1981), p. 194.

workers and could easily provoke a widespread and collective reaction. Tucker assumed that such disputes were occasioned by antipathy to the paymasters' 'Superior Fortunes' but this was not so. Woollen workers in the West in disputes invariably distinguished between the 'good honest gentlemen' who observed custom and those 'unmasterlike' masters who sought to destroy it by interfering with the workers 'rights' and independence.[52]

Closely bound up with these notions of independence were those of status. The craft specialisation of the West of England and the large degree of worker control over their own production emphasised the workers' belief that they were artisans and hence socially superior to those who were more directly controlled by their masters. Such beliefs were still to be found among weavers as late as 1838 at a period when their earnings had fallen even below those of many agricultural labourers.[53] In consequence, historians have been inclined to dismiss them as illusions, pointing out that at no period were wages comparable to those of the artisans of London or Birmingham and that the true hallmark of the artisan, formal apprenticeship, was almost entirely lacking. These points are true only up to a point. Certainly earnings never approached those of the highly skilled and organised Metropolitan crafts but West of England textile workers never encountered such men. Within their own communities they were well paid provided work was plentiful, the cloth dressers especially so, and the weavers and the scribblers could with their family economies earn incomes at least as good as those of local craftsmen such as bricklayers and masons and certainly well above those of ordinary labourers. Formal apprenticeship was indeed rare and only the cloth dressers were constantly able to exert effective limitation of entry to their trade. But all trades observed 'colting', the customary form of apprenticeship of being 'brought up in the trade' which, as clothiers were chagrined to learn in 1803, did have full legal sanction. We should not labour the point of defining exactly what was and what was not artisan status in the eighteenth century. As Rule has reminded us, a distinct 'artisan' culture was only gradually beginning to emerge late in that century, the gap between rural and urban craftsmen, between skilled and semi-skilled trades, only slowly beginning to widen.[54] The values of independence, self-help and the vigorous assertion of custom which

---

[52] These attitudes characterised many trades. Rule, *The Experience of Labour*, pp. 208–12.
[53] B.P.P., *Reports from the Assistant Handloom Weavers' Commissioners*, (H.C. 43–1), 1840, Vol. 23, Pt II, p. 456.
[54] Rule, *The Experience of Labour*, pp. 201–7.

characterised nineteenth-century craftsmen were widely shared in the century before.

'Artisan' status and 'independence' were most clearly manifested in a lifestyle which combined irregular bouts of industry with conspicuous consumption of leisure. The critics of this lifestyle believed that the root cause of all social ills lay in idleness which led both to moral depravity and to economic inconvenience. They believed that workers should work both for their own moral good and because that was their economic function. The woollen workers in the West did not share these cultural values. What clothiers and moralists saw as idleness they saw as leisure, as did the clothiers and moralists when enjoyed by their own class, of course. In valuing leisure as a mark of social status the workers were merely echoing an attitude shared by their rulers. This leisure was certainly not spent only in getting drunk. A thriving culture of sports, races, fairs, animal fights and the like drew weavers from the loom and shearmen from the finishing shops.[55] Social events, market day, bearing home day all made up a lifestyle which was not dominated solely by the uninterrupted grind of cloth production. This was why clothiers like Temple were convinced 'Nothing but necessity produces industry'[56] and why they believed that only by lowering wages could the workers be coerced into working a full seven-day week. Not unnaturally, the workers repudiated such attitudes. They saw their ability to take their ease, to come and go as they saw fit, as the mark of an artisan and felt superior to those workers who had to work steady hours under the eye of their employer. Their lifestyle was irregular because it suited them. It did not suit their employers and hence gave rise to growing friction.

Not all workers took St Monday or St Tuesday off whenever circumstances allowed. A few worked steadily and regularly and built up quite substantial assets. How far they did this with the aim of upward social mobility is less than clear. Certainly only a minority wished to cut themselves off from their class and to attempt what by the mid-eighteenth century had become a considerable leap into a very different cultural ambience. The majority were content to purchase their own loom or spinning wheel, to own a good suit of Sunday-best clothes and to have a supply of flour and ale in their cottages. These and some decent furniture marked the limits of most workers'

---

[55] Mann, *Cloth Industry*, p. 106; see also A. J. Randall, 'Labour and the industrial revolution in the West of England woollen industry' (unpubl. Ph.D. thesis, Birmingham, 1979), ch. 1.

[56] Temple, *A Vindication*, p. 33.

consumer ambitions for they constituted of themselves a clear indication to the world of superior status, of independence and of worth.

Certainly the woollen workers' lot was not all roses. And when
threats arose to their wages or work they complained loud and long,
exaggerating their miseries and their poverty. But an examination of
the cloth making communities of the West of England over the eighteenth century reveals a self-confident craft-conscious and proud community, vigorous in defence of its perceived 'rights and privileges'.
Discontents stemmed not from grievances about their role in the industry but from threats by their employers to that role. One comes
across no case in the eighteenth century of West of England workers
complaining about the structure of the putting out system. Indeed,
they glorified this system for it guaranteed them the independence,
status and autonomy which they so valued. Their protests were
centred on attempts to undermine or destroy the system as capitalists
sought to boost production or cut costs by weakening apprenticeship,
establishing loomshops or reducing wages. The character of these
protests was therefore essentially defensive, protecting a view of an
industrial structure and of industrial relationships which was essentially fixed and stable. This is not indicative of defeat or disillusionment
but of a vigorous and confident culture. It may be that these workers
were compensating for their undoubted proto-proletarian situation by
exaggerating their own sense of importance as specialist craftsmen.
Nonetheless, the putting out system offered them many valued economic and social compensations: an economy based on full family
involvement; social status; and a strong sense of community.

Custom, independence and status were equally important concepts
in the eighteenth-century West Riding woollen industry. Here, however, they did not constitute the same issues of potential conflict as in
the West of England since the structure of production meant that the
differences between the roles of capital and labour were much less
clearly demarcated. Independence was a vaunted symbol of the master
clothiers' lifestyle and status as producers of cloth. The cloth halls,
built and run by the master clothiers, stood as solid monuments to this
independence and their carefully regulated mechanisms reinforced it.
In effect the cloth halls acted as pitching markets, operating in exactly
the same way as the old paternalist model dictated that food markets
should be run.[57] According to their rules, all cloths had to be brought to
market and displayed there prior to sale. Thus, there could be no

---

[57] See E. P. Thompson, 'The moral economy of the English crowd in the eighteenth
century', *Past and Present*, 50 (1971), pp. 83–4.

1   West Riding master clothiers going to the cloth market
Source: G. Walker, *The Costume of Yorkshire* (1814).

forestalling and regrating by master clothiers selling direct to merchants. All transactions were confined to strictly determined hours.
The Leeds Mixed Cloth Hall opened for trading at 8.30 a.m. in the
summer, at 9.00 in the spring and autumn and at 9.30 in the winter.
After an hour the bell rang, warning that transactions must soon be
completed. Fifteen minutes later the bell rang again, announcing the
imminent end of dealing. Five minutes later all transactions ceased and
merchants who remained within the hall were fined 5s and a further
5s for every five minutes after that. When the Mixed Hall closed,
the White Cloth Hall opened, operating in exactly the same way.[58]
Cloths which were not sold remained in the hall until the next market.
Thus it was, in theory, impossible for the master clothier to undercut
the 'market' price by going round to the merchant's warehouse and
off-loading his unwanted pieces. The cloth halls were run and self-
regulated by trustees, fifteen for the Mixed Hall in Leeds, seventeen for
the White Hall, each elected for three years from among the master
clothiers of the various districts which traded in the halls. These
trustees had to be men 'of the Most Respectabillity and firstrate Character'. They were not only charged with maintaining the good order of
the halls, controlling the sale and leasing of market stalls and levying
fines on those who transgressed the rules; they also were responsible

[58] Heaton, *Yorkshire Woollen and Worsted Industries*, p. 376.

for amending and passing bye-laws, acting as the master clothiers' spokesmen in all dealings with the merchants and keeping a careful eye upon the interests of the trade. They also monitored the moral character of stall holders, dispossessing not only those who broke the rules or failed to pay their dues but also those who were convicted of frauds. In all, their aim was to maintain 'good order without oppression'. In return for these not inconsiderable burdens, the trustees earned both enhanced social status and the respect of their fellow master clothiers and the 'sumptuous banquet' which followed every annual meeting.[59] The cloth halls at Bradford, Halifax, Huddersfield and Wakefield operated in the same way.

The ethos of the cloth halls reflected the corporate pride and strong sense of independence evinced by the master clothiers. We must remember that while the halls were models of democratic self-government and regulation, the trustees did not control the prices or volume of transactions. Every master clothier had to compete on quality and price four-square with his neighbours. Deals were usually struck quietly even in times of depression when incentives to undercut rivals were strongest.[60] The ambience of the halls discouraged displays of desperate price-cutting though clearly merchants were adept at securing goods to their own advantage. While the halls housed a free market, however, while master clothiers competed, sometimes fiercely, with each other, they sold their goods within a framework and under rules and regulations which they themselves had made and monitored. Merchants might represent the life-blood capital which kept the industry thriving but they purchased their cloths only within a context controlled by the master clothiers. For the most part, the merchants were content with this arrangement. Indeed, in 1775 it was the merchants of Leeds who took the initiative in building a new White Cloth Hall when its predecessor proved too small to accommodate the booming trade of the district. Significantly, however, within a year they had handed over the hall to the trustees of the clothiers, on terms advantageous to them, for them to run and administer it.[61] Even though the development of the factory was beginning to put the cloth hall system under strain from the 1790s with a growing trade directly from producer to merchant, such was the vitality and collective spirit of the halls that they remained significant markets into the 1830s. The cloth halls, therefore, were major institutions preserving and displaying the independence of the master clothiers and acting as an effective buffer between clothiers and merchants.

[59] *Ibid.*, pp. 370–2, 374, 377.   [60] *Ibid.*, p. 376.   [61] *Ibid.*, pp. 367–70.

One further point is worth making. The cloth halls fulfilled an important market function. It is, however, debatable whether they were an especially economical method of exchanging cloths. Merchants were able to inspect a range of cloths at every market before deciding on their purchases. They could not, however, inspect these cloths with the same care with which clothiers in the West of England 'perched' cloths brought in to them by their outworking weavers since the halls lacked space, sufficient light or perching bars. Nor could they, therefore, so easily compute deductions for poor work. Merchants in the halls bought 'as seen'. Since the master clothiers were perhaps less inclined to maximise leisure opportunities when food was cheap, merchants may well have enjoyed rather more stable production rates than did the West Country clothiers. However, while the master clothiers had to compete on price on open terms when demand for goods was slack, the merchants equally had to compete in public with each other when demand was buoyant. West Country clothiers could more easily disguise the effects of market movements which acted to their own disadvantage. The time involved in attending the halls especially for clothiers from outlying parishes was also not inconsiderable since most markets were held twice weekly. This was a point emphasised by Arthur Young in 1793. He reflected that

such an immense number of men were idle, twice a week, to come from all parts of the clothing country, in order for half a dozen to execute business which might as well be performed by one woman: . . . one third of the productive time of such multitudes thus lost, to say the least, is a disadvantage attending this mode of spreading the manufacture.[62]

Markets were also times of social intercourse. Defoe recorded how the master clothiers earlier in the century had made their way to 'inns and public houses' before the markets and Heaton notes that clothiers coming into Briggate inns customarily consumed 'a "Clothier's two penny worth" which consisted of "a pot of ale, a noggin of pottage, and a trencher of boiled or roast beef for two pence"'.[63] Such social activity continued into the nineteenth century. The cloth halls, therefore, were not the most economically rational method of marketing. While they may have appeared prodigal in some respects, however, their strength lay in their reflection of and bolstering of a social system. The halls symbolised a stability, order and custom which was valued not just by the master clothiers but by the merchants too. Their

[62] Cited in Gregory, *Regional Transformation and Industrial Revolution*, p. 113.
[63] Defoe, *Tour*, Vol II, p. 611; Heaton, *Yorkshire Woollen and Worsted Industries*, p. 205.

economic inefficiencies were much less important than the cultural and social values they encapsulated.

The strong independence of the master clothiers did not, however, induce an equivalent sense of dependence on the part of the journeymen who worked for them. The mutuality of production within the master clothiers' workshops and the variety of tasks performed precluded this as a 'Poem Descriptive of the Manners of the Clothiers, written about the year 1730' suggests.

> Quoth Maister – 'Lads, work hard, I pray,
> Cloth mun be pearked next Market day.
> And Tom mun go to-morn to t' spinners,
> And Will mun seek about for t' swingers;
> And Jack, to-morn, by time be rising,
> And go t'sizing house for sizing,
> And get you web and warping done
> That ye may get it into t' loom.
> Joe, go give my horse some corn,
> For I design for t' Wolds to-morn.[64]

As in the West of England, custom played an important part in determining patterns and roles of production but, since the master clothier worked alongside his journeymen, work customs were shared rather than being sources of division. St Monday proved less of a 'problem' when masters and men alike enjoyed it, while the seasonal needs of the fields and small holdings of the clothiers provided flexibility and diversity *within* the Domestic System and did not directly conflict with the needs of cloth production as so often happened in the West of England.

While the organization of work was a major factor in helping to ease potential frictions between clothier and journeyman, equally important were the opportunities for the journeyman to set up as a little maker in his own right. Though becoming more difficult after 1790, the still real prospects of upward social and economic mobility played a major part in giving the journeyman a positive sense of his own place in the social hierarchy. The status division therefore between master clothier and journeyman was not sharply drawn. Rather it was one line within a spectrum across which men might move in either direction without major losses or gains in social esteem. The principal status division lay between master clothiers and merchants. However,

---

[64] The poem is transcribed in *Publications of the Thoresby Society*, XLI, Pt 3, No. 95, 1947, pp. 275–9.

provided the merchants stayed, both literally and figuratively, on their side of the table at the cloth halls and contented themselves with buying, finishing and marketing cloth – their customary business – conflict was kept to the minimum and hinged around market issues and not issues of production or autonomy. Only the Yorkshire cloth dressers fitted into the pattern of labour relations and attitudes evinced by the majority of woollen workers in the West of England since the organisation of their craft mirrored that of the West Country shearmen. They alone may be said to have developed the same clear labour consciousness with its closer regard for clear demarcation and aggressive defence and extension of custom. Even their labour relations, however, proved less acrimonious in the eighteenth century than did those of the West of England shearmen, not because they were any less effective in safeguarding their trade but because the whole tenor of capital–labour relations in Yorkshire was, until the advent of machinery, very much less conflictual than in the West of England.

To conclude: the West of England and the West Riding developed very different industrial structures and these gave rise to very different communities and cultures. In the West Riding where production remained in the hands of small producers and where ties to the land still had a vestigial economic and social importance, a society developed where class interests were blurred and economic frictions were soothed by interfaces such as the cloth halls which held advantages for all parties. In the West of England the putting out system increasingly polarised society into capital and labour, increasing class awareness and generating conflict. In the West Riding the Domestic System produced a society characterised by limited but extensive social mobility where lines of social and economic demarcation were relatively few and mutually acceptable to both sides of the divide. In the West of England the concentration on craft specialisation saw a proliferation of such lines of demarcation which were defined much more sharply and gave rise to many frictions. These differences led to markedly different reactions to the advent of machinery.

Chapter 2

Machinery, the factory and labour displacement

The advent of machinery constituted a major challenge to the industrial organisation and to the lives of the workers in the woollen industry in both the West of England and the West Riding. Mechanisation was somewhat more rapid in Yorkshire for resistance to the machine proved very much more widespread and tenacious in the West of England. In neither region, however, was the process of transformation as rapid or as thoroughgoing as in the cotton industry, the source of much innovation, both technological and organisational, in the Industrial Revolution. This comparative tardiness and delay in mechanisation has been explained by contemporaries and by historians by reference to the undoubted technical difficulties of adapting machinery developed for cotton to the needs of wool. The high tensile strength and length of the cotton staple made it much easier to draft and spin by mechanical means and the resultant yarn was remarkably tough. Worsted wool, having some of these characteristics, proved easier to convert into yarn using cotton spinning technology and for this reason the Yorkshire worsted industry led the way into factory development in that county. However, the short stapled woollen fibres presented more difficulties and it was some time before technical conversions developed machines which produced an acceptable product. Nontheless, technology can explain the relative delay only in part. We might equally well be asking why the cotton industry did not have problems adapting woollen machinery to its own use if technological innovation were the only reason. An equally critical factor lay in the industrial and social environment of the woollen industry. While both in Yorkshire and in the West of England the later eighteenth century offered examples of innovations in cloth types, in weaves and in finishing techniques, vested interests in both regions had strong reasons for wishing to retain the overall structures of their industries. In both regions gentlemen clothiers, master clothiers and cloth merchants thought in terms of perfecting the existing industrial organisation rather than of changing it. There was a marked reluctance on the part of most established capitalists to embark upon wholesale transformation, both from a conservative regard for the old institutions and customs and, perhaps, from a fear of committing their capital to an entirely new form of organisation.

In both the West Riding and the West of England it was a minority of enterprising men who, taking the examples of the cotton industry to heart, hastened the pace of change. This in turn put pressure on the rest, men whose roots and prejudices were firmly planted in the old system but who feared being left behind by the new forces of industrialisation. 'The increased level of investment in the 1780's', writes R. G. Wilson, 'led to changes in productivity which amazed contemporaries and allowed the bolder innovators to return a fat entrepreneurial profit.' But while 'technological innovations gave every master clothier his chance', it was the few rather than the many who took the risk. In Yorkshire, Wilson finds that the entrepreneurs were mostly 'the small struggling merchant, the merchant-manufacturers of the Halifax area, and above all the larger clothiers of Huddersfield, Bradford and the villages which stretched away south from Hunslet and Holbeck'. 'It was their vision, their capacity for hard work, their ability to save which lifted the Yorkshire textile industry out of the rut of domestic manufacture on to the rails of nineteenth-century factory production.' Men like Benjamin Gott from an established background were exceptional. Similarly, in the West of England the innovators were often modest gentlemen clothiers and men recently risen from small pretensions. These men brought new attitudes to the industry, regardless of tradition, contemptuous of worker resistance and with different social motivations to the merchant clothier whose ambitions were orientated towards the life of a solid country gentleman. These nascent manufacturers were to force the old controlling class to join them in building the factory system or to abandon the trade. Many old merchant families in fact eventually dropped out and 'stood aside to watch a new breed of masters, men without traditional obligations and authority, who built their mills across the country'.[1]

Gradually in the 1780s and 1790s machinery was introduced and buildings established or adapted to accommodate it. In the West Riding the first 'factories' were the scribbling mills of the Calder and Colne Valleys. Crump and Wilson[2] have argued convincingly that these mills were the pivot about which the Industrial Revolution was

---

[1] Wilson, *Gentlemen Merchants*, pp. 96–7, 108.
[2] Crump, *Leeds Woollen Industry*, pp. 12–29; Wilson, *Gentlemen Merchants*, pp. 91–6.

forced upon the Yorkshire industry but initially they did not harm but complemented the domestic trade, frequently being set up by master clothiers as small-scale joint-stock enterprises satisfying their own productive needs and taking work on commission for fellow master clothiers. In this way they worked just as the fulling mill had done for centuries, providing a service without threatening the organisation of production. However, the scribbling mills developed a momentum of capital accumulation and functional growth of their own and by the later 1790s were proving for many a springboard into factory production proper.[3] And as they developed, as their owners came to regard themselves not as master clothiers but as manufacturers, so disquiet and distrust grew. 'The outcry against scribbling mills of which many are at work is very great among the cloth makers', wrote William Cookson in 1802.[4] Mills were introduced a little later in the West Country and tended to house more processes. These mills, as Mann notes, 'were not, in most cases, the imposing piles familiar to a later generation, but small buildings, often converted tenements, which would house scribbling and carding machines, billies and sometimes jennies'.[5] But here too alongside the workshops and machine shops a few large factories began to develop, clearly presaging the inevitable triumph of large-scale capital. It was, perhaps erroneously, these large factories which caused most alarm. Benjamin Gott's factory at Bean Ing, Leeds, John Jones' imposing factory at Staverton in Wiltshire, Samuel Paul Bamford's mill at Twerton near Bath and Edward Sheppard's mill at Uley in Gloucestershire were all quite untypical in the late 1790s and early 1800s but they pointed the way ahead in an aggressively self-confident manner. 'Good God, Francis, it is no use your pretending to make cloth or any but those who have such places as me', Jones was said to have told a small Bradford on Avon clothier in 1802.[6] Of Bean Ing, Crump has written: 'The boldness of Gott's conception of a factory in 1792 is perhaps without parallel . . . Bean Ing sprang out of nothing; it was an ideal, a dream of the new age of industrialisation, materialised forthwith in bricks and iron, in steam and machinery.'[7]

It was this new age which these large mills so clearly foreshadowed which was the woollen workers' nightmare. The introduction of machinery aroused fears and hostility in both the West of England and the

---

[3] Hudson, *Genesis of Industrial Capital*, p. 72.
[4] W.W.M., F.45, 79, Cookson to Fitzwilliam, 16 Aug. 1802.
[5] Mann, *Cloth Industry*, p. 131.
[6] *B.P.P.*, 1802/3, Vol. 7, p. 195.   [7] Crump, *Leeds Woollen Industry*, p. 255.

West Riding. In both regions workers recognised the threat machinery posed to their jobs and to their way of life. These fears of technological redundancy were much more powerful in the West of England, however, because of its industrial organisation. The sub-division and specialisation of its workforce had enabled the production of fine quality cloths and had led to the development of skilled and craft-conscious communities. Such specialisation, however, made the West of England woollen workers especially vulnerable to machinery. There the mechanisation of any one task might threaten an entire specialist trade with redundancy without the compensating possibility of easy transfer to other activities. Hence it was that in the West of England reaction to machinery was so fierce, resistance so protracted. The organisation of work in the West Riding afforded workers some protection against such threats. The mechanisation of any one task in Yorkshire might cause a loss of work but the structure of the Domestic System meant that each worker was accustomed to a multiplicity of tasks. Thus energies released in one area could be redirected into others. Only in the case of the cloth dressers was this not so and here machinery encountered the same consistent and implacable hostility with which it was met by nearly all groups in the West of England.

The intensity and extent of hostility to machinery cannot, however, be explained simply by fears of redundancy. As will be seen, machinery was not suddenly introduced on a large scale in either the West of England or Yorkshire. It was brought in gradually and often in a low-key manner. Further, it was often introduced in times of prosperity when demand for labour was high. Yet such innovation was frequently met with resistance not merely from those in immediate danger of losing work nor even from those under longer term threat but also from other trades and groups not threatened in any way by the machine. Thus we find that it was not simply those fearing displacement who took to the streets to protest against the spinning jenny, the scribbling engine, the flying shuttle loom or the gig mill but a cross-section of the workforce as a whole. The machine innovator frequently found himself faced with the same community-wide hostility previously encountered only by the huckster, the forestaller and the re-grater. Nor were the ranks of the protesters confined to woollen workers. Small masters, petty capitalists and shopkeepers were often accused of overt or covert support for the machine breakers while rate-payers too made little secret of their sympathy for them. The machine innovators therefore faced a formidable uphill struggle. Why was this the case and why did machinery succeed in uniting so wide and disparate an opposition?

In many ways the fear which united this opposition was the fear of the factory and of the destruction of those modes of production which enabled labour to exercise autonomy over work. This fear of the factory came over strongly in the evidence given to the Parliamentary Select Committees in 1803 and 1806 and can be seen in the 1794 petition from the Yorkshire master clothiers; it was also behind much of the violent resistance to machinery in the West of England. This repudiation of the factory provides us with major insights into the attitudes of the woollen workers in both regions.

Historians, echoing contemporary apologists, have often denigrated the idea that the factory marked any tangible worsening of the workers' lot, either arguing that hostility to the factory has been exaggerated or seeking to explain it by the inertia of the workers. Thus, Hartwell concludes, 'the factory became the scapegoat for all the ills of industrialising England'.[8] Factory work, they argue, was no heavier and hours were no longer than in outwork and, moreover, it was better paid. Such views do not take account of the attitudes and fears of those engaged in outworking production. The image of the factory was amazingly powerful and fear of the factory widespread. In sheer size the factories at Bean Ing, at Staverton, Uley, Twerton and Otiwells dwarfed the workshops and fulling mills of the eighteenth century, symbolising a new power, a new centralised force in the industry. That many physically resembled workhouses furthered the popular association of the factory with places of confinement and loss of liberty. That such large mills were in every way untypical in 1800 or in 1812 did not diminish their impact. Bean Ing was familiar all over the West Riding, Staverton factory all over west Wiltshire and Somerset, to people who had never seen them. That they should be so famous (or notorious) is no surprise. These expressions of confident industrial capitalism proclaimed a future dominated by centralised production under the immediate sway of those few who possessed the resources and the courage to impose a new order upon the industry. Powered machinery necessitated some centralisation, but, as workers and employers realised, the factory offered a means of extending direct capitalist control over all processes, powered or not. The advantages of efficient quality and production control were attractive to innovators such as Gott and Jones and warned workers that their cottage economy was under

[8] R. M. Hartwell, *The Industrial Revolution and Economic Growth* (Methuen, 1971), p. 408.

threat. Thus John Phillis echoed a widespread belief when he stated in 1803 that the purpose of the clothiers' bill to repeal the old legislation was 'to build factories' and force the workpeople 'to go three or four miles to work and leave their families'. 'It is not done yet', his questioner replied. 'No, but the clouds seem to rise.'[9]

In both the West of England and the West Riding the dark clouds of the factory system grew progressively more threatening from the early 1790s. By then in Yorkshire the factory system was already a palpable presence, an encroaching menace marching eastwards towards it from the Lancashire cotton towns. It was not viewed with equanimity. Thus the building of the first steam mill in Bradford was hindered by large and hostile crowds.[10] In the West of England there was no cotton industry nearby, no adjacent region where the factory system was growing. Yet fears here were every bit as great. Staverton mill, the first large factory to be built in the heart of the woollen manufacturing area, from its inception met with constant hostility and sabotage from a workforce already afraid of the factory.[11] The image of the factory preceded the reality and aroused considerable alarm. Much of this alarm, it must be said, was highly inflated. As the decades after 1809 were to show, the grip of the factory over the industry was but slowly established. In Yorkshire the Domestic System proved remarkably tenacious and was only displaced by stages. In the West of England weaving remained a domestic labour until the 1840s. But contemporaries in 1800 could not know this. They viewed the factory system as an approaching flood which threatened to submerge them all.

The workers' arguments against the factory were imbued with moral imperatives. They assumed that the Domestic and putting out systems embodied the wisdom of ages, providing stable social and familial relations, the means of educating and socialising the young and bringing them up in trades which provided them with dignity and status. By threatening to destroy this moral system, the factory, they believed, must embody immorality. The immoral nature of the factory was confirmed in that it created monopoly. By concentrating power and control in the hands of the few able to raise enough capital to own one, the factory would lead to unfair competition, engrossing the trade of smaller capitalists and destroying the opportunities for upward social mobility. Society would thereby be polarised into a few rich

---

[9] *B.P.P.*, 1802/3, Vol. 7, p. 63.

[10] J. James, *History of the Worsted Manufacture in England from the Earliest Times* (1857), pp. 591–3.

[11] See below, pp. 158–9.

monopolists and a mass of impoverished, dependent labourers. Further, the experience of work in factories, to which they feared they would be consigned, was assumed to be degrading and demoralising. The lack of parental supervision, the destruction of the family economy, the licentious intermingling of the sexes were all deemed to lead to immorality and to the breakdown of social values.[12]

Historians armed with 'the enormous condescension of posterity'[13] easily dismiss such arguments. They know, of course, that the factory did not destroy outwork. Indeed, at first it stimulated a very great increase in the demand for outworkers. Nor did the factory lead to any immediate polarisation or monopoly. Many studies have shown that the capital requirements for entry into the class of factory masters were not very great and that such men were rarely recruited from the ranks of the most wealthy merchant manufacturers of the previous age.[14] The factory did not preclude social mobility. It may even have increased it. And as to the claims of immorality within the factory, these are seen as the hyperbole of threatened inertia. Hartwell, for example, notes that such allegations were far more frequent in domestic service and that opportunities for licentiousness within the factory day must have been limited.[15]

These opinions, however correct, are nonetheless the views of hindsight. The opinions of contemporaries, however misguided, cannot be simply dismissed for they informed the perceptions and actions of their day. The concern at the immorality of the factory system was to be found among the respectable clothiers as well as among the workforce. Thus John Anstie, a great supporter of the clothiers' case for repeal, was clearly acutely worried by the moral implications of the factory and its impact upon family life. In spite of his progressive belief in the efficiency of machinery, he refused to give up domestic spinning, a decision based on philanthropy and moral scruples and one which he subsequently blamed for his bankruptcy.[16] And Richard Oastler's father, a prosperous Yorkshire cloth merchant, gave up the trade rather than be forced to take up the factory system since he regarded

---

[12] These arguments are examined in Chapter 7.
[13] The phrase comes from Thompson, *The Making*, p. 13.
[14] Wilson, *Gentlemen Merchants*, p. 94; Hudson, *Genesis of Industrial Capital*, pp. 259–62; see also S. D. Chapman, *The Early Factory Masters: The Transition to the Factory System in the Midlands Textile Industry* (David and Charles, 1967), pp. 77–100.
[15] Hartwell, *Industrial Revolution*, pp. 397–8.
[16] W.O. 1/1082, Anstie to Sec. at War, 28 May 1795; see also J. Anstie, *Observations on the Importance and Necessity of Introducing Improved Machinery into the Woollen Manufactory* (1803), pp. 17–20.

the use of machinery 'as a means of oppression on the part of the rich and of corresponding degradation and misery to the poor'.[17] These fears of the impact of the factory upon the morals of the community, exaggerated or not, were deep-rooted.

The emphasis on the allegations of the immorality of the factory has, however, distracted attention from what to the workers was a more important area of concern, namely the amorality of the factory system. It was this aspect, the depersonalisation of the relationship between master and man, the imposition of the thraldom of the machine for the manly reciprocity of former industrial relations, which made the image of the factory one which was so much feared. The relationship between masters and men in both the Domestic and putting out systems was determined by the invisible but tenacious boundaries of custom. The factory would ignore custom, imposing a new, purely economic re-lationship in which men were mere hands, commodities to be bought and sold and set to work however and whenever market forces dic-tated. Under the old system custom protected the workers' rights, the workers' dignity. It was an impartial arbiter in disputes, the guardian of community morality. The factory would steamroller custom, turn the workers into slaves under an amoral regime dictated only by the factory master's profits. The factory would thus undermine all the values upon which the workers' culture and communities were predi-cated, replacing them with the new amoral imperatives of the market economy.[18] What was at risk was not just some workers' jobs. Machin-ery and the factory threatened the very fabric of existing social organisation.

The arguments advanced by the opponents of industrial change may easily be criticised, at worst for special pleading, at best for an extrava-gant idealisation of the real experience of eighteenth-century textile production. Workers fearing change might well idealise their past, picking out only the best times and conveniently forgetting the reality of drudgery, insecurity and poverty which were every bit as much characteristic. It is, indeed, an intrinsic human reaction to choose the very best of the past as a base line for future reference. Today, nostalgia is easily extracted from the rubble of inner city decay and renewal. We must note, however, that in 1803 and 1806 the woollen workers were not urging Parliament to restore to them a *lost* Golden Age. Their case was that they *already* had a Golden Age provided that the rules which

---

[17] C. Driver, *Tory Radical: The Life of Richard Oastler* (Oxford, 1946), pp. 17–18.
[18] See, for example, a letter 'In praise of Looker On', in *L.M.*, 15 March 1803.

enabled it to exist were enforced.[19] And those rules, those customs, precluded the advent of the factory and the spread of machinery.

The reaction to machinery and the response to its introduction was thus both a consequence of industrial organisation and informed by the cultural values such organisation had developed. The craft consciousness established by specialisation gave rise to a clearly defined conservative plebeian culture which was quick to react to threats to its economy. In the eighteenth century the woollen workers of the West of England and the cloth dressers of Yorkshire had shown themselves to be quick to resist any attempts to undermine or challenge their autonomy or standards of living. And in the West of England vigorous protests had extended out from industrial conflicts to embrace in particular food marketing and the price of provisions among other issues.[20] This tradition of protest generated its own momentum and engendered a powerful communal self-confidence. The threat of machinery was therefore met by a community with a history of active self-defence in the West of England, which, with the exception of the cloth dressers, was not the case in Yorkshire. In this way, industrial organisation made the West of England workers both far more vulnerable to machinery and also far more likely and able to resist machinery than did the Domestic System.

It is the purpose of this study to examine the character and development of this resistance to machinery but it is useful before examining the pattern of resistance to ask in what ways did machinery bring about changes in the workforce? In what numbers were woollen workers displaced by mechanical innovations? How many workers, conversely, were not affected by change? How did machinery alter the structure and the nature of employment in the industry and in what stages? These are clearly important questions if we are to understand fully both the chronology and impact of industrial change and the woollen workers' reaction to it. Yet textile historians have largely ignored the effects of mechanisation on the structure of the workforce except in its widest terms.[21] This is in part a consequence of the paucity of information. Contemporaries were for obvious reasons concerned

---

[19] For discussion of these views, see below, pp. 241–4.

[20] A. J. Randall, 'The Gloucestershire food riots of 1766', *Midland History*, 10 (1985), pp. 72–93.

[21] One of the few exceptions has been N. J. Smelser, *Social Change in the Industrial Revolution* (Routledge and Kegan Paul, 1959), which is concerned with the family in the Lancashire cotton industry. It is not, however, without its drawbacks. See M. M. Edwards and R. Lloyd-Jones, 'N. J. Smelser and the cotton factory family: a reassessment', in Harte and Ponting, eds., *Textile History*, pp. 304–19.

far more with the impact of specific changes than with the consequence of these changes for the industry as a whole. And when the effects of particular innovations were discussed, the evidence advanced was frequently of a fiercely partisan nature. Thus the historian is confronted with information which often is either so vague as to be of little use or so exaggerated as to present a highly distorted picture. For example, the clothiers of the West of England who met in Bath in October 1776 claimed that the spinning jenny would not lead to any unemployment whereas in fact it caused widespread distress when generally taken up in the 1790s. On the other hand, the Gloucestershire scribblers claimed in their petition to Parliament in 1794 that the scribbling engine could do the work of twenty scribblers and that the carding engine could do the work of eighty women, both claims being highly inflated.[22] Nor did the degree of opposition encountered by specific machines necessarily indicate their strategic impact on the industry as a whole. For example, the cloth dressers' resistance to the gig mill was the longest and most violent accorded to any innovation but in terms of labour displacement it was less significant than the spinning jenny or the scribbling engine. Again, not all machines provoked resistance or caused labour displacement. The slubbing billy was of crucial importance for the mechanisation and organisation of the preparatory stages of the industry but slubbing was a new trade, not having been previously needed,[23] and the billy provoked no opposition.

However, the historian of the woollen industry is fortunate in that the two handloom weavers' commissioners for the West of England both compiled evidence surveying the impact of mechanical change on the workforce over the period 1781 to 1838. W. A. Miles, the commissioner for Gloucestershire, chose to demonstrate the effect of machinery by discussing the changes which had affected each process in turn, but his colleague, A. Austin, commissioner for Wiltshire and Somerset, displayed his information in a series of tables showing the labour requirements for and the cost of producing a piece of broadcloth. These tables provide the historian with a wealth of evidence and constitute our most complete survey of the changing structure of the industry during the Industrial Revolution.[24] They cannot, however, be accepted without caution. The tabulated evidence ends with the year

[22] *G.J.*, 14 Oct. 1776; *J.H.C.*, Vol. 49, pp. 599–600.
[23] Mann, *Cloth Industry*, p. 288.
[24] *B.P.P.*, *Reports from the Assistant Handloom Weavers' Commissioners* (H.C. 220), 1840, Vol. 24, Pt v, W. A. Miles, Gloucestershire, pp. 369–74; B.P.P., 1840, Vol. 23, Pt viii, A. Austin, South-West of England, pp. 439–41.

1828, some ten years before Austin was writing his report, and doubts may be raised as to the accuracy of his figures purporting to relate to the period before 1796. Nonetheless, Austin was a scrupulously careful investigator as his whole report testifies. It is clear that in compiling the information for his tables he obtained evidence from clothiers whose businesses had spanned the years in question. Where possible, every effort has been made to check Austin's tables against other available sources but these are not numerous and are often equally open to question. While some of Austin's figures, particularly those for the pre-mechanised period, sometimes seem questionable, however, the general proportions of his conclusions appear to be largely borne out.

It must be emphasised that Austin's evidence of displacement related only to the West of England. As previously noted, the specialisation there made labour displacement very much easier to calculate than for the West Riding where many tasks were undertaken by the same workers. However, the scale of labour requirement changes effected by machinery would be the same in Yorkshire as in the West Country and may be equally effectually applied there. It will not, however, be possible to portray changes in the work structure with as much confidence as for the West of England.

Before investigating the tables compiled by Austin, it is necessary to note that the list of processes through which the wool passed given by Austin is incomplete. There is no mention of wool sorting, dyeing, oiling, fine drawing or marking.[25] None of these processes was affected by mechanisation nor did any employ a large number of workers per piece. Their numbers would have risen with increased production between 1790 and 1828 but their omission does not greatly detract from the value of the tables.

Austin chose to present his evidence concerning the numbers employed and the time taken to make one piece of superfine broadcloth in tables which represent five different periods. The first, reflecting the years from 1781 to 1796, represented for Austin the pre-mechanised period when the only powered machinery were the stocks of the fulling mills. Austin refers to fulling as 'felting'. His second table covers the years from 1796 to 1805 when, according to Austin, 'complicated machinery was introduced for scribbling and carding the wool, and for spinning the yarn, requiring large buildings,

[25] 'Oiling' involved adding fine oil to the scoured wool before scribbling and was performed by 'steady men'. 'Fine drawing' was the process of repairing damages in the cloth after finishing, and 'marking' involved sewing the cloth number, type, and often manufacturer's name, to the end of the cloth. Both were performed by women. *B.P.P.*, 1840, Vol. 24, Pt v, pp. 370, 374.

Table 1. *Labour required and costs to make a piece of superfine broadcloth, 1781–1796* (after Austin)

Employment	Quantity	Worker(s)	Time per piece hrs.	mins.	Cost per piece £	s.	d.
Cleansing the wool	- - 80 lbs.	- - one man	3	22	-	-	9
Picking	- - 80 lbs.	- - one woman	- - 101	2	-	8	5¼
Scribbling by hand	- - 75 lbs.	- - one man	- - 96	-	-	11	8
Spinning warp	- - - 26 lbs.	- - one woman & one child	260	-	1	12	6
Spinning abb	- - - 44 lbs.	- - one woman and two children	352	-	1	9	4
Spooling warp	- - - 26 lbs.	- - one old woman	- - 52	-	-	2	2
Warping	- - - 26 lbs.	- - one woman	- - 12	-	-	-	8½
Reeling abb	- - - 44 lbs.	- - one child	- - 12	-	-	-	6
Weaving	- - - 1 piece (34 ells)	two men and one child	364	-	2	15	6
Scouring	- - - 1 piece (34 ells)	one man and one boy	3	-	-	-	6
Burling	- - - 1 piece (34 ells)	one woman	- - 32	-	-	3	-
Felting	- - - 1 piece (34 ells)	one man and one boy	10	-	-	8	-
Raising or roughing	1 piece (34 ells)	one man	- - 88	-	-	14	2
Cutting or shearing	- - 1 piece (34 ells)	one man	- - 72	-	-	10	-
Pressing and finishing	1 piece (34 ells)	one man	- - 2	-	-	1	-
			Total £		8	18	2¾

Source: B.P.P., 1840, Vol. 23, p. 439.

great power to drive it, and considerable investment of capital'. This period, he believed, also saw the introduction of the flying shuttle loom and the gig mill which superseded the hand process of raising the nap prior to dressing the cloth. His third table, covering from 1805 to 1820, sees the introduction and proliferation of the shearing frame which mechanised the hand-dressing process. Austin's fourth table from 1820 to 1827 sees the frames superseded by rotary cutters and finally his last table details the industry in 1828 when, according to Austin, 'the introduction of mules for spinning lessened still further the quantity of human labour'. Austin's 'periods' have a certain artificiality. Clearly there was no such ordered progressive surge of machinery. Certainly the changes in the preparatory stages of scribbling, carding and spinning did largely pre-date other innovations in their take up, but they were widely used in Yorkshire long before 1796. Some areas were always in the van of change. Thus the area around Huddersfield saw the earliest and steadiest development of technological innovations whereas the area around Leeds generally was somewhat slower to take them up. The gig mill had long been used in Gloucestershire on white cloth before 1796 and the shearing frame was introduced here much earlier and on a wider scale than in Wiltshire. However, the gig mill was not widely in use anywhere outside of

Table 2. *Labour required and costs to make a piece of superfine broadcloth,*
1828 (after Austin)

Employment	Quantity	Worker(s)	Time per piece hrs.	mins.	Cost per piece £	s.	d.
Cleansing the wool - - -	80 lbs.	- - one man - -	3	22	–	–	9
Picking - - -	80 lbs.	- - one woman - -	101	2	–	10	2¼
Scribbling by machine	75 lbs.	- - one child - -	14	–	–	–	7¼
Carding by machine - -	75 lbs.	- - one child - -	13	21	–	–	7
Slubbing by billy - - -	25 lbs.	- - one man and two children	7	4	–	2	7¼
Spinning warp and abb by two mules - - -	75 lbs.	- - one man and one child	12	–	–	1	9
Reeling - - -	frequently dispensed with						
Spooling - - -	frequently dispensed with						
Warping - - -	25 lbs. -	- one woman - -	10	–	–	–	8½
Weaving - - -	1 piece (34 ells)	one man and one child	252	–	2	11	6
Scouring - - -	1 piece (34 ells)	one man and one boy	3	–	–	–	6
Burling - - -	1 piece (34 ells)	one woman - -	32	–	–	3	–
Felting - - -	1 piece (34 ells)	one man and one boy	12	–	–	8	–
Raising - - -	1 piece (34 ells)	one man and one boy	12	–	–	3	8
Boiling (new operation)	1 piece (34 ells)	one man - -	1	–	–	1	2
Cutting by rotary cutter	1 piece (34 ells)	one man - -	6	–	–	1	3[a]
Pressing - - -	1 piece (34 ells)	one man - -	2	–	–	1	–
			Total £		4	7	3¼

[a] On Austin's table a printing error has this as £1 3s. 0d. but it has been correctly added into the
total labour cost as 1s. 3d.
Source: B.P.P., 1840, Vol. 23, p. 441.

Gloucestershire until after 1803 when Parliament suspended the legislation which many believed forbade its use. The flying shuttle, or
spring loom as it was known in the West Country, was common in
Yorkshire by the 1790s but was rarely found in the West of England
before 1803. Indeed, its introduction to Frome in Somerset prompted
riots there as late as 1822. Rotary cutting machines had by no means
displaced shearing frames in the period 1820–27 for frames were to be
found in many mills into the 1830s.[26] Nonetheless, the tables indicate
well enough the general sequence of change everywhere.

Austin's first and final tables are reproduced in Tables 1 and 2. They
both represent the numbers employed, time required per process and
costs for a piece of superfine broadcloth of 34 ells or 51 yards woven
length and of about 38 yards finished length. This was because in

[26] For example, Thomas Spackman introduced rotary cutters into his Dunkirk mill,
Freshford, in 1832 or 1833. *B.P.P., First Report of the Commissioners for Inquiring into the
Employment of Children in Factories* (H.C. 450), 1833, Vol. 20, B. 2, p. 82. See also K. H.
Rogers, *Wiltshire and Somerset Woollen Mills* (Pasold, 1976), pp. 23–4.

fulling (felting) a cloth shrank by about a quarter. Austin's information suggests that the total labour required to produce a broadcloth fell by some 75% as a result of the introduction of machinery in the years between 1796 and 1828. The impact of mechanisation, however, was not experienced equally, those to suffer most being women workers, while adult males fared relatively best. The full impact of mechanical change on the workforce can be seen by comparing the labour requirements over Austin's five periods, taking labour in the period 1781–1796 as 100 as shown in Table 3.

Table 3. *Proportional labour requirements to produce one superfine broadcloth, 1781–1828* (after Austin)

	1 (1781–96)	2 (1796–1805)	3 (1805–20)	4 (1820–7)	5 (1828)
Men	100	41	36	35	31
Women	100	25	25	25	18
Children	100	30	30	30	25
Total	100	32	31	30	25

It is clear from Austin's figures that it was the first stage of mechanisation which made the greatest impact on the structure of employment and that women were particularly hard hit. However, following this first stage of change, female and child labour requirements per piece remained steady until the 1820s but that for adult male labour continued to fall. The individual changes between the five periods are summarised below.

Austin's first phase of mechanisation between 1796 and 1805 witnessed six major changes:

	Employment	Worker(s)	Time per piece hrs.	mins.	Cost per piece £	s.	d.
Period 1	Scribbling by hand	1 man	96	–		11	8
Period 2	Scribbling by machine	1 child	14	–			7
	Carding by machine	1 child	13	21			7
Period 1	Spinning warp	1 woman and 1 child	260	–	1	12	6
	Spinning abb	1 woman and 2 children	352	–	1	9	4
Period 2	Slubbing by machine	1 man and 2 children	7	4		2	7¼
	Spinning warp on the jenny	1 woman	38	17		11	1
	Spinning abb on the jenny	1 man and 2 children	34	17		11	5½

	Employment	Worker(s)	Time per piece hrs. mins.	Cost per piece £ s. d.
Period 1	Weaving on double loom	2 men and 1 child	364 –	2 15 6
Period 2	Weaving on spring loom	1 man and 1 child	252 –	2 11 6
Period 1	Raising by hand	1 man	88 –	14 2
Period 2	Raising by gig	1 man and 1 boy	12 –	3 8

As a result of these changes, Austin stated that labour costs per piece had fallen from £8 18s. 2¾d. to £6 3s. 5d., a fall of over 30%.

The only change cited by Austin as having been brought about between 1805 and 1820 was the introduction of the shearing frames:

	Employment	Worker(s)	Time per piece hrs. mins.	Cost per piece s. d.
Periods 1 and 2	Cutting by hand	1 man	72 —[a]	14 9
Period 3	Cutting with frame	1 man	18 —	3 9

[a] This figure is mistakenly given as 88 hours on Austin's table 2, but correctly as 72 hours on his tables 1 and 3.

The fourth period from 1820 to 1827 saw the introduction of rotary cutters, further displacing shearmen:

	Employment	Worker(s)	Time per piece hrs. mins.	Cost per piece s. d.
Period 3	Cutting with frame	1 man	18 —	3 9
Period 4	Cutting with rotary cutter	1 man	6 —	1 3

Lastly in 1828 spinning mules displaced the jennies:

	Employment	Worker(s)	Time per piece hrs. mins.	Cost per piece s. d.
Periods 2, 3 and 4	Spinning warp on the jenny	1 woman	38 17	11 1
	Spinning abb on the jenny	1 man and 2 children	34 17	11 5½
Period 5	Spinning warp and abb by 2 mules	1 man and 1 child	12 —	1 9

How far are Austin's figures to be relied upon? It is possible to compare his evidence both with that compiled by Miles, which is, however, less comprehensive concerning mechanical change, and with an 'Estimate of the cost of manufacturing a superfine broadcloth' which emanated from Trowbridge in 1798.[27] The purpose of the 'Estimate' was apparently to encourage clothiers to raise the price of cloth since it purported to show that each cloth was produced at a loss of £1 12s. 5½d. It was, therefore, essentially a piece of propaganda and not necessarily to be wholly relied upon. Taking the processes enumerated by Austin in turn, how far do these other pieces of information bear out Austin's figures? Austin stated that one woman picker would pick 80 lb of wool in 101 hours and earn from 4s. 6d. to 5s. 2d. per week or around ¾d. per lb. The 1798 estimate cited picking at 1d. per lb. Scribbling, however, presents a considerable disparity. Austin's figures indicate that hand scribblers before 1796 were paid at 1s. 9d. per lb. After machinery had taken over, the cost fell to 7d. for 75 lb, as did the cost of carding. Austin's figures also indicate that a slubber on the billy was paid at around 1d. per lb, a figure agreed by Miles. The 1798 estimate, however, cites the cost of scribbling as 2d. per lb, and that of carding and slubbing at 1½d. per lb each. These figures for scribbling and carding appear extraordinarily high, as high, indeed, as the cost of hand labour and must be viewed sceptically. The rates cited by Austin for spinning more or less correspond with those on the 1798 estimate but there is a disparity between the weekly earnings of the female warp spinner, supported by Miles' figures, and the cost per piece which probably indicates that the latter is an error. Austin cites a rate of 13d. per yard for weaving on the double loom, still used in Trowbridge in 1798, whereas the rate was then 15d. as given in the 'Estimate'. Further, he has allowed four weeks for weaving a broadcloth. While this may have been an average time for all cloths, such a cloth could have been completed in under three weeks.[28] Austin's figures also indicate that the spring loom would finish the same cloth in 70% of the time taken by the double loom. This is misleading. The spring loom was considerably slower than the double loom when first taken up, although greater experience and improving yarn quality helped make up the deficit.[29] The real difference was that weavers after 1800 began to work much longer hours in general than before and thus completed cloths more rapidly. The net result for labour demands, however, was

---

[27] Reproduced in full in Mann, *Cloth Industry*, p. 321.

[28] *Ibid.*, pp. 323–5; B.P.P., 1802/3, Vol. 7, pp. 8, 13.

[29] B.P.P., 1802/3, Vol. 7, pp. 10, 25, 78, 300.

much the same. A more serious weakness is Austin's assumption that the double loom was worked by two adult men. This was decreasingly the case throughout the eighteenth century and, while some looms were so worked, the majority of 'second men' by 1800 were women, youths or apprentices.[30] Austin's figure of 8s. per piece for the cost of fulling (felting) is at very great variance from that cited by Miles and the 1798 estimate, both 3s., but again his estimate of labour required corresponds with Miles' evidence. There is considerable discrepancy between Austin's figures for the cost of raising and shearing a cloth, about 4½d. per yard for both processes before 1796, and the 1798 estimate which cites 'dressing' at 15d. per yard. Austin's figures are far too low. The Bradford on Avon shearmen struck work in 1802 for their customary 7d. per yard for shearing and 4d. for raising.[31] The difference between the combined cost of 11d. per yard and the 1798 estimate would have constituted the master dresser's profit. Miles stated that about two days were required to gig mill a cloth in 1838 while Austin cited a figure of 12 hours. Miles seems to have taken some account of the trend towards heavier dressing in estimating the hours of labour required to shear a cloth on the rotary cutters in 1828 and after. Miles claimed 'In former years the cloth was thinly dressed, it was not cut more than six times, but now it is cut fifteen or twenty times.'[32] William Partridge noted in 1823 that a rotary cutter could shear the nap of a broadcloth 20 yards long in 15 minutes.[33] By this criteria a 38 yard broadcloth would need 28 minutes per 'kerf' or cut, making some twelve kerfs in the 6 hours designated by Austin in his fifth table, but improved design probably enabled a greater speed thereafter.

What then is it possible to conclude about the reliability of Austin's tables? Certainly his periods are artificial, his arithmetic is not always accurate and his estimates at times appear improbable. This weakness, however, relates more to wages and costs than to evidence of labour requirements. Indeed, as far as hours of labour in each of the trades which experienced change is concerned, Austin's evidence appears to

[30] *J.H.C.*, Vol. 27, p. 731; *A State of the Case, and a Narrative of Facts Relating to the late Commotions and Rising of the Weavers in the County of Gloucester* (1757), p. 20; J. de L. Mann, 'Clothiers and weavers in Wiltshire in the eighteenth century', in L. S. Pressnell, ed., *Studies in the Industrial Revolution, Presented to T. S. Ashton* (Athlone, 1960), p. 92; *B.P.P.*, 1802/3, Vol. 7, pp. 10, 28, 336.

[31] *B.P.P.*, 1802/3, Vol. 7, pp. 194, 198, 336, 341.

[32] *B.P.P.*, 1840, Vol. 24, Pt v, p. 373.

[33] W. Partridge, *A Practical Treatise on Dying of Woollen Cloth and Skein Silk with the Manufacture of Broadcloth and Cassimere* (New York, 1823; 1975 edn), p. 83.

Table 4. *Number of workers required to produce twelve superfine broadcloths in one week, 1781–1796, 1796–1805 and 1828* (after Austin)

	1781–96				1796–1805				1828		
Employment	Worker(s)	Time (hours)	Numbers required	Employment	Worker(s)	Time (hours)	Numbers required	Worker(s)	Time (hours)	Numbers required
Picking	1 woman	101	17W	Picking	same		17W	same		17W
Scribbling by hand	1 man	96	16M	Scribbling by machine	1 child	14	2C	same		2C
				Carding by machine	1 child	13	2C	same		2C
Spinning warp	1 woman and 1 child	260	65W / 65C	Slubbing by machine	1 man and 2 children	7	1M / 2C	same		1M / 2C
Spinning abb (weft)	1 woman and 2 children	352	88W / 176C	Spinning warp on jenny	1 woman	38	6W	Spinning warp and abb by 2 mules — 1 man and 1 child	12	2M / 2C
				Spinning abb on jenny	1 man and 2 children	34	6M / 12C			
Spooling warp	1 woman	52	9W	Spooling by machine	1 woman	24	4W	dispensed with		
Warping	1 woman	12	2W	Warping	1 woman	10	2W	same		2W
Reeling abb	1 child	12	2C	Reeling	same		2C	dispensed with		
Weaving	2 men and 1 child	364	61M (61M?) / 61C	Weaving on spring loom	1 man and 1 child	252	42M / 42C	same		42M / 42C
Burling	1 woman	32	5W	Burling	same		5W	same		5W
Felting	1 man and 1 child	10	2M / 2C	Felting	1 man and 1 child	12	2M / 2C	same		2M / 2C
Raising	1 man	88	15M	Raising by gig mill	1 man and 1 child	12	2M / 2C	same		2M / 2C
Cutting	1 man	72	12M	Cutting	same		12M	Cutting by rotary cutter — 1 man	6	1M

provide the historian with a good indication of the dimensions of change engendered by machinery.

While Austin's tables provide valuable information on the way in which machinery altered the labour requirements for each process, they do not indicate so clearly how the overall composition of the workforce was changed. I have therefore attempted in Table 4 to use the information contained in Austin's report relating to his periods 1, 2 and 5 to estimate the total number of workers required to produce 12 cloths per week, or 600 cloths per annum, the production level of a medium-sized 'respectable' West of England clothier, in 1781–96, 1796–1805 and 1828. I have estimated the working hours of all except the domestic spinners at 72 hours per week. The return to the Factory Commissioners by the Trowbridge firm J. & T. Clark in 1833 showed that the slubbing, scribbling, carding and drawing sections worked a $68^{1}/_{2}$ hour week, while the finishing sections worked 74 and $75^{1}/_{2}$ hour weeks.[34] Clearly working hours varied from trade to trade and from factory to factory. Working times in mills reliant upon water power often fluctuated considerably, but 72 hours seems a reasonable average figure for all working in shops or factories. Domestic weavers after 1800 may well have worked longer hours than this, just as certainly before 1790 they worked shorter hours. A working week of 72 hours probably represents a high average figure for them. Domestic spinners, however, clearly could not, or did not, achieve so high an average work rate. Spinning was for many a by-employment, to be put aside when other tasks became more urgent. The average production of domestic spinners was the subject of widely differing opinions. However, a pamphleteer in 1793 claimed that a woman with children could earn from 4s. to 5s. a week when work was plentiful and Mann believes that with the price for weft (abb) at 11d. per lb 'this would not have been impossible'.[35] This would mean a production rate of around $5^{1}/_{2}$ lb per week. According to Austin, a domestic abb spinner with two children could spin 44 lb in 352 hours or 1 lb in 8 hours. Thus, to produce $5^{1}/_{2}$ lb would necessitate a working week of 44 hours. I have chosen, therefore, to allow 48 hours for the working week of domestic spinners, recognising that this will produce a figure indicative of the very minimum number of female spinners required. I have chosen the limited period of one week fully realising that it was physically impossible to produce a broadcloth in so short a time because only in this way is it possible to arrive at any idea of the relative proportions of the

[34] W.R.O., 927/71, Clark's list of employees on 1 Jan. 1833.
[35] Mann, *Cloth Industry*, pp. 322–3.

Table 5. *Total labour required to produce twelve superfine broadcloths in one week, 1781–1796, 1796–1805 and 1828*

	1781–96	1796–1805	1828
Men	167	65	50
Women	186	34	24
Children	306	66	54
Total	659	165	128
Ratio	100	25	19

numbers involved in each trade. Contemporary estimates of the numbers employed by one loom are, as Mann notes, quite misleading since 'fullers and shearmen would perform their tasks much more quickly than spinners or weavers'.[36] It is for this reason that I have ignored Austin's one man employed cleansing the raw wool because he could cleanse sufficient wool for the piece of broadcloth in question in 3 hours 22 minutes or, in other words, every week he could cleanse enough wool for twenty-one cloths. I have also ignored time spent scouring the woven cloth. This process was almost always carried out by the millmen, being performed during the intervals between moving cloths in the stocks.[37] Finally, as I have noted before, these figures take no account of the wool sorters or dyers nor of the drawers or oilers. Their numbers were small and remained in proportion to production throughout the period under review. All figures for numbers employed have been rounded up or down to the nearest whole.

From the figures in Table 4 it is possible to conclude that the total labour required to produce twelve broadcloths in one week decreased between 1781–96 and 1828 as shown in Table 5. The figure for male labour in the period 1781–96 is probably over-large, a result of Austin's assumption that both weavers in the double loom were adult males. It will also be remembered that the figure for female hand spinners represents the very minimum number required. This being the case, the consequences of early mechanisation were relatively less severe for men and correspondingly much more severe for women and children. Even accepting the figures as they stand, it remains clear that it was the first wave of machinery which had the most sweeping consequences for the woollen workers as a whole and for women workers in particular. With the introduction of preparatory machinery the number of women required per cloth slumped to at most only 18% of its former

[36] *Ibid.*, p. 316.   [37] *Ibid.*, p. 294; B.P.P., 1840, Vol. 24, Pt v, p. 372.

2   Domestic spinning
Source: G. Walker, *The Costume of Yorkshire* (1814).

total as against a fall to 39% at worst for men. The main reason for this massive displacement was the demise of hand spinning and its replacement by the slubbing billy and jenny. When the latter were introduced, the work of 153 women and their 241 child assistants could be performed by just over 7 men, 6 women and 14 children. Here was labour redundancy on a massive scale. The blow, however, was to some extent cushioned for West of England woollen working families. The slowness of outworking spinners had forced clothiers there to put out wool over very wide areas to obtain sufficient yarn and very many domestic spinners were the wives of agricultural labourers and others living in purely rural areas.[38] Thus when machinery, the billy and the jenny, put an end to domestic spinning, those who suffered most were those families not primarily engaged in the woollen industry. Woollen workers' wives, of course, were made redundant, but they were better placed to take up newly created opportunities of work in mills, while the increased supply of superior machine spun yarn helped weavers to increase their earnings and growing trade encouraged their wives to take up weaving for themselves in the narrow loom or as journeymen

[38] S. Rudder, *A New History of Gloucestershire* (Cirencester, 1779), p. 711, stated that Stroud clothiers put out spinning 20 miles or more.

in the double loom. In the West Riding, where much less spinning was put out to the wives of non-textile workers, the displacement among women employed in the Domestic System occasioned by the billy and the jenny would have been much greater. As in the West of England some undoubtedly obtained work in the larger jenny 'factories'. More worked small hand-powered jennies in master clothiers' workshops but perhaps four in five women had to find other work. There is evidence that many took to the loom. However, prejudice against women weavers was if anything stronger in the West Riding than in the West of England and it may well be that women found themselves playing a more peripheral role within the industry after mechanisation, helping only with more ancillary tasks such as sorting, quilling or spooling, with perhaps occasional turns in the loom when deadlines were at hand.[39]

Two major adult male trades experienced severe displacement by machinery. Scribblers had constituted at least 10% of the adult male workforce in the West of England (more if we remember that the second weaver in the loom was often a juvenile or a woman) before the scribbling and carding engines replaced their skills entirely. Miles believed that only 75% of the scribblers were displaced,[40] presumably believing that one in four was employed to supervise the new machines. This does not appear to have been the case from the Clarks' evidence of 1833 where one slubber appears to have supervised carding and scribbling as well as his slubbing.[41] Nor is it likely that four out of sixteen men would have been employed to supervise four children working an engine each. The cloth finishers, responsible for raising and then cutting the cloth, were equally hard hit by machinery. The gig mill introduced during the initial phase of mechanisation displaced over six in seven men. The shearing frame, introduced in the period 1805–20 and not shown in Table 4, could perform the shearing process in 18 hours as against 72 hours required by hand methods and displaced three of the remaining four men. The rotary cutter introduced after 1820 further displaced two in three. Thus the work of some twenty-seven cloth finishers in the years up to 1796 could be performed by only three men and two boy assistants by 1828, a total displacement of eight out of nine men. Nor had the cloth dressers been a negligible

---

[39] See, for example, the evidence of the role of women in the West Riding woollen industry in Peel, *Risings of the Luddites*; B. Wilson, *Our Village* (1860); J. Lawson, *Letters to the Young on Progress in Pudsey in the Last Sixty Years* (J. W. Birdsall, 1887).
[40] B.P.P., 1840, Vol. 24, Pt v, p. 370.
[41] W.R.O., 927/71, Clark's list of employees on 1 Jan. 1833.

3   The slubbing billy
Source: A. Rees, *The Cyclopaedia*, Vol. xxxviii (1819),
'Woollen Manufacture', Plate i.

minority. They had constituted at least 16% of the total adult male workforce in the West, a quarter if all second men weavers are discounted, although their numbers likewise included apprentices.

What were the employment prospects for those adult males thus displaced by machinery? It is clear that the factory could not offer alternative employment to more than a handful. From Table 4 it can be seen that, up until the introduction of mules in about 1828, the factory offered employment to only one slubber and six male jenny spinners as against the sixteen scribblers and twenty-four shearmen displaced by machinery. The factory would have also offered supervisory jobs as overseers of machines, as foremen and as engine men to mind steam engines, unaccounted for by Austin's figures. However, their overall number would have been small in relation to the workforce as a whole. The picture of labour displacement may also be modified somewhat if we look at the situation around 1815. While the number of factory jobs and scribblers displaced would remain the same, the number of shearmen displaced would be significantly less, since only the gig mill was at all widely used by that date. The shearing frames in fact began to proliferate only in the period after 1815. This would mean that only thirteen shearmen would have been displaced at that time. Even so, twenty-nine men would have lost their work while only seven new jobs had been created. The only real alternative employment for such men was the loom. It was to the loom that John Collins, an ex-weaver, was referring when in 1803 he stated, 'since the scribbling and shearing machines have been introduced, they [the workers] have been thrown out of employ and have been obliged to apply themselves to other businesses; the young people have, a good deal'.[42] Weaving, in fact, became the only principal employment for adult males. Whereas before mechanisation weavers, even excluding second men in the double loom, had constituted 57% of the total male workforce in the West of England, by 1805 they were 65% and after 1828, 84%.

The position for displaced male workers was not, however, quite so calamitous in the period up to 1815–20 as it may appear. The reason for this was that the years from 1770 to 1820, and in particular the years of the French Wars, witnessed a period of exceptional growth which expanded demand for labour at the time when machinery was diminishing it. Figures for pieces of broadcloth milled in Yorkshire show that broadcloth production rose by over 50% between 1770–4 and 1785–9. Between 1785–9 and 1810–14, the period of most significant technological displacement, production of broadcloths doubled. Figures for narrow cloths were less spectacular. Between 1770–4 and 1785–9 production rose by some 80% but from 1785–9 to 1810–14 by only 13%. However, these cloths were on average some 30% longer and the output of narrow cloth in yards between these periods was some 46% increased. Further, it must be remembered that these were minimum figures. Cloths produced in the 'factories' and to direct orders which did not pass through the cloth halls were often missed. And the new 'fancy' cloths which increased rapidly in production from the 1780s were never included in these statistics.[43] The Stamping Acts which gave rise to these annual statistics did not apply in the West of England and here unfortunately there are no reliable figures to indicate the growth of production during this period. Export statistics, however, show that Spanish cloths, the major part of which would have come from the West, doubled between the decades 1781–90 and 1791–1800, while East India Company exports rose by around 60% from the early 1790s to the end of the war.[44] Enlistment in the army depleted the weavers' ranks and the years around 1808 were remembered as a period when 'a weaver was as precious as a jewel'. Austin was led to

[42] *B.P.P.*, 1802/3, Vol. 7, p. 96.
[43] B. R. Mitchell and P. Deane, *Abstract of British Historical Statistics* (Cambridge, 1962), p. 189; Wilson, *Gentlemen Merchants*, pp. 38–9.
[44] Mann, *Cloth Industry*, pp. 135–9, 310.

conclude that 'the increased trade of the districts [in the West of England] until 1820 had absorbed all the hands which the use of machinery had thrown out of work'.[45] This would appear a plausible supposition as far as adult male workers were concerned. Taking from Table 4 the information relating to adult males employed in Austin's first and second periods and assuming an average growth of 75% in production, the hypothetical answer is set out below in Table 6.

Table 6. *Adult male workers, mechanisation and economic growth,* *c. 1781–1805*

Austin Period 1	Austin Period 2	Period 2 × 75% growth
16 scribblers	1 slubber	1.75 slubbers
61 weavers	6 spinners	10.5 spinners
(61 assistants)	42 weavers	73.5 weavers
2 felters	2 felters	3.5 felters
27 shearmen	14 shearmen	24.5 shearmen
Totals 106 (167 with assistants)	65	113.75

It will be seen that a 75% increase in production would have re-employed most of the shearmen displaced by the gig mill either in cloth finishing or in milling and that the demand for adult male factory slubbers and spinners and for weavers would have absorbed all those displaced by the scribbling engine and accounted for all 'first men' weavers displaced by the flying shuttle loom. The sixty-one assistants or 'second men' weavers would not have all found work at the loom unless production had increased nearly threefold, but it must be remembered that the majority of these were women and youths, not adult males. In the West Riding growth almost certainly exceeded 75% in this period. In the West of England, where such an overall rate of growth may just have been achieved, the weavers' situation was helped by the fact that the spring loom did not oust the double loom completely until after 1820. Thus the demand for weavers would have been still stronger. It therefore seems quite possible that an increase in production of around 75% would have re-absorbed all displaced labour up to the end of the war, as Austin claimed. It was the end of growth after 1815 and, in the West of England, the beginnings of decline after 1820, which, coupled with the introduction of the frame, the rotary cutters and the mule, greatly increased the pressure upon the

[45] B.P.P., 1840, Vol. 23, p. 441.

Table 7. *Population growth in West of England and Yorkshire woollen towns, 1801–1831* (towns with a population of 2,000+ in 1801)

	1801	1811	1821	1831
Gloucestershire				
Bisley	4,227	4,757	5,421	5,896
Dursley	2,379	2,580	3,186	3,226
Horsley	2,971	2,925	3,565	3,690
Minchinhampton	3,419	3,246	4,907	5,114
Painswick	3,150	3,201	4,044	4,079
Stroud	5,422	5,321	7,097	8,607
Wotton	3,393	3,800	5,004	5,482
Somerset				
Frome	8,748	9,493	12,411	12,240
Shepton Mallet	5,104	4,638	5,021	5,330
Wiltshire				
Bradford on Avon	7,302	8,018	10,231	10,102
Calne	3,767	3,547	4,549	4,795
Chippenham	3,336	3,410	3,506	4,333
Melksham	4,030	4,110	4,765	4,722
Trowbridge	5,799	6,075	9,545	10,863
Yorkshire				
Dewsbury				
Birstall	1,637	1,911	2,436	3,317
Gomersal	4,303	5,002	5,952	6,189
Heckmondwike	1,742	2,324	2,579	2,793
Liversedge	2,837	3,643	4,259	5,265
Halifax				
Elland	3,385	3,963	5,088	5,500
Halifax	8,886	9,159	12,628	15,382
Heptonstall	2,983	3,647	4,543	4,661
Hipperholme	2,879	3,357	3,936	4,977
Huddersfield				
Almondbury	3,751	4,613	5,679	7,086
Huddersfield	7,268	9,671	13,284	19,035
Leeds				
Armley	2,695	2,941	4,273	5,159
Bramley	2,562	3,484	4,921	7,039
Holbeck	4,196	5,124	7,151	11,210
Hunslet	5,799	6,393	8,171	12,074
Pudsey	4,422	4,697	6,229	7,460
Wakefield				
Alverthorpe	3,105	3,756	4,448	4,859
Horbury	2,101	2,356	2,475	2,400
Wakefield	8,131	8,593	10,764	12,232

Source: B.P.P., Comparative Account of the Population of Great Britain in the Years 1801, 1811, 1821 and 1831 (H.C. 348), 1831, Vol. 18, pp. 100–8, 221–30, 278–85, 316–20.

workforce. The loom continued to offer the only hope of employment but it was employment in a rapidly over-stocking trade where wages and conditions were steadily to deteriorate into crushing poverty.

One final point requires attention. Was it possible that population growth negated the effects of growing production levels? The evidence, set out in Table 7, suggests that overall this was unlikely, though of course the lack of reliable figures before 1801 makes any conclusions suspect. The population in the main woollen towns in the West of England showed only a slow growth in the decade from 1801 to 1811, the largest growth rates being at Bisley and Wotton in Gloucestershire which grew by 12%, at Frome in Somerset which grew by 8.5% and at Bradford on Avon in Wiltshire, growing by 10%. It was the second decade of the century which saw the really remarkable growth of population in the West of England woollen towns. Trowbridge increased in size by 57% and Minchinhampton by 51% while Stroud, Wotton and Frome grew by over 30%. Only Shepton Mallet, undergoing a process of industrial collapse, and Chippenham failed to show substantial growth. Population increase was faster in the West Riding of Yorkshire. In the decade 1801–11 Bramley increased by 36%, Huddersfield, at the forefront of technological change, by 33%, while townships like Liversedge, Heptonstall and Holbeck increased by over 20%. The second decade of the century witnessed still faster growth. Bramley increased by another 41%, Holbeck by 40% and Huddersfield by a further 37%. Halifax rapidly increased by 38%, Pudsey by 33% and Wakefield, like Halifax stagnant in the first decade, also increased by 25%. The faster population growth in the West Riding was aided by economic growth in industries other than woollen cloth, of course, growth which continued to be sustained into the later nineteenth-century. Even concentrating our concern on woollen manufacture, however, it seems reasonable to conclude that population growth in neither region was such as to erode the prosperity of the war years or to wipe out the gains which growth set against the problem of technological displacement.

To conclude: the effects of mechanisation were sweeping and momentous for the woollen workforce as a whole. The transformation of two of the three principal adult male trades by machinery threw large numbers of men out of work and forced many towards the third trade, handloom weaving. However, the impact of the first wave of mechanical change was not fully felt by the woollen workers, partly because the heaviest blow fell on wives of agricultural labourers and others and also because favourable industrial circumstances created a demand for labour in the industrial areas which may well have counter-balanced the effects of displacement by machines. This did not mean that men thrown out of work suffered no ill-effects. Prosperity was far from uniform or permanent and a new job did not instantly beckon the displaced worker. Many skilled men faced the humiliation of the parish pay table with no expectations of alternative employment at hand. Nor, had they known of the opportunities for other work which growth might create, would they have modified their views on machinery. For mechanisation not only deprived them of their source of income; it also deprived them of a craft skill and of the social status which accompanied it. They believed that machinery could offer them no compensation for such a loss.

Chapter 3

The advent of machinery and community resistance

The advent of machinery in the last quarter of the eighteenth century alarmed workers and small-scale capitalists in the West of England and the West Riding alike. Nonetheless, while fears about the impact of machinery upon security of employment and economic and social relationships were general, the response to machinery varied widely. Innovations which in one area provoked spirited resistance in other areas were accepted without, or with little, demur. Two principal factors may be recognised as determining the response to machinery: the effect of the machine upon the structure and availability of work; and the character of the community within which that work was carried out.

A critical determinant of the response to machinery was without doubt the way in which the innovation in question might or might not be integrated into the organisation of production without detriment to employment or custom. Where this was the case the machine was taken up with minimum fuss. Where, on the other hand, machinery posed a direct threat to the trades of well-established labour groups, the consequence frequently was conflict. We can see this pattern in other industries besides the woollen. Thus early machinery in the Birmingham metal trades was taken up by the artisans without protest for it reinforced their work autonomy rather than threatening it. However, combing engines in the worsted industry threatened to destroy the wool combers' trade and their militant resistance delayed the take up of the machines for over a quarter of a century.[1] The introduction of preparatory machinery into the West Riding woollen industry, as will be seen, provoked only limited protest. Energies

This chapter develops an argument outlined in 'Work, culture and resistance to machinery in the West of England woollen industry', in P. Hudson, ed., *Regions and Industries: A Perspective on the Industrial Revolution in Britain* (Cambridge, 1989).

[1] For an interesting discussion of the take up of machinery in the early Industrial Revolution see Berg, *The Age of Manufactures*.

released by these machines were quickly re-absorbed within the Domestic System without substantially altering industrial relationships. The early scribbling mills in Yorkshire were likewise integrated without major conflict. In the West of England, on the other hand, preparatory machinery displaced large numbers of workers from specialist trades and began the process of concentration of production under the direct control of employers who were already clearly divorced from their workforces by wealth and function. However, where the structure of work was the same in both the West Riding and the West of England, as was the case with cloth finishing, the response was the same, as the Wiltshire Outrages and Yorkshire Luddism showed. Thus, it is necessary to examine how machinery impinged not only on a particular task but also on the workplace and on work practice if we are to understand its reception. The same machine might liberate labour from drudgery and open up more profitable and even more socially mobile prospects in one area and break down customary work relations, throw workers onto the scrapheap and widen the gap between capital and labour in another. Workers certainly did not view machinery in abstract. They recognised its direct relevance to their work and social status. And they judged its acceptability in terms of its impact upon their lives as a whole and the way it might support or challenge their autonomy over their work.

The contrasting responses to innovation occasioned by the different structures of work in the West Riding and the West of England can clearly be seen in the respective reactions to the introduction of the spinning jenny and scribbling engine. Spinning throughout most of the eighteenth century was performed by women and children within the family economy. In the West Riding this generally took place in the master clothiers' workshops, the work being undertaken by their wives and families, sometimes together with help from journeymen's wives and their families. This close familial work unit was characteristic of the multiplicity of small-scale production units which made up the Yorkshire woollen industry and was quite unlike that county's worsted industry where spinning was organised on the putting out system on a similar scale to that in the West of England. In the West the need to obtain sufficient yarn forced many clothiers to put out wool many miles to be worked up, and some established distant 'spinning stations' to organise and co-ordinate the work of such spinners.[2] There

---

[2] Mann, *Cloth Industry*, p. 287; P. H. Fisher, *Notes and Recollections of Stroud* (1871), p. 291; *Annals of Agriculture*, Vol. IX, pp. 298–9, cited in Hammonds, *Skilled Labourer*, p. 120; Anstie, *Observations on Machinery*, pp. 11–12.

4   The spinning jenny
Source: A. Rees, *The Cyclopaedia*, Vol. xxxviii (1819), 'Woollen Manufacture', Plate ii.

was also apparently a certain reluctance in some areas to put out wool
to the wives of woollen workers since 'the clothiers complain that our
poor spoil their yarn by dirtiness, bad spinning, damping . . . and
many other frauds'.[3] Spinning in the West of England provided supplementary employment for the rural poor in general and not simply
for the woollen workers' families.

   The spinning jenny, invented by James Hargreaves around 1764,
increased the number of spindles which one spinner could manage,
thereby greatly increasing the output. Early jennies were inexpensive,
hand powered and easily fitted into the domestic workplace.
However, because of their much greater productivity, they threatened
to displace very large numbers of spinners. F. M. Eden was informed
that jennies displaced nine in ten spinners, while the figures compiled

[3] *G.J.*, 9 Feb. 1784, report from Minchinhampton.

by Austin suggest that nine in ten weft spinners and six in seven warp spinners were displaced.[4]

The spinning jenny was introduced into the West Riding woollen industry in the 1770s from the Lancashire cotton industry. It first appeared in Holmfirth in 1776 and spread thence into the Huddersfield district and across the whole region.[5] The jenny seems to have encountered little opposition and was easily accommodated into the Domestic System. It was a major factor in the rapid expansion of the West Riding industry in the last quarter of the century, enabling the master clothier's household to produce most of the spun yarn needed without recourse to out-spinners. Its place was such that the membership card of the Clothiers' Community, an organisation of small-scale master clothiers established in 1803, depicted the jenny alongside the loom as symbols of the Domestic System. Even so, residual fears that machinery might lead to monopolies prompted demands in 1806 that the number of jennies owned and worked by any one concern should be limited by law.[6]

Clothiers in the West were not lagging behind their Yorkshire rivals in introducing the spinning jenny. In July 1776, a group of twelve Shepton Mallet clothiers attempted to introduce the machine to the town. Financed by these clothiers, jennies were set up in the workhouse as a public experiment with the blessing of the town's weavers. Mann suggests that the *quid pro quo* demanded by the weavers was the clothiers' agreement to restore the rate of 1s. 3d. per yard for superfine broadcloth set by the quarter sessions in 1756.[7] It is possible, however, that there had been earlier discussions relating to the jenny's introduction which had not been harmonious since dragoons were stationed in the town. This negotiated trial of the jennies did not meet with the approval of the woollen workers of the neighbouring woollen towns and on the night of the 10/11 July 'a riotous mob of weavers, shearmen etc., collected from the towns of Warminster, Frome, etc., assembled together and proceeded to the town of Shepton Mallet with the intention to destroy under cover of night a machine lately erected by the clothiers'. The clothiers had received intimation of their visit and had warned the magistrates, three of whom stationed themselves in an

[4] K. G. Ponting, *The Woollen Industry of South-West England* (Adams and Dart, 1971), pp. 54–5; Sir F. M. Eden, *The State of the Poor* (1797), Vol. III, p. 796.

[5] W. B. Crump and G. Ghorbal, *History of the Huddersfield Woollen Industry* (Tolson Memorial Museum Publications, 1935), p. 64; Crump, *Leeds Woollen Industry*, p. 7.

[6] *B.P.P.*, 1806, Vol. 3, pp. 36, 139.

[7] Mann, *Cloth Industry*, p. 12; *G.J.*, 22 July 1776; *B.C.*, 1 Aug. 1776; 1s. 3d. remained the standard rate until shortly before 1802; *B.P.P.*, 1802/3, Vol. 7, p. 62.

inn to await developments. By 2 a.m. the town was still peaceful and two magistrates left for their beds. The crowd, however, had hidden some way from the town and, believing that the coast was now clear, marched in, broke into the workhouse and destroyed the machines. They also broke all the windows and some 'forcibly entered one gentleman's house [and] destroyed all his furniture and drank two hogsheads of beer'.[8] The remaining magistrate, taking command of the dragoons, ordered the arrest of the 'ringleaders' and five or six were captured. The crowd counter-attacked the troops with stones. The Riot Act was read and, when the crowd refused to disperse, the troops were ordered to fire on them. One man was killed and six wounded. The crowd scattered and peace was restored.[9]

The riot drew the attention of all clothiers in the West of England to the spinning jenny and to the problem of possible worker resistance to its introduction. Thus, on 16 September, clothiers from Somerset, Wiltshire and Gloucestershire met at Bristol and issued two public resolutions. The first, signed by fifty 'principal manufacturers', declared that the introduction of spinning machines would greatly benefit the industry and recommended that clothiers in all woollen towns should follow the Shepton Mallet example and join together to set up public trials of the jennies. The second resolution, signed by over 100 clothiers, praised the 'spirited conduct' of the Shepton clothiers in introducing a machine which was 'conceived to be of general utility to the manufacture'.[10] A second general meeting in Bath on 1 October issued further resolutions in praise of the jenny. 'The working people in general will be thereby greatly benefitted, the trade extended and improved, and the wages in many branches of the business increased.' Failure to introduce this beneficent machine, however, would mean that Yorkshire clothiers, who did use it, would steal all the West's markets. These resolutions were intended primarily to influence public opinion and the clothiers were anxious to counter suggestions that the introduction of the jenny might push up poor rates by causing redundancies.

And whereas reports have been industriously propagated that the poor by the introduction of spinning machines will be deprived of a considerable part of their labour and consequently become burdensome to their parishes, they do,

---

[8] It is possible that this unfortunate gentleman was John Billingsley, a prominent clothier and later agriculturalist, and one of the twelve. Popular opinion labelled him as the motive force behind the jenny's introduction. *B.C.*, 1 Aug. 1776.

[9] *G.J.*, 15, 22 July 1776; *B.C.*, 18 July 1776.

[10] *G.J.*, 16 Sept. 1776.

upon the most mature consideration, declare that no mischievous consequences are likely to ensue . . . [However] they will be ready to discontinue the use of the machines if after a proper trial they shall be found in any degree prejudicial to the poor.

In the meantime, they announced their resolution to continue efforts to introduce the jenny.[11]

The woollen workers, even those of Shepton Mallet, were not convinced. A petition to the House of Commons from 'the wire drawers, card board makers, card makers, scribblers, spinners, twisters, weavers and others of Frome, Shepton Mallet and of Somerset', presented on 1 November, complained that the jenny threatened the livelihoods of many thousands of the industrious poor and prayed that Parliament would abolish the machine. Their petition was rejected.[12] They then tried a more conciliatory approach, publishing an address 'to the Gentlemen clothiers of Shepton Mallet' on 27 November. They agreed to support the present trial of the jenny, provided that the machine was used only in the workhouse and worked by able workmen to its full capacity for two months and subject at all times to inspection from two delegates appointed by the workmen. In this way they believed that 'the surprising utility which you have asserted, or the dangerous consequences which we have apprehended, may evidently appear'.[13]

This marked an end to the frictions over the spinning jenny in Shepton Mallet but the trial did not prove as successful as the clothiers anticipated. The early jennies were insufficiently delicate to cope with the fine yarns in which the West was increasingly specialising,[14] and the machine does not seem to have spread at all rapidly. While reports in April 1777 stated that the spinning jenny was being introduced into the Salisbury area 'with the greatest success' and in 1781 the machines were said to have proved successful at Shepton Mallet,[15] an attempt in June 1781 to introduce them to neighbouring Frome provoked violence. On Whit Monday a crowd collected and forcibly entered the house of a man who was working jennies and smashed the machines to pieces. The following day they reassembled and threatened to destroy the houses of a card maker and certain manufacturers but, according to the *Bath Chronicle*, they were dissuaded upon finding that the magistrates and gentlemen were armed to protect property.[16] The

---

[11] *G.J.*, 14 Oct. 1776.   [12] *J.H.C.*, Vol. 36, p. 7.
[13] *B.C.*, 28 Nov. 1776.   [14] Mann, *Cloth Industry*, pp. 126–7.
[15] *B.C.*, 24 April 1777, 14 June 1781.   [16] *B.C.*, 14 June 1781.

appeal for troops which ensued, however, indicated that the situation was anything but calm. The request claimed that 'the civil power was unequal to the suppression of the riots which have arisen at Frome in consequence of the machines lately introduced there for the spinning of wool'. A troop of dragoons was duly dispatched.[17] Two weeks after the arrival of the troops, three men and one woman were arrested for their parts in the disturbances. At the assizes in August the woman received one year's imprisonment and two men were found guilty but sentence was withheld until the following sessions, probably as an added inducement to others to keep the peace. The third man was freed in January 1782 after making a full public apology to his prosecutors for his part in the riot.[18]

It was only from the late 1780s that spinning jennies began to reappear in the West of England. They were introduced into Bradford on Avon around 1787 and spinning machines occasionally occur among the effects of bankrupt clothiers from this time on.[19] By 1790 trade in many branches was booming and some clothiers were unable to fill orders which encouraged them to introduce jennies and perhaps helped pacify workers' fears.[20] There was, however, still much suspicion. Although one Gloucestershire writer claimed that the jennies were hailed with delight by both masters and weavers, another Gloucestershire man recalled a much more distrustful climate.[21] There are no further reports of riots against the jenny in the West of England clothing districts, but it was only in 1792–3 that they were introduced in large numbers in Wiltshire, while it was not until 1794 that more distant towns like Marlborough were affected by the jenny. The major take up of jennies in Gloucestershire also occurred in the period around 1790–3.[22]

This pattern of response – the West Riding welcoming the jenny after initial scepticism, the West of England being unremittingly hostile for many years – was repeated with the introduction of scribbling

[17] W.O. 4/113, Jenkinson to Jesser, 7 June 1781 (refers to 'your letter of the 6th').

[18] *B.C.*, 21 June, 30 Aug. 1781, 31 Jan. 1782; *G.J.*, 30 July 1781.

[19] *S.W.J.*, 23 May 1791; *B.C.*, 4 Jan. 1787; *G.J.*, 15 Sept. 1788; *G.C.L.*, R115.118, catalogue of stock . . . of Thomas Tippetts, clothier, a bankrupt, 1789.

[20] H. Wansey, *Wool encouraged without exportation, by a Wiltshire Clothier* (1791), p. 68.

[21] *Stroud Journal*, 4 July 1868, cited by Mann, *Cloth Industry*, p. 129; Partridge, *A Practical Treatise*, p. 71.

[22] *A Letter to the Landholders of the county of Wilts. on the alarming State of the Poor* (Salisbury, 1793), pp. 3–4; Anstie, *Observations on Machinery*, p. 20; *S.W.J.*, 2, 9 June 1794; G. Turner, *A General View of the Agriculture of the County of Gloucester* (1794), p. 31.

and carding engines in the 1780s and 1790s. Scribbling was in essence carding writ large. It was the process of laying the short wool fibres roughly parallel, prior to being sent to the spinner for final hand carding and spinning. It was performed on a scribbling horse, an upright frame covered with cards set with wire teeth, the wool being worked across the surface with a large hand card also set with wire teeth. For high-quality yarns the wool would be worked many times with cards of varying degrees of fineness. Whereas in the West Riding scribbling was one of the many processes carried out by the master clothier and his journeymen, in the West of England it was a trade in itself, originating in the later seventeenth century with the development of medley cloth production.[23] Here adult male scribblers worked in shops owned by the clothier, thereby ensuring that the clothier was able to achieve more careful blending of wools and also that the wool delivered to the spinners was already well carded, helping to produce better yarn. The scribblers made up perhaps 10% of the adult male workforce in the West of England. A Gloucestershire clothier in 1803 described the scribblers as having been 'a poor, sickly, decrepit race of beings',[24] while a petition to Parliament in 1794 claimed that 'many individuals, who being advanced in age or by accident or misfortune disabled from working in other occupations which require bodily exertions, could be furnished with the means of the necessaries of life, without applying for parochial aid, by scribbling wool'.[25] Certainly scribbling did offer relatively light work but it is by no means the case that all scribblers were geriatrics. An appeal for public support for the scribblers in 1794 spoke of 'a great number of persons brought up to the business of wool scribbling'[26] and scribblers were quite capable of defending their industrial interests. For example, in 1761 a combination of Shepton Mallet scribblers attempted to establish a closed shop by evicting 'strangers' and met with some success.[27] Scribblers at Devizes formed a financially sturdy friendly society which met regularly at the Black Horse from at least 1765 until after 1782 with a membership of between 75 and 108. 'It is a very uncommon thing for the members of the club to apply to the parish on any occasion.'[28] Temple in 1738 grouped scribblers with shearmen in terms of idleness,

---

[23] See Mann, *Cloth Industry*, pp. 284–5.   [24] B.P.P., 1802/3, Vol. 7, p. 308.
[25] J.H.C., Vol. 49, p. 600.   [26] G.J., 5 May 1794.   [27] G.J., 10 Nov. 1761.
[28] Bath and West of England and Southern Counties Society, Bath, Archives, Letters and Papers addressed to the Society, Vol. 3, Paper from John Anstie on a friendly society at Devizes (1783).

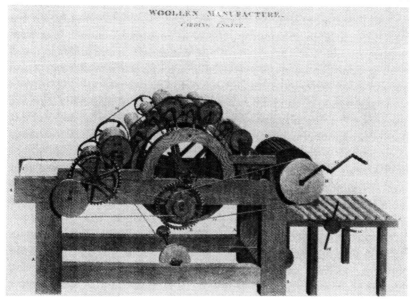

5   The carding engine
Source: A. Rees, The Cyclopaedia, Vol. xxxviii (1819), 'Woollen Manufacture', Plate iii.

drunkenness and difficulty of management.[29] Certainly the scribblers' response to scribbling machinery was far from feeble.

The basic concept behind the mechanisation of the scribbling process dated back to the inventions of Lewis Paul and Daniel Bourne in the mid-eighteenth century, but it was Arkwright who in 1775 patented one of the first practicable powered scribbling/carding engines. The scribbling engine consisted of a series of counter-spinning rollers set with wire teeth working against each other in much the same way as the hand card and scribbling horse. The machine delivered the scribbled wool in the form of a continuous web which was then fed onto the carding engine. This was essentially the same as the scribbling engine but with finer teeth and tolerances and it delivered the fibres not in a web but in short strips by means of a 'doffing comb', a final roller with teeth set only in short lateral ridges. The wool strips were pieced together by hand and fed onto the third machine in the sequence, the slubbing billy. This was the brother of the spinning jenny and worked in the same way. Like the jenny, the billy was hand powered. Cardings were drafted and given sufficient twist to turn them into rudimentary

[29] W. Temple, The Case as it now Stands between the Clothiers, Weavers and other Manufacturers with regard to the late Riot in the County of Wilts. (1739), p. 16.

yarn so that they could be wound onto bobbins and thence drawn out into fine yarn on the jenny. The slubbing billy filled a new role, apparently made necessary by the introduction of the scribbling and carding engines.[30] The billy thus deprived only those already made redundant of labour and appears never to have excited antipathy on its own account. Like the jenny, the billy probably came slowly into use from the late 1780s onwards and in greater numbers in the early 1790s. While the scribbling and carding engines were both powered, their requirements were not great. They were often set up in the lofts of fulling mills to utilise existing power sources or they were horse or even hand powered.[31] Boulton and Watt estimated that each engine required just over $1/2$ h.p. each in 1796, but in 1814 when machines were larger they were found to need only $1/3$ h.p. each.[32]

The scribbling engine made the scribblers' trade superfluous. It was claimed in 1794 that one man and a boy using the machine could perform the work of twenty scribblers.[33] Austin's figures suggested that the scribbling engine performed the work seven times faster than by hand, though if the time taken for the wool to be mechanically carded is added the difference was halved. The practice of employing an adult male to work the machines did not last long. Usually scribbling and carding engines were kept in a unit with an adult male slubber working with two children on two scribbling engines, two on carders and one child piecer. Machinery offered the scribblers no compensatory employment.

Scribbling engines were first introduced into the West Riding in the early 1780s as machines adapted from the Lancashire cotton industry. As with the jenny, the scribbling engines spread first into the south-western parts of the woollen districts and thence across the region.[34] By 1786 there were said to be some 170 in the district 'extending about seventeen miles south-west of Leeds' and nearly as many again in the rest of the Riding.[35] Unlike the jenny, however, the scribbling engine's reception was rather more mixed and not without conflict. Benjamin

[30] Ponting, *Woollen Industry*, pp. 46–55; Mann, *Cloth Industry*, p. 288.
[31] Crump, *Leeds Woollen Industry*, p. 12; Wilson, *Gentlemen Merchants*, pp. 91–2; Mann, *Cloth Industry*, p. 131, cites various examples of the latter power sources, while Francis Naish of Trowbridge was clearly employing horses for power in 1796. B.R.L., Boulton and Watt MSS, Out Letters, B. and W. to F. Naish, 1 Sept. 1796.
[32] B.R.L., Boulton and Watt MSS, In Letters, Box 6B, copy of letter to Mr Bush, Bradford, 28 May 1796; Muirhead I., James Watt, Jnr, notebook 1811–14, references to Cooper and Sons, Trowbridge and Mr Saunders, Trowbridge.
[33] *J.H.C.*, Vol. 49, p. 600.
[34] Crump, *Leeds Woollen Industry*, pp. 4–5, 7–9.
[35] *L.M.*, 13, 20 June 1786.

Wilson, Junior, wrote in 1860 of the reaction of the women of Bramley to the arrival of the machine. 'The first slubbing that came into Bramley that had been carded and slubbed by machinery came from Mr. Copley's at Hunslet. The women rose in a mob when the cart came with the slubbing, pulled it out of the cart, and trod it under their feet in the street!'[36] Copley was also one of the targets of a petition published in the Leeds papers in June 1786 which claimed that thousands had been thrown out of work by the introduction of scribbling engines. The petition claimed that each machine could do the work of ten men and that, once they were being worked round the clock, their effect would be to put out of work some 4,000 men and the same number of apprentices. The scribbling engines were said to impair the quality of the wool and the rate-payers were warned of the rapid increase in poor rates should machinery continue to be employed. In a subsequent public correspondence with Copley, the petitioners asserted that only 9 of the 1,700 clothiers who attended the Leeds Cloth Hall were in favour of the machines. The early engines, however, were small and easily accommodated into the clothiers' workshops. Indeed, a correspondent of the *Leeds Mercury* claimed that of the 170 in the area, '120 or 130 are very small and the small ones will not do more work than four men'.[37] However, from the later 1780s larger engines began to proliferate, frequently being grouped together with carding engines and slubbing billies and often some large jennies in water-powered mills, many of them fulling mills, frequently run by joint-stock companies owned by prosperous master clothiers. These scribbling mills not only prepared wool for their owner or owners; they also took in work on commission for other master clothiers as the fulling mills had always done.[38] The early scribbling mills were to prove pivotal in the transformation of the Domestic System into a factory-dominated industry, for from these small beginnings a new sort of clothier manufacturer such as Law Atkinson of Huddersfield was to arise. While many master clothiers viewed the proliferation of scribbling mills in the mid-1780s with initial disquiet, most became content to make use of the new public facility to get their wool ready for spinning and weaving much more rapidly than they were able to under their own roofs,

[36] Cited in Crump, *Leeds Woollen Industry*, p. 12. This event was recalled as an 'insurrection' of 'a parcel of old wives and worn-out scribblers' by a correspondent to the *Leeds Mercury* in March 1803.

[37] *L.M.*, 13, 20, 27 June 1786.

[38] Crump, *Leeds Woollen Industry*, pp. 11–12, 59–63; Wilson, *Gentlemen Merchants*, pp. 91–7.

thereby enabling them to concentrate on producing more cloth.[39] Their loss of control and independence was largely disguised by the growing prosperity of the region.

Scribbling engines encountered fierce and prolonged resistance in the West of England. This was particularly true of Wiltshire. Here trouble first broke out at Bradford on Avon in May 1791 upon the occasion of the first introduction of scribbling machines into the county. Joseph Phelps, a prominent clothier, set up a scribbling engine in the workshops behind his elegant house near the town bridge.[40] However, the scribblers 'did not choose to allow [this] lest by the introduction of such engines they should be thrown out of work'. A crowd of around 500 gathered and demanded that Phelps give them the machine and promise not to reintroduce scribbling engines. Phelps refused and stones were thrown. There were no troops stationed in the town and the only resident magistrate was ill, so the crowd, finding that they were unopposed, continued to stone the house, smashing all the windows and damaging furniture inside. Phelps and a friend in the house at first tried firing unloaded guns at the crowd in an attempt to frighten them off. The crowd were unimpressed. The defenders then tried firing small shot but the crowd still did not disperse and so finally Phelps began to fire ball, killing a man, a woman and a boy and mortally wounding two others. This action outraged the crowd and Phelps, his nerve broken, handed over the machine to be ceremoniously burned on the bridge. Eventually the respectable inhabitants of the town, armed and sworn as special constables, put in an appearance and the crowd dispersed. Four 'ringleaders' were committed. A coroner's jury subsequently sitting on the cases of the dead rioters returned a verdict of 'justifiable homicide'.[41]

The riot greatly frightened the clothiers and the magistrates, who urgently sent requests both for temporary military protection and for a permanent garrison, since 'such a measure is absolutely necessary to the peace and quiet of this county' as 'we are continually in expectation of another attack'.[42] Certainly the riot seems to have come as a surprise

[39] In praise of the scribbling engine, one correspondent of the *Leeds Mercury* wrote, 'a clothier may as he did formerly spend a fortnight or more in doing that which he may now get done in one day'. *L.M.*, 11 Nov. 1783.

[40] It appears to have been a converted carding engine. *Aris' Birmingham Gazette*, 23 May 1791: 'a carding machine upon which he was making some experiments'.

[41] *S.W.J.*, 23 May 1791.

[42] W.O. 1/1048, magistrates of Bradford to Sir George Yonge, 15 May 1791, Garth to Yonge, 18 May 1791; W.O. 1/1049, Capt. Lane to Yonge, 15 May 1791, Bethell to Lane, 15 May 1791; *S.W.J.*, 23 May 1791.

to the magistrates. George Bethell, the resident magistrate, wrote of 'an unforeseen outrage'[43] and certainly no troops had been stationed in the area in anticipation of disturbance. They did not make that mistake again. Some clothiers, however, had suspected trouble. The migration of Francis Hill, a major Bradford on Avon clothier, to Malmesbury, where the woollen trade was long dead, in order to set up many machines in a large corn mill took place shortly after the riot. Hill, however, had arranged the purchase of the mill well before the disturbance, indicating that he at least saw which way the wind would blow.[44]

The riot and the increasing spread of spinning jennies in Wiltshire provoked a growing public debate over machinery and the press frequently began to carry eulogies upon the values of mechanical innovation. I shall return to this debate later. Respectable opinion, however, was by no means wholeheartedly on the side of the clothiers. This was shown when those arrested for their parts in the riot were tried at the summer assizes and all were acquitted. Two of Phelps' neighbours were less fortunate. Phelps brought a successful action against them for the cost of damages incurred in the riot since neither had done anything to help him resist the mob. According to the *Salisbury Journal*, this clearly showed that it was not merely the duty but also in the financial interests of neighbours to assist to suppress riots. The judge took the opportunity to praise machinery and to warn that 'if machines are not used to enable the manufacturer to sell as cheap as other counties do now, they will be undersold'.[45] Phelps subsequently brought a similar action against the inhabitants of the town and was awarded further damages of £250 which can hardly have helped make innovators popular.[46]

The scribblers' antipathy to scribbling engines clearly remained strong and magistrates and clothiers clung to military protection. In early August 1791, reports of impending disturbances among the workers at Frome over the issue of machinery caused the troops quartered in Trowbridge to be dispatched there, much to the discomfort of the Trowbridge magistrates. 'We beg to observe that such a large populous town as this ought not to be without a military assistance especially at this time when the minds of the people are ripe for

[43] W.O. 1/1049, Bethell to Lane, 15 May 1791.
[44] Mann, *Cloth Industry*, p. 129; cf. Hammonds, *Skilled Labourer*, p. 121.
[45] *S.W.J.*, 2, 9, 22 Aug. 1791.   [46] *S.W.J.*, 12 March 1792.

riots.'[47] These fears were confirmed in September 1791. For some reason the soldiers were again temporarily removed and on the night of 16 September a crowd of between 400 and 500 assembled and 'behaved in a disorderly and riotous manner until nearly twelve o'clock'. The magistrates were insulted, the constables knocked down and those whom they had arrested were set free. The disturbance, however, was certainly directed against the clothiers, whether because they had introduced, or were preparing to introduce, machinery is not clear. The return of the troops was urgently requested 'or we are certain it will not be in the power of the manufacturers to carry on their trade'. The magistrates' request was augmented by another from the principal inhabitants, mostly clothiers, who warned that without military protection 'the trade of the town must be entirely at a stand owing to the riots and disorders that prevail'. Dragoons were sent from Frome and were retained.[48]

The pattern established in Wiltshire in 1791 was reproduced in the following year. Troops remained in all the main Wiltshire woollen towns until, in August 1792, miners from the Mendip pits struck work for increased wages and assembled in large numbers to prevent coal from leaving the collieries. The Sheriff of Somerset requested that troops be sent to Camerton and detachments of the dragoons stationed at Bradford on Avon and Trowbridge were duly dispatched, leaving only a few men in each town.[49] This weakening of the military force at Trowbridge encouraged the crowd to rise 'with the intention to destroy the machines'. The source of the crowd's ire this time was apparently not just scribbling engines but also flying shuttle looms.[50] They were dispersed only with great difficulty after those troops remaining in Bradford on Avon had been called in to help. But, said Lt. Col. Hubert, the officer commanding the dragoons, this raised further problems since 'Mr. Phelps of Bradford had given notice to the magistrates that he should soon again set up one of the machines which two years ago

[47] W.O. 1/1050, Mortimer and Gibbs to Yonge, 13, 21 Aug. 1791; W.O. 1/1049, Lt. Col. Newark to Lewis, 21 Aug. 1791.
[48] W.O. 1/1050, Mortimer and Gibbs to Yonge, 17, 27 Sept. 1791; Green, Bythesea, Waldron, etc. to Yonge, 17 Sept. 1791.
[49] *S.W.J.*, 20 Aug. 1792; W.O. 1/1053, Capt. Letharsham to Yonge, 15 Aug. 1792; W.O.1/1052, Lt. Col. Hubert to Yonge, 21 Aug. 1792.
[50] Mann, *Cloth Industry*, p. 140, refers to this riot as being over the flying shuttle and cites *V.C.H., Wiltshire*, Vol. IV, p. 167. The references cited here, however, to *S.W.J.*, 27 Aug. 1792, and to a pamphlet on sheep are inconclusive. That it was not over scribbling engines, however, is suggested by Hubert's apparent distinction between 'the machines' smashed at Trowbridge and the one, undoubtedly a scribbling engine, which Phelps intended to restore.

occasioned those riots that were attended with serious consequences.' Nor were the Trowbridge rioters easily dissuaded. The following night they reassembled and, Hubert reported, 'the people of Trowbridge carried their point and have destroyed the machines'. The crowd dispersed peacefully when the Riot Act was read but the situation remained tense. Hubert subsequently warned that, following the 'great inconvenience and loss to some of the manufacturers' at Trowbridge, 'there is every reason to expect very violent riots at Bradford shortly which it will be impossible to quell with the handful of troops remaining there'. The depleted garrisons in Trowbridge and Bradford on Avon were both reinforced. The colliers, the unwitting abettors of the rioters, won their strike and returned to work without, as Hubert wryly commented, showing the least indication to riot. The coal masters passed on their increased labour costs twofold in the price of coal to the consumer.[51]

It is impossible to assess how successful violence and the threat of violence proved in intimidating would-be innovators into postponing the introduction of machinery. The evidence suggests that, in the main Wiltshire woollen towns at least, the scribblers were remarkably successful. Some engines were set up in the more isolated parts of the county. For example, John Anstie, the Devizes clothier, had set up a new mill at Poulshot shortly before his bankruptcy in 1793 containing preparatory machinery while Hill's manufactory at Malmesbury, containing many scribbling engines, was at work by that date.[52] Such examples, however, were few and far between. In the main woollen areas resistance remained strong. For example, scribbling engines were 'not allowed' in Trowbridge in early 1795 and a clothier wishing to use them was forced to move to Marlborough.[53] Trade went into depression in 1793 which can only have served to increase fears of violence should machines be introduced. An attempt to set up scribbling engines in Shepton Mallet by William Jenkins, a prominent clothier, sparked off riots there in September 1794. Some warehouses belonging to Jenkins were burned down. Those mills in Somerset which contained machinery were defended by permanent detachments of troops.[54] Improved trade in 1794 does not appear to have greatly encouraged introduction of scribbling engines and this may be

[51] W.O. 1/1052, Hubert to Yonge, 21, 24 Aug. 1792; *S.W.J.*, 27 Aug., 1 Oct. 1792.
[52] *S.W.J.*, 5 May 1794, sale of Anstie's property; W.O. 1/1082, Anstie to Sec. at War, 28 May, 1795; *Wiltshire Notes and Queries* (1905–16), Vol. VIII, p. 438.
[53] Rogers, *Wiltshire and Somerset Woollen Mills*, p. 21.
[54] *An Account of the Proceedings of the Merchants, Manufacturers, and others concerned in the Wool and Woollen Trade* (1800), pp. 150, 153–5.

the reason why the Wiltshire scribblers did not join with those of Gloucestershire when they petitioned Parliament in May 1794 to abolish the machine.[55] However, Joseph Phelps, the Bradford on Avon clothier who had first introduced the engine into Wiltshire, had two scribbling engines and two carding engines when he died in the summer of 1794.[56]

Scribbling machinery seems to have been introduced into Wiltshire on a wide scale only during the boom in trade which began in 1795 and lasted until 1797 and in some branches until about 1800.[57] Thus, in July 1795 the *Salisbury Journal* reported that 'manufactures of all kinds are in a flourishing state, not a hand being out of work or likely to be so', while in August it reported that the woollen workers had so much work that few were leaving their looms to work on the harvest as was their custom.[58] However, the year 1795 was not a propitious one in which to introduce machinery since, as well as a trade boom, that year also experienced the legacy of a poor harvest in 1794 and a disastrous one in the early autumn, providing a background of tensions and ever-rising prices[59] against which old antipathies to machinery continued to be manifested. Food riots were mingled with occasional industrial disturbances or alarms and it was perhaps well for the clothiers that they did not generally rush to bring in scribbling engines since on many occasions the military presence was stretched so thin as to provide little real protection.

The clothiers of Westbury, however, were not so cautious. John Anstie, until his bankruptcy in late 1793 the leading spokesman of the Wiltshire clothiers, wrote to the War Office on 28 May:

the introduction of machinery into the woollen business has been gradual in this county and for some considerable time past no disturbance has been given to the manufacturers. But last week the scribblers at Westbury rose and demolished two scribbling engines. I was there on Monday and found the people were quiet – but the gentleman who owned the machines had been deterred by some slight opposition from taking up any of the people.

Anstie was now running one of his old mills at Poulshot for his brother who had bought it from him and he had recently begun to take in extra

[55] *J.H.C.*, Vol. 49, pp. 599–600.   [56] *G.J.*, 11 Aug. 1794.
[57] Mann, *Cloth Industry*, pp. 135–6.
[58] *S.W.J.*, 27 July, 31 Aug. 1795. The latter issue also carried an advertisement for a man to work a scribbling engine in Warminster.
[59] Thus the cost of a gallon loaf baked by George Sloper of Devizes rose from between 14d. to 16d. between February and May 1795; to 15½d. in June, and then to 19d. on 3 July; 21d. on 10 July; 25d. on 17 July; 28d. on 20 July; 27d. on 24 July. July in fact saw most food riots in the West. W.A.S.L., MS diary of George Sloper.

scribbling for a 'principal manufacturer' who 'had more work than his men could dispatch'. As a result, the Westbury scribblers had threatened to visit Anstie's mill and that of another manufacturer in the neighbourhood to destroy them.[60] It is clear that this was not the first threat to the mill. In August 1794, a report on the disposition of the Loyal Bristol regiment centred on Devizes showed that, while the main contingents were stationed in Devizes, Trowbridge and Bradford on Avon, detachments were also stationed in the villages of Rowde, where Anstie lived in 1795 and where he owned a fulling mill until 1794, and Potterne, both only 2 miles from the tiny hamlet of Poulshot.[61] After the May disturbances Westbury remained quiet until August when trouble once more erupted. The Westbury clothiers hastily requested more troops since 'They are apprehensive every day they shall have their houses either set on fire or pulled down. The use of a machine called a scribbling machine is the pretence for the complaint of those who threaten to destroy these gentlemen's property.' While the Yeomanry were always ready to act against rioters, 'I am sorry to say these riotous people appear at different places at one and the same time. Therefore the gentlemen have too great reasons to suspect that mischief may be done before the Yeomanry could arrive.'[62] A troop of dragoons was immediately dispatched but ironically the town was unable to find sufficient accommodation and many had to be quartered in Warminster, 4 miles away.[63] Shepton Mallet also remained in some fear of disturbances. In October 1795, the War Office was warned that troops were needed because 'new machinery lately erected there by some of the principal manufacturers requires some regular force constantly in it, at least till the price of provisions should be reduced and the working manufacturer a little reconciled to the modern necessary improvements'.[64]

The disturbances of 1795 appear to have marked the end of direct resistance to scribbling machinery in Wiltshire and Somerset. Trade continued to grow strongly in all branches until 1797 when the long and short cloth trades experienced severe depression, but the

[60] W.O.1/1082, Anstie to Sec. at War, 28 May 1795; Anstie's address was Rowde where he had owned another mill (*S.W.J.*, 5 May 1794) but Rogers shows that it was the Poulshot mill which Anstie's brother purchased. Rogers, *Wiltshire and Somerset Woollen Mills*, pp. 108–9.

[61] W.O. 1/1079, Lt. Col. Somerset to Wyndham, 3 Aug. 1794.

[62] W.O. 1/1093, Seymour, Long to Sec. at War, 7 Aug. 1795.

[63] W.O. 1/1082, a'Court, Long, Lambert to Sec. at War, 23 Nov. 1795, a'Court to Sec. at War, 23, 29 Nov. 1795.

[64] W.O. 1/1093, Stevens to Sec. at War, 1 Oct. 1795.

cassimere and Spanish trades, in which the area was most greatly concerned, appear to have experienced very healthy conditions until 1800.[65] With demand growing, workers leaving to join the war and food prices falling back after the 1796 harvest, the threat from scribbling machinery to jobs may well have receded. Clothiers and magistrates remained highly cautious, however, fearing that under a peaceful surface resentments were still harboured. There was no sudden acceleration of the take up of machinery after 1795. Eden reported of Trowbridge in 1797: 'the machines have been introduced chiefly within the last six or seven years; and as the people are so much averse to them, they are brought in only by degrees'.[66]

The different receptions accorded to the introduction of spinning jennies and scribbling engines into the West Riding and into Wiltshire and Somerset in the years before 1795 clearly indicate the correlation between resistance and the impact of machinery upon work. However, the reaction to any innovation was not simply a product of its capacity to displace labour, nor was it proportionate to the amount of labour displaced. Indeed, the response to a given machine varied widely, even though its impact upon employment was identical. The reaction to machinery was thus not merely economically determined but also, as importantly, socially produced. The reason for this variety of response, therefore, lay not only in the impact of the machine upon work itself but also in the character of the community within which work took place and which itself was largely a product of that work economy. Here the differences between the Domestic System of Yorkshire and the putting out system of the West of England, and between the textile-dominated woollen towns and villages of Wiltshire, Somerset and Gloucestershire and the more mixed economies of their surrounding parishes, led to different experiences of early industrialisation and to different responses to change. Some communities possessed a strong sense of community identity, a solidarity and collective self-confidence which was manifested in a tradition of and in a capacity to sustain vigorous and forceful protest when faced with challenges to accepted norms of economic relationships. Others did not and there machinery and changes to the structure of work and independence were tamely accepted.

What made some communities so much more self-assertive than others? At one level all the market towns and villages in the West of England and the West Riding of Yorkshire appear much the same,

---

[65] Mann, *Cloth Industry*, pp. 135–9.
[66] Eden, *State of the Poor*, Vol. III, pp. 800, 802.

collections of individuals inhabiting the same locality, linked together by ties of kinship and by the common experience of social intercourse around the market, public house, church or chapel. In every parish we would find some sense of community if manifested only in inter-parochial sporting contests or 'hooting' strangers who passed through. What distinguished some communities from the rest was their dynamic sense of social cohesion which arose from common experience of capitalist economic relations within stable single-indus-try economies. We can see this dynamic sense of community in many places in late eighteenth-century England: in the mining communities of Cornwall or of the North East and in the textile areas of the East Midlands or East Anglia. We can see it clearly in the woollen producing communities of the West of England.[67]

In many towns and villages of Gloucestershire, north Somerset and west Wiltshire full-time cloth making dominated the local economy and employment. Even though the industry was divided into many branches and production was highly specialised and sub-divided, the industry made for a strong unifying force amongst all involved in it. The fortunes of the industry, boom and slump, affected all workers and played a major role in their lives. The variety of products and markets might at first seem to negate such a claim. Indeed, those few villages which produced exclusively one particular cloth might well suffer very greatly if the market for this commodity collapsed while others producing different cloths might be unaffected. Most weavers in the West of England, however, owned both broad and narrow looms and switched into whichever branch offered work. And as, say, broad weavers shifted to narrow cloth, work there was spread more thinly so all experienced the decline of the broad trade. Fullers, dyers and cloth dressers too found the yarns and cloths on which they worked might vary with market demand but, like the weavers, they experienced the drop in overall production. This recognition of their mutual dependence upon the industry, this mutual experience of both prosperity and poverty, heightened the sense of community. Wage cuts in one branch had ramifications across the trade and rang warning bells in related trades. Attacks on apprenticeship in one trade sent shock waves throughout the industry. The introduction of labour-saving machinery fitted into this same pattern.

---

[67] For a discussion of this dynamic sense of community see A. Charlesworth and A. J. Randall, 'Morals, markets and the English crowd in 1766', *Past and Present*, 114 (1987), pp. 200–13. See also C. J. Calhoun, 'Community: toward a variable conceptualisation for comparative research', *Social History*, 5, 1 (1980).

While the pattern of prosperity generated common recognition of the industry's centrality to the community, it was the common experience of wage labour which gave this community consciousness its shape and focus. Piece work and the role of gentlemen clothiers as paymasters emphasised both the separation of the industry between capital and labour and the common economic status of wage earners. This awareness of their proto-proletarian status was emphasised by the specialisation of their industry. A strong craft consciousness characterised all the male trades, bolstered as it was by vestigial apprenticeship controls and a powerful belief in the 'artisan' status that the 'mystery of the trade' conferred upon its practitioners. The history of the industry in the eighteenth century is littered with conflicts over wages, apprenticeship and custom which occasionally afford tantalising glimpses of county-wide unions of all three male trades, though the basis of these larger organisations was certainly the permanent but mostly clandestine local box club, centred upon the sick club or burial society. Each trade was zealous to protect its own economic status and was well aware of its own history but craft exclusivity extended only so far. Weavers, scribblers and shearmen patronised different public houses but marriage and restrictions upon apprentice numbers made for close integration. This was reinforced by the numerous clubs, societies and looser associations occasioned by common needs for sickness and death insurance and for recreational, religious and cultural activities. This strong sense of mutuality was exhibited at times of crisis throughout the eighteenth century.

The common experience of dependence upon piece rate weekly earnings for survival was paralleled by common experience of dependence upon the market place for food supplies. Some textile workers had gardens and allotments but few had anything like sufficient space available to produce more than a small part of their subsistence needs.[68] Bread, the staple diet of the labouring poor, had to be bought for cash in the market place, either in its finished state, as flour or as grain. This great reliance upon wheat supplies from the Wold or the Downs made the food market a potential flash-point for disorders, as steep rises in price and diminishing availability of grain in 1766 and 1795 proved in both Gloucestershire and Wiltshire. The structure of employment in the industry thus led not only to a common experience as producers but also to a common experience as consumers, thereby reinforcing the strong sense of community consciousness. The same

[68] Mann, *Cloth Industry*, p. 102.

was true of leisure. Bearing home day developed and sustained contacts between workers while shortages of coin frequently necessitated group visits to local public houses where larger denomination promissory notes could be broken among several wage earners. In times of prosperity conspicuous consumption of drink and foodstuffs set markers for social status as did the universal practice of St Monday. The fairs, foot races and sports which punctuated such rest days emphasised the customs common to all and the independence which all woollen workers enjoyed from direct supervision at work.

Independence in work was matched by a remarkable degree of independence from external authority elsewhere. Housing, though rented, was rarely tied to employers, and local government in the woollen producing parishes rarely seems to have been a very effective agency of social control. Furthermore, these districts were not well provided with justices of the peace. The food riots in Gloucestershire in 1766 and 1795 forcibly drew the attention of the bench there to the paucity of magistrates local to the woollen parishes which contained between 40,000 and 60,000 inhabitants.[69] These disturbances clearly showed the means of maintaining law and order locally to be inadequate.

Finally, this common experience of capitalist industrial relations in the West of England gave rise to expectations and beliefs of life, work and society, in short a culture which informed attitudes and actions. This culture was built and premised upon the continuing stability and permanence of the existing economic and social system. At its core was a strong central belief in custom and customary rights which were bastions against the threat of detrimental change. This culture was not without its ambiguities. It was premised upon a capitalist economic system yet it assumed and expected fixed economic functions. It was the product of a market economy yet assumed that market forces might work only within the strict parameters of custom. These parameters were essentially moral ones, emphasising the 'rights' of labour over the rationality of the market. In such views we may discern the 'moral economy of the English crowd' so brilliantly delineated by E. P. Thompson in his work on eighteenth-century food riots, a belief in traditional rights and reciprocities which transcended market forces. The result was a community consciousness that was both dynamic and defensive. Here we see an example of that 'rebellious traditional culture' described by Thompson, forged elsewhere by similar

---

[69] Randall, 'The Gloucestershire food riots of 1766', pp. 72–93.

communities of non-agrarian independent workers, depending upon their earnings for food but divorced from the means of production.[70] 'Traditional' because, as has been shown, the woollen workers' culture put a premium upon custom and upon the maintenance of their 'rights and privileges'. But 'rebellious' because their common experiences gave them the collective basis from which to resist fiercely attempts to undermine their living conditions or way of life. It was because of this that the West of England woollen communities figured prominently in industrial disorders throughout the eighteenth century but this tradition of protest extended beyond industrial disputes. Other protests, food riots in particular, reinforced a habit of resistance to threats to existing notions of independence, fairness, order or custom.[71] The response to machinery therefore fitted into an established pattern. Where such a tradition of protest was not established, however, where workers had no successful background of collective action in support of living standards, the machine met with little resistance.

This can be seen clearly when we contrast the vigorous reaction against the spinning jenny in the main textile areas of the West of England with that encountered in the agrarian-based parishes around the peripheries. The protests of the Wiltshire and Somerset woollen workers delayed the main take up of the jenny until the early 1790s. Then a considerable expansion of trade eased its introduction for although the jenny displaced large numbers of domestic spinners, it could easily be accommodated into the domestic manufacture, while the trade boom offered alternative employment for those who had to abandon spinning altogether. The real casualties of the jenny were the wives of agricultural labourers to whom spinning constituted a major secondary source of family income and who received no compensatory employment for their loss. Many rural parishes in Wiltshire were devastated, having been heavily dependent upon spinning. Eden described the sad effects upon the chapelry of Seend where 'hand spinning has fallen into disuse . . . and the poor from the great reduction in the price scarcely have the heart to earn the little that can be made'. It was a scene duplicated in many parts of the county and served to generate a considerable groundswell of antipathy

---

[70] Thompson, 'The moral economy'; E. P. Thompson, 'Eighteenth-century English society: class struggle without class?', *Social History*, 3, 2 (1978), p. 154.
[71] Charlesworth and Randall, 'Morals, markets and the English crowd', pp. 202–3, 208–9.

to machinery among rate-payers.[72] But while the jenny had disastrous effects upon the agricultural parishes, these areas succumbed without demur. With no tradition of organised protest and within a tightly controlled and dependent environment, resistance had no community platform. The one non-textile community to generate resistance to the jenny was Keynsham, a colliery town where the miners' wives supplemented the family income by spinning. In March 1790, 'a lawless banditti of colliers and their wives' assembled to protest against the recent introduction of 'spinning engines', 'avowing their intention of cutting to pieces the machines'. The magistrates and two manufacturers were able to persuade the crowd to disperse without violence.[73] However, in June tensions rose again and dragoons were rushed to the town in time to prevent the destruction of the machines.[74] The Keynsham miners, like the workers in the woollen towns, had a long tradition of vigorous protest but, far from the towns where the clothiers who employed their wives lived, they had little chance of bringing their undoubted militancy to bear upon the jenny owners. The Keynsham disturbances marked the last resistance to the jenny.

The structure of the West Riding woollen industry gave rise to a community character significantly different to that found in the West of England woollen manufacturing parishes and this had important repercussions for the reception accorded to machinery. While the local economy of the woollen region of the West Riding was increasingly heavily dependent upon textile production, the dual economy of agriculture and cloth making which had typified the area in the early eighteenth century still survived with some vitality.[75] The small holdings of many master clothiers provided not only a source for credit or for capital to invest in new scribbling mills; they also provided a valuable economic cushion to mitigate sharp fluctuations in demand for cloth and a psychologically important sense of stability and security. The labour needs – caring for animals, haymaking, the harvesting of small patches of grains – likewise diversified a domestic economy already broken up by weekly trips to the cloth halls and to purchase

[72] Anstie, *Observations on Machinery*, pp. 11–12; Eden, *State of the Poor*, Vol. III, p. 796; T. Davis, *A General View of the Agriculture of the County of Wilts.* (1813), p. 215; see below, pp. 143, 234–5.

[73] H.O. 42/16, 17 March 1790, cited by Hammonds, *Skilled Labourer*, p. 121.

[74] *S.W.J.*, 7 June 1790.

[75] See, for example, 'The diary of Joseph Rogerson', in Crump, *Leeds Woollen Industry*, pp. 59–166. For a fascinating examination of the role of landownership in the industrial development of the West Riding woollen industry, see Hudson, *Genesis of Industrial Capital*, pp. 61–70, 85–104: 'The agricultural holding was still a valuable cushion against hard times' (p. 73).

wool and provided more areas where journeymen and master would toil side by side in common tasks. Further, the food supplied by small holdings and potato patches commonly attached to master clothiers' and journeymen's cottages reduced dependence upon the food markets and hucksters. Here too the more varied diet of the northern labourer contrasted strongly with the southern labourer's dependence upon fine wheaten bread and reduced the likelihood of clashes over one expensive staple in the market place. Food riots were not unknown in Yorkshire in the eighteenth century but they were nothing like so frequent nor so extensive as those found in the West of England.

The strong labour consciousness evinced in the West of England was not generally to be found in the West Riding. Yet the Domestic System produced its own sense of independence, a corporate sense of the pride of the master clothiers in their autonomous cloth production, epitomised in the cloth halls and their management structure.[76] Master clothiers were highly conscious of their independence and the 'little makers' were in many ways the progenitors of those characteristics which we today associate with Yorkshiremen: a bluff disregard for social graces, strong and forceful opinions and a fierce and zenophobic pride in their own achievements. But this emphasis upon independence was collective rather than individual. Master clothiers showed little sign of hostility towards nascent competitors but rather seem to have been very willing to offer help and credit to 'a young man of good character'.[77] Information on such matters as recipes for dyes were freely exchanged in a way of which gentlemen clothiers in the West of England would never have dreamed. Journeymen in the West Riding did not develop the clear labour consciousness found in the West of England because of their close relationship with their employer in the workplace and because of the clearer opportunities to become little makers in their own right. This is not to say that the majority did so rise. Indeed, towards the end of the eighteenth century as numbers of journeymen steadily increased, opportunities probably declined but journeymen did not really begin to see a clear division between themselves and the men who paid their wages until the rise of the early factory system in the later 1790s.

Like the West of England, the West Riding woollen industry was regulated every bit as much by the fixed parameters of custom which had developed over preceding decades as by industrial efficiency. However, the customary economy of the West Riding was not built

---

[76] B.P.P., 1806, Vol. 3, pp. 82–4.   [77] Ibid., Report, p. 10.

upon two clear competing interests as in the West of England but around the pivotal role of the master clothier. Part employer, part labourer, standing between journeyman and capitalist merchant, the master clothier gave the West Riding woollen region a community character unique in English textile production and one which inhibited and diffused the response to early machinery.

This can be seen in the response accorded to the introduction of the scribbling engine in the West Riding. As has been noted, the early scribbling engines generated much alarm and fear. However, the master clothiers' split status as labourer/capitalist diffused the reaction. As independent petty-producers they feared the consequences of a machine economy but as capitalists they recognised the opportunities for increased production and profits to be made from the new innovations. The solution of the joint-stock scribbling mills in which several master clothiers grouped together to finance small enterprises to do their own and other clothiers' wool preparation on commission epitomised much about the Domestic System with its unique combination of capitalist enterprise and collective caution.[78] Fears of lost autonomy were assuaged and within a few years the engines were numerous and in 1792 the first steam-powered scribbling mill was opened.[79] There was no further outcry against scribbling engines in the West Riding. However, the unease occasioned by the rise of the scribbling mills, that the machine economy would lead to new large-scale cloth manufacturers who would by-pass the Domestic System, remained if for the most part disguised by the rapid growth of the industry. It arose again in 1794 when fears of 'Merchants becoming Manufacturers' led to a large-scale petition seeking Parliamentary intervention to protect the clothiers' trade and broke out forcefully into the open in 1802 over the issue of the old regulatory legislation.[80] The enquiries of 1803 and 1806 revealed how deep the division occasioned by the rise of machinery had become. Even in 1806, however, the collective values of the master clothiers managed, if only briefly, to preserve a united and conciliatory front. The West Riding Domestic System thus generated a community character which, like that of the West of England, was both dynamic and conservative but it drew its spirit from the master clothiers, and their ambiguity towards machinery precluded the possibility of effective resistance to change. The

---

[78] See Hudson, *Genesis of Industrial Capital*, pp. 76–81.
[79] Wilson, *Gentlemen Merchants*, p. 92.
[80] See below, Chapter 6.

contrast between the response of the Yorkshire cloth makers and the Yorkshire cloth dressers was very marked, as we shall see.

The rebellious traditional culture of the West of England woollen producing parishes did not, however, give rise to identical reactions in all places. A previous proven capacity to resist detrimental change did not necessarily mean that machinery would be met with violence. The experience of previous conflicts might in some places inform and stimulate vigorous resistance but in others produce a more conciliatory response. Here the treatment of previous protests by the local authorities was an important determinant. This can be seen very clearly by contrasting reactions to machinery in Wiltshire and Gloucestershire. The disturbances of Gloucestershire weavers in 1727 and 1756 and the food riots there in 1766 had been handled with some discretion by a bench mostly composed of gentry. Their willingness to play their role in upholding the moral economy and weavers' rights was more apparent than real but it produced a much greater willingness on the part of the Gloucestershire woollen workers to consult the authorities in the hope of securing a negotiated solution than was the case in Wiltshire. There the shortage of gentry magistrates in and around the main woollen towns had given rise to the practice of appointing full-time clothiers to the bench. The consequence of this was a general and well-founded scepticism of the impartiality of the magistrates and a much more violent and bitter pattern of industrial relations as the riots of 1727, 1738 and 1766 showed.[81] This contrast, violence in Wiltshire and a willingness to try magisterial arbitration in Gloucestershire, characterised the respective responses to the scribbling engine and flying shuttle loom.

The introduction of scribbling engines into Gloucestershire was certainly less troubled than it was in Wiltshire and Somerset. The machine was introduced a year later than in Wiltshire and aroused a much less violent reaction. From 1791 onwards the *Gloucester Journal* constantly reiterated the message of the utility of machinery and the futility of opposing it.[82] How significant such propaganda was in persuading the Gloucestershire workmen to take a more passive view than their fellows in Wiltshire remains a matter for conjecture. The Gloucestershire response to the machine was much more legal and constitutional in approach, though no more successful than Wiltshire's

---

[81] A. J. Randall, 'The industrial moral economy of the Gloucestershire weavers in the eighteenth century', in J. Rule, ed., *British Trade Unionism, 1750–1850: The Formative Years* (Longman, 1988), pp. 29–51.

[82] *G.J.*, see, for example, 30 May, 18 July, 8, 22 Aug., 12 Sept., 13 Oct., 12 Dec. 1791.

direct action. Certainly the introduction of machinery in Gloucestershire was aided by a growing boom from 1794 in army cloth and cloth
for the East India Company, in both of which Gloucestershire clothiers
took a very large share,[83] but Wiltshire also experienced a growth in
trade in the 1790s, if not of such large dimensions. The disparity of
approach to machinery between the two counties was marked and is a
subject to which it will be necessary to return.

The scribbling engine first appeared in Gloucestershire in 1792,[84]
probably the first being at Woodchester where in April 1792 it provoked a minor disturbance. 'A considerable number of the more idle of
the people employed in the clothing trade' assembled, declaring their
intention to destroy some recently erected scribbling machines. 'They
proceeded to the different shops in order to seduce the work people to
follow them, but could not succeed, as they found them universally
convinced of the advantages the machines rendered the trade of this
country . . . The whole body of shearmen, weavers, etc., determined to
stand by their masters and to support them to the last.' Clothiers and
many workers were sworn in as special constables by Sir George Paul
who proceeded to lecture the rioters on the 'absurdity' of their conduct. 'The rioters, finding their cause desperate, dispersed as fast as
possible.'[85]

Scribbling machinery only began to be used at all widely in the
county from 1793–4 onwards. The effects of its introduction on
employment were probably worsened by a depression in trade in
1793,[86] but it was not until May 1794 that we have firm evidence of any
action by the Gloucestershire scribblers to resist their loss of work. It is
possible that scribbling engines contributed to the grievances which
found expression in disturbances in the southern woollen region in
October and November 1793, while workers in the Stroudwater area
were said to be concerned about the introduction of machinery in
December 1793. News of unrest in the county in these months was
deliberately suppressed by the authorities, so we cannot be sure what
were the causes.[87]

The number of scribbling machines seems to have increased in early
1794 when the trade in coarse cloth boomed, though the fine trade was

---

[83] Mann, *Cloth Industry*, p. 137.
[84] 'Within the space of two years or less, [scribbling] machines have been introduced.'
    J.H.C., Vol. 49, p. 600, May 1794.
[85] *G.J.*, 30 April 1792.
[86] Mann, *Cloth Industry*, pp. 130, 135.
[87] John Wallington of Dursley said in 1803 that scribbling engines were not introduced
    there until 1795 to 1796. *B.P.P.*, 1802/3, Vol. 7, p. 299.

depressed. George Turner wrote that 'the introduction of machinery for every process the wool goes through to the loom has thrown many hands out of employ'.[88] Among these were many scribblers and in May they petitioned Parliament to ameliorate their conditions. The petition was presented jointly with another from the Gloucestershire shearmen. The scribblers attempted to win the support of local respectable opinion by issuing a notice 'To the Landowners, Renters, and other persons affected by the poor', complaining that 'a great number of persons brought up to the business of wool scribbling are now nearly deprived of employment in consequence of a late introduction of scribbling machines' and warned that, unless 'proper and salutory' steps were taken, very large numbers would be thrown upon the parish. The notice stated that the scribblers intended to petition Parliament 'to suppress or otherwise confine the said machines to a specific number' but, being poor, they were unable to raise sufficient subscriptions for this purpose and solicited financial aid as well as signatures from well-wishers. Such aid was obviously forthcoming since the petition was presented and the combined scribblers'/shearmen's petition was said to bear 1,400 signatures, even though the clothiers organised a blacklist and dismissed any shearman involved in their petition and warned the public that 'the inconveniences attributed to these [scribbling] engines are the common objections raised against all machines' and that, should the scribblers obtain their demands, the industry would be ruined.[89]

The scribblers' petition, presented on 16 May, made much of the levels of unemployment and the consequent rise in poor rates ensuing from the scribbling engine. 'One man and a boy will do as much work in twelve hours as twenty men can do in a like space of time, and the carding machines will complete as much work as eighty women can industriously perform.' Card makers, card board makers and wire drawers would also be thrown out of work. They asked that Parliament suppress or limit the machines 'to such a number as will not engross the whole of the labour, but leave sufficient employment for the petitioners to support themselves and families'. However, the petition was presented too late in the session for action and the scribblers do not appear to have had the resources for a second attempt.[90]

The failure of the scribblers' petition appears to have put an end to all resistance to preparatory machinery in Gloucestershire. The following

---

[88] Turner, *General View of the Agriculture of Gloucestershire*, p. 31.
[89] *G.J.*, 5, 12, 26 May 1794.
[90] *J.H.C.*, Vol. 49, pp. 599–600; *G.J.*, 9, 16 June 1794.

year food riots swept through the cloth making areas of the county and, while magistrates like Paul feared that 'this is but the beginning of an evil that will turn to desperate consequences', he was more concerned with political sedition than with possible attacks on machinery.[91] There is no evidence that industrial disturbances accompanied the often extensive food riots in Gloucestershire. In early 1797 the suspension of cash payments by the Bank of England caused a lack of circulating coin in the county which coincided with a depression in the broadcloth trade but the clothiers feared riots over their inability to pay their workmen rather than because of hostility to machinery.[92] Fears of invasion from France prompted the formation of various volunteer corps in all the manufacturing areas and the clothiers were zealous volunteers. In April 1798 many clothiers were endeavouring to be allowed to form their workers into voluntary infantry companies. Paul was concerned that 'if too many of them should get under arms together and no enemy appear, they might take an opportunity of holding strong language to their masters on the sore point of increasing machinery'. The clothiers did not see it that way.[93] Certainly no such event did occur and, while increasing machinery may have raised hackles, only in a few instances concerning shearing frames did Gloucestershire workers use violence against machinery again during the war.

The sharply contrasting reactions of the Wiltshire and Somerset and the Gloucestershire woollen workers to the introduction of scribbling engines was reproduced in their respective responses to the one major innovation to affect the principal adult male trade, weaving, before the development of the power loom. Kay's flying shuttle, invented in 1733, enabled one man to work the broad loom instead of the two persons previously needed. Adapted to the narrow loom, which was always worked by one man, it enabled a faster rate of production. The loom was in general use in Lancashire from the 1760s and spread into the West Riding in the early 1770s. The major advantage for the weaver was, as one clothier said, 'it makes him independent of a journeyman'. It meant that the net earnings from a broad loom did not have to be divided between two workers. By the same token, in theory at least, the loom displaced one in two weavers. This, of course, was not strictly

---

[91] W.O. 1/1091, Paul to Sec. at War, 20 July 1795.
[92] H.O. 42/40, Earl of Berkeley to Portland, 3 March 1797; *J.H.C.*, Vol. 52, p. 463; *G.J.*, 3 April 1797.
[93] H.O. 50/41, Paul to Dundas?, 27 April 1798. See also Lloyd-Baker MSS, Box 55, letter book of Rev. William Lloyd-Baker, Lloyd-Baker to Cooper, 2 March 1797; H.O. 50/41, Austin to Berkeley, 17 March 1798.

true as many journeymen or second men were in fact apprentices or the wives and children of the weaver or master clothier. Further, the flying shuttle or spring loom, as it was commonly called in the West, was slower than the old double loom. John Clayfield, a Gloucestershire weaver who used the spring loom, estimated in 1803 that it took three weeks to complete a broadcloth on the spring loom as against two weeks on the double loom. This was because the weaver had to tie off ends and repair breakages on both sides of the loom. The spring loom also was said to require more physical effort to work it. If these ratios were roughly correct, and if both weavers from the double loom took up the spring loom, their combined output would have risen in the ratio of 3:4, double loom to spring loom. In other words the spring loom threatened to displace one in four weavers. William Clement, a Chippenham weaver, believed that the loom would displace one in three weavers. If the price of weaving per cloth remained the same, as it did in Gloucestershire in the late 1790s, this ratio of productivity would have meant that an individual weaver would have found his earnings had risen by one third. This, in fact, is what a prominent Gloucestershire clothier claimed had happened.[94] The figures cited by Austin in 1838 indicated that the spring loom was considerably faster than the double loom but these figures, if accurate for the period when the spring loom was generally used, do not accord with the evidence available for the 1790s.[95]

There is very little information relating to the introduction of the flying shuttle loom into the West Riding. The earliest evidence is from 1770 when it met with strong and vigorous opposition from the master clothiers. However, their riots and claims that it proved 'detrimental to the fabric and manufacture of cloth' do not appear to have persisted for long and the loom was in fairly general use in Yorkshire by the 1780s, aided by the rapid expansion of trade.[96] Weavers in the three western

---

[94] *B.P.P.*, 1802/3, Vol. 7, pp. 300, 10, 77, 78, 24, 300.

Thus 2 men in double loom produce	1 cloth in 2 weeks
	3 cloths in 6 weeks
1 man in spring loom produces	1 cloth in 3 weeks
	2 cloths in 6 weeks
Therefore 2 men in spring loom	4 cloths in 6 weeks

Earnings per man: P = wages for cloth
Double loom earns P/2 ÷ 2 weeks = P/4 per man per week
Spring loom earns P/1 ÷ 3 weeks = P/3 per man per week

[95] *B.P.P.*, 1840, Vol. 23, pp. 439–40. Austin stated that the double loom took 364 hours as against the spring loom's 252 hours to weave the same length of cloth.

[96] *L.M.*, 29 May 1770; Wilson, *Gentlemen Merchants*, p. 91.

counties also viewed the early introduction of the loom with alarm but here their opposition was more protracted.

The exact date when the spring loom was introduced into Gloucestershire is unclear. A weaver who had used the loom from its inception stated in 1803 that he had been doing so for nine or ten years, though he later said that he had bought the looms eight or ten years before, while John Wallington, a clothier, stated that the loom had been introduced into the county ten or twelve years before.[97] It seems probable that 1793 was the year in question. A Stonehouse clothier, Nathaniel Watts, introduced the looms into his weaving shops. This caused considerable alarm among the weavers and deputations were sent to Watts. The clothiers were also very concerned and met at Rodborough. Possibly this was the meeting convened for 21 March at The Fleece Inn, Rodborough, a favourite venue of clothiers' meetings, 'to consider measures for the general good of the trade'.[98] An 'immense number of weavers' assembled on Hartley Common (Wallington believed that there were 3,000 or 4,000 present, while Clayfield had heard that the crowd numbered 20,000) and delegates were sent to confer with the clothiers. The weavers said that they were afraid that the introduction of the looms would force them from their cottages to work in shops, that they and their families would be ruined and that the looms would decrease wage rates. The clothiers denied that they had any wish to drive the weavers into loom shops, stated that they would only introduce the loom if the state of trade made it necessary and that they would not lower wages. The clothiers promised to ask Watts to give up the looms which he did, selling them to some weavers, one of whom was John Clayfield who bought two 'by the week'. Antipathy to the loom was thus apparently assuaged if not entirely removed.[99] Clayfield found the looms advantageous but it was not until the period around 1798 when there was a great demand for weavers that the loom was taken up in any significant numbers, apparently by the weavers themselves. As the clothiers had promised, cloth made on the spring loom was paid at the same rate as that from the double loom, although Wallington said that the clothiers were thus out of pocket until the weavers mastered the new technique. By 1803 many weavers

[97] B.P.P., 1802/3, Vol. 7, pp. 9, 15, 299.
[98] G.J., 18 March 1793.
[99] It is possible but unlikely that the spring loom contributed to the disturbances in the Dursley–Uley area in November 1793, noted above. In their evidence, Clayfield and Wallington, himself a Dursley clothier, make no mention of any unrest after the Rodborough meeting.

had changed to the spring loom, though Daniel Lloyd stated that it was 'not at present universally used'.[100]

This negotiated introduction was very different to the response to the loom in Wiltshire. The spring loom was first introduced in Trowbridge in 1792 where it caused the riot mentioned earlier.[101] Thereafter, the loom was rarely seen in Wiltshire in the 1790s. George Wansey, the innovating Salisbury clothier, saw the loom on a visit to America in 1794, referring to it as 'the new invented spring shuttle' which indicates that it was not widely known.[102] Francis Hill used spring looms at his factory at Malmesbury but a weaver who had worked there and had returned to Bradford on Avon claimed in 1803 that 'Nobody else in Wiltshire uses them' as spring looms were 'not allowed'. There were in fact said in 1803 to be two or three spring looms in Chippenham where riots in 1801 may well have been sparked off by attempts to introduce them.[103] A Freshford weaver, who had been working in the North of England, tried to introduce the loom when he returned about 1801, but 'he worked with it only a few weeks on account of the riotous assemblage of the mob who made him relinquish it'.[104] James Jones, a master weaver from North Bradley, stated in 1803, 'I never saw a spring loom in my life.'[105] The strong antipathy of the Wiltshire and Somerset weavers ensured that the loom was not generally introduced there until well after the Napoleonic Wars.

There was therefore nothing automatic about the response to machinery as the history of the introduction of the spinning jenny, scribbling engine and flying shuttle into Yorkshire, Wiltshire, Somerset and Gloucestershire showed. The impact of the machine upon work was a critical factor but as important was the way in which the community responded and this was as much dictated by the character of that community and its previous history of industrial relations as by the technology itself. Diverse though they were, however, the protests against machinery did share many common features as comparison makes clear.

A characteristic of all protests against machinery in both the West of England and the West Riding was that they were pre-emptive

---

[100] *B.P.P.*, 1802/3, Vol. 7, pp. 15–16, 18–19, 299–300; *J.H.C.*, Vol. 58, p. 884.

[101] *S.W.J.*, 27 Aug. 1791; W.O. 1/1052, Hubert to Yonge, 21 Aug. 1792; see above, pp. 82–3.

[102] H. Wansey, *The Journal of an Excursion to the United States of America in 1794* (1796; ed. D. J. Jeremy, Philadelphia, 1970), p. 83.

[103] J. J. Daniell, *History of Chippenham* (1894), p. 91; Mann, *Cloth Industry*, p. 141.

[104] *J.H.C.*, Vol. 58, p. 885.

[105] *B.P.P.*, 1802/3, Vol. 7, p. 72.

responses rather than reactions of groups already displaced by technological innovations. Machines were not suddenly introduced in large
numbers nor did they always cause instant unemployment. Sometimes they were introduced to satisfy demands which hand work could
not supply. The West of England clothiers, indeed, were angered that
machinery was opposed whether or not men were out of work. The
workers there did not see it this way. They realised the implications of
machinery and sought to stem them at source. They did not need to see
large numbers thrown out of work to realise what machinery could
mean. This is not to argue that the West of England woollen workers
opposed all machines or all change. Machinery was only consistently
opposed where it threatened adult male employment. The workers'
attitude was, in fact, opportunistic. Thus, the Shepton Mallet weavers
were prepared to accept 'trials' of the jenny in return for a guaranteed
return to the old rate of 1s. 3d. per yard for weaving. The weavers and
shearmen of Woodchester helped to protect the newly established
scribbling engines from angry scribblers from Stroudwater in 1792,
presumably because they were indeed 'universally convinced of the
advantages the machines rendered the trade', particularly their own
trades.[106] And in the case of the spinning jenny, while opposition to its
introduction in the West of England was fierce until the late 1780s, it
seems to have encountered little resistance when it was brought in in
large numbers there in the early 1790s since booming trade offered
alternative employment for those woollen workers' wives who were
displaced by it. Paternalists and rate-payers were most acutely conscious that the real casualties from the jenny were the wives of agricultural labourers. The woollen workers found it advantageous to point to
this when trying to secure influential support but after 1790 they
showed no continued solidarity of support with the jenny's victims.

Whereas in the West Riding the initial fears of machinery were soon
assuaged, the main reaction of the woollen workers in the West of
England to the introduction of machinery in the 1790s was undoubtedly to resort to violence. How far were these riots mere spontaneous
uprisings or more premeditated affairs? It is difficult to give a categori-
cal answer. Certainly violence often erupted very shortly after the
establishment of any innovation but it was not an immediate response.
There was in all cases a gestation period in which the machine was left
undisturbed, in which popular resentment was primed and fostered.
Riots did not demand the degree of organisation and control required
for strikes but a general will and determination on action was

[106] *G.J.*, 30 April 1792.

necessary before disturbances occurred. Machine breaking riots in the early 1790s can perhaps best be compared with those patterns of protest seen in food riots. Indeed, the actions of the Westbury scribblers in 1795 in splitting their forces in simultaneous attacks on machinery and their owners in order to take advantage of the paucity of troops were very similar to those of the food rioters in Westbury in 1766.[107] If the crowds involved in the machinery riots were not 'organised', they were certainly not chance participants in an accidental incident. They knew what they were doing. Often large numbers were involved in machine riots. At Bradford on Avon in 1791 500 people were said to have assembled outside Phelps' house. Certainly, in no case were the disturbers of the peace merely those who had lost their jobs to the machine. The machines in question were few in number and their immediate effects upon the job market would have been limited. Therefore, very many others whose jobs were not directly at risk joined in the riots to destroy the machines. How far the unity of antipathy to machinery extended beyond the trade immediately threatened can only be suggested. We have little information concerning the occupations of the rioters because only a few were captured and tried and most were dealt with at quarter sessions where exact occupations were not recorded. Reports usually spoke only of rioters; only in the 1776 Shepton Mallet riot were 'weavers, shearmen, etc.' identified. Anstie, however, later stated that in Wiltshire in 1791 'serious apprehensions were entertained of the shearmen, and other persons in the manufactory, committing fresh outrages on the property of those clothiers who had more generally begun to scribble wool by machinery'.[108] The Woodchester rioters also included a cross-section of woollen workers. The role of women in the riots is interesting since they were the principal victims of the introduction of preparatory machinery. Women played prominent roles in the anti-jenny riots at Shepton Mallet, at Frome and at Keynsham. They were also involved in the Bradford on Avon riot in 1791 and took the leading part in the riot against machine-scribbled yarn at Bramley described by Wilson. The role played by women harmonises with what we know of their part in food riots and indicates further the strong community participation in anti-machinery riots before 1795.

The violence of the machinery riot was far from being uncontrolled. For the most part it was selective and the rioters showed considerable

---

[107] See Randall, 'The Gloucestershire food riots of 1766', pp. 82–6; *S.W.J.*, 29 Sept., 6, 13 Oct. 1766.
[108] Anstie, *Observations on Machinery*, p. 5.

restraint. This was seen in the Bradford on Avon riot of 1791. Although the crowd's anger at the introduction of a scribbling engine was exacerbated by Phelps' action in firing upon them, killing three of their colleagues, they did not attempt to exact vengeance upon Phelps himself or even upon his house or workshops once he agreed to hand over the machine. Innovators, in fact, appear to have suffered no personal harm whatsoever in the 1790s. Violence was directed against their machines and sometimes their other property but not at them. There were certainly attempts to intimidate them with threats but that was all. The other feature of the violence of the riots was the ceremony with which hated machines were often destroyed. Thus the ritualistic destruction of Phelps' scribbling engine on the town bridge served to symbolise the Bradford on Avon crowd's triumph over the machine and its owner. These displays of popular justice exacting its retribution upon machines and machine owners who were felt to have offended the moral principles of the woollen industry were very similar to those actions of food rioters punishing immoral traders. They also had parallels in the 'trials' of illegal warping bars and of blackleg weavers which were characteristic community responses to such 'offenders'.[109]

Disturbances would probably have been more frequent in the West of England had it not been for the continued presence there of troops. Thus Trowbridge clothiers were insistent: 'The disposition of the inhabitants of this town is such that upon the least innovation with regard to the manufactory, it is nothing unusual for the lower classes of people to assemble tumultuously . . . We therefore deem it absolutely necessary that the troops already stationed here should continue as a kind of protection to all the manufacturers.'[110] They were clearly of major importance in preserving peace. We have noted already that their removal, however temporary, or the weakening of their numbers could be instantly seized upon by the crowd. Troops were often drafted into an area in anticipation of trouble. This seems to have occurred at Shepton Mallet in 1776, for example. And, as a clothier in 1800 stated, small detachments of troops were used to defend such mills as appeared prime targets for violence.[111] This was borne out by evidence in 1802. If less true for Gloucestershire, it would be fair to conclude that the early mechanisation of the woollen industry in Wiltshire and Somerset was carried out in the coercive shadow of the

[109] See, for example, *B.P.P.*, 1840, Vol. 24, Pt v, p. 371; *G.J.*, 13 June 1825; and below, pp. 194–5.
[110] W.O. 1/1055, P. and J. Gibbs to Yonge, 7 Dec. 1792.
[111] *Account of the Proceedings of the Merchants*, p. 155.

protection of the military. This role was recognised by the War Office who responded promptly to claims that trouble was imminent. However, the War Office was anxious that troops should be used only when other means of pacifying a situation had failed. In 1781 Frome magistrates were recommended, 'in the strongest terms', 'that the military may not be called upon to act until every effort of the civil power has been exerted and proved ineffectual'.[112] Local magistrates were perhaps understandably quick to bring them to face a disorderly crowd but only at Shepton Mallet in 1776 were the troops used in a way calculated to cause serious injury to the rioters. The attitude of the 'respectable inhabitants' towards the troops was often ambivalent, however, since their presence and more particularly their cost in time of apparent peace was often resented. Thus in January 1795 Westbury refused to give back billets to troops previously stationed there, yet in May, August and November the town was desperately begging for their return to protect it from 'the mob'. Frome magistrates were grateful for swift military response to their fears of riot in June 1795, but by December of that year the innkeepers were petitioning for their removal. The problem was best encapsulated by Paul, writing in July 1795 following the food riots in the Gloucestershire woollen region. 'The appearance of a military force is necessary but, consistent with that purpose, we must let the pressure of their consumption be felt as little as possible in one point.'[113]

The rebellious culture of the West of England workers undoubtedly had an impact upon innovators. Their violent response to new machinery deterred all but the most determined from such confrontations, as repeated reports made clear. Many clothiers like Matthew Humphreys of Chippenham preferred not to risk the wrath of the workers. 'If we in this part of the Kingdom attempt to introduce [machinery]', he wrote in 1786, 'it must be with the risk of our lives and fortunes.'[114] The fear which the volatile communities of woollen workers engendered had influence far beyond their own immediate parishes for they did not recognise such artificial boundaries. The woollen workers took considerable interest in the activities of their neighbours and did not hesitate to visit violence upon them should innovations potentially

---

[112] W.O. 4/113, Jenkinson to Jesser, 7 June 1781.
[113] W.O. 1/1082, Anstie to Sec. at War, 28 May, a'Court to Sec. at War, 23 Nov. 1795; W.O. 1/1093, Seymour, Long to Sec. at War, 7 Aug. 1795, W.O. 1/1092, Sheppards to Rooke, 7 June, innkeepers of Frome to Rooke, 28 Dec. 1795; W.O. 1/1091, Paul to Sec. at War, 26 July 1795.
[114] P.R.O. B.T., 6/111, no. 39, cited in Mann, *Cloth Industry*, p. 126.

dangerous to a wider area be left unchallenged. Thus, the Shepton Mallet riots were occasioned by the woollen workers from the Frome area; and the rioters at Woodchester in 1792 were all strangers to the village. Even innovators far distant from the main woollen towns had good cause to worry. Samuel Paul Bamford was a highly progressive clothier of Twerton, a mile west of Bath, and sufficiently removed from the main woollen centres to encourage him to pioneer the introduction of most innovations. However, in February 1792 he wrote urgently to the War Office for immediate aid, 'having received some intimation of a combination formed by a set of scribblers in Wiltshire for the destruction of our worsted spinning mill at this place in which we have late set a scribbling machine at work'. He received similar threats in April 1793 and in December 1797 his mills were the target of an attempted attack by Wiltshire and Somerset shearmen which was prevented only at the last minute.[115] We must therefore avoid assuming that the impact of a riot was specific only to its immediate locality. By displaying so clearly both the potential consequences of introducing innovations and their readiness to issue forth from their strongholds to attack innovators, rioters in one place may well have curbed potential experiments over a much wider area.[116] Hostility to change therefore may have proved a major factor in delaying the mechanisation of the West of England woollen industry and thereby have contributed to its slower growth rate than that in Yorkshire. Worker resistance may thus have been responsible for depressed trade and not the reverse as economic historians have often concluded.

Direct action may have characterised the response of the West of England woollen workers to the early introduction of machinery but they, like the journeymen in the West Riding in 1786, also attempted to

[115] W.O. 1/1054, S. P. Bamford to Sec. at War, 5 Feb. 1792. The threats in April 1793 concerned Bamford's introduction and use of Cartwright's combing machines, which threatened to displace wool combers. These men were the labour aristocracy of the worsted and serge industries, but the combing process was more or less the same function of preparation as that carried out by the scribblers in the woollen industry. Bamford wrote to the War Office that the wool combers in the West of England 'have taken great umbrage against our method of working' and had made an agreement with the Mendip colliers to assist them in an attack on Twerton to smash all machines. Bamford's mill at Twerton figured prominently in evidence to the House of Commons which followed the Devon wool combers' petition in March 1794. There were well-organised wool combers in the Salisbury serge industry: W.O. 1/1056, S. P. Bamford to Young (sic), 26 April 1793; J.H.C., Vol. 49, pp. 322–3; B.C., 5 Aug. 1784; S.W.J., 30 Jan. 1792. For the 1797 disturbances, see below and H.O. 42/41, Bowen to Portland, 20 Dec. 1797.

[116] Charlesworth and Randall, 'Morals, markets and the English crowd', pp. 202–5, 213, makes similar points about food riots.

influence public opinion and to persuade the authorities to intervene
on their behalf. Their case was an amalgam of appeals to paternal
protection, warnings of the industrial consequences of mechanisation
and particularly appeals to rate-payer self-interest. As an argument
against machinery it was not wholly worked out, or rather not wholly
articulated, until 1802 but it was not without effect in influencing
landowners in the woollen districts. Appeals that machinery would
displace large numbers of workers and throw their families upon their
respective parishes were well calculated to worry rate-payers and the
Parliamentary petitions of 1776, 1786, 1794 and those of 1802 all
stressed this point. The Gloucestershire scribblers even appealed publicly for the help and support of rate-payers on this issue, apparently
with some success. The woollen workers also played upon the old
suspicions and enmities between clothiers and rate-payers, pointing
out that, while cost-cutting machinery was forcing up poor rates, the
clothiers had not passed on this saving to the consumer. On the
contrary, cloth prices had actually risen. The workers also stressed that
machines made inferior cloth, the scribblers claiming that scribbling
engines 'tear the wool from its true staple', while the shearmen in 1794
stated that the gig mill 'injures the texture or ground of a fine cloth'.[117]
Previous Parliaments had legislated to protect the quality and reputation of woollen cloth by ensuring that it was not 'deceitfully made'.
The workers clearly hoped that Parliament in the 1790s would follow
suit. Thus, the innovators were presented as would-be monopolists,
attempting to engross the trade and to make large temporary profits at
the expense of the labourer, the unwitting customer and ultimately the
reputation of the trade itself.[118] The woollen workers demanded, and
indeed believed that they were entitled to, protection against such
detrimental change, just as they claimed the right to protection against
the forestaller and engrosser in the market place. The innovator, in
introducing his machines, was seen as stealing the craft skills which
were the property of the displaced labourer and as threatening
traditional parameters of independence and control.

---

[117] *J.H.C.*, Vol. 49, pp. 599, 600. Apologists for machinery claimed that it led to better
cloth since in times of boom it ensured that quantity could be increased without loss
of quality.
[118] Very similar arguments were made by Nottinghamshire framework knitters against
cut-ups in 1811. They too demanded regulation. 'Let the wise and the great lend their
aid and advice Nor e'er their assistance withdraw Till full-fashioned work at the old
fashioned price is established by Custom and Law.' H.O. 42/119, cited in Thompson,
The Making, pp. 581–4.

To conclude: the response to the introduction of preparatory machinery into the woollen industry was varied and multiform. This response was only in part determined by the economic impact of labour-saving technology. As important was the character of the community into which the machine was being established. This community character led in some places to a grudging acceptance. In others it led to violent mass action. The impact of anti-machinery riots was considerable and in the West of England considerably delayed the take up of machinery. But while the community response was a powerful one, it was not without its weaknesses. The crowd was a strong agency of resistance only so long as it could be summoned to act and only so long as it represented a consensus of hostile opinion. After the initial set-backs, preparatory machinery was introduced by stealth and on the periphery of the woollen districts. There spinning jennies and scribbling and carding engines gradually established themselves, putting increased pressure on employers everywhere to follow, but also demonstrating that they held certain advantages for some groups of workers. Weavers found the benefits of stronger and more even yarn and their participation in support of spinners or scribblers could no longer be relied upon. It was in this way that the community response, at first so strong, could be undermined. Thus it was that the principal resistance to mechanisation came from a group which, while it could expect community support, nonetheless could rely upon its own industrial muscle to protect it from displacement: the cloth dressers of both the West Riding and the West of England.

Chapter 4

The cloth dressers, trade unionism and machinery

The introduction of preparatory machinery into the English woollen industry paved the way for the more bitter struggle which was to accompany the attempt in the later 1790s and early 1800s to mechanise cloth finishing and to introduce loomshops or weaving factories. As has been seen, the more aggressive reaction of the West of England, and in particular of the Wiltshire and Somerset, woollen workers substantially delayed the take up of preparatory machinery in that region as compared with the West Riding. By the mid-1790s, however, this new technology was increasingly securely established everywhere and was developing a momentum of its own which could not easily be retarded. The ever-present fears of the rise of a machine economy were temporarily stilled by the rapid expansion of trade, by the greater entrepreneurial opportunities available and by the need to compete with rival cloth producers. The superior yarn produced by the spin-ning jenny, the slubbing billy and the carding and scribbling engines made for faster weaving, increased production, more work and im-proved earnings for all in the industry but preparatory machinery also brought in its wake increased capital accumulation and capital concen-tration. In both the West of England and the West Riding the later 1790s saw the rise of a new breed of woollen cloth manufacturer, men who saw growing opportunities for wealth, status and success in further mechanisation of the industry. Some of these men were drawn from the ranks of the greater merchants and gentlemen clothiers and their accumulated wealth enabled them to pioneer the construction of the earliest large-scale factories. Benjamin Gott of Bean Ing, Leeds, and John Jones of Staverton in consequence became the most prominent of these early manufacturers in their respective regions. The majority, however, were drawn in the West Riding from the ranks of the larger master clothiers who had prospered with the establishment of scrib-bling mills and in the West of England from the ranks of the lesser clothiers. Ambitious, impatient with custom and older methods of production and increasingly confident that worker resistance had been overcome, in the later 1790s they began to press ahead with the next phase of industrialisation – the development of a closer control over the production of cloth afforded by loom shops and over cloth finishing by the introduction of the gig mill and the shearing frame. The scene was set for major conflict which reached its crescendo with the Wiltshire Outrages in 1802 which in turn led to two Parliamentary Select Committees in 1803 and 1806 to investigate the state of the woollen manufacture. It was as a result of these that Parliament chose in 1809 to repeal all the old regulatory legislation which for centuries had controlled various aspects of cloth production, thereby throwing open the industry to free market forces and entrepreneurial ambition. The decade from 1796 to 1806 therefore proved crucial in the attempt to drag the woollen industry 'onto the rails of nineteenth-century factory production'[1] and set the course which was inevitably to lead to the Luddite disturbances in Yorkshire in 1812.

Resistance to change in these years took on a rather different character to that which had greeted earlier technological changes. In part this was a consequence of the experience of those previous conflicts but it was mostly because mechanisation in this later period encountered in its path the most powerful labour interest in the woollen industry, the cloth dressers. The community resistance which had opposed preparatory machinery was, as has been seen, a potent force but it proved ultimately unsustainable. Community support was still a factor in the cloth dressers' battle against machinery. The cloth dressers, however, were better equipped than any other labour group to fight their own corner from their own resources. Their capacity to organise themselves into combinations had enabled them to become 'the aristocrats of the woollen workers'. That organisational capacity, that industrial muscle was now put to the purpose of preventing the cloth dressers from becoming 'an order of men not necessary to the manufacture'.[2] It was from the basis of a powerful trade union organisation that cloth dressers in the West Riding and the West of England launched and sustained their struggle against the finishing machinery which threatened the existence of their trade in the years from 1796 to 1809. The effectiveness of this opposition can be gauged by the fact that in Yorkshire it was not until after the repeal of the old protective legislation in 1809 that finishing machinery was introduced on any significant scale. And in Wiltshire, where earlier attempts to introduce the machines

---

[1] Wilson, *Gentlemen Merchants*, p. 97.
[2] Ponting, *Woollen Industry*, p. 71; H.O. 42/66, Fitzwilliam to Pelham, 27 Sept. 1802.

prompted major disturbances in 1802, it was not until 1816 that they began to proliferate. An examination of the cloth dressers' campaign in the years before 1809 therefore proves highly informative about the nature of the struggle, both physical and ideological, over the introduction of new technology into the woollen industry, about the character and methods of early trade unions and about the background and nature of Luddism.

The cloth dressers – known in the West of England as shearmen and in the West Riding as croppers and sometimes referred to in both areas as cloth workers – were responsible for finishing a piece of woollen cloth after it had been fulled. Fulling achieves three purposes. By pounding and compressing the cloth in a mixture of fuller's earth and water, the wool is cleaned, the fabric is shrunk to increase the weight to unit length ratio and thus resistance to wear, and at the same time the short stapled wool fibres used in woollens are felted together to form a close matt finish. The fulled cloth is left with an uneven pile and it was the cloth dresser's job to cut off this nap to leave a smooth and even surface. This involved two processes, raising a nap and then shearing it. Raising, otherwise known as roughing or rowing, was accomplished by hand, using a cross-shaped wooden tool to which teasels were attached, worked with a brushing action. It required considerable practice and experience to produce an even pile. The real skill, however, lay in shearing, for which large hand shears, standing perhaps 4 feet high and weighing up to 40 pounds, were used. The blades were curved and set at an angle of some 37° to each other. The shears were worked over a rounded bench called a horse, the cloth being fixed to the shearing board with one blade of the shears laid back-down onto it, resting on or against heavy weights called shear leads. The cutting action was achieved by pushing the free blade towards the other by a simple nog and lever device. Shearing required not only great skill but also considerable muscular power. 'It requires a deal of nicety to guide the shears so as to cut the work smooth and neat, and it requires a great deal of strength – little boys cannot do it.'[3] A piece of cloth required raising and shearing several times to provide a really good finish.

The business of the cloth worker is to take a piece of cloth in its rough state . . . as it comes from the fulling mill; he first raises the cloth; after that if it is a good piece, it is cropped wet; it is then taken and mossed and rowed; mossing is the filling up of the bottom of the wool after it has been cut with the shears wet . . . ;

[3] *B.P.P.*, 1802/3, Vol. 7, p. 196.

6   Cloth dressers at work
Source: G. Walker, *The Costume of Yorkshire* (1814).

after that it is rowed down with the cards, that is to make the wool lie closer; after that it is tentered; if a fine piece, it will receive three cuts dry after the tenter; when that is done, it is backed, that is the wool cut off the back side.

The cloth would then be burled, fine drawn and then pressed and finally gently raised again and perhaps also sheared slightly. 'Must a cloth worker and shearman understand the whole of that except fine drawing?', a cropper was asked in 1806. 'Yes', he replied.[4] It was a very highly skilled and complex trade. Indeed, the value of the finished cloth depended much on the quality of the cloth dresser's work. 'They can make a piece 20 per cent better or worse by due care and labour or the reverse.'[5] It was this vital role in the woollen industry which gave the cloth dressers their privileged status and strong bargaining position.

The cloth dressers worked in finishing shops, usually owned by a master dresser. Most merchants and gentlemen clothiers preferred

---

[4] *B.P.P.*, 1806, Vol. 3, p. 296, evidence of John Tate. Technically, cloth cut wet was 'cropped' while that cut dry was 'sheared'. 'Fine drawing' was the name given to the sewing up of small holes and flaws in the cloth.
[5] P.C. 1/43/A152, Observations respecting the combinations of workmen, 1799.

7   The preemer boy
The preemer boy cleared the flock off the 'handles' used by the cloth
dressers to raise a cloth – note the pile of clean handles at the dresser's feet
and the used ones beside.
Source: G. Walker, *The Costume of Yorkshire* (1814).

this system for they thus avoided any capital investment[6] and by-
passed the problems of direct disputes with the notoriously 'ill-dis-
ciplined' cloth dressers and of finding men work if trade grew slack.
This was not true of Leeds, the largest cloth finishing centre, where
merchants had gradually gathered the croppers under their own control. Thus by 1798 there were said to be only 22 master dressers to some
1,500 croppers in the town. Leeds, however, was untypical and it was
said that in the West Riding in 1806 there were some 500 masters and
between 5,000 and 6,000 croppers. In the West of England, where few
clothiers employed shearmen directly, there were perhaps 4,000
shearmen.[7]

The finishing shops retained much of the old trade guild atmosphere

---

[6] *The Trowbridge Woollen Industry as illustrated by the Stock Books of John and Thomas Clark,
1804–24*, ed. R. P. Beckinsale (Devizes, 1951), pp. 3, 10. The tools of the trade were
expensive. In Trowbridge in 1804, four pairs of second-hand shears cost £2 10s. od.,
while four new pairs cost over £10, a pair of shear boards were valued at £3 15s. od., on
top of which were needed brushes, teasels, shears, leads and such like.
[7] Wilson, *Gentlemen Merchants*, pp. 72–3; B.P.P., 1806, Vol. 3, pp. 249, 289; L.M., 29 Jan.
1803.

and independence. While he owned neither the tools of his trade nor the cloth on which he worked, 'the cropper strictly speaking is not a servant. He does not feel or call himself as such, but a cloth worker, and partakes much more of the nature of a shoemaker, joiner, taylor, etc. . . . Like them, he comes and goes, stops a longer or shorter time . . . according as he may chance to have work.'[8] Coming and going at will, that characteristic of many craft workshop trades, proved a source of antagonism to those manufacturers and merchants who did set up their own finishing shops. John Jones, the Bradford on Avon clothier, clashed with shearmen in his shop when he attempted in 1802 to rationalise their hours of labour to a working day from 6 a.m. to 6 p.m., allowing two hours for two meal breaks. The customary allowance was for five meal breaks during the working day, taken as and when the cloth dresser came to the end of a particular piece of work. Sometimes the break would be enjoyed in the workshop itself but equally often the journeyman would make his way to the local public house for drink and refreshment.[9] Such manifestations of the independence of the artisan did not in general cause friction with the master dressers. The cloth dresser was paid by the piece and by the quality of his work, and to maintain the life-style which he saw as commensurate with his social status he would work rapidly and steadily to make up his earnings when at his bench. Such irregularity, however, annoyed those men who were endeavouring to institute the more rigorous and formal regime of work which the factory age demanded. And indeed the uncertainty of production levels which such a capricious system of work could engender did cause difficulties when orders had to be filled. Most master dressers, however, shared their journeymen's attitudes, working alongside them at their benches and inhabiting the same social *milieu*. Some had risen from the ranks and by dint of hard work and careful saving had set up for themselves. Others were heirs of men who had made the same transition. Such upward social mobility was not as easy as that from journeyman weaver to master clothier but the gap between master and man in the independent finishing shops was nowhere near as wide as that between journeyman and gentleman clothier or merchant. Thus, while there was a clear economic division between capital and labour, a common perception of custom and tradition helped to mitigate conflict.

The cloth dressers were certainly among the best paid in the woollen industry, their wage traditionally being regulated at about 5% of the

---

[8] *L.M.*, 15 Jan. 1803, letter from 'A Looker On'.
[9] *B.P.P.*, 1802/3, Vol. 7, p. 336; K.B. 1/31/Pt 2, the King v James May, 27 Oct. 1802.

value of the finished cloth.[10] Evidence given in 1803 and 1806 suggested that Gloucestershire shearmen earned between 18s. and 21s. per week, while Wiltshiremen were said to average between 15s. and 16s. The latter figures were probably too low, for a witness in 1806 said that Gloucestershire shearmen were in general worse paid than those in Wiltshire and this would fit with other evidence about conditions of work. In peripheral towns in Somerset wages ranged from 12s. to 14s. Such figures are necessarily vague for, as Eden noted, 'They are seldom willing to own what [their wages] amount to.' Wage levels in the West Riding appear to have been somewhat higher, being said to range from 10s. 6d. to 30s., though 18s. to 25s. were probably nearer the norm.[11] Thus the croppers were said to be able to spend 'twice or three times as much money at the ale house than the weaver or dyer'.[12] These high wages reflected the cloth dressers' skill but they also reflected their careful regulation of recruitment into their trade. 'From time immemorial [they have] rendered their craft a species of monopoly by limiting the number of apprentices', noted an observer in 1799.[13] Each cloth dresser was allowed to apprentice only one son to the trade and to take only one apprentice at a time.[14] Since the trade required many years' experience and knowledge and this could be obtained only from a working cloth dresser, this regulation thereby ensured that the shearmen and croppers avoided the problem which perennially plagued the weavers, that of a surplus workforce. They were well aware that they were an elite and they were determined to remain so.

The key to the cloth dressers' strength lay in trade union organisation. Their capacity to organise for the common good had, by the 1750s, placed the cloth dressers in an enviable industrial bargaining position. Thus Earl Fitzwilliam wrote of the Yorkshire croppers in 1802; 'their power and influence has grown out of their wages, which enable them to make deposits that put them beyond all fear of inconvenience from misconduct'.[15] It was from this trade union platform that the resistance to finishing machinery was launched and sustained.

---

[10] P.C. 1/43/A152, Observations respecting combinations.
[11] *B.P.P.*, 1802/3, Vol. 7, pp. 115, 143, 196, 208, 255, 336; *B.P.P.*, 1806, Vol. 3, pp. 240, 278, 289, 303, 326, 434, 436, 438; Eden, *State of the Poor*, Vol. II, pp. 643–4, Vol. III, pp. 793, 800–2, 821, 847–8.
[12] *Manchester Exchange Herald*, 21 April 1812, cited in F. O. Darvall, *Popular Disturbances and Public Order in Regency England* (Oxford, 1934), p. 60.
[13] P.C. 1/43/A152, Observations respecting combinations.
[14] *B.P.P.*, 1806, Vol. 3, p. 231.
[15] H.O. 42/66, Fitzwilliam to Pelham, 27 Sept. 1802.

In examining this trade union base we encounter an initial problem of definition. The Webbs defined a trade union as 'a continuous association of wage earners for the purpose of maintaining or improving the conditions of their employment'.[16] As H. A. Turner has shown, however, 'continuous association' did not necessarily require formal organisation, regular meetings or recognised leadership.[17] Evidence of trade unionism among the cloth dressers before 1796 is fragmentary but, while an organised structure is only readily discernible in the years of crisis which followed, an informal and unspectacular organisation was certainly continuous and effective at all times at a parochial level. The nature of the cloth dressers' work fostered this. Working together in the finishing shops, the shearmen and croppers developed 'a deep sense of fellowship with their workmates which combined to give them a pride and sense of community in their work'.[18] In this atmosphere what Turner calls a 'natural association' and a strong sense of solidarity developed which did not require formalities, save only perhaps the appointment of a treasurer and secretary. At a local level everywhere the cloth dressers built up their union 'box', a fighting fund which was turned against any employer who refused to accede to a wage increase or who tried to violate the written and unwritten laws of the trade.

While the basis of collective action was undoubtedly the parochial association, we have very little evidence of these local organisations. However, at times the historian comes across larger, regional societies. How far these had any permanence is impossible to say but, since they were almost certainly federations of parochial units, there would have been little difficulty in establishing or dismantling them.[19] The combination of the Wiltshire and Somerset shearmen in 1769 provides a good example to examine for it was typical of both regional and parochial societies in its aims. This organisation seems to have been established early in 1769, much to the alarm of the master dressers and clothiers who publicly announced their intention of destroying it. Thus on

---

[16] S. and B. Webb, *The History of Trade Unionism* (Longmans, Green and Co., 1920), p. 1.

[17] H. A. Turner, *Trade Union Growth, Structure and Policy: A Comparative Study of the Cotton Unions* (Allen and Unwin, 1962), pp. 50–4.

[18] Ponting, *Woollen Industry*, p. 70.

[19] Some probably maintained a legal overt existence as friendly societies. For example, 'The Cloth Workers Club at the Crown Inn, Minchinhampton' until December 1784. The club was then dissolved although Richard Smith kept the club box, for which he was threatened with prosecution, and a new club formed at the Bell Inn in September 1785. *G. J.*, 19 Sept. 1785.

22 February the master cloth dressers of Melksham complained that 'a great number of loose and disorderly journeymen cloth workers in the counties of Wiltshire and Somerset' had established an 'unlawful and arbitrary combination' and had 'audaciously printed' their rules and orders. Treasurers and clerks had been appointed in each of the principal clothing towns and 'payments, exactions and contributions levied'. The rules laid down, among others,

That no Master shall take an apprentice but according to their rules, that every apprentice pay 1/2 guinea income, 1/2 guinea outgo, 5s. to what they call a fund, and a fee to the town clerk for taking up his freedom; that no Gloucestershire man shall be set to work by any master without payment of 2 guineas income, 5s. to the fund, with other quarterly payments to the same, and the freedom fee to the clerk; and [they] have fixed the particular work the master shall be obliged to do to each cloth without having any respect to the quality or nature the same will bear, thereby intending to raise their hours of work to six in four contrary to the constant method of five in four.

All journeymen were to be obliged to sign the articles of combination and to take up their freedom from the town clerk before any master should employ them. Should any master refuse to comply with their rules or employ any journeyman who refused to join their society, his shop would be blacked and all society men would leave his employment and receive 1s. per day each from the funds until the master in question gave in.[20]

The combination appears to have been particularly aimed against Gloucestershire incomers. The Bradford on Avon clothiers stated on 24 February that the shearmen there were 'setting heavy fines on some, utterly disqualifying others, and extorting unheard-of sums from the journeymen cloth workers of Gloucestershire for incomes and other impositions, and otherwise ill-treating them that they have been obliged to leave'. Like the Melksham master dressers, they announced that they were 'determined to suppress so dangerous an association' and that strangers would be 'set to work on the usual terms of 1s. income and their persons protected from the insults they have lately been subject to'. And if anyone were refused work by a master dresser, they guaranteed to find work for them. To emphasise their point, they detailed the law concerning combinations and that relating to assaults on or threats to employers in the trade. A very similar notice, dated Trowbridge, 1 March, was published by the clothiers and master

---

[20] *B.C.*, 2 March 1769; *G.J.*, 26, 13 March 1769.

cloth workers of Trowbridge, Bradford on Avon, Melksham and Chippenham.[21] In spite of their threats, however, the cloth dressers emerged victorious from this contest.[22]

The attempt to keep out Gloucestershire men was not new in 1769 – a shearman from Wotton wrote in October 1766 that during the food riots he had travelled to Wiltshire and Somerset to look for work, 'And I might as well have 'bided at home, for they shop no strangers'[23] – and the issue of incomers continued to be a vexed one into the 1790s. Thus, in May 1791 twenty-two of the leading clothiers and master dressers of Bradford on Avon published a warning that they intended to put a stop to an 'oppressive combination' of journeymen shearmen who had 'lately made it a custom to impose a large fine or income on strangers when set to work', stating that they would enforce the customary income of 1s.[24] A cloth workers' combination in Shepton Mallet in 1790 likewise attempted to enforce similar controls and fines.[25]

Cloth dressers' combinations proved resilient to pressure. Their carefully fostered independence and strength could not easily be ignored by employers and their vigorous prosecution of their 'rights and privileges' made cloth workers notoriously 'the least manageable of any persons employed in this important manufacture'.[26] The assertion of custom was not necessarily defensive. As the conflicts in the West Country in 1769, 1787, 1788 and 1791 showed, the shearmen were aggressive in protecting their position and were more than willing to force new regulations and practices on their employers. Once accepted, these too became enshrined as part of the customs of the trade. The West Riding croppers were equally effective in safeguarding their trade. This was why Fitzwilliam described the croppers as 'the tyrants of the country'.[27] However, while their industrial muscle offended clothiers, merchants and magistrates, it would be wrong to imagine that their superior financial position made cloth dressers aloof from the

---

[21] *B.C.*, 2 March 1769; *G.J.*, 6, 13 March 1769.

[22] *B.C.*, 9 March 1769; *G.J.*, 1 May 1769; *B.C.*, 4 May 1769.

[23] *G.J.*, 10 Nov. 1766. Trade, already depressed in 1766, grew worse thereafter. *G.J.*, 19 Jan. 1769: 'The miseries of the manufacturing poor are now inexpressibly great . . . provisions being so extremely dear, trade also languishing.' *G.J.*, 25 Jan. 1768: 'Bisley and Chalford bottoms particularly afford melancholy proof of how many wretches of the clothing district are prompted by despair to wander about and trust to the shelter of hedges and barns rather than starve under their own ineffectual roofs.'

[24] *G.J.*, 9 May 1791.

[25] *S.W.J.*, 3 May 1790.

[26] Darvall, *Popular Disturbances*, p. 60.

[27] H.O. 42/66, Fitzwilliam to Pelham, 27 Sept. 1802.

8   The gig mill
Source: A. Rees, *The Cyclopaedia*, Vol. xxxviii (1819), 'Woollen Manufacture', Plate iv.

other woollen workers. Certainly they patronised their 'own' pub but
so did the weavers. The cloth dressers shared the same social *milieu* as
the other woollen workers, they lived in the same small towns and
shared the same chapels while the limitation of apprentices probably
meant that many had close relatives in the other branches of the trade.
Shearmen and croppers were to be found taking an active role in the
crowd in food riots, in other popular protests and in riots against
jennies and scribbling engines.[28] Their close integration into this
society was most clearly seen in the years of the shearmen's campaign
in Wiltshire and later during the Yorkshire Luddite period when
popular encouragement and support for the cloth dressers was a
notable feature. They were to provide the woollen manufacturing
community with its most aggressive and articulate leadership in the
battle against machinery and the innovators with their most intractable
problem.
   The cloth dressers' battle against machinery in the years before 1812
was fought out largely against the gig mill. This simple machine

[28] See, for example, Randall, 'The Gloucestershire food riots of 1766', p. 82.

mechanised the hand-raising process by attaching the teasels to a rapidly revolving cylinder, supported between two upright posts. The fulled cloth was then drawn across this cylinder from a lower cylinder to one above. By hand, one man was reckoned to take between 88 and 100 hours on one piece. With the gig mill, a man with two boy assistants took just 12 hours.[29] Clearly the labour-saving potential of the gig mill was considerable. Thus William Shrapnell, a Bradford on Avon master clothier, expressed the fears of all shearmen in 1803 when he said, 'If the gig mill was generally established, in my opinion it would throw a vast number of those poor people out of employ.'[30] In their struggle against the gig mill, the cloth workers had one powerful weapon, the law. For, they claimed, the use of the machine in the woollen industry was forbidden under 5 & 6 Edward VI c. 22, 'An act for the putting down of gig mills'. There was always some doubt as to whether the gig mills prohibited by this statute performed the same function as those introduced in the eighteenth century. The act referred to 'gig mills for the perching and burling of cloth'. Perching, however, involved the examination of a cloth over a bench or bar after weaving or shearing to check for faults and burling was the process of mending them. Quite how any machine could have performed either of these tasks and thereby caused the cloth to be 'wonderfully impaired and . . . deceitfully made' as the act claimed is a matter for conjecture. Possibly the meaning of perching and burling had changed between 1552 and 1800. It seems altogether probable, however, that the gig mill was essentially the same throughout but that its use (or misuse) in the sixteenth century had been to over-stretch the cloths rather than merely to raise them. However, the vague wording gave the innovating clothiers encouragement to press their own interpretations and the matter was never clearly settled.

The gig mill had certainly been used in some places for a considerable time before the turn of the century. This was the case around Huddersfield. Richard Cockell believed that the gig mill had first been introduced here in 1784, but Law Atkinson in 1803 claimed from his own memory that they had been used there for thirty years, while his father could remember their being in use for some sixty years to dress coatings, a rough coarse cloth. Daniel Whitworth of Leeds could remember first seeing the gig mill when an apprentice in 1755, though he did not say where this was. It was probably not at Leeds, although one was found at work there on coarse quality cloth in 1761. There is

---

[29] Ponting, *Woollen Industry*, p. 71.   [30] B.P.P., 1802/3, Vol. 7, p. 201.

9   The shearing frame
Source: A. Rees, *The Cyclopaedia*, Vol. XXXVIII (1819), 'Woollen Manufacture', Plate V.

nothing to suggest that it was retained for any length of time.[31] The gig mill had long been in use in parts of Gloucestershire. William Watkins had been working gig mills for twenty-three years, probably at Wotton under Edge, while Edward Sheppard, the famous clothier manufacturer, said that they had been introduced at Uley about eleven or twelve years before 1803.[32] Mann, in fact, doubts whether the gig mill was ever discontinued in parts of Gloucestershire.[33] It was, however, confined to coarse cloths whose stronger texture was not damaged by the machine's action.

Even in Wiltshire, where hostility to the introduction of gig mills was most violent, there were gig mills to be found. Anstie, writing in 1803, stated that gig mills had been used for dressing coarse white cloth, 'even in the county of Wiltshire, longer than anyone can remember'.[34] They were, however, few in number – Kenneth Rogers' exhaustive survey notes only six before 1790, while I have come across two others

---

[31] B.P.P., 1806, Vol. 3, p. 253; B.P.P., 1802/3, Vol. 7, pp. 373, 226; Wilson, *Gentlemen Merchants*, p. 99.
[32] B.P.P., 1802/3, Vol. 7, pp. 103, 255.
[33] Mann, *Cloth Industry*, p. 140.   [34] Anstie, *Observations on Machinery*, p. 69.

– all in areas remote from the main woollen towns.[35] They never appear to have constituted any threat to the Wiltshire shearmen.

A more recent and potentially far greater threat to the cloth dressers' trade was the shearing frame. This contrivance, invented in 1787 and substantially improved in 1794 by a Sheffield clergyman, John Harmer,[36] consisted of several pairs of hand shears fixed into a travelling frame and operated by a revolving crank. Once developed, it was claimed the frame could shear cloth as well as most shearmen and in under a quarter of the time. William Barnard, a Gloucestershire cloth dresser, complained that the frame displaced two in every three shearmen, the master saving more than two men's wages because the remaining man's wage was reduced to 12s. for minding four shears since the task required less skill.[37] There was no prohibitive legislation concerning the shearing frame to which appeal could be made. This machine, then, threatened not only the cloth dressers' skilled status but their very livelihood.

The mounting threats to the cloth dressers' trade posed by the gig mill and shearing frame in the 1790s stimulated an increasing level of conflict which was to reach its climax with the Wiltshire Outrages of 1802. This conflict took several forms and in many ways may be seen as a dress rehearsal for events in Yorkshire in 1812. Indeed, in discussing the response to cloth dressing machinery in the years up to 1803 we are inevitably drawn into comparisons with Luddism for the problems confronted were much the same, save only that in 1812 there could no longer be recourse to the law since Parliament had repealed the old regulatory legislation in 1809. Examination of Luddism has been bedevilled by the compartmentalist approach adopted by many of its

---

[35] Rogers, *Wiltshire and Somerset Woollen Mills*, pp. 173, 175. Four of these eight gig mills discovered were situated on the River By Brook. Ford mill at North Wraxall contained a gig mill in 1725, as did Widdenham mill, Colerne, in 1752. When Weavern mill at Slaughterford was advertised for sale in 1769 it contained stocks and a gig mill, having been converted from a corn mill at some time since 1728. And Duncombe mill, North Wraxall, contained a gig mill in 1778. The By Brook, flowing north from Box, mid-way between Bath and Chippenham, the nearest woollen town, lies in the north-west corner of Wiltshire, and its comparative remoteness from the main finishing centres probably accounts for the lack of any worker hostility. However, in spite of its water power, the trade of the By Brook was clearly declining, at least from the mid-eighteenth century. By 1778 Ford mill had become a grist mill and the other three were all converted to paper mills, Duncombe mill not long after 1778, Weavern about 1793 and Widdenham possibly about the same time. *G.J.*, 11 Sept. 1769; Rogers, *Wiltshire and Somerset Woollen Mills*, pp. 173–5; Mann, *Cloth Industry*, p. 53, fn. 1.

[36] Mann, *Cloth Industry*, p. 302.

[37] *B.P.P.*, 1806, Vol. 3, p. 326.

investigators.[38] This approach is epitomised by Malcolm Thomis' monograph which sets out deliberately to segregate different forms of protest into hermetically sealed categories. Thomis writes, 'It is possible to recognise a labour approach that was concerned with the establishment of negotiating machinery, of the use of constitutional forms and procedures such as Parliamentary petitions, and these techniques betoken an approach quite different from that of industrial sabotage and direct action.' We should perhaps note that Thomis restricts his research to 'true Luddites', whom we are told not to confuse with 'the would-be revolutionaries or the Parliamentary reformers, the food rioters or the trade unionists ... They [the Luddites] were rather people who broke machinery as a deliberate calculated policy in a particular historical period.'[39] Such a blinkered view completely disregards the context from within which protest arose. Woollen workers in different trades or in the same trade in different places may have faced different specific industrial pressures but all shared the same problems of food prices and of political freedom, the same threats posed by industrial change and innovation. They also shared common cultural and community values, of which Thomis takes no account, which informed their response to these challenges. Moreover, such a view ignores the fact that violence was an effective weapon in the armoury of trade unions in both the eighteenth and nineteenth centuries and was used, just as the other weapons of the 'labour approach', with discrimination and purpose for specific ends. It is necessary, therefore, to recognise this common context and to attempt to examine the reaction to machinery as a whole rather than by setting out to impose a facile segregation of types of protest upon the evidence.

The response of the cloth dressers in both the West of England and the West Riding to the threat of displacement by machinery in the years up to 1809 in fact took three principal forms: recourse to the law; industrial action; and violence. These forms were in no way mutually exclusive, as we shall see. Each had a common basis in the cloth dressers' capacity to organise. Different methods were adopted singly or in combination as and when deemed appropriate both in the particular context obtaining at any one time and in the general context of

---

[38] For a critique of such approaches see F. K. Donnelly, 'Ideology and early English working class history: Edward Thompson and his critics', *Social History*, 2 (1976), pp. 219–38, and J. Rule, *The Labouring Classes in Early Industrial England, 1750–1850* (Longman, 1986), pp. 369–75.

[39] Thomis, *The Luddites*, pp. 132, 134, 27.

that community's tradition and experience of previous conflicts of a similar kind.

It is significant that the response of the Gloucestershire shearmen to the threat of machinery paralleled that taken by the scribblers and spinners in that county by preferring the legal and constitutionalist approach. As has been noted, Gloucestershire shearmen had long accepted the use of the gig mill for dressing coarse cloths. In late 1793 or early 1794, however, some clothiers began to use the machine on fine cloths as well. This caused the shearmen considerable alarm since the extended use of the mill threatened jobs for, although the coarse trade was booming in 1794, the fine was depressed.[40] Thus the cloth dressers faced a loss of work in a trade which was also declining. Several meetings were convened in Stroud in January and February which determined upon taking legal advice, including, apparently, that of the Attorney General, and subsequently upon petitioning Parliament to protect their interests. They engaged as their solicitor Henry Clarke of Stroud, who also acted for the Gloucestershire scribblers whose petition was presented jointly with that of the shearmen. An association later said to number over 500 was established to raise subscriptions and a committee was elected to organise support. This form of organisation was very similar to that established by the handloom weavers of the county in the years from 1755 to 1757 and revived again in 1793 and 1802. The shearmen believed that all gig mills were proscribed by law but they wanted Parliament to modify the act to allow use of the mill on coarse cloth only, in effect legitimising the situation which had existed in the county prior to 1794, while continuing the prohibition for fine cloth.

The decision to petition Parliament provoked a fierce response from some clothiers, presumably those who were already using the gig mill on fine cloth. They held a meeting at The Fleece, Rodborough, on 14 April at which, according to the shearmen, it was resolved that if the cloth dressers' committee did not immediately withdraw their attempted application to Parliament, the clothiers in question would dismiss all committee men in their employ, blacklist them, and would further ensure that the earnings of all members of the association were restricted to 7s. per week until they renounced their membership. The shearmen refused to be browbeaten and 'considerable numbers' were indeed discharged.[41] A bitter propaganda battle in the press ensued in which these clothiers asserted that the act against gig mills

[40] Turner, *General View of the Agriculture of Gloucester*, p. 31.
[41] G.J., 5, 12 May 1794.

was inapplicable and obsolete and the shearmen's meetings were 'not for the mere purpose of subscribing money to pay for applying to Parliament to remedy pretended grievances . . . but boldly to enter into combinations' and warned that all members were liable to three months' imprisonment.[42] The clothiers' allegations angered both Clarke and the cloth workers. In dignified letters, twenty-five shearmen, presumably the committee, denied that their actions had been illegal. 'However severely they may feel the pressure of their grievances, the cloth workers will seek relief in no other measures than are consistent with law and the character of honest and industrious men.'[43]

The petition was presented on 16 May. It recited the terms of 5 & 6 Edward VI c. 22 banning the use of the gig mill but stated that the machine had been found useful for dressing coarse and army cloths and had been generally used thus. However, when applied to fine cloths, as it had been recently, 'the true drapery of such cloth is considerably affected, deceitfully made, and rendered much less valuable to the wearer, as the gig mills are driven so violently by the impetuosity of the water that it injures the texture or ground of such fine cloth'. The extension of the machine would put 'a great number of men' out of work and would ultimately be the cause of the complete loss of the fine trade as customers realised the inadequacies of gig milled material. 'It is not the wish of the petitioners that the use of gig mills should be entirely suppressed, but only to confine them to the working of such cloth as cannot be hindered thereby, on namely the coarser sort, and which, if so restricted, would leave sufficient employment for the petitioners.' It was, they claimed, for this reason that they had not attempted to prosecute those who used the gig mill on fine cloth under the statute since this would encourage common informers to denounce all gig mill users and force the suspension of their use on all cloths.[44]

The petition was presented too late in the session for any further action to be taken. This point was taken up by Sir George Paul in a public reply to the cloth workers who had asked him to arbitrate. Paul's reply was scathing. The men had wasted money on expensive legal advice to discover if the law was still in force, had sent their petition too late and entrusted it to an M.P. strange to the county.

[42] *G.J.*, 12 May 1794. The signatories were Isaac Austin, John Wallington, William Phelps, John Tippetts, Edward Sheppard, Henry Hicks, Nathaniel Lloyd, Thomas Cooper, Paul Wathen and Samuel Wathen.
[43] *G.J.*, 19 May 1794.   [44] *J.H.C.*, Vol. 49, p. 599.

As to advice, I own that when I see a number of decent, orderly men with rational understandings who can relinquish a life of industry which produced a comfortable subsistence, and who determine to expose themselves to be dismissed by their employers and to live in common on the little capital derived from the surplus of their former earnings, for the purpose of laying a piece of useless paper on the table of the House of Commons – I cannot but presume that they are strongly biased by some motive adverse to reason.[45]

The shearmen replied that they had presented their petition prematurely 'in consequence of their subscriptions being stigmatised as combination'. They had not gone to the Attorney General to find out if the law was still in force: 'They were at that time and now are completely satisfied that it is in full force and effect.' The county M.P.s were not in London or they would have approached them and they had not wasted money on expensive legal counsel. This had cost them only 2 guineas. Nor had they 'relinquished' work. 'For their joining in a subscription to defray the costs attendant thereon, were they dismissed by their masters; and of their orderly behaviour during this time of their being unemployed, the public are already sufficiently convinced.'[46]

The petition of 1794 did, however, prove to be 'a piece of useless paper'. There was no further attempt in Gloucestershire to bring up the issue of regulation of gig mills, although it was said in June that the shearmen intended to ground legislation on their petition in the following year.[47] Whether the rapid growth in trade in the county from late 1794 to 1796 reconciled the shearmen to the extended use of the machine, or whether they were deterred by their employers is difficult to say. Edward Sheppard, one of their clothier protagonists in 1794, later claimed, 'they had the good sense to drop it'.[48] The gig mill was thereafter accepted for use on all cloth in Gloucestershire and the shearmen there never again managed to present much of a united front to resist further innovations. The capitulation of the Gloucestershire men had major repercussions for the shearmen of Wiltshire and Somerset. The growing use of the gig mill to dress fine cloth in Gloucestershire from 1794 onwards put pressure upon Wiltshire and Somerset clothiers to introduce the machine in an effort to remain competitive in the fine cloth market and this culminated in the sustained disturbances in Wiltshire in 1802. There is no sign of any interest in Wiltshire or

[45] *G.J.*, 16 June 1794.

[46] *G.J.*, 23 June 1794. Twenty-one names were appended to this reply but only ten had signed the letter published on 19 May.

[47] *G.J.*, 16 June 1794.   [48] *B.P.P.*, 1802/3, Vol. 7, p. 254.

Yorkshire in the 1794 petition. Certainly the Wiltshire and Somerset shearmen would have opposed any change to the act. Nonetheless, they may well have learned a lesson from the actions of their neighbours. The Gloucestershire men had characteristically pursued throughout a legal and constitutionalist course. The events of 1794, however, showed how little might be achieved by 'measures [that] are consistent with law and the character of honest and industrious men' when faced with resolute and ruthless innovators. In view of this, the Wiltshire shearmen probably felt there was every reason to be much more willing to take direct action against detrimental change.

The response of the Wiltshire and Somerset cloth dressers years before had indeed been recourse to violence when a Horningsham clothier, William Everett, attempted in 1767 to set up a gig mill only 4 miles from Warminster and 5 from Frome. On Saturday, 1 August, about 500 shearmen from Wiltshire and Somerset assembled on Corsley Heath,[49] marched on Horningsham and 'pulled down and destroyed a new gig mill just erected for dressing broad cloth, whereby a man and a boy can do as much work in two hours as thirty men could do in a day'.[50] Fifteen men were subsequently tried for complicity in the riot at the summer sessions in 1768. Twelve were acquitted, but William Fido, found guilty of destroying the gig mill, was sentenced to nine months' imprisonment, fined £20, and ordered to find sureties for future behaviour. Two others found guilty were ordered to be whipped and imprisoned.[51] Everett was later said to be manufacturing a variety of coarse cloths which 'cannot be dressed properly by any other means than by the gig mill' and because of this he and his father had for thirty years found it necessary to send such cloths to Gloucestershire to be gigged.[52]

Nonetheless, the Wiltshire shearmen were also prepared to use the courts as was shown in 1795 when an attempt was made to establish a cloth manufactory at Marlborough. The experiment sprang from the problems caused by the loss of hand spinning in the area.[53] Under the aegis of the Marquess of Ailesbury and following the example established at Kintbury in 1792,[54] the rate-payers decided to try to attract an experienced clothier to set up business in the town. This clothier was to be provided with a house in the High Street, with new workshops and

---

[49] Mid-way between Frome and Warminster.
[50] *B.C.*, 6 Aug. 1767.   [51] *B.C.*, 21 July 1768.
[52] *S.W.J.*, 24 Aug. 1767.   [53] See above, Chapter 3.
[54] Three miles east of Hungerford, in west Berkshire.

a dye house and a new mill at Elcot just outside the town. In exchange for these advantages, the clothier had to promise to use only hand spun yarn. A Trowbridge clothier, Samuel Cook the younger, accepted the opportunity and probably began work some time in 1796. Ailesbury's agent commented: 'It costs him a little more here to spin by hand than it did at Trowbridge by machine . . . But his great advantage will be by using scribbling and shearing machines. The former saves about cent per cent [sic], the latter about 3d. or 4d. a yard, and is a new invention which the people in the clothing [trade] will not suffer.'[55] The latter were Harmer's shearing frames making their first appearance in the West of England, the improved patent for them having been registered only the year before.[56] The mill at Elcot also housed a new double raiser gig mill. Thus the Marlborough experiment aimed to make use of the two machines which made the shearmen's skills redundant.

When Cook began full production is not clear but the formal lease on house, workshops and mill was made in January 1796. The Wiltshire shearmen could not attempt to repeat their Horningsham success of direct action since Marlborough lay some 15 miles east of Devizes and 13 from Calne, the nearest finishing centres. Nor were there any local shearmen in Marlborough who might have been able to help resist the machinery. Their recourse, therefore, was to law. At the summer assizes in 1796 an action was brought by 'certain shearmen of Wiltshire against Mr. Cooke of Marlborough for using a gig mill contrary to 5 and 6 Edward VI'. The case was dismissed, probably on the grounds that the gig mill proscribed by the act was not the same as that used by Cook.[57] Their defeat almost certainly persuaded the Wiltshire shearmen that their most effective deterrent against the gig mill was force rather than the law. They continued to believe that the gig mill now used was indeed that proscribed by 5 & 6 Edward VI c. 22, but they brought no further cases before the courts until 1802.[58] Cook's success opened the way for others to try to bring in cloth dressing machinery. One of the earliest was Paul Newman of Melksham, the first of a growing number of innovators to incur the shearmen's wrath. In September or October 1796, his property was attacked and a threatening letter sent to him.

[55] Rogers, *Wiltshire and Somerset Woollen Mills*, pp. 21–2.
[56] Mann, *Cloth Industry*, pp. 302–3.
[57] *G.J.*, 18 July 1796. This is clearly the action referred to by Read in H.O. 42/83, Observations on the shearmen's bill, 19 Feb. 1805; cf. Mann, *Cloth Industry*, p. 141, fn. 6.
[58] H.O. 42/83, Read, Observations on the shearmen's bill, 19 Feb. 1805.

W.T.N.B.C.M.C.B.

Sir, We have just gave you a Caution how we do intend to act as soon as
we can make it convenient, which we believe that it will be soon, so you
may go on with it as fast as Possible, the faster you go on the better it will
be for you, for we are determined to go forward with it as well as you you
and yours shall be in Flames you House and Machinery before you are 2
Months longer We are determined to do it and the rest of your neighbours shall share the same fate if ever we catch them out of town we will
waite upon them and make them rue the Day ever they was borned for
they nor you shall never tell ho hurted them

Your Humble Servant.[59]

Whether Newman was using a gig mill or shearing frames is not clear,
but the threats seem to have been effective. There is no further reference to machinery in Melksham before 1803.

Cook's gig mill and shearing frames do not appear to have caused
Wiltshire shearmen any loss of work and by 1799 Cook was bankrupt
and the Marlborough experiment came to an end.[60] However, the
Cook decision at Salisbury assizes, coupled with the increasing practice of using the gig mill on fine cloths in Gloucestershire,[61] can be seen
as beginning a period of growing pressure on the shearmen of Wiltshire and Somerset which culminated in the disturbances of 1802. By
that date the gig mills had begun to spread into the heart of the
Wiltshire region. Thomas Fowle reported that there were three or four
gig mills in Wiltshire in 1803 'and two more are erecting'. One of these
at Christian Malford had been at work for four years, supervised by a
mason and a labourer.[62] John Jones had finished building his new large
mill at Staverton by October 1801, incorporating a gig mill, while
Thomas Joyce at Freshford and Henry Wansey in Warminster, both
important figures in the area, were using gig mills by 1802. While
Nathaniel Edwards could still say in 1803 'there are scarcely any gigs in
Wiltshire', the presence of the machine in the mills of the most influential clothiers of the area gave them a significance disproportionate to
their numbers in the eyes of the shearmen. Further, other clothiers
who lacked the capital or the nerve to set up the machine themselves
were beginning to send cloths to Gloucestershire to be gigged. These
factors, combined with wartime dislocation of trade, meant that in 1803
there were 'a great number of shearmen out of employ' in Wiltshire.[63]

---

[59] *London Gazette*, 1796, p. 1002 (October 1796).
[60] *G.J.*, 29 April 1799.   [61] See below, pp. 154-5.
[62] B.P.P., 1802/3, Vol. 7, pp. 130, 359.   [63] *Ibid.*, pp. 212, 369, 337.

The West of England was not alone in feeling the mounting pressure from machinery. Similar trends were apparent in the West Riding. As has been noted, gig mills had long been used around Huddersfield but the croppers had managed to contain them to this area. In the 1790s, however, the croppers found themselves facing increasingly concerted threats to their power from would-be innovators. In Leeds this threat was made overt by the broadsheet issued on 18 November 1791 concerning a meeting, 'attended by almost every Merchant in the Town', to discuss 'the various kinds of MACHINERY for the better and more expeditious DRESSING of WOOLLEN-CLOTH ... lately invented'. The meeting noted that these machines were 'already made and set to work in different Parts of this County' and agreed it was 'absolutely necessary that the Town should partake of the Benefit of all sorts of Improvements that are, or can be made in the Dressing of their Cloths, to prevent the Decline of that Business'. In consequence the merchants set up a subscription to obtain 'one of each' of the innovations to try them out 'for the Inspection of the Trade, previous to their being brought into general use'. They concluded, defiantly, 'we will protect and support the free Use of the proposed Improvements in Cloth-Dressing by every legal Means in our Power'.[64]

In spite of this resolute rhetoric, however, nothing came of this plan when faced with the peaceful but plainly determined opposition from the powerful Leeds croppers. Such was the strength of their organisation that it was not until 1799 that any merchant dared to attempt to establish a gig mill in the town. It was immediately destroyed. Benjamin Gott attempted to introduce a gig mill into his Bean Ing factory in July 1801 but was compelled to abandon the attempt.[65] However, while Leeds resisted any machinery, from the mid- and late 1790s the gig mill did begin to spread into the periphery of the mixed cloth districts. Thus Thomas Brunton claimed in 1806 that many croppers in Wakefield were only partially employed as a result of the increasing numbers of gig mills, while in Huddersfield croppers stood idle whilst gig mills were at work. And, as in Wiltshire, some West Riding merchants began to send cloths away to be gig raised, often to Huddersfield, in preference to hand raising. William Cookson, the Leeds merchant and magistrate, was one of these. He claimed in 1806 that he had sent over 1,000 cloths to Huddersfield and to Halifax to be experimentally raised by machine.[66]

---

[64] See Crump, *Leeds Woollen Industry*, pp. 317–18.
[65] *Leeds Intelligencer*, 6 Dec. 1799; Crump, *Leeds Woollen Industry*, p. 327.
[66] B.P.P., 1806, Vol. 3, pp. 278, 290, 366–72.

The mounting threat to their trade posed by machinery together with the legal reversals of 1794 and 1796 prompted the cloth dressers to bolster their already formidable organisation by the establishment of an extended trade union organisation which replaced the more haphazard inter-parochial camaraderie for a wider, better organised unity, better able to resist innovation. This was the so-called Brief Institution which, according to John Tate, was formed in Yorkshire in 1796 to prevent illegal workmen from following the trade.[67] That function, however, was but one of many, if we are to believe the Privy Council's paper on combinations.

Their system has received great energy from having now formed a general purse to which each branch contributes, and from which they are supported as long as their respective contests with their masters shall last.

The fund belonging to . . . the cloth workers is said to amount to above £1,000 and the despotic power they really possess and exercise almost exceeds belief . . . They are now nearly all associated under the denomination of Ticket Men and none others are allowed to be employed from the moment the men of any shop so ordain – all interference of the master would be fruitless – the man he sets on must become a Ticket Man (which binds them to unite always in a common cause) or not another man would remain in the shop. To contend with the men in their now united state would be very imprudent in every master. They know and feel their power and it gains such accession by every struggle that it becomes a matter of discretion now not to attempt resistance.[68]

It was almost impossible to break their ranks, William Cookson, then mayor of Leeds, lamented in 1802, 'so simple is the plan, so faithful are the men to their oaths'.[69]

Organisationally the Institution was an extension of the existing parochial trade unions. The 1806 Committee summarised it thus:

In each of the principal manufacturing towns there appears to be a society composed of deputies chosen from the several shops of workmen, from each of which town societies, one or more deputies are chosen to form what is called the Central Committee which meets as occasion requires at some place suitable to the local convenience of all parties. The power of this Central Committee appears to pervade the whole Institution.[70]

In this way the Brief Institution did not replace the local branches but built upon them, welding them into a coherent whole. According to

---

[67] *Ibid.*, p. 231.
[68] P.C. 1/43/A152, Observations respecting combinations.
[69] W.W.M., 79, Cookson to Fitzwilliam, 16 Aug. 1802.
[70] *J.H.C.*, Vol. 61, p. 701.

John Tate, Yorkshire Central Committee meetings took place between four and five times per year and business consisted of choosing delegates to represent the cloth workers in London, receiving their reports and settling their expenses and presumably deciding on the financial quota expected from each town towards the liabilities. Instructions to delegates were apparently verbal and loosely framed, Tate being given power 'to act in the manner which I thought most conducive to the interests of the body of cloth-workers'.[71] All of which is very well. We must not forget, however, that in the face of persistent badgering, Tate and the other shearmen delegates were anxious to show the Institution in its most strictly legal form, that is, as a society whose sole aim was to petition Parliament on certain industrial grievances. But as the 1806 Committee concluded, 'various circumstances render this explanation far from satisfactory'.[72] The Brief Institution in fact vastly augmented the industrial power of the cloth dressers. It provided the means, far better than before, of scrutinising recruitment to the trade by issuing membership cards, of enforcing closed shops and of regulating the tramp system. It enabled information on disputes to be diffused more completely than before and, most important, it ensured that any employer standing out against his workmen's demands faced the weight and financial resources not only of the local cloth dressers but of all the region. 'This sense of power which union and implicit adherence in a common cause gives to the workmen, operates upon their minds.'[73]

The Central Committee in the West Riding frequently met at The White Swan, Birstall, though there were also meetings at Roberttown in 1803.[74] While the powers of the Central Committee certainly did pervade the whole Institution, however, and while the Committee probably met more often than Tate said, it could not have been in session permanently. All the evidence, in fact, suggests that the motive force behind the Institution, and the centre of power when the Central Committee was not in session, lay at Leeds, the Yorkshire croppers' stronghold. Of the personalities involved at Leeds we know very little, except of the ubiquitous shoemaker, George Palmer. All correspondence between Yorkshire and the West of England appears to have been channelled through him, as was the croppers'

[71] *B.P.P.*, 1806, Vol. 3, pp. 244–6.
[72] *J.H.C.*, Vol. 61, p. 701.
[73] W.W.M., 62, Cookson to Fitzwilliam, 27 July 1802.
[74] *B.P.P.*, 1806, Vol. 3, p. 241; H.O. 42/70, Hainsworth to Palmer, 20 May 1803.

correspondence with other trades.[75] When in December, William May, the West of England shearmen's emissary, went to Leeds, he 'Waited on Mr Palmer who received me very kindly and as I informed him of my business, he called the C- together, and it was agreed that he and myself should set off for Huddersfield and other places on Monday morning.' And we should note that it was the Leeds committee, not a meeting of the Central Committee, with whom May worked out the proportions in which the payment of 'Mr W', Mr Wilmott, the cloth dressers' solicitor, should be allocated between the West Riding and West of England 'in order that our petition may be immediately carried into Parliament'.[76] Leeds certainly was a key place in the West Riding croppers' organisation. 'This place is headquarters', wrote Cookson, 'and until an effectual extinguisher be applied here, I am convinced no efficient measures to prevent combinations among shearmen will be practicable.'[77]

Our evidence about the Brief Institution is drawn mainly from the West Riding. This was because somehow the Parliamentary Committee which investigated the woollen trade in 1806 obtained many of the books of the Institution and grilled its representatives unmercifully. When the Institution was established in the West of England is not entirely clear. Rumour said that it had existed in the West before 1799 and in 1806 William Howard, a Bradford on Avon master shearman, told the Committee that the Institution existed in Wiltshire though he knew no details. 'The masters never enquire into those things.' James Read, the Bow Street magistrate sent to Wiltshire in 1802, reported, 'These clubs [in Wiltshire] are certainly not of many months standing and I think their government is at Leeds – a letter has been seen as coming thence, directing the formation of clubs and committees of correspondence and to write as sensible a letter as they could and direct it and any other letters to George Palmer, Duke Street, Leeds.' Read's assumption that prior to the West Riding approach the Wiltshire shearmen had had no organisation was clearly wrong. His

---

[75] H.O. 42/66, Cookson to Fitzwilliam, 18 Aug. 1802. See also W.W.M., 114, J.R. to Palmer, 28 Dec. 1802; H.O. 42/70, Thomas to Palmer, 17 March 1803; see also H.O. 42/62, Palmer to Tucker, 27 Aug. 1802. This copy is in fact dated 1801 and not 1802, but this is clearly a copying error. The copy in the Fitzwilliam papers, W.W.M., 84, is dated 1802. The original was sent on.

[76] H.O. 42/66, Griffin to Gentlemen, 5 Sept. 1802. It is possible that Palmer was himself a West Countryman, for he concluded his letter to Mr Tucker, 'I remain your countryman and well-wisher, George Palmer', and it is also possible that he was related to 'James Palmer, Painter, Trooper Street, Frome', to whom the two Yorkshiremen were sent. H.O. 42/66, May to Tucker, 16 Dec. 1802.

[77] H.O. 42/62, Cookson to G. H. Tugwell, Bath, n.d. (Aug. 1802).

mistake probably arose because in the early summer of 1802 new national rules were printed and circulated and new membership tickets, corresponding exactly to those issued in the West Riding, were engraved and given to each member. Every member also had to swear a new oath of allegiance.[78] Whether the Institution was ever present in Gloucestershire is uncertain. Walter Hilton Jessop, the Gloucestershire weavers' attorney, said he believed an understanding had always existed between the Gloucestershire shearmen and the Yorkshire croppers.[79] The shearmen there certainly supported the campaign before Parliament but it is possible that they stayed aloof from the national society, maintaining their local institutions or perhaps the countywide association which they had formed in 1794.

Just as Leeds appears to have been the dominant force in Yorkshire when the Central Committee was not in session, in Wiltshire Trowbridge seems to have been the focus. While the two Yorkshire delegates were sent to Frome in early September 1802, the letter concerning their visit was directed to Trowbridge.[80] Here, according to evidence extracted from a shearman, Thomas Bailey, we know that

> The committee consists of thirteen, and meets on Wednesdays – that there is a Chairman, clerk, and two stewards, that the oath – 'To be true to the shearmen and see that none of them are hurt and not to divulge any of their secrets' – was administered to him by the clerk, that he has a printed ticket which he states to be the same as is used by the shearmen's clubs in Yorkshire.[81]

It was to the Trowbridge committee that William May reported the results of his meetings with the committees in Leeds and Huddersfield and it appears to have had the task of deciding the allocation of the West's part toward the legal fees incurred by their joint campaign to Parliament.[82] The secretary of the committee was James May who, said Read, 'appears to have been a very considerable actor in forwarding the views of the society'. He was the brother of William May, the emissary to Yorkshire in December 1802 and agent for the Wiltshire and Somerset shearmen in the 1806 enquiry.[83] Chairman of the

[78] *B.P.P.*, 1806, Vol. 3, pp. 354–6, 308; H.O. 42/66, Read to Pelham, 10 Aug. 1802. See also Read to Pelham, 9 Aug. 1802, re-evidence of Thomas Bailey that 'lately he has been called upon to take an oath' to be true to the shearmen; ASSI. 25/2/8, trial of the Trowbridge committee, and P.C. 1/43/A152.

[79] *B.P.P.*, 1806, Vol. 3, pp. 304, 367.

[80] H.O. 42/62, Palmer to Tucker, 27 Aug. 1802.

[81] H.O. 42/66, Read to Pelham, 9 Aug. 1802.

[82] H.O. 42/66, May to Tucker, 16 Dec. 1802.

[83] H.O. 42/66, Read to Pelham, 10 Aug. 1802; *B.P.P.*, 1806, Vol. 3, p. 321.

10 Membership ticket of the Brief Institution
Source: H.O. 42/65.

committee may have been a man called Howell who acted as spokesman for the Trowbridge shearmen at their meeting with the clothiers
which ended their strike in July 1802. He had also presented a paper to
the Grand Jury at Salisbury that month, complaining of the illegal
introduction of gig mills.[84]

While the Brief Institution extended through Yorkshire and the West
of England, it did not impose a monolithic trade union structure over
the various parochial branches, nor did it create an all-powerful executive which controlled it. The Institution was a pyramidal structure
which allowed full freedom of action on a local scale within a wider
union of interests. 'The system exists more in general consent to the
few simple rules of their union than in any written form.'[85] Clearly the
West of England and the West Riding were autonomous, though
parallel, in structure and their co-ordination was a matter rather of
liaison than of direct orders from one to the other. This can be seen in
the interchange of delegates. The two croppers sent to Frome in
August 1802 clearly carried the decisions of the Yorkshire croppers to
the Wiltshire shearmen but they gave advice rather than instruction.
James Griffin, a member of the Trowbridge committee, wrote back 'by
order of the Community' that these suggestions had been agreed to,
'except for one or two little plans which is but very little, consequently
that the whole country will be harmonised'.[86] This harmony was seen
when a deputation of shearmen, conferring with John Jones on terms
for ending the Bradford on Avon cloth dressers' strike in July 1802,
rejected Jones' offer 'on behalf of the Body of Shearmen who deputed
them, and declared it was the resolution throughout England, Scot-
land and Ireland not to work after machinery'.[87] There was considerable co-operation between the regions in preparing petitions and
footing the bills for Parliamentary expenses, the Yorkshiremen paying
two-thirds of the costs because they out-numbered their West Country
colleagues in that proportion. The agent for the Gloucestershire cloth
workers in 1806 proved to be John Tate, a Halifax man, and an active
delegate of the West Riding Institution who had been sent to Gloucestershire in 1804 to ascertain whether the shearmen there would join
with the West Riding petition.[88] We would be wrong to envisage an
all-powerful centralised authority. Complex trade union structures

---

[84] H.O. 42/66, Read to Pelham, 6 Sept. 1802.
[85] P.C. 1/43/A152, Observations respecting combinations.
[86] H.O. 42/66, Griffin to Gentlemen, 5 Sept. 1802; see also H.O. 42/66, Read to Pelham,
    1, 5 Sept. 1802.
[87] H.O. 42/65, John Jones, Sen., to John King, 28 July 1802.
[88] B.P.P., 1806, Vol. 3, pp. 249, 352, 357.

and constitutions looked very impressive on paper but proved impossible to work in practice, as all trades who attempted to implement such
in the early nineteenth century found.[89] The Institution was as much a
means of federating local union branches as a force in itself.

Subscriptions for the Brief Institution were collected weekly or
monthly from shop to shop,[90] the sum collected varying from place to
place. In 1803, Bartholomew Horsell at Twerton was paying 3d. a week
to 'a committee', while John Hanson of Huddersfield paid between
1¹/₂d. and 1s. 0d. and 1s. 6d. per week to 'some committee' and
sometimes more.[91] In Halifax, while subscriptions in 1802 had been
negligible, amounting in all for the year to only 2s. 6d. or 3s. 0d., in
1803 they 'often paid 1s. 0d., 18d., 2s. 0d. and as high as 2s. 6d. per
week' to meet the costs of Parliamentary expenses and 'every man paid
regularly'.[92] 'The sick used to be collected for in Leeds 1d. per man, but
in Halifax they collected 3d. per man; in Leeds there are probably eight
times as many cloth workers as at Halifax and therefore 1d. per man
used to raise more than 3d. at Halifax.'[93] Joshua Shaw's total weekly
contribution in Leeds was usually only about 6d.[94] Subscriptions
varied depending upon the needs of the local branch and Institution
central fund. In times of trouble they were increased, in calmer days
probably just a few pence were collected weekly to cover the box for
sickness and death benefits to members. In acting as a sick club, the
local branches of the Institution complemented or filled the role of the
friendly societies, though some shearmen belonged to both.[95]
However, though the local boxes did fulfil the welfare function which
all cloth dresser witnesses claimed was their sole task, the cloth workers were not coy about using their funds to finance strikes.

The Brief Institution claimed virtual 100% membership of all the
cloth dressers in the West Riding and West of England. Indeed, John
Tate said he doubted if there were twenty workers in Yorkshire who

---

[89] The most obvious example of such was the Grand National Consolidated Trade
Union. See G. D. H. Cole, *Attempts at General Union: A Study in British Trade Union
History, 1818–1834* (Macmillan, 1953).
[90] B.P.P., 1802/3, Vol. 7, p. 219.
[91] Ibid., pp. 124, 223.
[92] B.P.P., 1806, Vol. 3, p. 239. This was not always the case. In May 1803, William
Hainsworth, secretary of the Halifax croppers, wrote to Leeds for information on two
defaulting subscribers, one of whom, Jonathon Wilson, 'says that he as paid a great
deale in at Leeds but he as been hat Halifax all winter or nearly all winter and as been
very backward at paying since he came'. H.O. 42/70, Hainsworth to Palmer, 20 May
1803.
[93] B.P.P., 1806, Vol. 3, p. 250.   [94] Ibid., p. 282.   [95] Ibid., p. 251.

were not members.[96] Members received a ticket on which was printed the insignia and arms of Leeds but, instead of the town's motto, around the shield was printed 'May Industry and Freedom Unite Us in Friendship' and, underneath, the name of the local centre, the date of issue, the words 'Trade and Commerce' and then two empty lines for the member's name and number. These cards acted as both membership card and tramping ticket.[97] A non-member, besides receiving no benefits, would have experienced difficulty in finding a shop where his unionised colleagues would accept him. 'There is the utmost reason to believe that no cloth worker would be suffered to carry on his trade other than in solitude who should refuse to submit to the rules and obligations of the society.'[98] Tate told the 1806 Committee, 'there are so few who are not [in the Institution], they are conspicuous enough without tickets', but some, however, succeeded. Thus from Halifax came news of 'one John Bottomly, that is com'd from Leeds and as got work hear about a month or five weeks since without a tramp card, but we blame the shop where he works more than him'. For the most part, however, there is every reason to believe that non-members 'must stay where they are'.[99]

The most important factors behind the Institution's full and active membership were the cloth dressers' sense of community and their realisation that machinery could not be opposed successfully at a parochial level. The slow spread of the gig mills and shearing frames was weakening their position generally. Cookson wrote to Fitzwilliam that the resolutions of the Bath meeting of the West of England clothiers to introduce machinery had 'alarmed the cloth dressers [of Leeds] because they well know the use of machinery in the West would inevitably lead to its use here or carry away a great part of the trade from hence'.[100] It was for this reason that the cloth workers of the West and of Yorkshire were prepared to hand over a not inconsiderable part of their weekly wages to the Institution to defray the very heavy costs of the campaign before Parliament, which between 1802–3 and 1806 were said to have come to about £10,000 or £12,000 at least.[101]

The Brief Institution strengthened the cloth dressers' bargaining position against their employers. But how far were orthodox trade

---

[96] *Ibid.*, p. 232.
[97] H.O. 42/66, Read to Pelham, 9 Aug. 1802; a ticket seized at Trowbridge in 1802, and in H.O. 42/66, is reproduced on p. 135.
[98] *J.H.C.*, Vol. 61, p. 701.
[99] *B.P.P.*, 1806, Vol. 3, pp. 232, 250; H.O. 42/70, Hainsworth to Palmer, 20 May 1803.
[100] W.W.M., 83, Cookson to Fitzwilliam, 30 Aug. 1802.
[101] *B.P.P.*, 1806, Vol. 3, p. 239.

union sanctions applicable or effective in the face of the determined onslaughts of the innovators on the cloth dressers' privileged position?

The cloth dressers were formidably equipped to use industrial sanctions to protect their trade especially after the establishment of the Brief Institution. Strike funds were available initially from the local branch box and subscriptions collected locally but, if the issue proved important or the local box insufficiently replete, funds were provided from other centres, probably from the regional committee of the Institution, and sometimes from even further afield. For example, it was said that the Gott strikers, out from 27 September 1802 until 29 January 1803, were supported by funds subscribed from all over the West Riding, while money was sent from Yorkshire to Warminster and Trowbridge in 1802 to support strikes there.[102] In June 1804 a further £189 was sent to the West of England and the central fund was also used to send money to other trades in dispute with their employers during this period.[103]

The threat of blacklegs was largely obviated by the highly skilled nature of a cloth dresser's work since only another experienced cloth dresser (or a machine) could take his place and, because the establishment of the Brief Institution extended union influence nationally, finding able blacklegs presented the employer with almost insurmountable problems. 'As the men refused to do any work ... till the point was complied with, masters were under the necessity of advertising for other men, the futility of which was soon apparent ... so far indeed from getting any workmen by these advertisements – the master found that they only rendered the workmen united.'[104] In an attempt to break the strike of his croppers in 1802, Gott even tried recruiting labour from Wiltshire and Somerset where unemployment among the shearmen was quite high and where, owing to the exertions of James Read, a government magistrate, and the presence of large numbers of troops, their combinations were under considerable pressure. Two agents were sent to Trowbridge and Frome, armed with handbills stating – 'WANTED IMMEDIATELY AT LEEDS, in Yorkshire, A NUMBER OF JOURNEYMEN SHEARMEN, sober, steady, good workmen will meet with constant employment and good wages by applying to Messrs. Wormald, Gott & Wormald, at their manufactory NEAR LEEDS.'

---

[102] *Ibid.*, p. 251; W.W.M., 117, Beckett to Fitzwilliam, 28 Jan. 1803; H.O. 42/66, Cookson to Fitzwilliam, 18 Aug. 1802.

[103] *B.P.P.*, 1806, Vol. 3, p. 356; H.O. 42/66, Read to Pelham, 16 Aug. 1802; H.O. 42/66, Cookson to Fitzwilliam, 18 Aug. 1802; *B.P.P.*, 1806, Vol. 3, pp. 355, 356–7.

[104] P.C. 1/43/A152, Observations respecting combinations.

There is no evidence that the offer was taken up, nor was Gott able to get labour from Huddersfield or Wakefield either.[105] Indeed, one of the agents informed Read that he did not expect many recruits.[106] The blackleg ran the gauntlet of his fellow workers' ire which was often more violent towards traitors than to employers. 'A workman daring from gratitude to stand by his master in the hour of his need becomes a proscribed *Isolé*. He can never be allowed to work where a ticket man is till he has abjured his neutrality and paid the penalty they please to impose.'[107] Croppers who broke ranks to work for Law Atkinson at Huddersfield in 1802 were 'beaten, knocked down, dragged by the hair of the head, and the men swore they would gig them as they gigged at Bradley mill'. Daniel Baker, a Warminster shearman who refused to join the strike in 1802 and who impeached on a fellow shearman, was threatened and abused. Read wrote, 'Baker is . . . the only instance I have met with in being true to his master, and which he has done at the hazard of his life, having been frequently insulted and once had his dwelling fired into.' Four Warminster shearmen, including Baker, remained at work and two at least, Joseph Tucker and J. Jones, suffered similar treatment. Jones, namesake of the Bradford on Avon clothier magistrate, was warned:

> J. Jones
> The journeymen shearmen of Bradford, Trowbridge, Melksham, Chippenham, Calne and Devizes Have a Greed to Pay you 4 that are at work a Vizett that cuteth after the Giggar Raiser But if you will Leve of that a Bomable acton you shall Be Free after the Public Notes But if you dont Leve of you may espect Shearmans Law; that is to be Cuartered And your flesh and Bones Burnt and your aishes Blown away with the weend I send you this as a frind; and Please to let your Master know that there is sum thing concerning him But at present I cannot let you know But I Beleve it will be Greate Sevearitys for they will Componhim as a thefte in the night.[108]

The similarities between these examples and the treatment of the Yorkshire Luddite turncoat, Benjamin Walker, in 1813 are readily apparent but such men were exceptions. The overwhelming majority followed their union's line and blacked goods, paid subscriptions to

105 W.W.M., 117, Beckett to Fitzwilliam, 28 Jan. 1803.
106 H.O. 42/66, Read to King, 3 Oct. 1802.
107 P.C. 1/43/A152, Observations respecting combinations.
108 H.O. 42/66, Read to Pelham, 10 Aug. 1802; H.O. 42/65, Jones to Pelham, 29 July 1802; S.W.J., 20 Dec. 1802; *London Gazette*, 1802, p. 386 (2 April 1802); Ponting, *Woollen Industry*, p. 76, is mistaken in assuming this letter was sent to the clothier. It is significant that Warminster is not mentioned in the letter.

support and came out and stayed out on strike when such action was decided upon, even if their wives grumbled.[109]

Further, the Brief Institution could ensure that the strike sanction bit deep into the employer's purse by preventing the boycotted manufacturer having his cloths finished elsewhere. Gott initially received numerous promises of help against his striking croppers but he was informed that the cloth workers would not 'suffer him to evade the effects of their displeasure by getting his cloths finished at the workshop of another merchant, his friend. Any person presuming to do so would incur the same penalty; he likewise should be proscribed.'[110] Gott was unable to get his cloth finished. All Bradford on Avon dressers refused to touch John Jones' cloths when his shearmen struck work over Jones' attempt to cut their wages and the striking Warminster shearmen successfully foiled an attempt by their employers to send cloths away to be finished. Such actions were not always successful. As previously noted, in certain parts of the West Riding the croppers' position was weak. And the major cause of the growing pressure on the Wiltshire shearmen was the impotence of the Gloucestershire cloth dressers who were gig raising and probably shearing a great deal of Wiltshire cloth.[111] Gloucestershire and the old-mechanised parts of Yorkshire apart, however, the cloth workers appear to have well learned 'that the cause was a common one, and that by sticking to each other on this and future occasions the advantage would become certain and general'.[112]

Formal confrontation between masters and men in the major finishing centres was probably infrequent. 'It is generally hinted by some indirect mode to the master what the expectations of the workmen were, and the master must either comply or his workmen will drop off one by one.'[113] According to a report to the Privy Council in 1799, demands were usually met: 'it becomes a matter of discretion now not to attempt resistance'.[114] In Leeds where the croppers were extraordinarily strong this was certainly the case. 'I have little expectation that any measure of vigour ... will be taken at Leeds just now', wrote Fitzwilliam in September 1802. 'The intimidation is too strong.'[115] And following the success of the Gott strikers in January 1803, John Beckett

[109] H.O. 42/66, Read to King, 18 Oct. 1802.
[110] H.O. 42/66, Fitzwilliam to Pelham, 27 Sept. 1802.
[111] *B.P.P.*, 1802/3, Vol. 7, pp. 336–7, 254; *B.P.P.*, 1806, Vol. 3, pp. 306, 311.
[112] P.C. 1/43/A152, Observations respecting combinations.
[113] *B.P.P.*, 1806, Vol. 3, p. 369, evidence of William Cookson.
[114] P.C. 1/43/A152, Observations respecting combinations.
[115] H.O. 42/66, Fitzwilliam to Pelham, 27 Sept. 1802.

bitterly noted that the merchants 'must endure slavery yet longer, they are beyond the power of help'.[116] Leeds, however, was abnormal and elsewhere, where the cloth dressers were not so numerous, resistance to their demands was more widespread.

When necessitated strike action did not require wholesale walk-outs. The usual manner of conducting a withdrawal of labour from an obnoxious employer was for his journeymen to quit his shop after finishing the piece on which they were working, for otherwise they could be prosecuted under the Elizabethan Statute of Artificers.[117] Where large numbers were employed, however, as in the case of Gott who employed eighty croppers at Bean Ing or, on a lesser scale, Atkinson who employed twenty-five in Bradley mill, the cloth dressers might quit in a body. In Warminster in 1802 most of the shearmen quit work as a result of the introduction of gig mills, while at Trowbridge the move of eight or ten clothiers to increase the work load of their shearmen without increasing wages led to a strike which immediately closed their finishing shops.[118] Overt action like this had the disadvantage that it could scarcely be misconstrued by the authorities as anything other than a deliberate violation of the combination laws. Nevertheless, the shearmen's position was strong. Their strikes were solid and their skills vital to the employer. Thus, according to Cookson, 'The master must and has given way in every struggle.'[119]

Some manufacturers were more resolute. Atkinson had been using the gig mill for many years before 1802, despite intermittent pressure from the Huddersfield croppers, but in that year Atkinson precipitated industrial action in his dressing shop, probably as a result of the cloth dressers' national determination 'not to work after machinery'. Cookson wrote to Fitzwilliam on 30 August 1802, 'Within these last three weeks all the gig mills at Huddersfield, some of which had been at work for 20 years, have been totally stopped from working – masters learnt by chance as it were that gig mills were not to be allowed. Men soon afterwards gave notice of an intention to quit their employ.'[120] All but three of Atkinson's croppers immediately turned out when he ordered that they must either hire till Christmas and thus continue to work with the gig mill or leave. His timing was shrewd. Unable to find work elsewhere as trade dropped off, all except two went back. By this

---

[116] W.W.M., 117, Beckett to Fitzwilliam, 28 Jan. 1803.
[117] 5 Elizabeth c. 4; see Thompson, *The Making*, p. 533; see also B.C., 15 Jan. 1778.
[118] W.W.M., 111, Fitzwilliam to Pelham, 25 Sept. 1802; B.P.P., 1802/3, Vol. 7, pp. 374, 194, 212; J.H.C., Vol. 58, p. 886; H.O. 42/66, Read to Pelham, 6 Sept. 1802.
[119] W.W.M., 79, Cookson to Fitzwilliam, 16 Aug. 1802.
[120] W.W.M., 83, Cookson to Fitzwilliam, 30 Aug. 1802.

action Atkinson seems to have broken the resistance of his workmen. Despite threats from other croppers, he told the 1803 Committee, 'They have again hired for us for the present year.'[121] Atkinson, however, was an exception. Cookson lamented, 'rather than lose the shipping season, or the timely sale of their goods, the masters, as is always the case, gave way and the law against gig mills is now as complete in effect – nay, more so – than if enacted by Parliament'.[122]

During disputes cloth dressers were active in recruiting public sympathy, the success of which can be gauged from the response of the innovating manufacturers. William Hughes had dolefully informed Pelham in June 1802 that 'The inhabitants of this town [Warminster], partly through fear and partly from a disgust to the introduction of machinery, do not come forward to take any active part in showing their detestation of these outrages.'[123] And by August the Wiltshire woollen manufacturers' Bath committee resolved anxiously 'That the Chairman should be desired to caution the public against the scandalous and false reports circulated by the shearmen and others; and also to caution all persons against illegal contributions.' This appears to have done no good for in October the committee was offering 10 guineas reward.

Whereas many scandalous and false reports have been circulated by the shearmen . . . pretending that in consequence of the introduction of machinery they have been deprived of employment, whereby the benevolent have been induced to commiserate their situation and bestow relief – the manufacturers think it necessary to caution the inhabitants of the clothing neighbourhoods against such impositions as they may be assured that there is full employment for all workmen disposed to labour in the manufactures . . . Any person found offending . . . will be prosecuted.[124]

During the Gott strike the Leeds croppers obtained the opinions of a Lincoln's Inn barrister favourable to their interpretation of the apprenticeship regulations which were printed and circulated to good effect.[125] The cloth dressers were clearly aware that appeals to the old moral economy would strike sympathetic cords in the public at large, a fact which the clothiers tried strenuously to change with alarmist accusations.

[121] B.P.P., 1802/3, Vol. 7, pp. 373–4.
[122] W.W.M., 83, Cookson to Fitzwilliam, 30 Aug. 1802.
[123] H.O. 42/65, Hughes to Pelham, 23 June 1802.
[124] S.W.J., 23 Aug., 11 Oct. 1802.
[125] W.W.M., 115 and 116, Cloth dressers' case, etc.; Resolutions of the merchants, etc.

Formal negotiations with an employer, though intimidated by the Combination Acts after 1799, nevertheless took place because it often proved to be in the interests of the manufacturer to end a strike. As has been shown, strong union organisation ensured that strikes were not easily broken. Consequently an employer in dispute with his workers would find himself with an increasing pile of unfinished goods on his hands, his circulating capital considerably curtailed and his credit thus tightening. 'Mr Gott is not only precluded from manufacturing in future, but there remains upon his hands all that has passed through the first stages of manufacture without the possibility of being rendered saleable.'[126] Very large concerns like Wormald, Gott and Wormald could withstand such sanctions for longer than a smaller firm but eventually it affected all to some degree. Consequently it became a matter of prudence not to invoke the Combination Acts as this would only create more trouble for the firm. The Gott strike saw various attempts at a negotiated settlement but the possibility of using the Combination Acts against the croppers never seems to have been seriously considered. Beckett wrote that this could not be done because the informant would lose his trade for the three months before the case was tried, during which time his cropping shops would be 'under an interdict'.[127] Cookson confirmed, 'during the interval, the prosecutor would be obliged to suspend his business entirely and be exposed to incalculable injuries'.[128] John Jones, against whom much of the Wiltshire shearmen's animosity was directed, was pressed by the Home Office to institute proceedings for conspiracy against the deputation of seven shearmen who visited his home in July 1802 in an attempt to negotiate a settlement to the strike of the Bradford on Avon cloth workers. Jones himself was later to state 'the conduct of these men was certainly combination'[129] and the meeting was attended by several local worthies, including Benjamin Hobhouse, M.P., so any legal action would not have lacked trustworthy witnesses, but no action was taken. Jones wrote to Pelham, 'the seven men . . . were promised that no advantage should be taken of their attendance upon that occasion by the person who persuaded them to see me, and although it is most certainly desirable to make examples without delay, yet I am of the opinion that I shall personally become reprobated for an

---

126 H.O. 42/66, Fitzwilliam to Pelham, 27 Sept. 1802.
127 W.W.M., 117, Beckett to Fitzwilliam, 28 Jan. 1803.
128 H.O. 42/66, Cookson to Fitzwilliam, 8 Sept. 1802. The Leeds merchants, in fact, wanted stiffer penalties for combination. See H.O. 42/65, Fitzwilliam to Pelham, 28 July 1802, and H.O. 42/66, Cookson to Fitzwilliam, 8 Sept. 1802.
129 B.P.P., 1802/3, Vol. 7, p. 342.

apparent deception towards these men'.[130] Jones could not risk adding further to the odium the shearmen felt towards him, or causing the campaign of strike action and incendiarism against him and his property to be escalated. Jones was a determined man but his major hope must have been to reach some sort of settlement and get his mill working again.

While combinations of cloth workers prompted aggressive counter-combinations of employers, these were on the whole far less successful. Their mainspring tended to come from the new progressive manufacturers, since many master dressers, like their workers, did not want change. The jealousy of competitors, smaller employers' fears of the innovating manufacturers' ambitions of monopoly and the inertia of the old-established merchant clothier class ensured that any employers' combination was inevitably weakened and loyalties ambiguous. Thus F. Manuel, writing of the Luddite disturbances amongst shearmen in the southern departments of France, notes 'Sometimes the detailed study of a local incident reveals the Luddite movement less as an agitation of workmen than as an aspect of the competition between the backward and progressive shop-owner or manufacturer.'[131] In Wiltshire, James Read felt, 'The master shearmen are, I believe, considerably instrumental in keeping up the prejudice [against machinery] behind the curtain, and I also believe that the smaller manufacturers are not dissatisfied with the opposition.'[132] At one stage Jones lamented, 'I have spared neither offers of Reward nor personal Exertion to gain intelligence of [the shearmen's] schemes', but he found that when it came to offering a reward for informants, 'Mr Bush, a considerable Clothier acting as Magistrate in Bradford ... absolutely declines to join in a Subscription or to publish the name of the firm of his own Concern to any offers of Reward.'[133] The defiant resolutions of the merchants of Leeds in 1791 to introduce cloth dressing machinery came to nought when faced with determined workers' resistance. Gott's struggle against his croppers was sold out by a

---

[130] H.O. 42/65, J. Jones, Sen., to King, 28 July 1802, Opinion of the Law Officers of the Crown, 28 July 1802, Jones to Pelham, 30 July 1802. Hammonds, *Skilled Labourer*, p. 174, write of this meeting that 'these negotiations were poisoned like all negotiations of the kind by the existence of the Combination Acts'. The negotiations, however, broke down because the Bradford on Avon shearmen refused to work after the gig mill. The Combination Acts were not mentioned until news reached the Secretary of State's Office. H.O. 43/13, King to Jones, 29 July 1802.

[131] F. E. Manuel, 'The Luddite movement in France', *Journal of Modern History*, 10 (1938), p. 186.

[132] H.O. 42/66, Read to Pelham, 5 Sept. 1802.

[133] H.O. 42/65, Jones to Pelham, 29 July 1802.

compromise reached by the other merchants with the croppers in January 1803. Beckett was highly critical of the large numbers of merchants who were ready 'to rat it'.[134] And again, in August 1805, though a meeting of eighty-five firms, including Gott's, declared its 'Determination . . . to resist by all legal means such combinations . . . the injurious effects of which have been lately felt by many of their employers' and agreed 'not to employ any workman who shall on or after the First Day of October next be or become a Member of what is called *the Institution*, or any other illegal combination', the position of the Leeds croppers was little challenged until after 1812.[135]

How potent a weapon was industrial action? John Jones felt that 'the effects of such combinations are more to be dreaded than even open attacks'.[136] It was certainly a powerful weapon used when the employer was experiencing good trade or when he had a contract to fill in a limited time, 'when the shops are full of work, and when it is well known that to have their work stand still will be of the greatest prejudice to the masters'.[137] The West Riding croppers were not slow to strike to keep their wage rates up when wartime inflation sapped the purchasing power of static wages. 'Some have advanced wages two times within four years', it was stated in 1799, 'and whenever advanced, no reduction is allowed, however unfavourable the times may be for the employers. It is well known that several branches have already agreed to demand further increases of wages whenever trade is brisk.'[138] West Country shearmen also increased their wages in this period. The strike, then, was an effective offensive weapon. After 1800, however, strike action was instituted more as a reaction to worsening conditions than as an aggressive weapon of improvement. This was a direct result of the attempted introduction of cloth dressing machinery. The Bradford on Avon shearmen struck work some time during July 1802, ostensibly over an attempt by Jones to reduce their wages. However, the cloths Jones was trying to have sheared had been previously gig milled at his Staverton factory. In Trowbridge the strike in that month was also superficially financial. Some of the clothiers 'took upon themselves to fall the time generally allowed for finishing a piece of goods from twenty-three to twenty' without any corresponding change in wages The attempt, however, was in the context of the growing practice of some clothiers there sending cloths away to

---

[134] W.W.M., 117, Beckett to Fitzwilliam, 28 Jan. 1803.
[135] *Leeds Intelligencer*, 2 Sept. 1805.
[136] H.O. 42/65, Jones to Pelham, 27 July 1802.
[137] P.C. 1/43/A152, Observations respecting combinations.   [138] *Ibid.*

Gloucestershire, to Twerton and probably to Staverton to be gig milled. Industrial violence combined with strike action forced the Trowbridge clothiers to climb down but Jones refused to give way and introduced shearing frames into his mill, thus totally severing the need to employ unionist shearmen. 'Mr. Jones at this time has not a single shearman at work for him. That part of their labour he is obliged to supply by shearing frames set in motion by machinery, where one person attends four pairs of shears and that person need not be a shearman.'[139] The Warminster and Huddersfield cloth dressers actually went on strike against the gig mill itself. In Huddersfield they were generally successful. At Warminster, however, the strike dragged on, becoming increasingly bitter, while some manufacturers followed Jones' example in introducing shearing frames. In Leeds the issue was disguised in several contests over apprenticeship of which the struggle with Gott was crucial for, while this strike apparently bore no relation to machinery, the Leeds croppers regarded Gott as their greatest adversary, a man who had already tried to set up a gig mill and who was clearly more than willing to try again. Trouble was provoked when Gott took two youths, both over the age of fourteen years, as apprentice croppers. All his men walked out. Gott tried to rally other merchants to the cause. The result was the formation of an 'Association for the support of the laws' whose members agreed to employ 'no shearmen that might quit any other shop', to circulate a 'black list' of those who did do so and to support all merchants whose shops were 'deserted'. The Gott strike thereby became a general strike affecting large numbers of Leeds croppers. When the men struck they had an allowance of 18s. a week out of their common fund, 'but being about 1,500 in the whole of which a great many claimed the allowance, the fund lessened so fast as to alarm the manager of it, so the allowance was reduced to 10/od.' The fund, however, outlasted the merchants' nerve. Whether or not large numbers remained on strike until agreement was finally reached on 18 January 1803 we do not know. Gott's men were certainly out until that date. It is thus little wonder that when in January the merchants capitulated 'the croppers gave out they had got a victory'.[140] There were no more attempts to weaken the croppers' position by expanding the workforce with illegal apprentices. 'Two or three years ago, our dressers by combining together brought us to agree not to take them after they were fifteen; and since then we have

---

[139] *B.P.P.*, 1802/3, Vol. 7, pp. 194, 212; H.O. 42/66, Read to Pelham, 5 Sept. 1802.
[140] *L.M.*, 2 Oct. 1802; W.W.M., 117, Beckett to Fitzwilliam, 28 Jan. 1803.

not dared to take any apprentice after they were fifteen years old.'[141] 'They are virtually a perpetual monopoly in themselves.'[142]

On the issue of gig mills, however, no negotiated settlement proved possible. Offers of never using machinery whilst men stood idle or of finding them other jobs at other trades appeared to the cloth dressers to be empty rhetoric. Jones offered the Bradford on Avon shearmen 'always to give a preference to the employment of men of the said parish rather than use the frames for shearing of cloth whilst any such men should want work' and added that, in future, 'no gigging or shearing shall be done for hire by him on account of other manufacturers'.[143] However, Jones' gig mill would remain in action and the shearing frames ready to be put to use whenever Jones decided work exceeded shearmen. The cloth dressers could not even contemplate negotiated phased introduction of gig mills even had they trusted their employers. For they realised that to accept the gig mill would have irretrievably weakened their position and ability to organise a collective defence against further mechanical incursions. Nor was it tactically sound to modify their intransigence and join in talks about the gradual introduction of the gig mills when they could still hope to implement 5 & 6 Edward VI c. 22, 'An act for putting down gig mills'. The machine had to be resisted down the line. And for this, while the sanction of a strike brought considerable pressure to bear on an employer, direct action offered a more immediate method of driving the pernicious machines away.

[141] *B.P.P.*, 1806, Vol. 3, p. 163, evidence of John Hebblethwaite, Leeds merchant.
[142] W.W.M., 111, Fitzwilliam to Pelham, 25 Sept. 1802.
[143] H.O. 42/65, J. Jones, Sen., to King, 26 July 1802.

Chapter 5

Industrial violence and machine breaking – the Wiltshire Outrages

The community-based resistance to early preparatory machinery relied, as has been seen, principally, though not exclusively, upon direct action and above all upon the machine breaking riot. Machine breaking and violence proved effective methods of protest for groups of workers who, like the spinners and scribblers, lacked strong trade union organisation. Historians have in consequence often chosen to see industrial violence as symptomatic of organisational immaturity, as a 'pre-industrial' method of resisting change utilised by labour groups insufficiently sophisticated to organise more orderly forms of protest. Thus Bythell, writing of the Lancashire weavers' riots against power looms in the 1820s, refers to them as 'blind vandalism' and 'pointless physical violence'. They were 'a throwback to the disorganised activities of a pre-industrial age and not a forerunner of modern collective bargaining'. Hunt, likewise, portrays machine breaking as a consequence of industrial weakness and an incapacity for organised 'orthodox trade unionism'. Hobsbawm's delineation of the concept of 'collective bargaining by riot' only partially counters such views. While he reminds us that 'wrecking was a technique of trade unionism in the period before, and during the early phases of, the Industrial Revolution', he however qualifies this by noting that 'organised unions hardly as yet existed in the trades concerned'. Collective bargaining by riot was therefore an early step towards the acquisition of that 'habit of solidarity which is the foundation of effective trade unionism'. This view of violence as a transitional stage has been developed by Stevenson who also emphasises the difference between direct action and organised industrial action, advancing a developmental theory of labour protest in which the riot and violence of the pre-industrial crowd gives way with the advent of the Industrial Revolution to more orderly and sophisticated means of articulating grievances, namely the

This chapter includes material developed from my article, 'The shearmen and the Wiltshire Outrages' which appeared in *Social History*, 7, 3 (1982).

strike, collective bargaining and industrial arbitration. This reflects the view asserted by Thomis who argues that Luddism took place only where labour was not effectively organised. Violence, he claims, 'occurred not through established trade union machinery but in its absence'.[1]

This teleological view of labour history cannot be sustained, as careful examination of the response of the cloth dressers to the challenge posed to their livelihood by finishing machinery in the years before 1809 clearly demonstrates. As has been seen, cloth dressers' combinations were formidably equipped to undertake strike action. However, while they did indeed initiate industrial sanctions and have recourse to the courts – what Thomis describes as 'a labour approach', 'an approach quite different from that of industrial sabotage and direct action'[2] – neither technique proved entirely appropriate responses to the threat posed by machinery. For this reason cloth dressers in the West of England in the years from 1797 to 1809, like those in Yorkshire in 1812, showed no hesitation in also resorting to direct action. Violence was not the spontaneous reaction of men driven to despair as Briggs assumes when he refers to the Luddites as 'the helpless victims of distress'.[3] While the gig mills and shearing frames introduced before 1809 threatened jobs, their numbers were limited. The cloth dressers' actions, like those of the scribblers and spinners, were essentially pre-emptive, recognising that, once machinery was allowed to secure a significant share of the trade, all employers would be forced to introduce them in order to compete and the dressers' trade would be irretrievably undermined. Violence was selective, controlled and aimed at specific targets, supplementing and reinforcing the more orthodox sanctions of their combinations. We must firmly resist a simplistic imposition of nineteenth- or twentieth-century models of 'appropriate' trade union behaviour upon the actions and activities of eighteenth-century combinations regardless of their very different context and culture.[4] Machine wrecking, arson, violence, or threats of such, represented some of the most easily and most frequently

---

[1] D. Bythell, *The Handloom Weavers – A Study in the English Cotton Industry during the Industrial Revolution* (Cambridge, 1969), pp. 180, 181; Hunt, *British Labour History*, p. 196; Hobsbawm, *Labouring Men*, pp. 7–8; J. Stevenson, 'Food riots in England, 1792–1818', in J. Stevenson and R. Quinault, eds., *Popular Protest and Public Order* (Allen and Unwin, 1974), pp. 62–3, 67; Thomis, *The Luddites*, p. 134.

[2] Thomis, *The Luddites*, p. 132.

[3] Briggs, *The Age of Improvement*, p. 182.

[4] See Rule, *The Experience of Labour*, especially ch. 6; and Randall, 'The industrial moral economy', pp. 44–9.

implemented industrial sanctions available to an eighteenth-century trade union. Violence was in no way an alternative to Thomis' 'labour approach' but a major weapon of the trade unions, reflecting the organisation, culture and community from which they developed.

While the failure of the Wiltshire shearmen's action against Cook at the summer assizes of 1796 for using a gig mill at Marlborough seems to have encouraged at least one clothier, Paul Newman of Melksham, to set up the machine, the shearmen's threats and violence against him seem to have had the desired effect, forcing Newman to give up his attempt and dissuading others in the main woollen producing towns from following his example. Left alone, the Wiltshire and Somerset shearmen might have held off the gig mills for some time by such methods but an important external factor began from that time onwards to add a new pressure to the situation. The failure of the Gloucestershire shearmen in 1794 to prevent the clothiers there from using the gig mill on fine cloths gradually put pressure on Wiltshire and Somerset. From around 1797/8 clothiers in these counties found themselves losing trade in the superfine market to Gloucestershire and this forced them to consider either sending cloths away to be gig raised or else risking the setting up of gig mills for themselves. In the period from 1797 to 1802 we can discern three phases in which gig mills crept ever closer to the strongholds of the Wiltshire and Somerset shearmen. The earliest and a persistent threat came from the woollen mills at Twerton, west of Bath. Three mills there produced woollen cloth, Twerton Upper and Lower mills and Weston Lower mill on the opposite side of the River Avon. At least two, Twerton Upper and Weston, housed gig mills in 1797, Twerton Upper having had one from 1787.[5] It seems clear that by 1797 they had begun to raise cloths for some Wiltshire and Somerset clothiers as well. These mills were a long way from the main Wiltshire and Somerset finishing centres and possibly their activities might have been tolerated had not Samuel Bamford, owner of Twerton Upper mill, also introduced shearing frames in that year.[6] This marked a clear challenge to the shearmen and they were quick to respond. One Thursday night in December 1797, 200 or 300 men with faces blackened and armed with bludgeons,

entered the house of a shear grinder at Nunny [about 3 miles from Frome] and demolished about £30 worth of shears belonging to the manufactory of Messrs. Bamford, Cook and Co. of Twerton . . . after committing this outrage the rioters

---

[5] Rogers, *Wiltshire and Somerset Woollen Mills*, pp. 168–9; B.C., 4 Jan. 1787.
[6] S.W.J., 19 July, 1802; this caused major unemployment among Twerton shearmen – see B.P.P., 1802/3, Vol. 7, p. 121.

assembled in another place to the amount of 8 or 900 and resolved to proceed to Twerton in order to hang up Bamford and two of his men, to burn down his works and those of Collicott and Co. on the opposite side of the river.[7]

The shears were almost certainly from Bamford's shearing frames. The attack on Twerton was set for the Sunday but the plan was leaked and J. Bowen, a Bath magistrate, prepared a military defence. Rumours that 1,500 rioters would assemble at Norton and that 2,000 more were expected to join them induced the worthy justice to assemble a considerable force on the night in question, consisting of one troop of 'the Surrey fensible cavalry', 22 subalterns and 20 light dragoons, together with 200 infantrymen and a field piece. They waited all night, 'but no rioters appeared – having heard, I suppose, of the preparation which was made to receive them'. At midday all was still quiet and Bowen dispatched the troops back to their quarters. He was about himself to leave 'when an Express arrived of the rioters having assembled and were coming down within a half a mile of the village to the amount of 150'. He immediately sent word for the military to return and remained to observe a group of thirty or forty men armed with bludgeons, 'two or three of whom went into a cottage inhabited by one of Bamford's own men who was said to be disaffected to him'. The cavalry were soon back upon the scene and Bowen resolved to launch an offensive, ordering the troops to surround the cottage and capture the would-be rioters. He was disappointed. 'They had been apprized of the approach of the cavalry and were escaped. However, I then ordered the roads to be scoured.' The troops took up seventy-two men in this way and escorted them to Bath. Each was closely questioned but, because he 'could not fix anything like an outrage upon them', Bowen had to dismiss them. However, he considered the effect of the severe reprimand he gave them salutory for 'They seemed much frightened and made very fair promises.' A further troop of cavalry and 100 Berkshire militia were drafted into the Bath area and Bowen recommended stationing further detachments at Frome, Bradford on Avon, Trowbridge and Beckington, 'as it will convince those deluded men of the impropriety of their conduct and of the impossibility of succeeding in their intentions'.[8]

---

[7] The shearmen were said to be from Trowbridge, Bradford, Frome and Beckington: *S.W.J.*, 15 Jan. 1798.

[8] H.O. 42/41, Bowen to Portland, 20 Dec. 1797. Bowen's actions appear ponderous and somewhat risible, but his situation and that of fellow magistrates in possession of similar information was difficult. If he dismissed reports as exaggerated, their fulfilment could incur for him the charge of neglecting his duty. Yet if he did call out the troops and nothing occurred, he would be termed 'alarmist'.

The military presence stifled further outrage for a while but, beneath a calm surface, trouble was brewing. By 1799 other clothiers around Bath had set up gig mills and began to take work from Wiltshire on commission. One such was John Bell who bought Batheaston fulling mill in 1794 and had erected a factory there by 1799[9] which certainly housed a gig mill and possibly shearing frames as well. In April 1799, he was warned:

I send you this to inform you that we the cloth workers of Trowbridge, Bradford, Chippinham, & Melkshom are allmost or the greatest part of Us oute of worke and Wee are fully convinst that the greatests of the Cause is your dressing work by Machinery. And we are determind if you follow this practise any longer that we will keep som People to watch you Abought with loaded Blunderbuss or Pistols and Will Certanly Blow your Brains out it is no use to Destroy the Factorys But put you Damd Villions to death. And that you will may depend up on will be don the county then but make up your lost when your soul is blown into Hellfire and this shall be done as sure as you are Alive give your Brother Brown a Caution of this as hee will shear the same fate and Cook and Bamford Allso. There is everything gott in readyness for the Business now you know what you have to Trust to it will be no use For you to cry out when to late you have been in Hell I mean you was better perswade your Mother from her evill Ways in it or shee will shear the same fate do Consider and put a stop to it in time or Death and Damnation will be your fate. We are yours the cloth workers of the afforsaid Towns.[10]

'Brother Brown' was probably Ebenezer Brown who had bought Twerton Lower mill by 1800 and converted it into a large factory. A gig mill was also probably at work in the mill at Bathwick at this time.[11] Several Wiltshire clothiers were by now sending cloths to Bath to be finished and they were warned, rather more politely:

Gentlemen, If you persist in the plan you have adopted, others certainly will follow which will distress many poor families. This is to give you timely notice to discontinue it and if you do not perhaps you may experience a return from a quarter you little suspect. Depend on it a honest man has no need to arm himself against his fellow citizens.

Clearly some clothiers were seriously alarmed by the shearmen's threats but cloths continued to be sent. Another letter was more menacing.

Gentlemen clothiers al i hope that you will a warn tak an not send no more cloth to Turten for if you do your own ruen will be for we are determed to go

---

[9] Rogers, *Wiltshire and Somerset Woollen Mills*, p. 167. Bell also owned workshops in Trowbridge: p. 140.
[10] *London Gazette*, 1799, p. 507 (May 1799).
[11] Rogers, *Wiltshire and Somerset Woollen Mills*, pp. 169, 168.

throo with it as nou we be gon it fore next time that wecom we will set all the mishenery a fiere if ther is any more sent from Fesh ford ar Stoke for we have gote the math all ready made for it for we migh so well be hong ought of the as storve to deth for we have put up with long a nose i think pear teoker fresh ford meall but as for devel Joice the marder an the Welch Goate we will burn them both as soon as we hood other doges and we are the thrmed to have down stavern factry if tha dont look dam shap we will begin the—very soon and we will drive the devls before us.[12]

The only mill at Limpley Stoke was owned from 1796 by John Newton, a partner in the Bradford on Avon firm of Bush, Newton and Bush. Newton also owned Clifford mill at Beckington which was burned down by the shearmen in 1802 and which may have housed a gig mill. The partnership also leased Freshford mill from 1796 and extended it to a factory. The other mill at Freshford, Dunkirk mill, was a large factory built by 1795 by Thomas Joyce and his partner John Moggridge (perhaps the 'Welch Goate'). This partnership also owned workshops in Bradford on Avon. Staverton mill ('Stavern factry') was still in its last stages of completion at this date[13] but it was soon to represent the major threat to the Wiltshire shearmen for it was only a few miles from Bradford on Avon and Trowbridge and its owner, John Jones, was sending cloths away to Gloucestershire to be gig milled. How far any of these threats were successful in dissuading the practice of sending cloths to Bath is unclear. There were also two other gig mills at work in Wiltshire at this time. One was that owned by Francis Hill at Malmesbury, many miles from the main clothing towns, but the other was set up by Abraham Lloyd Edridge in the village of Christian Malford, not far from Chippenham.[14] Neither seem to have incurred immediate trouble.

It was the downturn of trade from 1800 onwards and fears that Gloucestershire was getting ahead of them[15] that prompted a speeding up of the introduction of cloth finishing machinery in 1801 and 1802 which in the latter year led to major disturbances. In 1801 Jones set up a gig mill at his Staverton factory while other gig mills were also set up around Chippenham, one owned by Uriah Tarrant at Christian Malford and another at Calstone Wellington owned by a clothier named Baily. At Frome one of the major firms, W. H. and G. Sheppard,

---

[12] *London Gazette*, 1799, p. 507 (May 1799).
[13] Rogers, *Wiltshire and Somerset Woollen Mills*, pp. 166, 196, 194, 97.
[14] H.O. 42/66, Read to Pelham, 5 Sept. 1802; *B.P.P.*, 1802/3, Vol. 7, pp. 333, 359.
[15] Mann, *Cloth Industry*, p. 139.

began to send cloths to Gloucestershire to be finished.[16] However, it was at Warminster that trouble flared first in April 1802. Two manufacturers, Henry Wansey and Peter Warren, both set up gig mills in their workshops and both were soon the victims of strike action. Wansey, and probably Warren, was threatened and he wrote asking the government for overt assistance for, while he was prepared to pay a reward, 'what I want is the sanction of Government and to show my workmen that Government have taken up the business'.[17] Four of his workmen stood by him and refused to join the strike and were ill-treated and threatened by their colleagues.[18] The shearmen's threats against the clothiers were supplemented by the cutting down of a row of young trees, probably the property of Wansey, and on the night of 22 April a large hayrick belonging to Warren was set on fire but this was discovered and extinguished. The strike at Wansey's continued, probably spreading to other manufacturers' shops or to their cloths, for in evidence in 1803 George Wansey said that three-quarters of the Warminster shearmen had at one stage struck work over the introduction of gig mills.[19] Probably several local clothiers were availing themselves of Wansey's or Warren's mill.

The strike continued into May but no more outrages appear to have occurred until 20 May when 'the cart of Mr. Bayley of Calstone Mills near Devizes, returning from Warminster loaded with cloths, was overtaken on the Downs by six men with blackened faces who took out the cloths, cut five or six of them to pieces and damaged fourteen others to the amount of £200'.[20] This ended the attempt of the Warminster clothiers to break the effects of the strike by sending their cloths to be raised by Baily's gig mill, noted above. The strike held firm and on the night of 15 June, 'between 12 and 1 o'clock, a rick of oats worth about £20 belonging to Mr. Peter Warren, clothier, was maliciously set on fire, and entirely consumed. A dog kennel at some distance therefrom, the property of the said Mr. Warren and others, was at the same time also set on fire and partly consumed.' This fire was put out by the timely arrival of dragoons for 'not a labourer in that place would assist in any degree to save from destruction either corn or premises'. The striking Warminster shearmen were giving Warren another warning. 'There is no doubt but this daring outrage was committed by some of

[16] B.P.P., 1802/3, Vol. 7, pp. 333, 138, 142, 368; Rogers, *Wiltshire and Somerset Woollen Mills*, pp. 76, 82.
[17] H.O. 42/65, Wansey to King, 9 April 1802.
[18] See above, p. 140.
[19] J.H.C., Vol. 58, p. 886.
[20] H.O. 42/95, printed list of Wiltshire Outrages, 25 Sept. 1802.

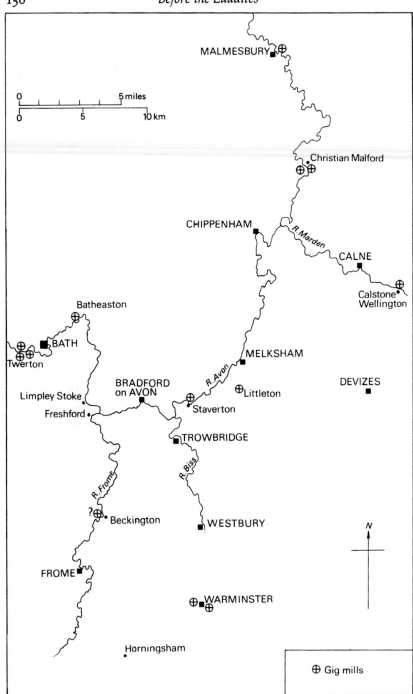

Map 4
Gig mills in Wiltshire, 1800–1802

the workmen usually employed in the woollen manufactory, who now and have for many weeks past refused to work on account of some machines being introduced which they consider as obnoxious.'[21] A week later a gun was fired into the lodgings of another renegade cloth worker, an employee of Messrs. Bleek and Strode, 'in the dead of night'. The violence took on a wider significance when on the evening of 29 June workmen from Trowbridge, Westbury and other cloth finishing towns met in Warminster, probably for a union meeting, and 'about 1 o'clock in the night a gun was fired into the chambers of Mr. Henry Wansey but happily did no mischief except breaking the windows'. Firearms again featured a week later when on the night of 6 July the homes of J. Jones and Daniel Baker, Wansey's loyal workmen, were fired into without casualties. And on the night of 13 July, a barn and stable owned by Warren were burned down. The clothiers, however, refused to give in, even though one received a letter threatening 'by Almighty God to have his life within a month'.[22]

Meanwhile clothiers elsewhere were coming into conflict with their shearmen. At Trowbridge a strike ensued following the announcement by eight or ten clothiers that they were cutting the time allowed for finishing a piece of cloth. Quite when this occurred is not clear. Read believed that the strike did not begin until 14 July but Nathaniel Edwards later stated that the dispute began towards the end of June.[23] The latter may well have been the case for on the night of 23 June there was an abortive attempt to fire a rick belonging to a Trowbridge manufacturer named Dunn, while on the night of 6 July a gun was fired into the house of William Stancomb, a Trowbridge clothier, 'but the bullets striking against the wall, flattened and fell down'.[24] Industrial action also disrupted the finishing shops at Bradford on Avon at this time following a general refusal by the shearmen there to finish cloths which John Jones had raised on his gig mill at Staverton. Jones offered to pay the shearmen only 4d. per yard for shearing when 'the accustomed price, time out of mind, was seven pence'. Jones later claimed that, because of the superior quality of the raising, the shearmen would have earned between 15s. and 16s. at this rate and that he had promised to make up the wages of any who failed to earn this sum. However, he expected the shearmen to work from six in the morning to six at night and to take only two instead of the customary five breaks,

[21] H.O. 42/65, Matthew Davies to Pelham, 15 June 1802; see also Hughes to Pelham, 23 June 1802; W.R.O., 9, Ailesbury MSS, Yeomanry papers, Pettit to Bruce, 16 June 1802.
[22] H.O. 42/65, Jones to Pelham, 29 July 1802.
[23] H.O. 42/66, Read to Pelham, 6 Sept. 1802; B.P.P., 1802/3, Vol. 7, p. 212.
[24] H.O. 42/95, printed list; H.O. 42/65, Jones to Pelham, 29 July 1802.

thus increasing their hours of work.[25] It is probable that the Trowbridge clothiers were trying to force this same abandonment of customary breaks. Other Bradford on Avon clothiers also had cloths raised at Staverton and one, Thomas Tugwell, was soon the victim of the shearmen's antipathy when on the night of 26 June one of his ricks was burned. This was only part of his warning, for he found the following letter under the door of his workshops:

Death or Glory to you T. & M. Tugwell. We will burn you and your Horses we will Cut your heart out and Eat him you ot to have your Dam heart cut out of your Body you will Go to Hell for Starveing the Poor thee Shot Shaw fly by night for some of you.[26]

These disputes formed the background to the first attack on Staverton mill on the night of 14 July and to the destruction of John Newton's mill at Beckington the following night. Jones wrote to Pelham,

On Thursday . . . a considerable armed body attacked without any provocation the works belonging to myself and Partners and effected much mischief by firing for more than half an hour back slug and small shot into the mill and dwelling house of the resident onlooker but happily no lives were lost . . . I attended with every possible haste with a detachment of the Queen's Dragoon Guards . . . but the Rioters had dispersed before our arrival, hearing (I conjecture) of our approach.[27]

Staverton mill epitomised the future that all the woollen workers of Wiltshire most feared. Properly named 'The Staverton Superfine Woollen Manufactory', it was an imposing edifice of 'not less than six different floors and having 65 windows in front'. According to P. A. Nemnich, the German traveller, the mill 'is filled with every sort of newly invented machinery so that every kind of process except weaving can be done there'.[28] From its inception, the mill met with harassment from the workers of the neighbouring towns. On 30 November 1801, Jones was sufficiently alarmed at their attitudes to write to the Secretary of State requesting that further troops should be drafted into the area to intimidate the workmen. Pelham wrote back that he had received the letter 'stating the difficulty you have experienced in establishing your manufactory at Staverton in consequence of a combination entered into by the workmen in that neighbourhood to oppose it'. He felt the troops already stationed in the area should prove

[25] B.B.P., 1802/3, Vol. 7, pp. 194, 336.
[26] H.O. 42/95, printed list; *London Gazette*, 1802, p. 692 (July 1802).
[27] H.O. 42/65, Jones to Pelham, 18 July 1802. There were, in fact, two attacks on Staverton mill and not just the one as Ponting, *Woollen Industry*, p. 76, implies.
[28] *Devizes Gazette*, 5 Nov. 1824; P. A. Nemnich, *Neueste Reise durch England, Schottland und Irland* (1807), p. 222.

sufficient but that, 'should it appear that any outrages are likely to be committed', he would see that more soldiers were dispatched to 'effectually secure the tranquility of that part of the country and enable you to proceed in the work you have undertaken without further molestation'.[29] When the Bradford on Avon shearmen struck work and blacked Jones' cloths in 1802, they also managed to induce many of the workers at Staverton mill to leave 'under a pretence that they had been threatened and forced to do it'. It was, wrote Jones, 'a most wicked attempt to ruin our manufacture by threats ... whereby one whole branch of our business is wholly stopped'. Jones, however, was not to be beaten for he immediately began to set up shearing frames in the mill, operated by non-shearmen.[30] His action could hardly have exacerbated the situation more. The shearing frames, however, were not in action until after the shearmen's first attack. There does not appear to have been any serious attempt to break into the mill and destroy the machinery inside on the night of 14 July, though the assailants in their haste left behind a pickaxe together with part of a powder horn and powder and shot.[31] The attack may have been yet another gesture but it is more likely that the mill proved too well fortified and guarded, as on the second assault. Troops had been stationed to protect mills around Shepton Mallet in the later 1790s and it is probable that soldiers were detached to guard Staverton mill following the scares in late 1801. Certainly after the attack on the mill, two companies of infantry were drafted into the area 'for the purpose of assisting the magistrates by acting as sentries or guards upon sundry mills'.[32]

The following night the mill and dwelling house owned by John Newton at Clifford, near Beckington, was set on fire and burned to the ground. It is possible that the mill contained a gig mill.[33] Newton certainly had been using the Twerton gig mill before this. His loss was estimated at £1,500. Part of the mill might have been saved 'but the populace would not permit it'. Newton was highly alarmed and asked for special protection for his other mill at Limpley Stoke which he believed might be attacked next.[34] On the following night Trowbridge

[29] W.A.S.L., *Wiltshire Cuttings*, Vol. 14, pp. 138–9, Pelham to Jones, 5 Dec. 1801.
[30] H.O. 42/66, Read to King, 4 Oct. 1802; H.O. 42/65, Jones to Pelham, 27 July 1802; H.O. 42/66, Read to Pelham, 5 Sept. 1802.
[31] H.O. 42/65, Jones to Pelham, 29 July 1802.
[32] *Account of the Proceedings of the Merchants*, p. 155; H.O. 50/392, Brownrigg to King, 29 July 1802; H.O. 42/65, Jones to Pelham, 18 July 1802.
[33] Rogers, *Wiltshire and Somerset Woollen Mills*, p. 184, notes that in 1795 two pairs of stocks were removed, presumably to enable the use of other powered machinery, and in 1802 the mill was described as a spinning, scribbling and fulling mill.
[34] H.O. 42/65, Newman to Jones, 16 July, Jones to Pelham, 18, 29 July 1802.

shearmen attacked and 'demolished' the house of Stephen James, probably a blackleg.[35]

Events in Wiltshire were building up to some sort of climax. On Monday, 19 July, a large rick, the property of Mr Tanner, a Bradford on Avon clothier, was burned.[36] It was a prelude to the dramatic attack on the scribbling and fulling mill at Littleton in the parish of Steeple Ashton, the property of Mr Francis Naish, a prominent Trowbridge clothier and one of the shearmen's most determined opponents in their strike there. Naish bought the isolated mill in 1797, installed scribbling and spinning machinery and let it to Ralph Heath who came from Calne where he had described himself as a machine worker in the woollen manufactory. It seems certain that Naish set up a gig mill at Littleton or, as Rogers says, that he set up shearing frames, possibly in consequence of the strike.[37] Certainly the Trowbridge shearmen were determined to destroy this mill rather than Naish's more extensive and more accessible workshops in Trowbridge. Heath, who described himself as 'a millman and spinner', had for some time been living in fear of an attack and, together with his three workmen, had been guarding the mill every night. On the night of 22 July, at about eleven o'clock, Heath received a message from Naish stating that he believed the shearmen might attack that night and to be on his guard. Heath was angry that Naish had not sent any soldiers. The defenders sat and waited in Heath's cottage adjacent to the mill, occasionally patrolling outside, until at about one o'clock Heath believed that he had heard a noise outside and sent one of his three servants, Daniel Goodship, to investigate. According to Heath:

> Immediately upon the said Daniel Goodship having opened the Door, four or five Men, some of them with their Faces Blacked and all of them Armed with Muskets, Pistols, Bayonets and other Weapons Rushed into the Room crying out 'Stand you Buggers', at the same time presenting their arms and swearing 'that no one should stir'.

The leader, a small man with his face blacked and carrying a small musket with a fixed bayonet, demanded, 'Damn your eyes, is there any soldiers or guards here?' He immediately went out to check, leaving one young shearman, with 'his face blacked and a pistol in his hand', to stand guard. This man pointed his pistol at Heath and swore

---

[35] ASSI. 25/2/8, indictment of Samuel Baker.

[36] H.O. 42/65, Jones to Pelham, 29 July 1802.

[37] Rogers, *Wiltshire and Somerset Woollen Mills*, pp. 112, 83. Ponting, *Woollen Industry*, p. 78, claims that the shearmen stated they intended to burn the mill 'because you are going to introduce shearing frames' but gives no source.

'he would blow out their brains if anyone offered to move'. Soon the 'little man' returned and told Heath, 'Damn your eyes, we are come to set fire to it and we will.' Shortly afterwards a glow outside the cottage showed the mill was indeed on fire. The shearmen left the cottage and shortly after Heath made to follow but he was met at the door by a guard and ordered back inside. Heath 'immediately returned into the cottage and waited there some time and on his going out again he found the mill completely in flames'. He managed to save a few cloths 'at the hazard of his life' before the mill was totally consumed. An unsigned draft copy of the information of John Pearce, who with Goodship and Stephen Richardson had been present with Heath, shows Heath in a somewhat less heroic role. Pearce stated that when the shearman announced their intention to burn the mill, Heath had replied 'you may do as you like, burn it down or let it stand. We can't hinder you, if you burn it down I shall sleep in peace which I have not done for a good while.' The shearman replied they would burn the mill 'for it was their lives as well as it was ours'. Also, according to Pearce, when the 'short man', who was the leader, returned to the cottage, he 'went up stairs and took out a child that was in bed and gave it to the mother [Mrs Heath], told her what cloths were in her husband's care he might get out as quick as he could'. These presumably were the cloths which Heath saved.[38]

Littleton mill was totally destroyed and the loss was said to amount to £8,000.[39] The attack was perhaps the most successful of all the shearmen's outrages but it was also to prove the most tragic. Heath later claimed that he had recognised the man who had stood guard over them and threatened them with a pistol as Thomas Helliker or Hilliker, a shearman's colt, who worked for Naish at Trowbridge. Helliker was arrested in Trowbridge on 3 August.[40]

The destruction of Littleton mill broke the nerve of the Trowbridge clothiers who had tried to force their shearmen's wages down. The next morning they agreed to a meeting and 'acceded to the terms of the shearmen, and they went to work again. The shearmen afterwards

[38] H.O. 42/66, information of Ralph Heath, 6 Aug. 1802; K.B. 1/31/Pt 2, draft copy of the information of John Pearce, n.d. It is clear that this is Pearce's deposition, although it is unsigned, since the witness was at Littleton from 11 o'clock and was responsible for summoning both Richardson and Goodship to the mill.

[39] H.O. 42/65, Jones to Pelham, 29 July 1802.

[40] H.O. 42/66, Jones to Pelham, 3 Aug. 1802. The spelling of the name has become fixed as Helliker in popular memory since his tomb has it thus. But it is clear that the family generally favoured the spelling Hilliker. I am grateful to Ms. Sue Hilliker for this information.

printed and circulated a paper of what had been agreed to.'[41] For the Trowbridge cloth dressers, then, direct action had achieved success. Events were not so salutory elsewhere. On the night of the 24th, an alarm at Twerton mills caused troops to be dispatched to guard it whilst in Melksham Paul Newman, a target for violence in 1796, lost two more ricks. The Melksham Yeomanry were also mounting a permanent guard over the mill of Edward Phillips at this time.[42] The Bradford on Avon shearmen were induced to hold negotiations with Jones and on the night of the 26th a deputation of seven men met him at his house. No solution could be found however. One man, Samuel Jones, in fact declared 'he would rather be hanged than recommend the shearmen to accept Jones' offer'.[43] Thus the strike continued. This, together with Jones' new shearing frames, was almost certainly the factor which prompted the second attack on Staverton mill on the night of 28 July. This time there was a definite attempt to get into the mill. The attackers were spotted scaling the high surrounding wall by 'the sentinells on guard' who fired many shots at them. Their fire was returned from three separate localities without scoring any hits. The alarm bell summoned a patrol of mounted dragoons who had been stationed at hand in anticipation of such trouble but though the soldiers scoured the roads and fields they could find no one. The following night an unoccupied dwelling house at Bearfield, near Bradford on Avon, owned by Jones, was set on fire and burned down. It was said that the house had been 'intended for the reception of machinery' and that the attack had been an attempt to draw off the troops protecting Staverton. This did not occur.[44]

The second attack on Staverton mill marked the beginning of the end for direct action in Wiltshire. On 31 July a Trowbridge shearman named Howell presented a paper to the Grand Jury at the Salisbury Assizes complaining of the introduction of gig mills and shearing frames as a nuisance. The case came to nothing as there was some doubt as to the validity of 5 & 6 Edward VI c. 22 to the gig mills in question, but it was scarcely likely anyway that the shearmen's case

---

[41] H.O. 42/66 Read to Pelham, 6 Sept. 1802.

[42] H.O. 42/65, Jones to Pelham, 29 July 1802; *B.J.*, 2 Aug. 1802; H.O. 42/65, inhabitants of Melksham to Pelham, 26 July 1802; W.R.O., 9, Ailesbury MSS, Yeomanry papers, Anon. to Bruce (Melksham, n.d., probably late July 1802).

[43] H.O. 42/65, J. Jones, Sen., to Pelham, 26 July 1802.

[44] H.O. 42/65, Jones to Pelham, 29 July 1802; *B.J.*, 2 Aug. 1802; W.O. 40/17, J. M. Rogers to ?, 4 Aug. 1802; W.R.O., 9, Ailesbury MSS, Yeomanry papers, Anon. to Bruce (Melksham, n.d., probably late July 1802).

would have been upheld in the light of the series of outrages.[45] On 3 August Helliker was arrested. That night the workshops and dwelling house owned by Naish in the Conigre, Trowbridge, were set on fire and burned down. 'Dates and circumstances are much connected in these transactions.' Naish had been a particular opponent of the Trowbridge shearmen and had been responsible for the arrest of Helliker.[46] The real change, however, was marked by the arrival of the chief Bow Street magistrate, James Read, dispatched to Wiltshire by the Secretary of State to 'assist' the local magistrates.[47] His 'active' policy soon led to a number of shearmen being sent to gaol, either to await trial or for examination. These included several of the Trowbridge committee of thirteen shearmen which probably was the co-ordinating committee of the area. Under constant, unrelenting pressure from Read and large numbers of soldiers drafted into the region, violence declined rapidly. The Warminster shearmen maintained spasmodic violence. On the night of the 30th, two cottages, a stable and outhouses belonging to Warren were burned down. The magistrates and Read had met in the town that day and convicted two local shearmen, 'one for endeavouring to intimidate and withdraw a workman from his master's employ, and the other for distributing weekly payments to the refractory shearmen'. 'Mr. Warren was instrumental in bringing forward one of the cases we convicted upon', wrote Read, 'which I suppose provoked this mischief.'[48] Only three more incidents occurred in the town. Between 9 and 10 on the evening of 9 September, 'a gun was fired into a sitting room in the house of Mr. John Bleek of Warminster'. On the night of 22 November 'three guns loaded with shot and bullets were discharged into the windows of different persons in the town ... by persons unknown, but who, from the objects they have selected for their malice, too plainly appear to be connected with the discontented shearmen'. And on 15 December, a gun was fired through the window of Joseph Tucker, another loyal workman.[49] Elsewhere relative quiet returned as the Wiltshire and Somerset shearmen set about organising their petitions and case to be put before Parliament. As Read wrote to John King on 20 December, 'Whilst they are so much occupied, we may rest secure against any Riots in Wiltshire.'[50]

---

[45] H.O. 42/66, Read to Pelham, 6 Sept. 1802.
[46] W.A.S.L., *Wiltshire Cuttings*, Vol. 14, p. 139, Read to Pelham, 6 Sept. 1802.
[47] H.O. 42/66, Pelham to Earl of Pembroke, 3 Aug. 1802.
[48] H.O. 42/95, printed list; B.J., 13 Sept. 1802; H.O. 42/66, Read to Pelham, 1 Sept. 1802.
[49] H.O. 42/95, printed list; B.C., 2 Dec. 1802; S.W.J., 20 Dec. 1802.
[50] H.O. 42/66, Read to King, 20 Dec. 1802.

The Parliamentary campaign seems, as Read predicted, to have absorbed most of the Wiltshire shearmen's energies from 1803 to 1806, though the continued military presence was another obvious disincentive to further outrages. Frustration with the legal processes, however, was probably mixed with their usual antipathy to finishing machinery when violence broke out briefly in Bradford on Avon in late 1807 and in 1808. The target this time was the firm of Divett, Price and Jackson, doubly disliked because they were a 'foreign' firm, having moved into Bradford on Avon in 1807 from London, and had erected a new mill in which they set up machinery 'to a considerable extent and having thereby excited the envy and malice of the shearmen of Bradford on Avon'. 'A daring and alarming attack' was made on their mill on the night of 11 October 1807. 'A party of armed ruffians' attempted to set fire to the factory but 'An alarm being given, the villains fled, leaving in their haste two large bags and two glass bottles which had contained combustibles, a loaded pistol and two ladders.' The mill was probably permanently guarded. The *Salisbury Journal* noted, 'we are informed that active measures are taking by the magistrates to bring to condign punishment the offenders and to protect the persons and property of the clothiers in case of further riotous proceedings among the workmen who still continue under the grossest error to oppose the use of machinery'. Divett, Price and Jackson, however, were very nervous and begged the magistrates that 'for the security of the property and lives of the inhabitants of Bradford on Avon as well as our own, we do entreat you most earnestly to apply for military aid'.[51] Troops were returned to Bradford on Avon but removed again in the summer of 1808.

The presence of the troops, however, had failed to prevent a deliberate attempt to murder John Jones on the evening of 20 January 1808, as he rode home from Staverton. Either a horse pistol or blunderbuss, Jones guessed, was fired at him from close range, the priming injuring his eyes. 'I escaped further mischief from the ill-direction of the piece', he wrote. 'My horse, frightened by the report, instantly ran off with me, which I consider to have prevented a repetition of the act, as these evil disposed men appeared to be divided into Parties at a certain distance.'[52] Despite the offer of free pardon and a reward of £500 for information leading to the conviction of the would-be assassins, no clue as to Jones' assailants came to light until May 1812 when three

[51] H.O. 42/91, Divett, Price and Jackson to Jones, Bush and Hobhouse, 12? Oct. 1807; *S.W.J.*, 17 Oct. 1807; Mann, *Cloth Industry*, p. 226.
[52] H.O. 42/95, Jones to Hawkesbury, 20 Jan. 1808.

men, James Ball, a shearman, William Timbury, a slaymaker, and John Gibbs were arrested, Ball and Gibbs on suspicion of having been involved in the shooting and Timbury of being at a committee meeting which had decided upon the action. 'Their dream of security is over', crowed the *Salisbury Journal*, 'information has been obtained.' However, at the assizes in July it was clear that the evidence against them was inadequate and Ball was acquitted and the case against Timbury dropped. Gibbs was never brought to trial.[53]

Nor did the troops prevent a riot at the house of John Adams in Bradford on Avon in February 1808, 'which appeared to originate in the aversion of the shearmen to the use of machinery'. Eight shearmen and one carpenter received prison sentences of one or two months for their parts in the affair.[54] The removal of the troops in the summer of 1808, however, encouraged the Bradford on Avon shearmen to put pressure once more on Divett, Price and Jackson. The firm wrote another timorous letter to the magistrates, stating that they were 'under great apprehensions for the safety of our manufactory and the good order of the town of Bradford in consequence of the riotous conduct of the shearmen which manifests itself at this instance – and is emboldened by the withdrawing of the troops'. Again they asked for the troops to be returned.[55] Shortly afterwards five Bradford on Avon shearmen were convicted at the town's petty sessions for combination, apparently for having blacklisted and refused to work with one of their fellows. However, the shearmen appealed against their conviction at the subsequent quarter sessions and, although the chairman of the bench delivered an admonitory address to them, their convictions were quashed.[56]

The campaign of industrial violence in Wiltshire in 1802 may well

---

[53] *S.W.J.*, 10 May, 20 July 1812. Why information was suddenly forthcoming about the Bradford shearmen in 1812 is unclear. It may have been connected with the attempts to recruit Wiltshire shearmen serving in the army to infiltrate Yorkshire Luddite organisations, though this was a failure. See H.O. 42/120, Radcliffe to Beckett, 4 March 1812; Hammonds, *Skilled Labourer*, p. 256. Besides Ball, Timbury and Gibbs, one other shearman found himself awaiting trial in June 1812. He was Edward Spinnels, alias Pinnel, who was accused of taking part in the attempted arson of Divett and Co.'s factory in October 1807. Spinnels had previously been convicted for a riot and assaults in Warminster in 1802 and sentenced to four months' imprisonment, and for the riot in Bradford in 1808 at the house of John Adams, for which he received one month. Like his three fellows, however, Spinnels was acquitted in 1812. *B.C.*, 20 Jan. 1803; *S.W.J.*, 21 March 1808, 15 June, 20 July 1812.
[54] *S.W.J.*, 21 March 1808.
[55] H.O. 42/95, Divett to Hawkesbury, 22 July 1808; Divett, Price and Jackson to Jones and Bush, 25 July 1808.
[56] *B.J.*, 17 Oct. 1808.

have declined of its own accord. Threats and incendiarism had broken the nerve of the Trowbridge clothiers but the Bradford on Avon shearmen had been unable to force Jones to take down his gig mill and the Warminster shearmen had failed to stop Warren and Wansey. Left to themselves the conflicts would eventually have been settled, some *modus vivendi* reached which would have depended upon the strength of the shearmen relative to their employers. This is what occurred elsewhere, where the government was not tempted to intervene. However, the scale of the outbreaks of violence in Wiltshire greatly alarmed a government fearful of Jacobinal conspiracies. Troops were dispatched to the area in considerable numbers. Shortly after 26 July, the principal manufacturing towns of west Wiltshire and Somerset were accommodating eleven troops of cavalry while seven more troops which could not be quartered there were stationed around Bristol as reinforcements. In addition, two companies of infantry were guarding mills. These were supplemented shortly afterwards by 'A Body of Infantry'.[57] Many manufacturers using machinery saw the troops as the final barrier before anarchy and as the only means of coercing their employees to work. William Henry and George Sheppard of Frome wrote to Pelham of a rumoured withdrawal of the troop of dragoons from the town in August: 'The principal mills which have hitherto been protected by the cavalry and thereby become odious to the disaffected must inevitably be burnt, Order will never be restored nor will the people return to their work.'[58] The military were only part of the government's response, however. Fears that the Wiltshire rioters might have ambitions beyond machine breaking prompted the Secretary of State also to send Read to Wiltshire to investigate the trouble. His influence led to a considerable change in the attitude of the local authorities to the shearmen.

Until Read's arrival, the local authorities had made little headway in putting an end to the disorders. They had indeed tried to implement the advice which came from the Home Office, best summarised in a letter from Pelham to Matthew Davies.

I should advise the magistrates in the first place to appoint to be special constables as large a number as circumstances will allow of the most trustworthy persons . . . and secondly, to publish Resolutions expressing the determination to bring to speedy justice all those who are concerned in the outrages

[57] H.O. 42/65, Brownrigg to King, 26 July 1802, King to Jones, July 1802; H.O. 50/392, Brownrigg to King, 29 July 1802; W.O. 4/186, 187.
[58] H.O. 42/66, W. H. and G. Sheppard to Pelham, 5 Aug. 1802.

that have been committed, and thirdly to offer on the part of the county or hundred a handsome reward for the discovery of the offenders.[59]

Resolutions and rewards were duly published and offered, though finding people willing to be special constables was not easy. Jones wrote 'Many persons have refused to be sworn constables' and asked if an example might be made of them to 'encourage' the others.[60] Nevertheless, results were not encouraging. Thomas Helliker had been arrested and Jones had discovered the existence of the Trowbridge shearmen's committee before Read arrived but these were the only definite results.[61]

The Home Office and Read were not quite attuned to the situation in expecting more. They found it hard to accept that the woollen community was tightly-knit, that the perpetrators of the outrages were condoned by the great majority and that the magistracy, most of them engaged in the woollen industry and all of them members of the local community, might think twice about unleashing the full rigour of the law on their workmen, knowing where such action would rebound. Colonel Ogle, a die-hard who had seen 'active service' as a High Constable and magistrate in Ireland during the Rebellion, was 'sorry to observe the *supineness* of any well-disposed subject but particularly that of the magistracy, in short some in this neighbourhood [Chippenham–Melksham] have refused to act'. Ogle wanted more 'coercive' measures.[62] John Jones was certainly not 'supine' – indeed Pelham praised his 'laudable activity'[63] – but many justices did refuse to take an active part against the shearmen. Some clearly were concerned lest their firms incurred the wrath of the militant shearmen[64] but others clearly felt sympathy for the men, sharing their suspicion of the innovators and their machinery. Read, on the other hand, saw the problem solely in terms of law and order.

Pelham wrote to Jones that the disorders 'can only be effectively crushed by an open manifestation of the determined resolution of the civil power to apprehend and prosecute offenders'. The authorities' problem, however, was lack of evidence. Jones hoped that by seizing

[59] H.O. 43/13, Pelham to Jones, 27 July 1802; H.O. 42/65, Brownrigg to King, 26 July 1802; H.O. 42/66, Pelham to Pembroke, 3 Aug. 1802; H.O. 43/13, Pelham to Davies, 18 June 1802.
[60] H.O. 42/66, Jones to Pelham, 1 Aug. 1802.
[61] H.O. 42/66, Jones to Pelham, 3 Aug. 1802; H.O. 42/65, Jones to Pelham, 20 July 1802.
[62] H.O. 42/66, Ogle to Jones, 30 July 1802.
[63] H.O. 43/13, Pelham to Jones, 21 July 1802.
[64] H.O. 43/13, Pelham to Hughes, 24 June 1802; H.O. 42/65, Jones to Pelham, 29 July 1802.

the Trowbridge committee he might find some. Spencer Perceval from the Law Office advised, however,

it does not appear to me that [the outrages] are sufficiently connected by evidence as yet with the committee as justify a seizure of the committee and its papers. Such a measure would only be justified by what was found and it is most probable that they are too cunning to keep any papers but such as would be referable to little more than a friendly society. The misery and difficulty in all these cases is the want of legal evidence.

Pelham directed that the justices should meet regularly 'for the purpose of taking examinations and receiving information'. The trouble was that no one would willingly give evidence, not even when the rewards were 'of such a magnitude as shall enable the person discovering to support himself in any other part of the Kingdom distant from Wiltshire'. Perceval likewise believed evidence would only come 'by offers of reward and assurances of protection ... The protection is more difficult to be effected than the reward ... because [of] the peril the informer is subjected to.' Nor did it prove possible to get information from 'spies and scouts'. While Pelham might think it advisable 'to employ some trustworthy persons to act as spies and if possible to mix with and get into the confidence of the persons concerned in these proceedings', such proved impracticable.[65] The techniques employed against Jacobinal clubs and revolutionary societies could not succeed in this case, nor in the Luddite period in Yorkshire either. No shearman could be persuaded to turn spy and spies who could shear cloth proved impossible to find.

Read decided to break down the wall of silence by ignoring legal niceties. He described his methods thus:

Two or more justices meet daily at one or other of the manufacturing towns, and as the Combination Acts afford a very convenient pretext for summoning and examining upon oath any suspected persons, I have continually some before them. It answers the double purpose of keeping the magistrates at their post and of alarming the disaffected.[66]

Those who would not give information, or who would not provide the right information, were thrown into gaol and given a chance to change their minds. One such was Thomas Bailey, a Trowbridge shearman. Bailey was accused of having been sent by the shearmen to ask his master, Jonathon Symes, 'what he meant to do in the business as to

[65] H.O. 43/13, Pelham to Jones, 21, 27 July, Pelham to Croome, 1 Oct. 1802; H.O. 49/5, King to White, 21 July 1802; H.O. 48/11, memorandum from Perceval, 22 July 1802.
[66] H.O. 42/66, Read to King, 13 Sept. 1802.

acceding or not to the shearmen's terms of working; and upon the manufacturer saying he should do as other employers did, he desired him to be cool and take care what he said as he had taken an oath to tell the committee everything he said'. Bailey cracked and told Read about the Trowbridge committee, where it met and by whom the oath had been administered to him. On his evidence James May, the secretary, and four other members of the committee were immediately arrested and remanded in prison for administering illegal oaths.[67] Further, Read obtained the testimony of Daniel Baker, the 'loyal' Warminster shearman, against Samuel Baker who was on this evidence imprisoned, accused of being one of those involved in the attack on Staverton on 14 July. A local newspaper hoped these arrests had broken the shearmen's combination but clearly they did not.[68] Read did obtain one conviction on 30 August of a Warminster shearman for disbursing strike pay and by 1 September he had imprisoned four men under the Combination Acts, together with two men for refusing to give testimony. This aggressive use of the Combination Acts was in marked contrast to the reluctance of the clothiers to use the statutes and suggests that, while recent historians have tended to assume that they were a dead letter, they could have proved extremely coercive had they been widely implemented in such a way. 'I am bringing forward as many cases as I can under the Combination Acts, and by forcing some to give evidence against others I hope to provoke quarrels amongst them and by that means to be able to bring some of their deeds to light.'[69]

All the Trowbridge committee produced identical defences against Bailey's charges, claiming that they had all been in The New Cross Keys public house by chance, having a drink during one of their meal breaks. They claimed they had fallen to discussing the problem of truck since 'for many years past it has been found very inconvenient to the cloth workers to be paid their wages in goods . . . which some of the master clothiers have frequently insisted upon'. It had become the practice of the shearmen to 'censure' anyone who accepted truck 'for setting what was considered a bad example'. Bailey, suspected of this, was called into the room and 'admitted he had been paid his wages in goods, but said he should not do so again'. To show he meant it, Bailey then voluntarily picked up a bible 'which was in the said room

[67] H.O. 42/66, Read to Pelham, 9, 10 Aug. 1802.
[68] *S.W.J.*, 16 Aug. 1802.
[69] *B.J.*, 16 Sept. 1802; H.O. 42/66, Read to Pelham, 1 Sept. 1802. On the Combination Acts see, for example, Hunt, *British Labour History*, p. 199: 'The Combination Acts, in short, were of little significance.'

accidentally' and swore on it.[70] Five other members of the Trowbridge committee who were also charged with assisting May and the others in administering an illegal oath to Bailey made similar affidavits. This second group, which included William May and James Griffin, were clearly out on bail for William May was at large in Trowbridge in September and he was in Leeds soliciting funds to help pay Mr Wilmott, the shearmen's solicitor, in early December 1802.[71] The five principal accused, James May, the secretary, George Marks, John Hilliker (the older brother of Thomas Helliker), Samuel Ferris and Philip Edwards were, however, denied bail. In late November they brought an action for their release before the King's Bench on the grounds of an insufficiency of evidence against them and on a legal technicality. They rehearsed their defence against Bailey's accusations, but also they claimed that the act under which Read had charged them, 37 George III c. 123, made it a felony to administer oaths only where the object of the association was to stir mutiny or sedition, which did not apply in this case. There was in fact some doubt in the court's mind on this but Lord Ellenborough believed that the law was open to a wider interpretation and the shearmen's application ultimately failed.[72]

The prisoners on remand were given plenty of time to cool their heels. The Trowbridge shearmen were not tried until 17 March 1803, seven months all but a week in prison and the Warminster men tried in January had probably been in gaol since September.[73] The experience was not pleasant. 'Your Uncle James has been used very bad since he have been in gaol', Phoebe Warren wrote about James May to her son, Joseph Warren, who had fled to Yorkshire.[74] Hopes that a taste of prison would break the shearmen's confidence and loosen their tongues, however, were disappointed. The gaoler at Salisbury thought Samuel Ferris would impeach, 'which when his present expectation of being bailed becomes disappointed he may be yet disposed to do', but Read's hopes were not fulfilled, nor was his prediction that 'much advantage may be derived' from the imprisonment of Thomas

---

[70] K.B. 1/31/Pt 2, the King v James May, Philip Edwards, and others. The lack of further evidence concerned the Law Officers, but they were consoled by the thought that any witnesses for the defence 'must necessarily appear in the nature of accomplices as having been there'. H.O. 49/5, King to White, 1 Jan. 1803.

[71] H.O. 42/66, Read to King, 3 Oct., May to Tucker, 16 Dec. 1802.

[72] K.B. 1/31/Pt 2; *The English Reports*, Vol. cii, King's Bench Division, xxxi (1910), pp. 557–61, ref. 102 ER 557.

[73] *S.W.J.*, 14 March 1803, 4 Jan. 1803.

[74] H.O. 42/66, Read to King, 3 Oct. 1802, enclosure.

Helliker.[75] The youth refused to give any evidence about his colleagues, maintaining his innocence throughout. Local tradition says
that Helliker was indeed innocent, but, even were this so, the lad must
have known something of material interest to Read.[76]

Local tradition may well be correct. As an eighteen-year-old apprentice it is unlikely that he would have been allowed fully into the
shearmen's counsels or permitted to take part in attacks on mills. In
addition, serious doubts must be raised of Helliker's guilt by two
papers which exist in the King's Bench. One is a signed draft deposition of Joseph Warren, in which Warren claimed that at 10.30 p.m. on
the night Littleton was burned he had met Helliker outside the house
of John Walter where Warren had been visiting. Helliker was very
drunk and Warren helped him into the Walters' kitchen, locked the
front door and took the key upstairs, putting it under the door of the
room where Walter and his wife were sleeping. He and Helliker had
slept in the kitchen until 5 a.m. when he retrieved the key and let
Helliker out to work. He believed it impossible for Helliker to have left
during the night, since he did not know where the key had been put.[77]
This may not have been a very genuine alibi. Warren and Helliker were
said by Read to be great friends and both worked for Naish at Trowbridge. Ann Waller, or Walter, was Warren's sweetheart, doubtless
the reason for his visit and her parents may have been prepared to
support a claim which also gave Warren an alibi. Warren made his
statement shortly after the arrest of Helliker on 3 August. When Naish
heard about it, he 'interviewed' Warren about his claim. The following
morning Warren disappeared, to turn up in Leeds in September. Read,
who himself wished to interview Warren, believed that the Trowbridge shearmen had sent him away with a reference and some money
'for fear of discoveries' for Read would undoubtedly have locked him
up. Three letters sent to Warren, via George Palmer, were intercepted
at Leeds. One from Ann Waller said: 'I know that you cannot come to
me yet unless you do mean to involve yourself in trouble and put it out
of your power to do any good for your friend.' She urged him to take
care of his money, 'for you will not be sure to have work till the time
you must come home which will not be till March next'. That was the

---

[75] H.O. 42/66, Read to King, 18 Oct. 1802, Read to Pelham, 5 Aug. 1802.
[76] The story of Thomas Helliker, the 'martyr of Trowbridge', entered the folk heritage of
nineteenth-century west Wiltshire and is still perpetuated today. Belief in Helliker's
innocence was and is general, and has been reinforced by rumours of a posthumous
Royal pardon said to have been in the Helliker family in the early twentieth century.
See *Labour Weekly*, 26 April 1985.
[77] K.B. 1/31/Pt 2.

date of the assizes and Helliker's trial. William May, his uncle, wrote, 'you must not come here by no means. There was a report that you were seen at Beckington, but I knew better but let it go, so much the better that they are ignorant.'[78] Warren never turned up for Helliker's trial.

The other paper in the King's Bench which is of significance is the draft information of John Pearce, one of Heath's assistants at Littleton, which in certain crucial points disagrees markedly with Heath's version of the shearmen's attack. At Helliker's trial, Heath stood by his original statement that Helliker was the second man to enter the room, that his face was blacked and that he carried a pistol with which he had threatened those present. On cross-examination he claimed that Helliker's face was not so black as to be unrecognisable and that, while he had at one time claimed not to recognise Helliker, he had done so 'from a dread that his life was in danger if it had been understood that he could convict him'.[79] Pearce's draft deposition, however, made no mention of the second man and claimed that only one man, the 'short' man who had entered the room first, had carried a pistol and that the rest had been armed only with bayonets fixed on poles. Heath claimed the first man had a musket, Helliker a pistol and the rest muskets, pistols and bayonets. Further, Pearce stated that 'There was only one man with his face blacked' while the others had their jackets and great coats pulled up to hide their faces. Most significant of all, however, are the concluding lines of Pearce's deposition. 'Mr. Heath never looked up the whole time the men were present but kept his hat on his face looking to the ground, this was the whole time after the first man appeared.'[80] Yet twelve days later Heath was able positively to identify Helliker. Pressure from Naish, his employer, who was clearly convinced of Helliker's complicity and the prospect of a £500 reward may have helped Heath make up his mind. His testimony sent Helliker to the gallows. Neither Pearce nor Goodship were called at Helliker's trial.

Helliker was certainly seen as a martyr by the woollen workers who took his body from the authorities after the hanging at Salisbury, placed it on a cart and pulled it in procession back to Trowbridge. There it was said that girls in white dresses led thousands of mourners in accompanying the body to the parish church where they forced the curate to bury Helliker in the churchyard with full rites. There his body

---

[78] H.O. 42/66, Read to King, 3 Oct. 1802, and enclosures.
[79] *S.W.J.*, 14 March 1803; H.O. 42/66, information of Ralph Heath, 6 Aug. 1802.
[80] K.B. 1/31/Pt 2.

still lies, commemorated by a fine tombstone 'erected by the cloth making factories of the Counties of York, Wilts and Somerset'. His mother received an allowance from the Institution.[81]

The shearman on whose evidence the Trowbridge committee had been put in prison, Thomas Bailey, also found himself in gaol until the assizes in March 1803. Read felt it safest to send him to Marlborough bridewell 'for the protection of his person so that may be forthcoming when wanted'[82] for Bailey was the only prosecution witness. Somehow, however, pressures were brought to bear upon him by the time of the trial.

> Bailey had twice before positively sworn to and very frequently repeated to his master and others the form of the oath, yet on his examination in court, his recollection failed him and he could not repeat it again. And on account of the oath not being proved ... the prisoners were acquitted. Thus through the sudden failure of the memory of one of their comrades have these men escaped the punishment their improper conduct deserves.[83]

While Read pursued his single-minded course, however, and while the Home Office worried that the business would drag on, Pelham was not going to be drawn into more wholesale repression. He declined Ogle's offer of help, writing that 'it might be prudent to curb rather than stimulate his activity'.[84] After consultations with the Law Office, who believed the evidence too thin, he advised that a master shearman named William Brice, who, wrote Jones, 'had made it a practise to utter very strong declarations against me', should be cautioned but no further action should be taken.[85] He recommended, however, that when it was possible to arrest any individual for a part in an outrage, he should be 'publicly sent to the county gaol under a sufficient military escort'. It was important to make an example of someone, for this, it was hoped, would bring a return of public tranquillity.[86] It was unfortunate for Thomas Helliker that he was to be the scapegoat which the government wanted.

Incendiarism and industrial violence in the West of England were

---

[81] Ponting, *Woollen Industry*, p. 107; B.P.P., 1806, Vol. 3, p. 355; Hammonds, *Skilled Labourer*, p. 143, fn. 181, mistakenly refer to Mrs Helliker as Thomas' widow. Rumours that the Wiltshire shearmen intended to rescue Helliker before his execution sent troops immediately to Salisbury. H.O. 51/154, King to Brownrigg, 14 March 1803.
[82] H.O. 42/66, Read to Pelham, 10 Aug. 1802.
[83] B.C., 10 March 1803.
[84] H.O. 42/66, King to Read, 14 Sept. 1802; Pelham to Pembroke, 9 Aug. 1802.
[85] H.O. 42/70, Jones to King, 2 Jan. 1803; H.O. 48/12, pp. 23, 25, 27, 29; H.O. 43/13, King to Jones, 9 March 1803. Brice offered to give £5 for Jones' heart and £6 for his head 'to set in my garden to frighten the birds'.
[86] H.O. 42/65, Pelham to Jones, July 1802.

not simply the products of despair nor the wild anarchy of 'lawless banditti'.[87] This is not to say that distress was non-existent nor that the industrial pressures on the shearmen were as Read wrote 'in a great measure imaginary'.[88] The years from 1795 to 1801 were marked with rapidly rising food prices which generated acute distress nationally. Even with the Peace of Amiens grain prices decreased only slowly. More significantly, the woollen industry, subject to fairly violent fluctuations of market during the Revolutionary War, slumped badly with the Peace.[89] It had been reported in September 1801 that 'the woollen manufactures are in a very depressed state all over the kingdom'.[90] Thereafter the contraction of trade multiplied distress. Even the few gig mills set up before 1802 had caused some structural unemployment. 'If you persist in the plan you have adopted, others will certainly follow which will distress many poor families', gig mill users were warned in 1799, and Tugwell was told in 1802, 'You will go to Hell for starveing the Poor.' Demobilised soldiers came home to find no work and to swell the ranks of the partially employed. William Lambeth, a Stroud cloth dresser about thirty years old, told the 1803 Committee, 'I have been a soldier and when Peace was then I was discharged: I went home and could get no work: I was a soldier five years.'[91] Benjamin Hobhouse received a letter from 'a souldier returned to his wife and weeping orphans':

We hope [you] will intercede for us so that we may have labour to earn our daily bread some of us may perhaps more or less servd in his Majesty's survice some six Eight or ten years, in Defence of him and his Country now the contending Nations are at Peace with each other we are send home to starve ... we know that it have been mentioned to our great men and Ministers by them that have Factorys how many poor they employ forgetting at the same time how many more they would employ were they to have it done by hand ... the Poor house we find full of great lurking boys ... the burning of Factorys or setting fire to property of People we know is not right but Starvation forces Nature to do that which he would not nor would it reach his Thoughts had he sufficient Employ we have tried every Effort to live by Pawning our Cloaths and Chattles so we are now on the brink for the last struggle.[92]

We must beware, however, of seeing the industrial violence of 1802, or indeed of the years from 1796 to 1808, in purely economistic terms of

[87] H.O. 42/65, Pembroke to Pelham, 7 Aug. 1802.
[88] H.O. 42/65, Read to Pelham, 5 Sept. 1802.
[89] B.P.P., 1802/3, Vol. 7, p. 213; Mann, *Cloth Industry*, pp. 138–9.
[90] B.C., 17 Sept. 1801.
[91] B.P.P., 1802/3, Vol. 7, p. 171.
[92] H.O. 42/65, 'A souldier' to Hobhouse, July 1802.

'distress'. Shearmen were not being laid off wholesale because of machinery in 1802 nor was their response a blind reaction to the fact of displacement by machines. At most there were only around a dozen gig mills at work in Wiltshire and Somerset by the late summer of 1802. It was not the unemployed Twerton cloth workers who marched into the village 'to hang up Bamford . . . and burn down his works' in 1797 nor local residents who burned Newton's mill at Clifford in 1802, although they would not allow it to be saved, but rather the shearmen from the neighbouring cloth finishing centres whose security and livelihoods these isolated mills were threatening. The outrages were calculated and deliberate, 'carefully controlled within limits imposed by the moral culture of the working community'.[93] Victims of industrial violence were not chosen at random. They and their property were attacked because, with their machines, they were usurping the shearmen's trade and status and attempting to destroy their customs and their community. Indeed, to the shearmen it was these men who were engaging in immoral and illegal practices.[94] Nor, as has been shown, did 'the burning of Factorys or the setting fire to property of People' occur in isolation. In Wiltshire it was clearly very much a part of an industrial struggle, supplementing and enforcing the more 'orthodox' sanction of the strike, always directed to a specific end.

Threatening letters and incendiarism were not confined to Wiltshire and Somerset. Even in Leeds, where the croppers were most numerous, best organised and consequently the most powerful of all cloth workers, industrial violence was several times employed against machinery. In 1799 'a most daring and outrageous riot' took place 'and a mill used for the raising of cloth by Messrs. Johnson of Holbeck was pulled down and totally destroyed'.[95] This may have been the gig mill referred to in the Privy Council paper on combinations.

One house actually erected a gig mill, the partners of which were insulted and reviled by the workmen whenever they appeared in public. Their lives and property were threatened, their servants abused, and still persevering to work their machine – a numerous mob took advantage of a dark night to assemble and destroyed the work completely and though many hundred people were present both as assistants and spectators – though very great rewards were offered by Government and by the magistrates here – the fact could not be

[93] Thompson, *The Making*, p. 563.
[94] Note the threatening letter to 'Gentlemen' sent in 1799 (see above, p. 153), *'a honest man* has no need to arm himself against his fellow citizens' (my italics).
[95] *L.M.,* 25 Nov. 1799.

brought home to any *one* individual: other machines which another house had in contemplation to set up, were seized by a mob of women and children and actually burnt in the streets without the possibility of detecting the instigators.[96]

In 1801 Gott was intimidated into taking down a gig mill he had recently set up[97] and in February 1803 the *Leeds Mercury* reported that cloths had been maliciously cut up in the tenter grounds and many 'inflammatory sentences inscribed against the doors and walls in this town', advancing 'villainous, horrid and murderous ideas'. 'It is not difficult to determine from what quarter both proceed', the *Mercury* continued, hopefully asserting 'that by far the major part of the cloth workers hold all such scandalous practices in the utmost destestation'.[98] In November 1803 cloths in a tenter ground at Wakefield were cut up and destroyed. Again the croppers were blamed.[99] At some point during 1803, Messrs. Horsfall, probably the same Horsfall to die a victim of the Yorkshire Luddites nine years later, lost their mill in mysterious circumstances, though suspicions pointed towards the croppers as Horsfalls 'use the same kind of obnoxious machinery', namely gig mills and shearing frames. And in December 1804, Bradley mills near Huddersfield, the property of T. and L. Atkinson, the prominent and successful opponents of the local croppers and long-term gig mill operators, were burned down. The Royal Exchange Insurance Company received a letter postmarked Huddersfield on 25 September 1805, warning:

> Gentlemen Directors,
> At a general but private meeting of the Chairmen of all the committees of cloth workers in this county, it was ordered to desire you (for your own profit), not to insure any factory where machinery was in belonging the cloth workers. For it was ordered again to petition Parliament for our rights; and if they will not grant us them by stopping the machinery belong us, we are determined to grant them ourselves but does not wish you to be any loser thereby. By order of the cloth workers. N.B. Only remember Bradley mill in this county which did not do 1/6th of what was wished for.[100]

As in the West of England, therefore, the highly organised and unionised Yorkshire croppers were perfectly willing to utilise violent sanctions against their employers.

[96] P.C. 1/43/A152, Observations respecting combinations.
[97] See above, p. 130.   [98] *L.M.*, 12 Feb. 1803.
[99] *L.M.*, 5 Nov. 1803.   [100] *B.P.P.*, 1806, Vol. 3, pp. 312–13.

It is worth comparing the experience in Wiltshire and Yorkshire with that in Gloucestershire. The failure of the Gloucestershire shearmen, concentrating entirely upon legal and peaceful methods, to mount an effective resistance to the use of gig mills on fine cloth in 1794 irredeemably weakened their position. Even the early introduction of the shearing frames into the county from late 1799 onwards failed to stimulate much resistance. The Woodchester firm of Paul and Nathaniel Wathen were pioneers in the use of the frames and they experienced some labour problems in this connection in January 1800. On the night of the 13th 'some evil disposed person' cut up and destroyed three cloths belonging to the firm which were in the rack grounds of George Hawker at Rodborough and later the same night destroyed nine more cloths in Wathens' own grounds at Woodchester. Wathens offered a reward of £100 for information leading to the conviction of the culprits, indicating the seriousness with which they viewed the attack.[101] On 23 January, the Gloucestershire clothiers met at The Fleece, Rodborough, to discuss the trouble and offered an additional 500 guineas reward. They did, however, take a conciliatory line towards the shearmen who were clearly suspected of the outrage.

And at the same time that we are determined to oppose and suppress every illegal proceeding, we are desirous that no real cause of injury should happen to the working people; and it is therefore recommended to such manufacturers as may adopt the use of shearing machines to do it in such a manner as not to deprive any of their shearmen of Employ.[102]

Joseph Stephens was eventually captured and tried at the summer assizes for the crime. He was found guilty and hanged. Before his execution, he expressed due contrition and 'frequently expressed hopes that his shop mates would be warned against any attempt to revenge his deserved punishment'.[103] There appears to have been no further manifestation of antipathy towards the frames in 1800 or in 1801 so it is possible that the clothiers' desire for moderation was observed.[104] Wathens continued to use their shearing frames for in 1801 Warner saw them at work at Woodchester and believed that Wathen had actually invented them.[105] In September or October 1802,

---

[101] *G.J.*, 20 Jan. 1800.   [102] *G.J.*, 27 Jan. 1800.   [103] *G.J.*, 4, 18 Aug. 1800.
[104] There was, however, considerable friction between the clothiers' volunteer forces and the food rioters who stopped barges containing wheat on the canal in the food riots of July 1800. *G.J.*, 7 July 1800.
[105] R. Warner, *Excursions from Bath* (Bath, 1801), p. 323. The description indicates that it was Harmer's machine.

however, the firm once more became the object of the shearmen's resentment, receiving the following threatening letter:

Paul Wathen you Hare a Damd in Fernald Scoundrel and We will Teack yuir Damd Life from you if Dont teack care of yuirself. And We Hear in Formd that you got Shear in mee sheens and if you Dont pull them Down in a Forght Nights Time Wee will pull them Down for you Wee will you damd infernald Dog. And Bee four Almighty God We will pull down all the Mills that heave Heaney Shearin me Shens in Wee will cut out Hall your Damd Hearts as do Ceep them and Wee will meack the rest Heat them or els Wee will searve them the seam.
Thear Read this and Weep do you For your Time is but shourt Hear your Damd Villian Raskell.[106]

These threats were not made good, though in February 1805 Thomas Croome, a Stroud magistrate, wrote to Hawkesbury of the malicious destruction of three cloths in the tenter grounds belonging to Cooper, Wathen and Co. at King's Stanley.

The mills and works of Messrs. Cooper, Wathen and Co., are very extensive, and like all other manufacturers they are in the habit of using those machines which the Ingenuity of Mechanics has produced to save manual labour – the Ignorance of the workmen had Induced them to consider the introduction of such machinery as prejudicial to their interest, and they have been guilty of repeated acts of malicious mischief and of sending anonymous letters of a threatening and diabolical tendency to the principal manufacturers. Among other methods of showing their mischievous disposition, they have frequently resorted to that of cutting the cloths in the tenters during the Night and notwithstanding an Offender was detected and punished with death . . . a few years back, yet that example had its effect only for a short period.[107]

'Acts of mischief', however, never escalated into outrages comparable to those in Wiltshire or even in Yorkshire and the Gloucestershire clothiers, proceeding cautiously, continued to introduce shearing frames. Both William Lambeth and William Barnard stated in 1803 that the machine had put many Gloucestershire shearmen out of work. Lambeth complained that, on returning home, he could get no work 'by reason of so many machines, the shearing frames and gigs, taking entirely all the work'.[108] Frames appeared, usually in small numbers, in many mills offered for sale or let from 1803 onwards. Thus in 1806

---

[106] Anon. to Messrs Paul and Nathaniel Wathen, Oct. 1802, reprinted in D. M. Hunter, *The West of England Woollen Industry under Protection and Free Trade* (Cassell, 1910), p. 21.

[107] H.O. 42/82, Croome to Hawkesbury, 13 Feb. 1805.

[108] *B.P.P.*, 1802/3, Vol. 7, pp. 165, 170–1, 255.

Jenners mill at Pitchcombe included three frames while the mill of the late Thomas Went at Uley contained an unspecified number. A mill at Wallbridge housed three of Harmer's frames in 1807 while Harmer's frames were offered with mills at Alderley and Horsley the following year. By 1814 Stonehouse mill contained fifteen frames[109] and thereafter frames were almost commonplace in Gloucestershire. Again, there appears to have been no protest from the shearmen. Having failed to stem the early trickle of machinery, the Gloucestershire shearmen found themselves unable to prevent it becoming a torrent as their employers, with consumate skill, chose to open the floodgates by degrees and not in a rush. Here, then, we can see the fruits of what Thomis labels 'the labour approach'. Constitutional methods, petitions and attempts at negotiation proved impotent unless supported by direct pressure.

For a general uprising against machinery the toll of damage in the Wiltshire Outrages was unspectacular. Only three mills were destroyed – Clifford, Littleton and Naish's workshops in Trowbridge – while at least six ricks, one barn, two dwelling houses, one stable, several outhouses and one dog kennel were burned down, trees were cut down, numerous windows broken and much general property damaged. This indicates not only that gig mills were both few and, after July, too well guarded; it also shows that the Wiltshire shearmen's aim was of success achieved by limited use of force. Actual attempts to destroy the machinery and the mills which housed them were very much a last resort. Thus the outrages must be seen in terms of a mounting level of industrial intimidation rather than as an out-and-out struggle of man against machine as witnessed in Yorkshire in 1812. 'Great Enoch' was not prominent in Wiltshire, nor in Yorkshire in the earlier period, and violence and outrages were far more intermittent and discriminatingly applied than in 1812 because in 1802 the cloth dressers had more options left open. Until 1809 hopes could be raised that salvation might be at hand in the protective legislation which the cloth workers tried so hard to keep in force. Thereafter, however, with no external authority to appeal to, the struggle had to be won on the local stage alone.

The violence directed at property was not matched by violence against the person. Certainly innovators received many threats to their lives in the form of anonymous letters. Mr Bell was warned in 1799, 'It is no use to destroy the Factorys But put you Damd Villions to

---

[109] *G.J.*, 7 July, 29 Dec. 1806, 9 March 1807, 16, 23 May 1808, 14 March 1814.

Death.'[110] And an inflammatory paper stuck up at Freshford in January 1803 urged all shearmen to procure arms:

As it is requested that if government gives the business unfavourable to the shearmen, it is the determination of the shearmen to do the business by force of arms . . . and destroy all clothiers that encourage such machinery likewise their families . . . Upon them and cut them up like Chaff for they have oppressed us long enough.[111]

For all their blood-thirsty rhetoric, however, the shearmen recognised that actual attacks on employers would rapidly prove counter-productive. Intimidating a clothier into abandoning the use of the gig mill was one thing. Physical attacks which caused him to abandon the trade altogether was another. Besides, public sympathy would be forfeit by such an escalation. Certainly shots were fired into the homes of two clothiers, Wansey and Stancomb, but there is no indication that murder was the aim. The same is probably true of the shots fired into the houses of the three blacklegging Warminster shearmen, though blacklegs were certainly more likely to be the victims of physical violence than employers.[112] However, as in Yorkshire in 1812, some shearmen were prepared to resort to murder. When all threats failed to frighten him and all attacks on his mill had been beaten off, William Horsfall, owner of Ottiwells mill, was shot when out riding in April 1812. A similar attempt was made on the life of William Cartwright, owner of Rawfolds mill.[113] In the same way, in January 1808 there was a deliberate attempt to murder Jones, the Wiltshire shearmen's most implacable adversary. Owner of Staverton mill and the most active local magistrate, Jones was also chairman of the combined committee of the Gloucestershire, Somerset and Wiltshire clothiers which in 1808 had so nearly achieved its object in securing the repeal of the protective legislation concerning the trade. He could well have seemed a key figure in the shearmen's miseries. He had been threatened before. He told the 1803 Committee that he knew of 'four men now at large who have sworn to put me to death'.[114] The attack in 1808 does not appear to have been a freelance affair but a planned operation, the product of years of frustration. Before this, however, there are few signs that the cloth dressers were prepared to resort to murder to win their way. This, indeed, was in keeping with what was the essentially low-key nature of violence in this earlier period.

---

[110] *London Gazette*, 1799, p. 507 (May 1799).
[111] *S.W.J.*, 7 Feb. 1803.   [112] *B.J.*, 26 July 1802.
[113] Thompson, *The Making*, pp. 624–5.   [114] *B.P.P.*, 1802/3, Vol. 7, p. 347.

Details about the organisation of, and the numbers and personnel involved in, the outrages variously committed between 1799 and 1808 are scant. The authorities tried various methods to induce people with information to come forward but they met with a wall of silence. Thomas Helliker, the only cloth worker tried and found guilty of participating in an outrage, was taken up and hanged solely on the evidence of Ralph Heath, the mill's manager. Consequently the authorities only heard vague reports of 'a considerable armed body', 'a considerable number of people', 'a numerous mob' or 'a body of armed men'.[115] The organisation and tactical skill of the depredators led some contemporaries to assume that their leaders had military experience, views enhanced by reports of their armaments, 'Musquets, Pistols, Swords, Bayonets and other offensive weapons'.[116] 'It is not an assembly of the common Mob', wrote John Jones' father, 'but a body of armed, regulated and systematic people, composed principally of militia men and marines.'[117] Jones himself believed cloth workers had obtained their arms and training as members of the associated corps 'who originally having purchased their musquets still retain them'.[118] The handbill found at Freshford which called on all shearmen having arms to meet 'and mutually agree to be commanded by officers appointed by the majority of 13 of the oldest soldiers or engineers' likewise suggested an ex-military presence among the shearmen.[119] Mann indeed believes that demobilised soldier shearmen 'with their military experience behind them were probably the instigators of most of the attacks'.[120] In fact, evidence suggesting that the movement was dominated by ex-soldiers is difficult to substantiate. While such men, 'sent home to starve', were certainly disgruntled, we must remember that the cloth dressers as a body bitterly resented machinery. Eighteenth-century authorities, when faced with prolonged disorder, often tended to equate organised and effective action with military training and to hold ex-soldiers and militiamen responsible both for the crowd's actions and indeed for their initiation. Such was the case in the food riots in the region in 1766.[121] Certainly many members of the crowd would have had army or militia experience. However, a military career was no substitute for local knowledge nor did it automatically

[115] See, for example, H.O. 42/65, Jones to Pelham, 18, 29 July 1802.
[116] H.O. 42/65, Resolutions of the magistrates of Wiltshire, 24 July 1802.
[117] H.O. 42/65, J. Jones, Sen., to King, 26 July 1802.
[118] H.O. 42/65, Jones to Pelham, 18 July 1802.
[119] *S.W.J.*, 7 Feb. 1803; Mann, *Cloth Industry*, p. 149, fn. 4.
[120] Mann, *Cloth Industry*, p. 142.
[121] See Randall, 'Labour and the industrial revolution', pp. 137–42, 154–8.

make one a leader of men. Organisation, secrecy and careful regulation characterised many disturbances, consumer as well as industrial, in this period and the cloth dressers had always been effective in maintaining what Fitzwilliam referred to as the croppers' 'system of terror' to maintain their union's security.[122]

There is, moreover, limited but persistent evidence to suggest that there were inter-parochial union links behind the more spectacular displays of violence. The assembly of workmen who fired shots into Wansey's house were said to have included many from Trowbridge, Westbury and other towns as well as the local Warminster men. There is also reason to believe that the two attacks on Staverton were joint enterprises of the workers of the region. There were reports of the Trowbridge and Bradford on Avon shearmen meeting beforehand and Samuel Baker, the Warminster shearman, was supposed to have warned Daniel Baker on 18 July, two days after the first attack, 'We have been to Staverton and we are coming here next.' Further, Read was informed that the Trowbridge committee had always met 'on the same night when any violence has been done'.[123] And the attempted murder of Jones in 1808 was attributed to a decision of a meeting of Bradford on Avon shearmen.[124] While window breaking, rick burning, tree felling and the punishment of blacklegs were probably the work of local men, the cloth dressers of the region were combined in their efforts to pressurise the innovators into abandoning the use of machines which all knew would ultimately undermine their position everywhere.

The rioters were for the most part clearly cloth dressers although among those arrested for the disturbance in Bradford on Avon in January 1808 was a carpenter, Samuel Fussel, and one of the two men charged with the attempted murder of Jones was a slaymaker.[125] It is unlikely, however, that many people other than cloth dressers would have been admitted into the shearmen's counsels though we may note that sundry trades were later involved in Yorkshire Luddism.[126] Nevertheless, there are certain similarities. Thomis finds that the activist croppers in 1812 were young, in their late 'teens or early 'twenties.[127]

122 H.O. 42/66, Fitzwilliam to Pelham, 27 Sept. 1802.
123 H.O. 42/65, Jones to Pelham, 29 July 1802; Ponting, *Woollen Industry*, p. 76; H.O. 42/66, Read to Pelham, 10, 9 Aug. 1802.
124 *S.W.J.*, 10 May 1812.
125 *S.W.J.*, 21 March 1808, 10 May 1812.
126 Thompson, *The Making*, pp. 609–16. Thomis, *The Luddites*, pp. 109–10, dismisses such evidence, arguing that those not directly in conflict with the shearing frames could have had no interest in the struggle.
127 Thomis, *The Luddites*, p. 112.

Helliker was only eighteen years old when he was arrested. James May, secretary of the Trowbridge committee, was twenty-eight whilst committee members Samuel Ferris, George Marks, John Helliker and Philip Edwards were thirty-three, twenty-eight, thirty and twenty-four years old respectively. Samuel Baker, the Warminster shearman, was fifty years old but he was almost certainly exceptional.[128] Dodging dragoons around damp fields in the night was not the place for men of riper years.

Likewise, the Wiltshire shearmen, like the Yorkshire Luddites, enjoyed a wide measure of public support. Weavers, as we shall see, had their own reasons for distrusting the innovators while many master dressers and some small clothiers covertly and in some cases overtly supported their men.[129] John Anstie, a major apologist for machinery, admitted in 1803, 'there are a considerable number of persons of respectability in the three counties who . . . still continue to consider the introduction of machinery into the woollen trade as unfriendly to the general interest and peculiarly injurious to the poor'.[130] No one in Warminster 'would assist in any degree' to extinguish the fires which destroyed Warren's ricks and dog kennel while 'the populace would not permit' Newton's agents to save any part of his blazing mill at Beckington.[131] Nor would anyone come forward to give evidence against any shearman. It was a measure of the general hostility towards the innovating clothiers evinced by the woollen working community.

What, then, is it possible to conclude about outbreaks of industrial violence in the cloth finishing trade up to 1808? Primarily we must cease to view the depredators as 'industrial primitives'. The timing of the introduction of gig mills into major cloth finishing centres in Wiltshire in 1802 was unfortunate, coinciding as it did with a trade slump and the demobilisation of many woollen workers. However, while 'distress' was a factor in the outbreak of violence, the shearmen were not so near starvation as they sometimes claimed. Violence was the pre-emptive, calculated choice of a powerful labour elite, not the desperate last gasp of a demoralised trade. Violence was controlled and specifically directed against men who in the cloth dressers' eyes were engaging in immoral and illegal practices. The Wiltshire

---

[128] ASSI. 25/2/Pt 1, indictments.
[129] H.O. 42/66, Read to Pelham, 5 Sept. 1802.
[130] Anstie, *Observations on Machinery*, pp. 7–8.
[131] H.O. 42/65, Davies to Pelham, 15 June 1802, Jones to Pelham, 29 July 1802.

shearmen were pragmatists, not pyromaniacs, and the outrages must be seen in terms of a mounting level of industrial intimidation against key innovators, seeking to force them back into compliance with the established customs of the trade. If to achieve this it was necessary to fire a few ricks and barns, this was justified by the innovators' own disregard for customary negotiation and legitimated by an Act of Parliament which the courts, on dubious grounds, refused to enforce.

Direct action did not occur in isolation. It was very much part of an industrial struggle, supplementing and enforcing more 'orthodox' sanctions. The cloth dressers saw no division between a 'labour approach' and 'industrial sabotage'. Indeed, they made use of all aspects of Thomis' 'labour approach'. They used the courts, recognising that victory there could put them in an unassailable position. They were to fight their case, that regulatory legislation should be retained and indeed bolstered, with great skill and dignity before two Parliamentary Select Committees. They sought with some success to influence public opinion in their favour. They used the 'orthodox' (and illegal) industrial weapons of the strike and blacking the goods of obnoxious employers. These actions reflected the powerful trade union base the cloth dressers had developed. Yet, while strikes were effective against smaller employers, the weapon was inappropriate for tackling more powerful innovators who were prepared to throw down the gauntlet, to turn their mills into armed fortresses, to introduce gig mills and shearing frames and bid the shearmen defiance. Nor could negotiation and conciliation reconcile two such conflicting views of the rise of a machine economy. Therefore, the cloth dressers consciously and deliberately made use of industrial violence, initially in an attempt to frighten innovators into compliance or, when necessary, in an attempt to destroy the threatening machinery. These machine breakers were not simply a 'minority movement' or 'true Luddites', easily distinguishable from the trade unionists. To compartmentalise the cloth workers in this way is flagrantly to disregard their trade, their community and their industrial culture. Certainly there would have been hot-heads and those who consistently favoured direct action. It is, however, ludicrous to envisage such men as being totally divorced from their workmates, pursuing their campaign of dedicated terrorism *in vacuo*. The threat of machinery was met by a well-organised and united trade which knew well the importance of corporate solidarity. The Thomis thesis, that 'violence occurred not through trade union machinery but in its absence',[132] simply does not stand up in the case of the cloth finishing trade in 1802 or, for that matter, in 1812 either. The centres of the Wiltshire Outrages were the towns of Trowbridge, Bradford on Avon and Warminster where the shearmen's organisation was strongest. This indeed was one of the factors which most alarmed the authorities.

[132] Thomis, *The Luddites*, p. 116.

Chapter 6

Custom and law: the weavers' campaign

The year 1802 proved to be one of crisis not only for the cloth dressers but also for the weavers and master clothiers in the woollen industry. The Peace of Amiens ushered in a severe economic depression resulting in unemployment or partial employment and rapidly falling living standards. The reduction in work opportunities exacerbated fears in both the West of England and the West Riding about the mounting threats to the traditional structure of weaving and cloth making, fears which had been growing increasingly acute from the early 1790s. The considerable tensions caused by the bitter conflicts over the introduction of cloth dressing machinery further added to the general air of insecurity which pervaded the industry. It was in this climate of impending crisis that the weavers of Gloucestershire commenced a concerted attempt to safeguard their trade and customs through an aggressive utilisation of the old regulatory statutes governing the industry. Their action was to provoke a major confrontation with the innovators in the county, precipitating the latter's application to Parliament to have all the old restrictive legislation repealed. From this petition in late 1802 onwards, the issue of structural change in the woollen industry ceased to be merely a local or regional struggle between innovation and custom. It became a national issue of economic policy. On this national stage that issue was emphatically decided in favour of innovation. The weavers' campaign thus became inextricably bound up with that of the cloth dressers as both vainly tried to persuade Parliament to uphold the legislative pillars which for so long had supported the whole structure of custom.

Weaving was always the most populous male occupation in the woollen industry. As previously noted, in the West of England the great majority of weavers were independent journeymen owning their own looms and working at home under the putting out system. Though in effect proto-proletarians, they saw themselves as independent artisans, socially superior to those who had to answer directly to a

master. Their strong sense of community and craft had been manifested throughout the eighteenth century in a vigorous tradition of self-
assertion and of resistance to any threat to their customary work
practices. While the majority of weavers in the West were such independent journeymen dealing directly with a clothier, there were still
many master weavers who employed journeymen to weave alongside
them in small workshops. Unlike the master clothiers of Yorkshire,
however, the master weaver in the West of England remained in effect
an outworker, owning, like the independent weaver, only the tools of
his trade, never the materials on which he worked. The Domestic
System of the West Riding, on the other hand, was built around the
independent production of the master clothiers, buying and sorting
the wool and then working it up into cloth with the aid of their families
and journeymen who lived in. By the latter part of the eighteenth
century there were also increasing numbers of independent journeymen weavers in Yorkshire who took work from the master clothiers in
much the same way as in the West of England. While there was some
gradual erosion of the Domestic System, however, master clothiers
and journeymen in the West Riding were just as conservative of their
customary work structures and relations as their equivalents in the
West of England, equally determined to uphold the rights and privileges of their trade. In both regions, however, these customary relationships were coming under growing pressure from the late 1780s as
the mechanisation of the preparatory stages of cloth manufacture
established a new model of industrial production.

The early introduction of preparatory and spinning machinery into
the woollen industry did not have immediate adverse consequences
for the weavers. Indeed, machine spun yarn proved more uniform and
less prone to breakage than hand spun yarn and enabled the weaver to
increase production. Yarn supply proved no longer an impediment to
expansion and these factors, coupled with the war, produced a boom
in trade in the 1790s. And, as men flocked to the colours, demand for
weavers rose everywhere. Nonetheless, buoyant conditions did not
disguise the fact that the growth and gradual but inexorable mechanisation of the industry carried with them growing threats to the weavers'
trade. Three aspects in particular need to be noted: the consequences
of the introduction of the flying shuttle loom; the increase in 'illegal'
weavers, that is, men who had not served the customary apprenticeship in the trade; and the rise of large loomshops or weaving 'factories'.
All three were seen as a threat to wage rates while the flying shuttle and
illegal men also appeared to threaten jobs. Only the flying shuttle loom

could be said to be a new threat to the weavers. As has been previously noted, the flying shuttle was taken up in Yorkshire fairly extensively from the early 1780s following initial riots and protests there but in the West of England its reception was much more troubled. Gloucestershire weavers' protests gave way after 1793 to a gradual acceptance but this was mostly because the loom was not introduced in large numbers and because it was used mainly by independent weavers of narrow cloth, not of broadcloth, the county's principal production. The loom, however, was not accorded even this grudging treatment in Wiltshire or Somerset. Indeed, extensive disturbances continued to greet attempts to introduce the flying shuttle or spring loom there as late as 1822 and few were in use until after the Napoleonic Wars.[1] While the flying shuttle posed new problems of redundancy, the threat of illegal weavers was a perennial one and loomshops had been threatening the weavers' independence intermittently since the sixteenth century when William Stumpe took over Malmesbury Abbey and filled it with 'lumbes to weve clooth yn'.[2] However, with the rise of a mechanised industry under way, all three problems became greatly exacerbated since all, and loomshops in particular, seemed to provide means to enable innovators to extend their control over the industry and thereby undermine the old organisational structure of cloth manufacture. Indeed, the problem of loomshops was central to all. Loomshops threatened the autonomy of the putting out and Domestic systems and heralded an extended factory system. Men 'not bred up to the trade' who turned to the loom, attracted by the high earnings of the 1790s or as a result of displacement by machinery, were frequently set to weave under the immediate supervision of trained weavers in loom shops where they were paid at lower rates than outworkers. Likewise flying shuttle looms were frequently used first in shops, partly because of fears of attack but also because they could substantially cut costs this way. In 1802 a crisis point had been reached. It is worthwhile investigating how this came about.

The eighteenth century had witnessed various intermittent and individual attempts in the West of England to establish loomshops or weaving factories where large numbers of journeymen laboured under a regime of strict discipline quite alien to the putting out system. However, from the 1780s the introduction of loomshops took on a more concerted and threatening character. Loomshops offered mixed blessings to the innovator. They enabled him to maintain a much closer

---

[1] Mann, *Cloth Industry*, p. 161.
[2] Rogers, *Wiltshire and Somerset Woollen Mills*, p. 50.

control over production and quality than was possible under the putting out system and also to keep a tighter check on embezzlement. Costs per piece could be kept down by paying lower wage rates than those paid to outdoor weavers and by deducting from wages a sum for sizing and quilling for which one man was usually employed. The shop weaver also had to pay rent for his loom, harness and slay. Where the cloth being produced was of low quality, shops made it easy to employ untrained and illegal weavers at even lower wages under the supervision of a skilled foreman who would set up looms and monitor progress. Not all shops, however, produced cheap cloth. Loomshops were introduced into Wiltshire in the 1780s so that the clothiers could supervise production of the new, complicated and expensive fancy cassimeres and many shops in Gloucestershire were also set up in the early 1790s for the same purpose.

The major disadvantage of loomshops as far as the West of England clothiers were concerned was that they tended to generate considerable hostility from the weavers. The weavers disliked everything about loomshops. They disliked the time discipline enforced in the shops, or 'factories' as they often called them, and they resented the close supervision to which those working in them were subject. They resented the loss of independence and the slur which supervision was felt to cast on their dignity and craftmanship. Shop work also broke up the family work unit since quilling and other tasks normally performed at home by the family were done by the clothier and had to be paid for.[3] This dislike of loomshops was in very few cases informed by direct experience. Most weavers had no intention of working in them if at all possible. This was why the spread of shops aroused so much resentment. The weavers feared that loomshops would undermine the whole structure of outwork and that it was the aim of the innovators to draw all weaving into the 'factories'. Such fears grew with the development of scribbling mills and machinery. Loomshops, therefore, were felt to threaten the whole customary fabric of the putting out system. Moreover, the weavers believed that loomshops were not merely immoral but also illegal. In this respect they were not wholly correct, for while 2 & 3 Philip and Mary c. 11 stated that no clothier might own more than one loom, nor let out looms for hire, this was applicable only to those persons who lived outside a city, borough, market town or corporate town. For this reason the loomshops set up by Trowbridge clothiers producing narrow cloth in the 1780s were deemed 'not in practice contrary to the law' by the magistrates in 1787

[3] B.P.P., 1840, Vol. 24, p. 437.

for the town had a market charter. However, the weavers were correct when they claimed in 1792 that Nathaniel Lloyd 'had no right to keep looms in his house' in the village of Uley.[4]

The most extensive display of antipathy to loomshops was seen in Wiltshire in 1787. Shops had only recently been established in Trowbridge to produce fancy cassimeres and these had been a cause of unrest in September 1785. Rev. John Clark recorded in his diary, 'The weavers were rising round the country and intended to come and destroy all the looms of their masters.'[5] Little information survives of these disturbances but in early 1787 trouble broke out again as some clothiers attempted to extend the use of loomshops from fancy cloths to plain cassimeres. The first disturbances occurred at Bradford on Avon on 22 January. They were caused by an influx of riotous Trowbridge weavers, concerned at local wage agreements.[6] Anstie subsequently wrote that 'the weavers [have] for some time past threatened the clothiers of Trowbridge with their intention of pulling down the shops erected for the purpose of weaving cassimeer'.[7] Facing such threats and following the Bradford on Avon riot, a meeting of cassimere manufacturers from Trowbridge, Devizes, Melksham and Chippenham was convened in Trowbridge on 6 February. The chair was taken by Anstie, himself the owner of a weaving shop said to contain 300 narrow looms.[8] This meeting agreed a series of propositions 'grounded on the complaints of the narrow weavers which may tend to reconcile those differences which now exist between the clothiers and the weavers' and offered to submit them to the magistrates for their judgement. Basically these propositions were that the clothiers would promise to erect no more shops if the weavers agreed to accept a cut in wage rates from 11d. per yard to 10d. It is clear that there were considerable dissensions within the clothiers' ranks between those who had set up shops and those who had not and some were not at all happy with the proposals. The weavers for their part completely rejected the offer.[9]

The initial judgement of the bench who had assembled on the 17th to arbitrate in the dispute favoured the weavers. They recommended 'to the clothiers the giving up of weaving plain cassimeres in their houses if it could be effected', recognising, however, that for some fancy cloths

[4] V.C.H., Wiltshire, Vol. vii (Oxford, 1953), p. 143; Statutes at Large, Vol. 2 (1758), p. 299.
[5] The Trowbridge Woollen Industry, 1804–24, ed. Beckinsale, p. xix.
[6] B.C., 1, 8 Feb. 1787; G.J., 5 Feb. 1787; Mann, Cloth Industry, p. 115.
[7] B.C., 1 March 1787.
[8] W.A.S.L., MS diary of George Sloper, 4 April 1788.
[9] B.C., 8 Feb. 1787.

it was necessary that the clothier should be able to supervise their manufacture. This judgement greatly displeased those clothiers who had set up shops and they 'represented in forcible terms' the losses they would accrue from such a ruling. The justices consequently withdrew their judgement, accepting the clothiers' claim that loomshops were not 'in the practice contrary to the law'. They recommended that the weavers accept the clothiers' original proposals 'as being the only proper mode of preventing the further erection of shops'. The weavers did not accept the proposals but agreed to take a copy to discuss among themselves, promising to be guilty of no disorders.[10] However, three days later on the 20th trouble broke out again. A large number of narrow weavers from the weaving villages around Trowbridge entered the town and 'compelled the clothiers by force and violence to promise that their shops should be discontinued'. It is interesting that these rioters came from outside the town, perhaps fearing that the town weavers might now accept the clothiers' proposals. The riot was put down with considerable force.[11] Angered by the rejection of their proposals and by the riot, the narrow clothiers commenced a lock-out of all weavers. Loomshops were shut and no work was given out to domestic weavers in an attempt to force an agreement on them. It seems to have been widely effective.[12]

On 7 March a further attempt was made to resolve the friction between those clothiers who owned shops and those who did not by 'equalising the advantages'. The clothiers agreed that their previous offer of 10d. per yard to out-weavers should stand but that those clothiers who owned shops should not reduce their rates below 8d. per yard. Since they all agreed that it was 'highly expedient to permit those weavers to begin working who are sensible of the reasonableness of the above proposals', they resolved that the lock-out of the plain cassimere weavers should end on 10 March when clothiers would give out work 'at 10d. per yard and no less'. Many clothiers who owned loomshops were not pleased with the outcome and declared that they would no longer weave plain cassimeres in their shops, while others who had contemplated setting up shops declared that they were now content to continue as before.[13] Thus the clothiers' initial offer to the weavers became a *fait accompli*. The three-week lock-out clearly had

---

[10] *B.C.*, 22 Feb. 1787.

[11] *B.C.*, 1 March, 22 Feb. 1787.

[12] *B.C.*, 1 March 1787. Anstie himself was clearly unhappy with the outcome of events – 'this disagreeable business'. *B.C.*, 22 Feb. 1787.

[13] *B.C.*, 15 March 1787.

reduced the weavers' resistance. Perhaps many were prepared to believe the clothiers' assurances that shops would not now spread and genuinely accepted their terms. Many certainly returned to work. Not all were happy, however. On the evening of Tuesday, 20 March, a mob of weavers from Devizes and its neighbourhood marched into Melksham 'with the intention to oblige the journeymen of that place to forego the agreement they had lately made with their masters, in consequence of which they were again settled in their work'. The magistrates and manufacturers broke up the mob who dispersed without succeeding in their aims.[14]

The disturbances in 1787 in Wiltshire, and, perhaps more importantly, the agreement among cassimere clothiers to peg rates 'equalising the advantages' between shops and outwork, ensured that the spread of loomshops in that county in the 1790s was slowed. Some clothiers may indeed have given up their shops after 1787. Francis Naish advertised for twenty weavers to work in his loomshop in Trowbridge in 1791, but this may well have been the shop containing twenty looms occupied by John Cook in 1803, the only shop in Trowbridge mentioned in evidence to Parliament that year. The largest shop in the county, that owned by John Anstie at Devizes, closed following his bankruptcy in 1793. Most shops remained relatively small – William Sheppard at Frome had weaving shops containing fourteen or twenty looms at this time – but there were also new large mills growing on the periphery of the woollen district which housed increasing numbers of looms from the early 1790s. The mill of Francis Hill at Malmesbury contained some forty broad looms, all of them spring looms, from the middle of the decade, while Samuel Bamford's large factory at Twerton, outside Bath, had even more, probably over 100. By 1818 it housed some 160 looms.[15]

A few loomshops existed in Gloucestershire before the late 1780s but it was really the introduction of narrow cloths and especially cassimeres from perhaps as early as 1788,[16] but certainly from 1792 onwards, which gave the impetus to their growth. Shops were set up, principally in the southern woollen district around Dursley, purportedly to train the weavers prior to their returning to domestic

[14] *G.J.*, 2 April 1787.
[15] *S.W.J.*, 8 Aug. 1791; Naish left Trowbridge for Twerton in 1802; *B.P.P.*, 1802/3, Vol. 7, p. 98; Rogers, *Wiltshire and Somerset Woollen Mills*, p. 105; *B.P.P.*, 1802/3, Vol. 7, pp. 369, 86, 266; *S.W.J.*, 17 July 1802, 8 June 1818. The mill does not seem to have been extended but in the 1790s part of the premises were used for worsted production. *J.H.C.*, Vol. 49, pp. 322–3.
[16] Mann, *Cloth Industry*, p. 137.

production. Probably the largest of these shops was that owned by Nathaniel Lloyd at Uley mentioned above. Rates in the shops were lower than those paid to outdoor weavers and this gave rise to considerable ill-feeling and suspicion. However, it was the issue of rates paid by Lloyd to one of his out-weavers which occasioned disturbances at Uley in 1792.[17] On the morning of 1 June 1792, a mob of about fifty weavers assembled outside the cottage of John Teakle, a narrow weaver of Uley, and accused him of 'working under price' for Lloyd. They claimed that he had taken work '3d. per yard under foot'. Teakle denied this although he was working for either 9d. or 9½d. per yard as against the 11d. per yard which was the standard rate. Lloyd subsequently claimed that Teakle was working a loom owned by Lloyd for which Lloyd found both harness and slay, but in Teakle's own home. Thus, in effect Teakle was employed on the same terms and was paid as a shop weaver while working as an out-weaver. The implications of this for the outdoor weavers were obvious. The mob forced Teakle to remove the work from the loom and take it with them to Lloyd's workshops, threatening Teakle that if he refused, his house would be pulled down and he would be ducked in a neighbouring pond and carried through Nailsworth and Stroud as a public example. When they arrived at Uley, however, they found that Lloyd was away and the shops locked up by his wool-loft man who had been apprised of their arrival. Lloyd's brother-in-law, George Harris, himself a clothier, came to parley with the mob, denying that the work had been given out under-price and insisting that Teakle take back the cloth and finish it. The crowd were equally insistent that the work was under-price and that it should not be taken back. They asserted that 'if work was not worth 1¼d. per yard, it should not be wove in their parish for less than 11d'. Several threatened to smash up Lloyd's looms 'for he had no right to keep looms in his house'. The cloth was thrown on the ground and the mob threatened to kill anyone who removed it. However, when they left, Teakle's wife picked it up and took it to the cottage of her brother-in-law, William Webb, who lived next door to them. Leaving Lloyd's yard, the mob dragged Teakle to a local public house and drank some beer while others obtained a stinge, a large pole used for carrying cloth. Teakle was forced to sit astride the pole and was carried by the mob towards Owlpen where he was ducked in a mud hole. Then,

---

17 Nathaniel Lloyd was succeeded in trade by his son, Daniel, who gave evidence about the loomshop in 1803. It may well have been at Angeston, near Uley. Tann erroneously states that it was Daniel who experienced the labour problems in 1792. Tann, *Gloucestershire Woollen Mills*, pp. 120, 136, 11.

stopping at various ale-houses to refresh themselves, the mob paraded him on the stinge through Horsley and Nailsworth. This was the traditional manner in which Gloucestershire weavers humiliated blacklegs. Finally in the evening they brought him home. Arriving back in Uley, the mob heard that Teakle's wife had re-possessed the cloth and they insisted that Teakle should go into Webb's house and bring it out. Teakle, however, chose his moment to bolt into Webb's house and Webb barred the door. Incensed, the crowd began to break down the door, smash the windows and also began to unroof the cottage. Those inside defended themselves as well as they could and after three hours of damage the mob left, threatening to return the following morning. By then, however, the authorities had been alerted and order was restored, though Webb was too frightened to leave his house for some time. Forty-four people were subsequently charged with riot at the Epiphany sessions in January 1793, but those found guilty received only light sentences, being fined 10s. 6d. and ordered to make a public apology for their crime.[18]

How far animosity to loomshops continued to be expressed in the southern woollen producing area of the county in the early 1790s is not clear. However, the way in which shops could be used to employ illegal workers and to lower rates for outworking weavers may well have been behind the undoubted tensions that existed in the county and the disturbances which occurred in the southern area in November 1793. Evidence is fragmentary and we know very little of the riots which occurred since the authorities deliberately suppressed news of them. The Rev. Wiliam Lloyd-Baker wrote, 'I perfectly agree with your friends that government do wisely to keep it secret. The less riots are talked of, the less likely they are to increase or succeed.'[19] The disturbances may have concerned loomshops but they may also have been occasioned by the extended use of gig mills from coarse to fine cloth which occurred about this time in the area.[20] It is

---

[18] G.C.L., RV 319–6, Uley – riots of weavers, 1792, No. 51, brief to the prosecution, Epiphany sessions 1792, the King v 44 people for riot; No. 35, Easter sessions, 1793, notice; No. 37, draft apology of rioters; No. 9, examination of William Webb. Many of those convicted received good character references. The vicar and churchwardens of Horsley claimed that ten of their parishioners who had been convicted were variously 'men of sober and orderly conduct' and of 'a well known, peaceable and good character'. The same could not be said for their victims. 'The evidence of William Webb and Richard Teakle (old inhabitants of a prison) should be received with a suspicious caution.' No. 17, memorial from vicar and churchwardens of Horsley.
[19] Lloyd-Baker MSS, Box 55, letter book of Rev. William Lloyd-Baker, Lloyd-Baker to William Pitt, Cirencester, 30 Nov. 1793.
[20] B.P.P., 1802/3, Vol. 7, p. 254.

clear, however, that outdoor weavers were very concerned about threats to their trade and that the Dursley–Uley area was the centre of disturbances.

The first indication of unrest comes with a notice which reported a meeting of the master broadcloth and narrow cloth weavers held in Stroud on 2 November, at which 'The Gloucestershire Society of Broad and Narrow Cloth Weavers' was established. The meeting had been called because 'divers infringements, irregularities and abuses have crept into the said trades from many persons of the lower order who have illegally undertaken to weave cloth at reduced prices when not regularly bred up to the business as the law requires' and because of 'a report being circulated that a small part of the clothiers meant to lower the price of weaving'. The master weavers resolved to form a society to secure 'our just and fair regulated and accustomed prices for weaving; for the maintenance of good order and regulation; ... and for the termination of all discord, anarchy, and confusion'. The society resolved to punish anyone who 'shall be guilty of any outrage, or any open violation of the law – it being the fixed determination of this society that the property and persons of all people, of whatever denomination, shall be held sacred and inviolable'. A committee of twenty-five were appointed and a fund commenced 'for allowing stipends, gratuities and other rewards for those weavers who shall stand according to law for the accustomed prices'. The society published these resolutions 'in order publicly to manifest the intentions of this society'.[21] Trade in Gloucestershire was suffering from depression in 1793[22] and it was at such times that illegal weavers were most resented, but the master weavers had most to lose from the spread of loomshops and the Teakle affair the previous year had shown how shops could be a means of decreasing wages for all.

Around the middle of November disturbances broke out and troops were urgently dispatched to the county to restore order. By late November everything was again peaceful. Just who was involved in these disturbances is not clear, but it may well have been journeymen weavers for the master weavers' notice reported that the journeymen were very 'dissatisfied' at rumours of wage cuts. Lloyd-Baker, an active Uley magistrate, and his fellow justices met some of the master weavers' leaders. 'The men who appeared as of the committee were considerably alarmed when they found how far matters were carried and [I] have every reason to believe that there is not a man of them who would

[21] *G.J.*, 11 Nov. 1793.   [22] Mann, *Cloth Industry*, pp. 130, 135.

not stand forth to suppress a riot.'[23] They were warned that their society was of dubious legal status and liable to prosecution should it get involved in wage disputes. The magistrates were 'confident that the failure of this business . . . will most probably have a good effect in suppressing anything which might otherwise have been attempted to be brought forward'. The southern area, however, remained tense throughout December. Paul reported that while a military presence was no longer required at Stroudwater, 'the people of Wotton and Dursley are not so well disposed and [the magistrates] still think the place in danger if without a ready application to a military force'.[24]

The threat of loomshops thus remained a potent concern for the weavers in the West of England at the turn of the century. Their fears, however, were greatly exacerbated in 1802 by two factors: the economic consequences of the Peace; and the increasingly aggressive tone of the innovators in their pronouncements in the bitter struggle over cloth dressing machinery which indicated, they believed, ambitions to move towards much greater centralisation of control of the industry by the new machine owners.

Peace in Western Europe brought major problems for the West of England woollen trade. The wartime demand for woollen cloth for military and ancillary purposes, not only for the British armed forces but also for her continental allies, abruptly ceased. The re-opening of the shipping routes ended the days of British monopoly and European competitors attempted to revive their commerce with aggressive trade restrictions on British goods. At home, rapid demobilisation, not only of regular servicemen but also of the inflated militia regiments into which many woollen workers had enlisted or been balloted since 1793, threw many weavers onto the labour market just as work was rapidly diminishing. Quite how many men were so placed is difficult to estimate but the number was not small. Over 800 men from the Frome area alone were said to have entered the army by late 1795 and recruitment seems to have received a boost in 1797.[25] While the pattern of trade varied between the different branches of industry, it seems clear that the worst effects of depression were experienced in the year or so from early 1801 to mid-1802. Overseers' accounts for Trowbridge and Bradford on Avon in Wiltshire and for the extensive parish of Bisley in Gloucestershire show relief payments reaching a peak at this time and

[23] Lloyd-Baker MSS, Box 55, Lloyd-Baker to Pitt, 30 Nov. 1793.
[24] W.O. 1/1063, Paul to Yonge, 10 Dec. 1793.
[25] Eden, *State of the Poor*, Vol. II, p. 643; *J.H.C.*, Vol. 58, p. 889; see also H.O. 50/42, Pembroke to Dundas, 19 May 1798.

thereafter gradually declining.[26] Almost every branch of the trade came
to a near standstill in early 1802 but by the winter and into 1803 the
broadcloth trade was showing vigorous signs of revival. The narrow
trade, however, remained depressed. It was probably because
Gloucestershire was less heavily involved with the latter trade that the
effects of recession were apparently less severely felt there than in
Wiltshire. The improving state of the industry in 1803 enabled those
clothiers who gave evidence to the Parliamentary Committee considering their petition that year the opportunity to claim that there was no
unemployment among their weavers and, indeed, that there was a
scarcity of hands. The weavers denied this but their evidence tended to
be drawn from the narrow trade. Thus Thomas Richmond of Trowbridge claimed that there were 169 looms and 55 weavers wholly
unemployed in the town, while others had been forced to leave to seek
work. James Jones, a weaver from North Bradley, claimed that in
January 1803, over 300 looms had stood idle in the parishes of Trowbridge, Westbury, Beckington, Rode and North Bradley. Many of
these would have been narrow looms. A Trowbridge clothier who gave
evidence on behalf of the workmen stated that while the broadcloth
trade was recovering, narrow cloth 'is a dead article'. 'We have not had
such a dead time since the war began', a Trowbridge weaver
concurred. The clothiers for their part claimed that narrow looms stood
idle because the broad trade had need of all the available hands. John
Jones claimed that the shortage of weavers had led to many women
taking up the loom while Abraham Lloyd Edridge, a Chippenham
clothier, stated that he had been forced to put out work some 10 miles
to find sufficient broad weavers. Both sides had considerable incentives to exaggerate their case but it does seem clear that conditions
were improving by late 1802.[27] However, it is also clear that the prosperity which had existed before 1800 was never regained and that
while many found some work after mid-1802 their employment was
only partial. John Mills, a Gloucestershire weaver, made this clear in
1806. 'The greater part of our country . . . are not so well off as they
were: I knew many at that time [before the Peace] who could have good
beer in their houses and a sack of flour, who cannot have anything of
the kind now.'[28]

It is difficult to ascertain if the number of loomshops had increased

[26] Randall, 'Labour and the industrial revolution', Appendix.
[27] *B.P.P.*, 1802/3, Vol. 7, pp. 98, 100, 71, 213, 335–6, 361; see also pp. 11, 17, 21, 29, 55 and
    279, 265, 250.
[28] *B.P.P.*, 1806, Vol. 3, p. 338.

in the years immediately before 1802. In Wiltshire and Somerset it seems probable that they did not increase beyond those noted previously. Nonetheless, the factories at Twerton and Malmesbury loomed larger in popular concerns with the start of the new century and fears were growing that John Jones intended to establish a weaving factory alongside his large Staverton mill, so widely hated by the cloth dressers. In 1803 Jones denied he had any such intention, stating that the costs made such a building uneconomic. However, before he went bankrupt in 1813 he had indeed built a factory containing forty spring looms.[29] It was fear that loomshops might spread, fears increased by the development of the atypically large factories like Staverton, which galvanised the Wiltshire weavers into action. In Gloucestershire there does seem to have been a growth of loomshops in the years immediately before 1802 though for the most part these appear to have been of small scale. John Mills listed nine 'factories' in 1806, the largest two housing only twenty and twenty-three looms respectively, two more with ten and eleven looms and the remaining five holding eight or less. Most were situated in the southern woollen area around Dursley and Wotton where they seem to have increased since the mid-1790s, but they were also to be found in the north around Painswick and also at Woodchester and Stonehouse. There were none in Stroud but the fear that shops would expand further was very real. The Gloucestershire clothiers were anxious to disclaim any suggestion that they intended to establish larger factories or more shops. 'The expenses of such a building would be prodigious', claimed Edward Sheppard, and it was 'furthest from my inclinations'. Lloyd claimed that he was keen to close his large loomshop, which then housed around fifty looms because he needed the space.[30] Yet shortly after this Sheppard was to build his 'Great Factory' for weaving, while it seems clear that Lloyd's factory continued to produce cloth.[31] Certainly the threat which such factories were deemed to pose to their way of life preoccupied the weavers. 'If they were to take the trade into factories, they would draw the people into factories', warned Cornelius Bancroft. The clothiers' moves to repeal the protective legislation was seen as a deliberate attempt to open the way for factories. Joseph Bailey stated, 'We understood that the gentlemen clothiers had brought in a Bill to say that all the work should be brought into shops', while John Clayfield said that the weavers had petitioned 'that we might not be sent to the factories'.

[29] *B.P.P.*, 1802/3, Vol. 7, p. 344; Rogers, *Wiltshire and Somerset Woollen Mills*, pp. 98–9.
[30] *B.P.P.*, 1806, Vol. 3, p. 334; *B.P.P.*, 1802/3, Vol. 7, pp. 16, 249, 266.
[31] Tann, *Gloucestershire Woollen Mills*, p. 48.

John Mills believed the clothiers were deliberately attempting to destroy the basis of outwork.[32]

While the West of England weavers' greatest fear was the spread of factories, the issue over which they clashed with their employers in 1802 was that of illegal workmen. Such men were always resented because they were felt to deprive those who had served a full apprenticeship of work and to threaten wage rates since they were usually prepared to weave under-price. They were also often employed in loomshops. The circumstances of 1801–2 increased these resentments as many legal weavers returned from the army to find that there was no work for them. Further, the growing mistrust of the larger clothiers' intentions over factories induced many to believe that the clothiers were trying to use illegal weavers as another wedge to soften up weavers' resistance to detrimental changes. Thus Edward Sheppard, the leading Gloucestershire innovator, was said to give a preference to illegal weavers in allocating work.[33] 'Who first encouraged the illegal workmen?', John Clayfield was asked in 1803. 'The clothiers', he replied, 'by setting up large factories and drawing us from our homes to work for them.'[34] How far the illegal weavers made any substantial impact in increasing or prolonging unemployment in 1802 is difficult to ascertain. There was a shortage of weavers around 1798 after increasing enlistment into the army in a depressed period of 1797 had been followed by a sudden growth in trade[35] and illegal men had helped to make good the deficit. The shortage of weavers also prompted the more rapid take up of the spring loom in Gloucestershire[36] and this also made for less work for journeymen when trade declined in 1801. Just how many illegal workers turned to the loom during the war is unclear but the numbers certainly ran into many hundreds. The Gloucestershire weavers threatened prosecutions against 150 illegal men soon after the establishment of their county-wide society in 1802 and these were only the more notorious offenders.[37] The Wiltshire weavers' solicitor also issued a notice threatening to prosecute illegal men, but the clothiers' bill prevented any action from being taken and we have no idea how many might have been involved.[38] The problem, however, seems to have been greater in Gloucestershire. While the weavers there were always better

[32] *B.P.P.*, 1802/3, Vol. 7, pp. 88, 58, 26; *B.P.P.*, 1806, Vol. 3, p. 335.
[33] *B.P.P.*, 1806, Vol. 3, p. 345.　　　[34] *B.P.P.*, 1802/3, Vol. 7, p. 16.
[35] *J.H.C.*, Vol. 58, p. 889.　　　[36] *B.P.P.*, 1802/3, Vol. 7, p. 300.
[37] G.C.L., JF.13.9(1).　　　[38] *B.P.P.*, 1806, Vol. 3, p. 349.

organised, the Gloucestershire broadcloth trade benefited more from the great demand for military wear than that of Wiltshire or Somerset which concentrated on higher quality cloths. Army and navy cloth required little skill in the weaving and it was in such branches that illegal weavers most readily found work. Among the intruders were agricultural labourers, blacksmiths, carpenters and tailors, but it is clear that many were woollen workers displaced by machinery. Most were scribblers but some in Gloucestershire were ex-shearmen. 'Since the scribbling and shearing machines have been introduced, [men] have been thrown out of employ, and have been obliged to apply themselves to other businesses, the young people have a good deal', stated a retired weaver from King's Stanley in 1803.[39] The 'other businesses' almost always meant weaving.

It is significant of the constitutional tradition of the Gloucestershire weavers that they chose to resist the spread of loomshops and the increase of non-apprenticed workers by legal rather than by illegal means. Doubtless there was some intimidation of the intruders and perhaps of shop owners but this was limited. Rather, the weavers turned to the legislation which regulated the woollen industry, in particular to the statutes 5 Elizabeth c. 4, which prohibited all who had not served an apprenticeship from weaving cloth, and 2 & 3 Philip and Mary c. 11, which limited the number of looms which might be kept by any one person. Between them, these acts appeared to ban both the interlopers from taking up the loom and the clothiers from setting up loomshops. The weavers thus felt that their case at law was strong.

Legal action was commenced by an association of weavers at Bisley. Bisley parish was primarily a weaving community whose economic focus was the Chalford Vale. Following the decline of the broadcloth trade, Chalford clothiers had turned in the 1790s to specialise in cheaper cloths, particularly a variety known as 'Spanish Stripes' produced mainly for the East India Company. These cheaper cloths were easy to produce and consequently the clothiers, under increasing pressure from the Company's factors to cut costs, were accused of being among the most notorious encouragers of illegal weavers and shops. In the summer of 1802 the local weavers determined to attempt to discourage this trend and they hired a Cheltenham solicitor, Walter Hilton Jessop, to prosecute a Chalford clothier named Webb for employing illegal weavers in a loomshop. The case came up at the

[39] *B.P.P.*, 1802/3, Vol. 7, pp. 58–9, 96; *B.P.P.*, 1806, Vol. 3, pp. 334, 335.

summer assizes and, the *Gloucester Journal* noted, hinged on 'whether the defendant, a clothier, was entitled to exercise the trade of a weaver *without being apprenticed to or following* the business for seven years'. The matter was settled out of court when Webb undertook to cease employing the illegal weavers and a juror was withdrawn and the matter compromised. Webb did not, in fact, keep his promise. The weavers of Bisley, however, believed they had won an important battle. Before commencing the action Jessop had consulted with a number of local gentry and had apparently obtained their approval for the prosecution. Furthermore, though the judge was never called upon to make a formal adjudication, he added remarks by way of a conclusion which must have greatly heartened the weavers and worried the innovating clothiers. 'Mr. Justice Lawrence expressed his approval of the issue of this business', the *Gloucester Journal* reported, 'observing that the statute most explicitly and incontestibly establishes that a legal apprenticeship or following of a trade for the customary period was the only protection for the undisturbed exercise of it by any person whatever.'[40]

The outcome of the Bisley weavers' prosecution of Webb was the formation of a county-wide association, the Woollen Cloth Weavers' Society, founded on 13 September 1802, following a notice published by Jessop on 1 September.

> By an Act of Parliament made in the reign of Queen Elizabeth inflicting certain penalties on persons following or exercising trades without becoming an apprentice; and the trade of a woollen cloth weaver being in the said Act mentioned, which is now illegally followed or exercised by numerous persons . . .
>
> A meeting will be holden at the Berkeley Arms at Cam on Monday 13th September at 11 a.m., where one weaver (and no more) out of the parish he represents is desired to attend in order to determine on prosecuting those who unlawfully exercise or follow the said trade of a weaver; and it is not feared but the peaceful temper and disposition will continue with the lawful weavers which the learned Judge at the last Assizes observed did honour to them.[41]

About 100 delegates duly met and founded the Weavers' Society. Its aims were clearly stated in its rules and articles: 'to raise a fund for the protection of the trade and to prevent the same from being illegally followed'. Jessop was unanimously chosen as president and by October the *Gloucester Journal* was reporting a membership of 3,000.[42]

---

[40] *B.P.P.*, 1802/3, Vol. 7, pp. 44–5; *B.P.P.*, 1806, Vol. 3, p. 351; *G.J.*, 9 Aug. 1802.
[41] *G.J.*, 6 Sept. 1802.
[42] *B.P.P.*, 1802/3, Vol. 7, p. 46; G.C.L., J.11.53, Rules and Articles; *G.J.*, 4 Oct. 1802.

The Woollen Cloth Weavers' Society did not spring out of nothing. There were precedents in 1756 and in 1793 as noted before and, while these larger organisations appear to have declined after short periods, local societies enjoyed a semi-permanent existence. Some of these were primarily friendly societies such as that to which John Clayfield belonged at Stroud in 1802, but Clayfield also claimed to belong to a society at Stroud which was concerned with trade matters which was in existence at the time of the Wiltshire Outrages in June and July 1802, several months before the establishment of the county society.[43] The Bisley weavers were clearly well organised before they began their prosecution of Webb and probably similar trade societies were to be found in all the main weaving parishes. It was because the weavers were relatively well organised at a parochial level that it was possible to establish the larger society so easily and so effectively.[44]

The Gloucestershire weavers took care to ensure that their organisation was legally constituted, even submitting their rules to 'several gentlemen of the Bar' for approval.[45] The society was modelled on benefit societies and indeed the rules referred to the club as a 'Friendly Society' for on paper at least the society had a dual function, both to protect the trade and 'for the relief and support of certain members . . . who may become indigent and poor'. Relief, however, would only be given when the society's funds could remain in excess of £200. It is unlikely that this aspect was intended to do more than give the society an aura of respectability. Most subscribers were, and continued to be, members of local benefit societies.[46] Any 'regularly apprenticed' weaver could join but no one else would be admitted. Members paid an entry fee of 1s. and thereafter a monthly subscription of 6d. Meetings were to be strictly regulated and a list of fines were drawn up for failing to pay regularly, refusing office, swearing and drunkenness, in the manner of friendly societies. Meetings of members in each parish were to be held on the first Monday evening in every month, at which subscriptions were payable, thereby ensuring a good attendance. The parish stewards were to meet together quarterly, delegates from the southern district meeting in Dursley and those from the north in Stroud.[47]

The society did not wait long before showing its teeth. Rule XII ordered that 'whenever any member shall discover any person using

[43] *B.P.P.*, 1802/3, Vol. 7, pp. 25–7.
[44] Randall, 'The industrial moral economy', pp. 32–50.
[45] *B.P.P.*, 1802/3, Vol. 7, pp. 45–6.
[46] *Ibid.*, pp. 21, 25.   [47] G.C.L., J.11.53.

or exercising the trade of woollen cloth weaver illegally, he shall make it known to the stewards of his parish who shall report the same at the next quarterly meeting or by letter to the solicitor'. Names of such persons were readily forthcoming and in October Jessop served notices of prosecution on 150 illegal weavers.

> I hereby give you notice that you will be prosecuted for setting up, occupying, using, or exercising the trade of a woollen or broad cloth weaver not having served an apprenticeship thereto ... And also I give you further notice that if you cease to follow the said trade ... within the space of one month ... no prosecution will be commenced, as this is intended to give you a reasonable time to dispose of those articles or utensils you might so have in your possession as a weaver.

As a result of these warnings, Jessop believed that around 100 did in fact give up the trade.[48]

The remarks of Justice Lawrence and the formation and rapid growth of the Weavers' Society had greatly alarmed the innovators, but it was the threatened prosecutions of large numbers of illegal weavers which galvanised them into action. On 14 October several of them met and agreed to form a committee and to raise a fund to apply to Parliament for the 'revision' of certain laws, in particular, no doubt 5 Elizabeth c. 4 and 2 & 3 Philip and Mary c. 11. Further, they agreed to contact the committee of Wiltshire and Somerset clothiers which had been formed to institute proceedings against the riotous shearmen there, in the hope of persuading them to join the application to Parliament. The Bath committee had in fact shown signs that they too were thinking along similiar lines when on 16 August they had appointed a sub-committee under John Jones to 'examine the several statutes relating to the woollen manufacture'. On 4 November the two committees met at Bath and, without consultation with the subscribers to the Wiltshire fund, joined together to form a United Committee to apply to Parliament.[49]

This was just the kind of counter-reaction which the weavers did not wish to provoke. After the first meeting of the Gloucestershire clothiers, the Weavers' Society issued a notice affirming that the aim of their club was merely to protect their trade and to confine their business to those who properly understood it, expressing the hope that the clothiers would not find it offensive. The weavers, it noted, considered their society to be framed upon the same principles as the clothiers'

---

[48] G.C.L., J.11.53, JF.13.9(1); *B.P.P.*, 1802/3, Vol. 7, p. 45.
[49] G.C.L., JF.13.25, minutes of the manufacturers' committee; *S.W.J.*, 23 Aug. 1802; *B.P.P.*, 1802/3, Vol. 7, pp. 134, 137–8, 259, 340.

association and recommended the clothiers to buy a copy of the society's rules, offering to modify any part which the clothiers felt was improper. Nevertheless, the society confirmed that it would prosecute illegal weavers, although it hoped that the latter would voluntarily discontinue the trade.[50] If this was intended to mollify the clothiers, it failed, for the agreement of the Gloucestershire clothiers in October set in motion the train of events which led in 1809 to the repeal of the old legislative code on which the weavers' hopes were pinned. On 9 December, Vansittart introduced the manufacturers' petition into the Commons. It complained that, 'from the present altered and improved state of the woollen manufacture', many of the old protective statutes 'are now rendered impracticable, detrimental, or useless'. 'The petitioners and others have been and are at this time harrassed and threatened with divers vexatious prosecutions . . . though for many years past and until recently no such prosecutions have taken place and such statutes have usually been considered as obsolete.' The clothiers prayed that it was necessary 'not merely for the benefit and advantage of the woollen manufactory . . . but even for its existence that the said statutes should be altered, amended, or wholly repealed'. The Commons immediately passed a suspension bill, pending an enquiry, but this was delayed by the Lords. However, in July 1803, after a Commons Select Committee had investigated the industry, both Houses agreed to suspend the old statutes. They were never implemented again.[51]

The Gloucestershire clothiers also appear to have endeavoured to undermine the Weavers' Society by suggesting that the organisation intended to prosecute anyone who had not served a formal apprenticeship. The weavers hastily denied this. 'Those persons who have followed the trade of a weaver seven years and those who have served in any regular military capacity are empowered as much as those weavers who have been apprenticed agreeable to the statute . . . and will be admitted members of the said Society.' The notice re-affirmed that the aim of the organisation was 'to preserve peace and good understanding between the weavers and their employers',[52] but by then battle had been joined and no further rapprochement was possible. The two sides had by this time been further sundered by a minor strike of weavers at Wotton. The men struck work because their employer, a clothier named Symons, had given them slubbings to weave instead of spun yarn which made their task much more difficult. It transpired that

---

[50] *G.J.*, 25 Oct. 1802.
[51] *J.H.C.*, Vol. 58, pp. 75, 641, 649, 690.   [52] *G.J.*, 13 Dec. 1802.

strike action had been decided upon at the monthly meeting of the local branch of the Weavers' Society and the Dursley district meeting of parish stewards later agreed to support them, although the Stroud district meeting disavowed the strike. Eight weavers of Wotton were taken up under the Combination Acts and found guilty, whereupon they were expelled from the society. The episode clearly demonstrated the problems which the Weavers' Society faced, torn between a desire to act within the law and yet also to safeguard their conditions. It also showed the dangers of its dependence upon its parochial branches to act 'responsibly'. The clothiers saw the strike as confirmation that the society intended to embark upon aggressive industrial action. Jessop later claimed that the society had always intended to expel the eight, realising that they had broken the law, but did not do so until after their trial to avoid prejudicing their case.[53] In view of the support initially given by the Dursley district meeting, this can hardly have been true.

The suspension bill brought home to the weavers of Wiltshire and Somerset the dangers to their trade should the clothiers of the United Committee achieve their aim. As in Gloucestershire, there were local societies of weavers in most of the larger parishes and these seem to have collectively sent a delegation to confer with the Gloucestershire weavers at Stroud. Their mission led to a reciprocal visit by Jessop who met twenty or thirty delegates at Bradford on Avon in January. He also arranged a meeting with weavers and clothiers at Trowbridge and with some clothiers at Bath. These clothiers were probably representatives of the smaller non-'respectable' clothiers who feared the intentions of the larger innovators and who were to give valuable help to the weavers' and shearmen's cause before the 1803 Parliamentary Committee. As a result of his visit, the Wiltshire and Somerset weavers formed themselves into a society modelled upon the Gloucestershire one with the same rules and articles. They employed a Frome solicitor, James Frampton, as their attorney and he immediately issued a notice in the papers that the society would prosecute all illegal weavers in the Bradford on Avon and Trowbridge area who did not voluntarily abandon the trade. No prosecutions were commenced, however, perhaps because the statutes on which they would have been based appeared likely to be suspended.[54]

There is contradictory evidence concerning the total membership of

---

[53] *B.P.P.*, 1802/3, Vol. 7, pp. 46–8, 34. The three weavers committed to prison for combination in December may well have been members of this group. *G.J.*, 27 Dec. 1802.

[54] *B.P.P.*, 1802/3, Vol. 7, pp. 50, 52–3, 56, 71.

both societies. According to the *Gloucester Journal*, the Gloucestershire society numbered over 3,000 by early October, only three weeks after the Cam meeting, but Jessop told the 1803 Parliamentary Committee that he believed the club had only between 1,200 and 1,300 members, though he thought there were between 2,000 and 3,000 in the Wiltshire and Somerset society. Clearly not every weaver was prepared to subscribe. John Niblett, a Stroud weaver, joined only in January 1803 after the society had canvassed for members. However, the large sums of money said to have been spent by the weavers required a large and regular membership to provide them. Jessop stated in 1803 that the Gloucestershire society had spent only £150, although Dauncey for the clothiers asserted the truth was five times this sum. In 1806, however, Jessop admitted that the weavers had spent some £1,500, while Frampton claimed £3,000 had been spent. Possibly Jessop's figure was the Gloucestershire weavers' share of the joint costs. Compared with the £10,000 to £12,000 which John Tate claimed the croppers and shearmen had raised and spent between 1802 and 1806, this sum does not seem large. Yet to raise £3,000 over three years would have required over 3,000 contributors to have paid their entry fees of 1s. and then their 1½d. per week regularly throughout that period. Nor were the Parliamentary expenses the only drain on resources. It was claimed that the Wiltshire weavers had also spent £300 on the defence of a member at the Salisbury Assizes.[55] Clearly, therefore, a very large number of weavers must have joined and remained loyal to the two societies over this period.

Fears of the spread of loomshops and of increasing numbers of non-apprenticed workers were not confined to the West of England. The structure of cloth production in the West Riding had enabled the earlier mechanisation of the preparatory processes and the flying shuttle to be absorbed into the Domestic System without threatening existing relationships. However, the growth of the joint-stock and single-owner scribbling mills began a slow but inexorable process of capital concentration in the hands of the innovators and a growing polarisation between the nascent merchant manufacturers and the small master clothiers and journeymen. Growth of production – an increase of some threefold in the years between 1781 and 1800[56] – assuaged worries for a time. However, by the mid-1790s increasing numbers of small master clothiers were coming to realise

---

[55] *Ibid.*, pp. 49, 52, 32, 51, 74; *B.P.P.*, 1806, Vol. 3, pp. 348–50, 239. The Gloucestershire weavers also owed Jessop £100 in 1803 and £170 in 1806.
[56] Wilson, *Gentlemen Merchants*, p. 96.

that prosperity and growth masked trends which threatened to sub-
vert the old methods and organisation of production.

The development of the few very large-scale factories excited most
concern but the greatest impetus to change in the West Riding came, as
Crump and Wilson have shown, not from the capitally endowed
merchants but from the ranks of the larger master clothiers who recognised first the entrepreneurial possibilities of the new technology. In a
detailed recent work, Pat Hudson has shown how such men accumulated and concentrated capital, not generally by the establishment of
large purpose-built factories but by an extension and multiplication of
workshops and existing mills.[57] Employing ever-larger numbers of
workers, these nascent manufacturers were establishing organisational forms and industrial relationships quite alien to the old Domestic System. It was the area around Huddersfield and Halifax which
led the way. Here was first seen the new breed of manufacturer, men
like Law Atkinson, a large master clothier who had steadily installed all
the new preparatory and finishing machinery available in his mills and
workshops and who was increasingly marketing his cloths directly,
thereby by-passing the cloth halls and the merchants.[58] Such men,
however, were not content to control only the preparatory and finishing processes. Increasingly they also developed loomshops where
growing numbers of journeymen wove under a strict regime of discipline, often for wages rather lower than those generally found in the
Domestic System. In part the development of loomshops here was
facilitated by the area's concentration on the production of narrow
cloth since, as in the West of England, narrow looms of the flying
shuttle variety proved most suitable for such concentrations. It was
here, too, that we can see the impact of the cotton and worsted
industries upon the woollen industry felt most clearly. The new attitudes and entrepreneurial aggression so visible in the cotton factories
in neighbouring parishes just over the county boundary provided such
men with a new model for self-advancement. But they also had certain
cultural 'advantages' over other woollen districts, since the tripartite
pivot of master clothier, cloth hall and merchant, so central to the
whole *mentalité* of the Domestic System in the Leeds–Wakefield region,
had never been so deeply entrenched in the area around Huddersfield.[59] With a longer tradition of independence, the large master

[57] Crump and Ghorbal, *Huddersfield Woollen Industry*, pp. 90–1; Wilson, *Gentlemen Merchants*, pp. 93–7; Hudson, *Genesis of Industrial Capital*, pp. 70–84.
[58] *B.P.P.*, 1802/3, Vol. 7, pp. 371–7.
[59] Wilson, *Gentlemen Merchants*, pp. 95, 105–6.

clothiers of this district had fewer inhibitions at taking an axe to traditional modes and methods.

While the impetus for change came initially from the Halifax–Huddersfield area, there were men everywhere willing to follow their successful pioneering and to take the risks of the necessary capital investment to embark upon the factory system. The most famous, and in many ways the least typical, was Benjamin Gott. Gott's great factory at Bean Ing in Leeds, built in 1792, had a profound impact all over the West Riding. This was in part because of its sheer size and scope but it was also because Gott was a prominent cloth merchant. His example of a merchant eschewing the traditional limited role of cloth marketing and establishing himself as a major manufacturer-cum-merchant stimulated wide and growing alarm. Bean Ing was designed from the start to house not just preparatory, spinning and finishing machinery; it was also intended to contain weaving. By 1799 there were extensive weaving shops in the ever-growing complex. Evidence presented to the Select Committee in 1806 did not clarify the number of weavers employed there but in 1812 the mill housed no fewer than 133 looms.[60] Gott's determination to rival the West of England in fine broadcloth production may have been one factor inducing him to take this step. It was a step, nonetheless, which could not but be seen as a direct threat to the Domestic System. Gott did not employ weavers in Bean Ing directly, in effect sub-contracting control over weaving to supervisors within the factory. Nonetheless, master clothiers and journeymen, and indeed many merchants too, saw this concentration of weavers, however managed, as a major challenge. The former feared that Bean Ing would be followed by other merchant-owned weaving factories which would by-pass the small independent producers, forcing them either to establish their own factories, an impracticable and distasteful prospect, or be forced down into a growing mass of journeymen weavers. Many merchants also feared that the rise of such merchant manufacturers would undermine the cloth halls and thereby destroy the profitability and volume of trade conducted in the old, agreeably gentlemanly ways.

The impact of Bean Ing may be judged from the reaction of these groups in the early years following the factory's opening. In 1793 the Leeds cloth halls buzzed with various schemes by which the Domestic System could be protected from the supposed threat posed by new merchant manufacturers. Meanwhile the Leeds merchants, concerned

---

[60] Crump, *Leeds Woollen Industry*, p. 33.

11   The Leeds Cloth Hall at work
Source: G. Walker, *The Costume of Yorkshire* (1814).

to maintain the existing separation of functions and worried that the example of the new master clothier manufacturers of the Huddersfield–Halifax area was being copied in the broadcloth trade, proposed to petition Parliament to implement legislation which would forbid such dual functions in the industry. They shrank from this step, however, when they heard that the master clothiers were considering tightening up their apprenticeship regulations on those taking up stands or stalls in the cloth halls, thereby potentially reducing the number of cloth suppliers. In consequence, the Leeds merchants issued a curiously ambiguous statement in favour of freedom and condemning restriction, a statement which in turn further alarmed the master clothiers who interpreted it as confirmation that the merchants did indeed intend to emulate Gott's example.[61] Thus, in March 1794 the trustees of the cloth halls organised Parliamentary petitions of their own, three in all, representing the narrow, white and mixed cloth trades. The petitions warned that the Domestic System, by which master clothiers and journeymen were 'maintained with decency and comfort', was 'now in danger of being broken in upon and destroyed by the introduction of the Modes which have prevailed in other parts of

[61] Wilson, *Gentlemen Merchants*, pp. 98–9.

the Kingdom . . . which Modes are founded on a Monopoly erected and supported by great Capitals and set on foot by . . . Cloth Merchants becoming Cloth Makers'. The petitioners claimed that many in Leeds and Halifax had taken this step and many others had shown a 'disposition to follow their example by establishing large factories for making woollen cloth'. They sought leave to bring in a bill to prevent such monopolies. In April a Select Committee took evidence from the master clothiers' witnesses, including Joseph Stancliffe who claimed 'that from this comfortable and independent situation, should such innovation prevail, the petitioners must separate from their families and be reduced to a state of servitude to gain their bread'. Permission was given to bring in a bill, but, for reasons which are far from clear, no further action was taken by the trustees and the matter lapsed.[62]

From 1794 onwards, however, tension, mistrust and conflict increasingly began to divide the West Riding woollen industry. Other merchants, like Brook and Fisher, did indeed follow Gott's lead and develop factories of their own. More numerous, large master clothiers like James Walker of Wortley – 'half a factory man' as he described himself in 1806 – likewise adopted the role of manufacturer, employing men both in their new and expanding factories and shops and in the workers' own homes on an out-working basis.[63] The accelerating production of cloth continued to give the industry every appearance of buoyancy but this growth brought with it yet further dilution of the old Domestic System, increasing insecurity for journeymen and small clothiers alike and increasing economic polarisation.

This gradual undermining of the Domestic System can be seen in the changes beginning to affect cloth marketing. Boom conditions brought increasing numbers of men to the loom especially in the cheap coarse trade where many set up as petty-producers. A very large percentage of these incomers had neither been 'brought up in the trade' nor served a formal apprenticeship to a master clothier. The trustees of all the cloth halls were, as noted above, initially resolute to resist accepting such men into their halls, thereby providing them with a place to market their wares. This only led, however, to the development of the Albion Street Cloth Hall, popularly referred to always as the Tom Paine Hall, which ignored the restrictiveness which both characterised and stabilised the older halls. Samuel Waterhouse, an Eccleshall clothier, complained that anyone could use the Tom Paine Hall, 'shoemakers and tinkers and any persons who were not brought up to the trade'.

[62] *J.H.C.*, Vol. 49, pp. 275–6, 431–2.
[63] *B.P.P.*, 1806, Vol. 3, pp. 174–8, 104.

Such was the concern about the impact of this new hall on the trade that the trustees of the White Cloth Hall, the hall most threatened by these new petty-producers in the coarse trade, tried to drive it out of business by holding its own markets on the same days and times, but this did not prove a successful tactic. Indeed, in an attempt to retain some regulatory control, the White Cloth Hall was forced in 1797 to re-word its bye-laws to allow in men who had served an apprenticeship of only five years, not the seven years previously insisted upon.[64] While cloth production continued to rise, however, it was clear that the number of master clothiers selling through the old halls was not keeping pace, and, indeed, according to many witnesses, was actually decreasing. Thus the value of stands in the established halls had fallen by 1806, clear evidence of decreasing competition for marketing space.[65] Furthermore, there were growing grumbles from all areas of the West Riding that the master clothiers were under increasing pressure. These surfaced clearly before the 1806 Select Committee. Numbers of master clothiers were said to have declined at Eccleshall, Holbeck, Idle, Morley and Armley. Indeed, James Ellis reported that at Armley, while since the late 1790s some seventeen new master clothiers had set up in trade, some forty-seven had given up business. Many were said to have gone bankrupt. James Walker, a spokesman for the innovating manufacturer master clothiers, claimed that it had never been easier to set up as a master clothier since earnings were high and credit cheap, but it is clear that the majority of clothiers did not accept this contention. Numbers of clothiers had risen at Pudsey where the trade was entirely in coarse cloth but the increasing numbers entering the trade at Armley did so as journeymen, not as master clothiers. The story was reiterated elsewhere.[66] The growth in production, therefore, was seen as taking place at the expense of the small master clothiers and the Domestic System. These clothiers felt increasing resentment at this attack on their economic and social status. 'Many who were masters are brought to be workmen', Ellis complained, voicing the bitterness which many felt. Without exception they blamed the new factories. It was the factories which had caused the bankruptcies at Holbeck. It was the factories which were 'likely to take the trade out of the hands of the legal manufacturers' since the merchant manufacturers 'have the privilege of taking the best of the orders'. They were already moving to monopolise the fine trade, Joseph Coope complained, forcing the master clothiers to turn to the coarse trade to eke

[64] *Ibid.*, pp. 96, 205, 101, 200.
[65] *Ibid.*, pp. 84, 72.   [66] *Ibid.*, pp. 94, 71, 125, 130, 59, 138, 182, 50, 64.

out a living. The large profits of these merchant manufacturers would encourage all merchants to build yet more factories, Robert Cookson believed, destroying the clothiers' trade. 'We have been in the habit of making those goods which they will make themselves.'[67]

This sense of insecurity likewise affected the growing numbers of journeymen weavers. The onset of war and the rising cost of food made living-in servants of all sorts an increasingly unattractive proposition to employers and this was also true of the West Riding woollen industry in which journeymen had traditionally formed part of the master clothiers' household. Increasingly it became the practice for journeymen to be hired for shorter periods and to live out, often in cottages constructed on the periphery of lands owned by the clothiers. By 1806 Cookson claimed that 'it is not common now' to hire by the year. Indeed, his journeymen were hired by the day.[68] In effect the Yorkshire journeyman was becoming much more like his West Country equivalent, save for the fact that he usually did not own his own loom. Such weavers increasingly looked, or had to look, for work in the weaving factories. In the fine trade rates were often rather higher, though expenses tended to be heavier and the work was more arduous and intensive. But all agreed that factory work was much less regular and reliable. In slack times men were turned off wholesale while 'troublemakers' found themselves victimised. John Atkinson told in 1806 how he had gone from factory to factory chasing work.

I had a large family . . . and Mr. Knibley was making a great deal of white cloth and I could do better than what I could otherwise do at that time of the year, though I was not partial to factory work; that induced me to go and I did not wish to apply to the parish.

Weavers who had worked in the factories emphasised their resentment of the discipline found in them, seeing this as an affront to their craft and pride. Indeed, many referred to themselves as journeymen clothiers to emphasise their claims to skilled status rather than the ascription of 'hands' used by their employers. Factory work in Yorkshire, as in the West of England, was also condemned for the way it broke up the family work unit. Said Joseph Coope: 'the greater evil is this, that if the factory system prevail, it will call all the poor labouring men away from their homes into factories where they will . . . not have the help and advantage from their families'. As in the West Country it was the innovators, the men who sought to overthrow customary relationships, who incurred the most odium. William Child saw a

---

[67] *Ibid.*, pp. 16, 73–4, 96, 47, 76.   [68] *Ibid.*, p. 69.

deliberate policy to wreck the Domestic System and reduce the journeymen to dependent status. 'The opulent clothiers have made it a rule to have one third more men than they could employ and then we have to stand still part of our time.' They were the ones who reduced wages, putting pressure on the smaller master clothiers to follow.[69] The experiences of men like Child and John Atkinson were to develop a new, more militant, industrial consciousness on the part of the journeymen weavers in the West Riding, more akin to that of the West of England weavers than the old values of the Domestic System.

By the end of the 1790s the Domestic System was showing signs of fracture at each of its various levels. However, whereas in the West of England machinery and loomshops simply polarised still further an already economically clearly differentiated structure, the effect of these changes in Yorkshire was rather more confused. The changes divided merchants between the new innovators like Gott and Fisher and the more traditionalist merchants who did not wish to exchange their comfortable gentlemanly lifestyle for the uncertain profits and perceived lower social status of the manufacturer. The ranks of the master clothiers were fractured between the new entrepreneurial master manufacturers and the determinedly conservative small master clothiers, with a large number of clothiers in between, torn between ambition and security. This ambiguity characterised all future actions by the clothiers and was seen clearly in the deliberations of the trustees of the cloth halls after 1794. As Joseph Stancliffe was to remark ruefully in 1806, 'after the introduction of machinery the trustees were never unanimous'.[70] And the journeymen weavers were likewise divided between those who still worked entirely in the Domestic System and had the traditional aspirations of in time setting up as master clothiers and those who now worked in the factories who had begun to develop a new industrial consciousness of their own.

It is important to remember, of course, that these changes were only in their infancy in the 1790s. Historians well know that the Domestic System managed to survive for many decades the coming of the factory. The fears of the conservatives were easily ridiculed as gross exaggerations by the 1806 Select Committee, as were those of the West of England weavers in 1803. It was pointed out that only three prominent Leeds merchants had established factories, that these merchants continued to buy in the cloth halls and that their factories produced only 8,000 cloths per annum or one sixteenth part of the production in

---

[69] *Ibid.*, pp. 117, 49, 111, 107.   [70] *Ibid.*, p. 192.

the town, while the Domestic System produced some 300,000 broad-cloths and 166,000 narrow cloths.[71] But the interrogators of the master clothiers and journeymen in 1806 deliberately chose to miss the point of their argument. The spokesmen for the Domestic System recognised the *trend* and the economic implications of the rise of the factory system. Like the cloth dressers they did not need to see this innovation triumphant before they could determine its effect upon their lives. It is significant that the man who likewise recognised most clearly the inevitability of the trend, Benjamin Gott, was not chosen to be a witness on behalf of the merchants and manufacturers in 1806. Per-haps Gott could not be trusted to be economical with the truth when questioned about the direction the woollen industry was taking. It was this direction, well recognised, which the master clothiers sought to resist. Increasingly from the late 1790s it became clear that the major bastion of custom in the West Riding, as in the West of England, was the old regulatory legislative corpus. Indeed, as early as 1796 the dynamic master manufacturers of Huddersfield were considering pet-itioning Parliament to repeal all the old restrictive acts, though nothing came of it. In the end these deliberations were pre-empted by the actions in the West of England.

News of the West Country clothiers' petition seeking to repeal all the old regulatory legislation threw the West Riding woollen industry into turmoil. The master manufacturers of Halifax and Huddersfield had no doubts and petitioned at once to ensure that repeal would also include the Yorkshire industry.[72] The journeymen were equally clear: they wished to oppose repeal at all costs. The Leeds and Wakefield mer-chants, forced at last to choose, enthusiastically or reluctantly by degrees, opted for repeal. It was the master clothiers who found decision most difficult. The divisions in their ranks had been apparent from the mid-1790s but their culture of corporate response focussed through the cloth halls threw these divisions into stark contrast. It is clear that the great majority of clothiers were horrified at the prospect of repeal, believing that it would mark the death knell of the Domestic System. However, the acknowledged leaders of the master clothiers, the trustees of the Leeds cloth halls, were very reluctant to act. Some now owned their own large shops and factories. Others were probably contemplating such a step. Some had, perhaps genuinely, come to believe that repeal would not harm the industry. This view was epitomised by Joseph Stancliffe. In 1794 the spokesman who had

[71] *Ibid.*, pp. 75–6, 94.   [72] *J.H.C.*, Vol. 58, p. 379.

condemned the factories, by 1806 he was sure that the factories would not usurp the woollen trade and claimed that all the respectable clothiers agreed with him.[73] This use of the term 'respectable', echoing its similar use in the West of England, is significant in pointing up the growing cultural divisions in the ranks of the previously undifferentiated master clothiers.

The 'respectable' master clothiers' ambiguity was soon shown in two ways. They assiduously spread rumours that if repeal was rejected the old laws would be enforced absolutely, thereby exposing many customary but technically illegal practices which made up many aspects of the Domestic System. They particularly emphasised fears concerning apprenticeship legislation. Secondly, they deliberately and calculatedly rejected attempts by the West Country weavers to co-ordinate their efforts to oppose repeal. In the early spring of 1803, Jessop, acting for the Gloucestershire and Wiltshire weavers, sent his agent, Thomas May, to Leeds to this end. May, however, was refused admission to the meeting of the trustees of the Mixed Cloth Hall and was both insulted and assaulted for his pains.[74] It became increasingly obvious that the traditional spokesmen and organisers of the master clothiers did not intend to take positive action. Growing disillusionment and distrust of their old leaders eventually was to prompt the formation of a new and independent organisation made up of the small master clothiers and journeymen, namely the Clothiers' Community.

There exists a certain confusion in delineating the Clothiers' Community, a confusion fostered by the 1806 Parliamentary Committee. In the early days of their enquiry they heard evidence from Joseph Coope, William Child, John Atkinson, William Illingworth, Richard Fawcett and Joseph Stancliffe concerning an organisation variously referred to as 'the Clothiers' Community' or 'the Institution'. Depending on these witnesses' viewpoints, the objects of this organisation ranged from acting as a sick club, or for petitioning Parliament, to a means of drawing together the lower orders of society and for illegally raising wages. Allegations of intimidation of non-member workers and of attempts to enforce closed shops were also made, together with others of sinister links between the organisation and others in the West.[75] So similar were these allegations to those levelled at the cloth dressers' Brief Institution that the Select Committee from the first appeared to conflate the Clothiers' Community with the croppers'

---

[73] *B.P.P.*, 1806, Vol. 3, p. 199.
[74] *Ibid.*, pp. 191, 203.   [75] *Ibid.*, pp. 36, 188, 114, 125, 192–3.

organisation. That they were distinct entities was clearly indicated when they produced a document entitled 'The Rules and Orders of the Clothiers' Community, Leeds, 1803', which Stancliffe recognised as being the rules of that organisation.[76] John Tate, however, specifically denied that these were the rules of the Institution to which he belonged, the West Riding croppers' Brief Institution; indeed, they bore no resemblance at all. These rules, it may be noticed, bore the date 1803 whereas Tate claimed his organisation's rules had ceased in January 1803 and had not been renewed.[77] The Committee appeared somewhat muddled but continued apparently to assume that the Clothiers' Community and the Institution were the one and the same thing. This confusion was added to by Robert Cookson, who referred to Child, Atkinson and Illingworth as representatives of the cloth *workers*, a term normally used to describe cloth dressers.[78] Heaton, in fact, implies that Child was a cropper when he cites his evidence as descriptive of the militancy and illegal activities of the croppers' union. But Atkinson and Illingworth stated their trade as journeyman clothier and weaver respectively and, while Child never said so formally, it is clear that he too was a weaver. The institution or Clothiers' Community to which these men belonged was in fact a distinct and separate organisation to the Brief Institution and not, as the 1806 Committee and some historians subsequently appear to have supposed, the same organisation under a different name.[79]

The origin of the Clothiers' Community is rather difficult to unravel, but it is clear that the initiative came from the small master clothiers, angry at the procrastination and apparent duplicity of the trustees. Determined to support the West Country weavers and to carry their case for upholding the old legislation to Parliament and denied access to the funds available in the cloth halls' coffers, in the spring of 1803 they established their own organisation. Members paid subscriptions towards the costs of sending delegates to London and also for a sick fund, receiving a membership ticket on which was engraved a picture of a jenny and a loom.[80] It was clearly this organisation 'of clothiers, masters and journeymen' and *not* the cloth dressers' Institution into which the 'men of respectability' with whom Richard Fawcett had done business and the 'many' master clothiers of whom Stancliffe

---

[76] *Ibid.*, pp. 36, 189.   [77] *Ibid.*, p. 230.   [78] *Ibid.*, p. 208.
[79] Heaton, *Yorkshire Woollen and Worsted Industries*, p. 320; *B.P.P.*, 1806, Vol. 3, pp. 116, 129, 110. See, for example, Thompson, *The Making*, p. 573.
[80] *B.P.P.*, 1806, Vol. 3, p. 36.

knew were supposedly forced against their wills by threats of industrial violence.[81]

According to Joseph Coope, the Clothiers' Community had ceased to exist by 1806 because the trustees of the cloth halls had decided, albeit reluctantly, after all to lead the campaign to retain legislative protection.[82] But during its lifetime the Community showed many similarities to the cloth dressers' Institution. It, too, held 'extensive' delegate meetings and established links with the West Country weavers.[83] Further, its members endeavoured to develop and maintain a strong solidarity. 'Artful and plausible people' like William Child spent much time going round, 'getting the workmen to stand up for their rights and encouraging them to join the organisation'. Though Stancliffe said he believed that the workers were 'not feeling any real grievance arising from their present situation', it is clear that, on the contrary, the woollen workers as a whole were immensely concerned with the implications of the repeal of the old protective legislation.[84] And, even when the trustees took over the campaign against repeal, the more militant members of the Community continued their own separate efforts, the organisation in consequence becoming a more distinctly industrially motivated one. This reflected the growing numbers of journeymen factory weavers in the West Riding who had come by 1805 to dominate the membership. By then, it was claimed, one of the Community's aims was 'to keep up and regulate wages' and the journeymen weavers were using strike action and intimidation of blacklegs to bring their employers to heel.[85] In May 1805 there were disturbances at Wortley when members of a journeymen weavers' society were turned out, according to Child because they intended petitioning Parliament, according to a report in the *Leeds Mercury*, 'under a pretence of breaking up an institution formed for the purpose of relieving each other when sick'.[86] And in August that year there was 'a very extensive turn out of journeymen clothiers in the West Riding', including 400 in the neighbourhood of Leeds, over the manufacturers' declared resolution 'to dismiss from their service all persons who should persist in remaining members' of the union.[87] We should perhaps note that the latter phase of the Community was part of a more

[81] *Ibid.*, pp. 185, 193, 188.
[82] *Ibid.*, p. 35.   [83] *Ibid.*, pp. 192, 190.   [84] *Ibid.*, p. 193.
[85] *Ibid.*, pp. 179–81, 188, 189–90.
[86] *Ibid.*, p. 110; L.M., 4 May 1805.
[87] L.M., 24 Aug. 1805.

general wave of trade union activity of the period and that there is some evidence to link the Institution with it as a mentor. It is also possible that some members of the organisation drifted into the orbit of the Brief Institution itself after 1805 and formed some of the 'various other classes of artificers' which the 1806 Committee found so disturbing a feature of the Institution's membership and influence.[88]

To conclude: by the end of 1802 the woollen industry in all its branches had been precipitated into conflict. In the West of England the weavers had now mobilised collectively to defend their trade as the scribblers and shearmen had done before them. In the West Riding fears of the rise of weaving factories and of the increasing numbers of illegal workmen were beginning to cause the old community of master clothiers and journeymen to fragment, fracturing under the strains imposed by the twin prospects of economic advancement and social debasement. These pressures on the weaving trades were not new. But the circumstances of 1802, not just those of economic depression but more importantly the bitter clashes over the introduction of finishing machinery which stretched old industrial relations patterns past the breaking point, heightened the sense of crisis. And it was for the most part the same men who could be seen as precipitating detrimental change in finishing trade and in cloth making alike. Innovators like Gott or Walker, like Sheppard, Lloyd and Jones, were challenging the woollen industry as a whole to follow them into a new, mechanised, factory-based industry or risk being left behind in economic decline. Their nascent factories were seen as more than receptacles for preparatory and potentially finishing machinery. The factory was now universally recognised as a potent organisational force regardless of the existence of powered machinery. The factory was recognised as the destroyer of customary practice regardless of craft. The factory was recognised as the encourager and employer of men without traditional skills, traditional training or customary expectations. The factory was recognised as the weapon of men prepared to sweep away the structures of the past. As with the cloth dressers, therefore, the events of 1802 heightened the awareness of weavers in the West of England, master clothiers and journeymen in Yorkshire and innovators in both regions that the last bastion to stem wholesale industrial change lay in the old legislative code which

[88] *B.P.P.*, 1806, Vol. 3, Report, p. 16.

governed their industry and in particular the acts relating to apprenticeship, cloth production and machinery. It was thus to Westminster that all sides were to look to settle the issue and before Parliament that they were to lay their cases.

Chapter 7

The political economy of machine breaking

Just as, in the summer of 1802, the threat of industrial change prompted the weavers and master clothiers to look to the old statutes for a means of protecting their trades, the cloth dressers likewise were increasingly turning their attention to the law, in particular to 5 & 6 Edward VI c. 22, 'An act for the putting down of gig mills'. The 1806 Parliamentary Committee implied that the cloth dressers had only 'discovered' this 'obsolete' act in 1802 but this, as we have seen, was not so.[1] Cloth dressers both in the West of England and the West Riding were well aware of the statute long before the Wiltshire Outrages. The Gloucestershire cloth dressers had sought its modification in 1794 and the Wiltshire shearmen had invoked the act in their case against Cook in 1796, though this had shown that the clothiers could use the vagueness of the statute to claim that it was inapplicable. Nevertheless, the Wiltshire shearmen remained convinced that they had a strong case at law. Circumstances in late July 1802 prompted them to try the courts again. By then they had succeeded in intimidating most of the clothiers who had attempted to set up gig mills in Wiltshire. However, key opponents like Jones and Wansey still stood firm and the growing numbers of troops being drafted into the county made attacks on their mills increasingly dangerous. This was a situation very similar to that reached by the Yorkshire Luddites in March 1812. In 1802, however, the Wiltshire cloth dressers still had the remaining weapon of the law in their armoury and they resolved once more to utilise it. This time, though, they chose a different approach. Rather than bring a case against any one particular gig mill user, the shearmen pursued a general attack, presenting a paper to the assizes which indicted all gig mills as a nuisance and contrary to law. This paper, presented by the Trowbridge shearman, Howell, to the

An earlier version of the argument in this chapter appeared in my article 'The philosophy of Luddism', in *Technology and Culture*, 27, 1 (1986).

[1] *J.H.C.*, Vol. 61, p. 696.

Salisbury Grand Jury on 31 July 1802, began a new and crucial phase of the campaign for, although it was rejected,[2] it galvanised the leading innovators into action. A committee of clothiers had been set up at Bath to raise a fund to prosecute rioters. It had not proved a success. However, on 16 August 1802, alerted by the Salisbury case, the leaders of this committee set up a sub-committee to consider petitioning Parliament to repeal the regulatory legislation which they realised provided the workers with a legitimate weapon to oppose change. This sub-committee was chaired by John Jones and was made up of Henry Wansey, Thomas Joyce, Abraham Lloyd Edridge and William Sheppard, all prominent gig mill users, while Jones and Wansey also owned shearing frames. Before many of the general members of the prosecution committee realised it, this sub-committee had turned their funds entirely towards a Parliamentary campaign.[3]

While this sub-committee began clandestinely to organise their petition and to lobby local worthies and M.P.s for support, the innovating clothiers in Gloucestershire likewise were being forcibly reminded of the threat which the old statutes could pose to change. The statement of Justice Lawrence at the summer assizes in August, the founding of the Weavers' Society in September and Jessop's notices to quit in early October clearly showed the danger of a thorough-going implementation of the existing laws. As noted, on 14 October they formed themselves into a new committee, subscribed funds and contacted the Bath committee of the Wiltshire and Somerset innovators. On 4 November they joined forces and within a month this United Committee had presented a petition to Parliament seeking that the old statutes should be 'altered, amended or wholly repealed'.[4] Like it or not, the cloth dressers and weavers therefore found themselves forced into a campaign to safeguard their 'rights' before Parliament.

The United Committee's petition had major repercussions for the woollen industry for it was forcibly to divide it into two antagonistic camps. The clear intention of the petitioners to bring about the repeal of all the old regulatory legislation confronted all those involved in the trade with a clear choice between tradition and progress, between an industry run and structured within traditional parameters of control and one in which these would be overturned by machinery and capital. It is important to emphasise the significance which all in the woollen industry attached to the old legislation. Certainly much of it was

[2] H.O. 42/66, Read to Pelham, 6 Sept. 1802.
[3] Mann, *Cloth Industry*, pp. 145–6; *S.W.J.*, 23 Aug. 1802.
[4] See above, pp. 204–5; *J.H.C.*, Vol. 58, p. 75.

archaic and ignored in the daily business of making cloth. A great deal of it was observed vaguely in the spirit of the law though not to the letter. And regional difference made for different practice and observance. Thus, in the West Riding the laws relating to searching and sealing of cloths to ensure that they were not stretched beyond prescribed limits were generally, if sometimes fairly cavalierly, obeyed whereas in the West of England the practice had long since fallen into desuetude. Custom had accepted the gig mill in Gloucestershire and in north-west Wiltshire for use on coarse white cloths, even though all shearmen believed that legally this was an offence. Elsewhere no such bending of the law was generally tolerated. However, if the legislative code was not slavishly enforced in all respects, psychologically it loomed large in the perceptions of all in the trade, providing a sense of order, stability and continuity to the industry. To the woollen workers these were indeed 'statutes which they thought their protection'.[5] Their restrictions were seen as bulwarks against structural change, defining and delimiting roles and freedoms in much the same way as the legislation controlling the marketing of foodstuffs had regulated roles and freedoms in the market place. The already strong fears that these roles were about to be subverted were greatly heightened by the United Committee's petition. For although the repealers, both from the West of England and from the West Riding, were to argue their case in the years from 1802 to 1809 on technocratic lines, positing the old statutes as being outmoded and irrelevant to the present needs of the industry, their real concern was to open up the trade to just that sort of unfettered capitalist rationalisation which these statutes prevented. Behind the bland words about improving industrial efficiency through the removal of outworn inconveniences lay the ambition to build a factory system on the corpse of the old outworking system. Their opponents' fears of the imminence of this take over were exaggerated, as the repealers and the 1806 House of Commons Select Committee were to emphasise. The outworking system proved to have a resilience and ability to adapt that few in the first decade of the nineteenth century expected. Nonetheless, the repealers' opponents were correct to discern the image of the factory behind the mist of the repealers' fine words. The principal spokesmen for change were all leading innovators, men who had introduced gig mills and shearing frames, had built factories or were planning their construction and who had already sought to undermine the customs of the trade. Their rosy vision of the future was to their opponents a nightmare. 'It is not done yet',

[5] *B.P.P.*, 1802/3, Vol. 7, p. 46.

the 1803 Committee taunted John Phillis, a Shepton Mallet weaver, over his statement that the aim of the repealers was 'to build factories' and put an end to outwork. 'No', he admitted, 'but the clouds seem to rise.'[6]

It was not just the woollen workers who viewed with alarm the attempt of the innovators to repeal the old statutes. The United Committee's petition also split the ranks of capital with the larger and ambitious clothiers, master clothiers and merchants supporting repeal and the smaller makers and merchants opposing it. For example, the Gloucestershire clothiers' association frequently asserted that nearly all the respectable clothiers in the county supported their efforts but in fact only eighty-three firms signed their petition and only seventy-eight firms subscribed to the organisation.[7] The 'inferior' clothiers whose numbers were probably at least four times this were unwilling to subscribe and were mostly hostile. The same pattern was true of Wiltshire. John Jones claimed that seven-eighths of the trade in that county supported repeal but he was weighing franchises, not counting them. The great majority of Wiltshire clothiers opposed the measure. Thus, in Chippenham only four or five of the fifteen or sixteen clothiers supported repeal and of the twenty-eight or thirty clothiers in Bradford on Avon only four were in favour.[8] Certainly the largest producers generally sided with the innovators, but even this was not always so. There were several very prosperous clothiers in the West of England who were conspicuous by their absence from the repealers' ranks. In Yorkshire the petition caused a major rift in the ranks of the master clothiers, leading, as previously noted, to the formation of the Clothiers' Community which united journeymen weavers and small master clothiers in common concert against the proposed repeal and in opposition to many of the larger master clothiers who dominated the cloth halls. The Yorkshire merchants too were split over the measure. The prosperous merchanting firms of Leeds and Wakefield showed little inclination to extend their functions into manufacturing and for the most part remained aloof from the petitioning, though few were prepared to exert themselves to oppose repeal. The merchants of the Huddersfield, Halifax and Bradford districts, however, were generally strongly in favour of repeal and were active in its support. Thus, capital was undoubtedly split by the move for repeal. The prosperous and the ambitious everywhere favoured removal of all and any restriction. The

---

[6] *Ibid.*, p. 63.
[7] G.C.L., JF.13.27, fol. 91; Mann, *Cloth Industry*, p. 145.
[8] *B.P.P.*, 1802/3, Vol. 7, pp. 133, 201, 194, 205, 339–40.

modest and the cautious believed that such a course would lay clear the way whereby the larger capitalist could monopolise the trade. This was the view almost entirely shared by the master dressers in Yorkshire and the West of England. While they sometimes recognised the need for gig mills for dressing some cloths, they believed repeal would herald the demise of independent dressing shops.

The battle lines were soon drawn but the powerful lobbying of the clothiers, merchants and manufacturers did not secure the easy victory they had expected. The House of Commons, recipients of their most active lobbying, proved generally favourable and, within nine days of the reading of the clothiers' petition, had passed a bill to suspend all the old statutes pending further investigation and repeal.[9] The House of Lords proved less easily swayed, however, and the cloth dressers' and weavers' representatives directed much of their energies in this direction. Indeed, when in February 1803 the Lords postponed discussion of the suspension bill, in fact to enable consideration of future repeal, the Wiltshire weavers were jubilant. 'Barton the Weaver has written to his comrades in Bradford that their Enemies are defeated, that praise was due to Mr. Jessop and that they had obtained a complete victory', John Jones acidly recorded on 10 February. The following day the church bells were ringing in Trowbridge and weavers paraded the streets of Bradford on Avon wearing blue cockades. 'Barton came home with the others in Post Chaises.'[10] Such rejoicing proved premature. In March a small committee of the Commons cosily interviewed the petitioning West of England clothiers and, on their evidence, recommended immediate repeal. Thus on 7 April the House gave leave for a bill to repeal all the old legislation concerning the manufacture and stretching of cloth, the use of gig mills, the number of looms which might be owned and the law on apprenticeship. In response, counter-petitions began to flood in. The weavers in Gloucestershire joined with their fellows in Wiltshire and Somerset in a joint petition of protest. The West of England and Yorkshire cloth dressers sent in separate but identical petitions. And eventually the Yorkshire master clothiers sent in their protests. In the face of this mounting pressure, the Commons set up a new large Select Committee to hear evidence from all sides, with the exception of the Yorkshire master clothiers who had yet to agree their position. Here again the arguments of the innovators carried the day and the Committee recommended

[9] *J.H.C.*, Vol. 58, pp. 75, 88, 106.
[10] *J.H.L.*, Vol. 44, pp. 43, 48, 49, 51; H.O. 42/70, Hart to Jones, 10 Feb., Jones to Pelham, 11 Feb. 1803.

repeal. The Commons concurred but the Lords were still less easily convinced and they themselves interviewed in committee counsel for all groups involved. As a consequence they rejected the repeal bill. However, a compromise measure proposed by Vansittart on 27 July and rapidly accepted by both Houses suspended the old statutes for a period of one year to enable closer scrutiny of the problem.[11]

Thereafter the affair dragged interminably onwards. Circumstances or design, or both, hindered an early decision. War returned, ministries changed and the problem was repeatedly shelved. Every year until 1809 the Suspension Act was renewed. Every year until 1806 the repealers failed to bring forward the 'bill for a general revision and regulation of the said laws' they had suggested in 1803. In 1804 the master clothiers of Yorkshire proposed counter-measures which would reinforce the old laws against illegal workers and the numbers of looms which could be employed under one roof. Yet this was allowed tamely to lapse in the face of another suspension.[12] In 1805 tempers and purses, especially in the West of England, had worn thin. The West Country clothiers grew increasingly despondent and had difficulty in making their Yorkshire allies pay their share of the campaign expenses, which by then had amounted to some £6,557. Even the Chancellor protested at the continuing delay and forcibly hinted that he expected action in the next session.[13] The year 1806 did in fact see action. The cloth dressers demanded 'that the affair should at last be taken up', complaining of 'the very heavy expenses which we have been already subject to'. And the Yorkshire master clothiers again sought leave to bring in their own bill to tighten the legislative code. Thus in March 1806 a new Select Committee was set up to investigate the matter. Its composition can have done little to hearten the repealers' opponents for prominent within it were Henry Lascelles and Sir Robert Peel, both committed advocates of deregulation, James Graham who was well connected with the Leeds merchant community and William Wilberforce, the Evangelical and close friend of Pitt.[14] The Committee got through its work quickly. Most witnesses for both sides came from Yorkshire. This reflected not only the way in which the

11 *J.H.C.*, Vol. 58, pp. 252, 334, 351, 352, 358, 375, 379, 386, 398, 413, 414, 455, 472, 477, 572–3, 580; *J.H.L.*, Vol. 44, pp. 203, 310, 311, 317, 321, 324, 335, 345, 366, 378, 397; *J.H.C.*, Vol. 58, pp. 641, 642, 649, 677, 690.
12 *J.H.C.*, Vol. 61, p. 45, Vol. 59, pp. 226, 341.
13 G.C.L., JF.13.27, minutes of the manufacturers' committee; *Hansard's Parliamentary Debates*, 27 June 1805.
14 H.O. 42/83, Tate, Wood and May to Hawkesbury, 10 Feb. 1806; *J.H.C.*, Vol. 61, pp. 78, 136.

preceding campaign had sapped the financial resources of the West Countrymen, but also the Committee's assurance to them that their evidence of 1803 would also be reconsidered.[15] There is little reason to suppose that they did in fact do this. The 1806 Committee proved to be crucial. After brow-beating and ridiculing the witnesses for the weavers and master clothiers and treating the cloth dressers to a witch-hunt over their union activities, the Committee came out firmly on the side of the repealers, lauding in ringing tones the advantages of freedom from control and disparaging the fears of a factory system. Even their panegyric for repeal failed to move Parliament from the fence, however. For three more years Suspension Acts were passed until in 1809 the repealers were given their way and the old statutes at last consigned to the legal dust-bin.[16] The woollen industry entered the brave new world of the nineteenth century.

The campaign before Parliament proved disastrous for the woollen workers but it offers the historian a unique insight into their attitudes towards the threat of machinery which ultimately was to engulf them. We have seen already that the response of most groups of workers in the industry to the advent of machinery was direct and frequently violent. This violence was far from being uncontrolled. Rather it was limited and purposefully directed, its aim being to ensure the withdrawal of innovation and a return to customary work relations. Further, as the Wiltshire shearmen's resistance to the gig mill in 1802 demonstrated, this violence took place within a wider organised resistance to machinery which had its basis in a strong and united trade unionism. However, we would be wrong to see resistance to machinery as being only a physical response, as an understandable but limited reaction of virility towards a threat to economy and status. The response to mechanisation was informed by more than just rational self-preservation. Underlying the workers' reaction to change was an alternative intellectual perception to that of the image of progress offered by the innovators. This view was not just the special pleading of self-interest but was based in an essentially eighteenth-century reading of economics and social relationships which placed a premium on stability, regulation and custom. The woollen workers recognised that the nascent machine economy represented a value system quite alien to this and they therefore sought not only to combat machinery itself but also to refute the whole ethic of *laissez-faire* industrial capitalism which it represented. The struggle over the industrialisation of

[15] Mann, *Cloth Industry*, pp. 146–7; B.P.P., 1806, Vol. 3, pp. 1–4.
[16] J.H.C., Vol. 64, p. 405.

the woollen industry was more than just a physical confrontation. It was an ideological struggle as well. The innovators, by taking the issue of machinery to Parliament, inadvertently opened up the possibility of a major public debate and presented the woollen workers and small master clothiers with a legitimate and effective platform from which to expound their views. Such platforms were rarely available to other groups facing similar crises and their intellectual arguments have in consequence been lost. The woollen workers offer us one of the few examples whereby we can begin to understand the political economy of labour groups before the age of the factory.

In examining their ideological arguments against the spread of machinery, it might be asserted that I am crediting the woollen workers with ideas which were not their own, in that the wider arguments against machinery were put not by them but by lawyers and anonymous pamphleteers on their behalf. The implication here is that clever men gave the workers some intellectual decorations with which to drape their narrow self-interest. Such an argument fails to appreciate the context. Until the working classes acquired an authentic voice of their own with the rise of the Unstamped press in the 1830s, their values remain for the most part historiographically silent. Without a platform and without a medium to transmit them, such views are irrecoverable directly. The historian generally can only extrapolate their attitudes by careful examination of the actions of the crowd.[17] This does not mean, however, that they did not have such views and attitudes. The circumstances of the years 1790–1809 in the woollen industry were exceptional in that the workers could argue that they had the law on their side, a claim which could not easily be ignored, and because in 1803 and 1806 Parliament itself provided them with a platform. While workers were called to give evidence, however, this took the form of answering interrogatory questions. Their overall case had to be put for them by solicitors, lawyers and agents. Only such people were given the opportunity to air wider views since witnesses were kept closely to the issues as defined by their interrogators. Did the workers brief their counsel – they certainly paid them – or did they leave it up to them to 'get them off' with whatever fancy arguments they chose? Neither contention can be proved but it seems to me to be unduly patronising to assume that the men who paid the piper not only knew no tunes but were also tone deaf. That both workers and innovators sought to utilise the economic theories of their age in

---

[17] Thompson, 'The moral economy', was of major influence in pioneering such 'decoding' of the actions of the eighteenth-century crowd.

making their case should not predispose us to consider that their espousal of these doctrines was merely the expedient appropriation of concepts which legitimised special pleading. Self-interest was certainly strong on both sides. Nonetheless, ideologies were embraced only in so far as they harmonised with the economic and social experiences of that self-interest and reflected its aspirations. Economic and social theories provided only the cipher for messages which were already formulated by the culture of the counting house and of the workplace. And those messages, alternatively the need for freedom of capital or the need for order and stability, were the banners of men who genuinely believed that their own special needs were uniquely relevant to and mirrored the needs of the country as a whole.

It is irrelevant for the purpose of examining this debate whether or not these ideologies were ultimately proved correct. The fact that the rise of an unrestricted machine economy brought eventual national prosperity is in this case of no consequence. Nor is it necessary to examine the validity of the workers' claims that machinery would transform their industry and destroy jobs. That it did both seems to me to be clear but hindsight should not distort our analysis of the perceptions of the protagonists at the time. In arguing their cases both were doing more than protecting incomes or capitals. They were defining their own view of the nature and legitimacy of society. William Reddy, in discussing *mentalités* in the French textile industry of this period, has argued that it is necessary to 'recognise how deeply any society's organisation of its productive activity is informed by its culture, that is, by fundamental conceptions of the nature of the world and of human relations to it'.[18] It seems to me that this is putting the cart before the horse. Culture and conceptions of economic and social relations are informed by experience of the economic process and mediated by one's role within it. It was the experience of work and of the organisation and culture of work which principally determined the values expressed by both sides in the debate and which informed their beliefs concerning the legitimacy of economic, social and political relationships generally. It is my belief not only that such views are worthy of understanding in their own right. They also provide the only way by which we may really understand the nature of the conflicts which the Industrial Revolution precipitated.

The debate on 'progress' in the woollen industry, which reached its peak in the years from 1803 to 1806, had its antecedents in the 1780s and early 1790s in the protests over the introduction of preparatory

---

[18] Reddy, 'The spinning jenny in France', p. 52.

machinery and the extended use of the gig mill. While the innovators' case for freedom from restriction voiced then was modified only a little by 1803, the case against change was subsequently much amplified. In the earlier period it essentially contained only two aspects, an amalgam of appeals for paternal protection and to rate-payers' self-interest on the one hand and general warnings of the industrial, economic and social consequences of mechanisation on the other. Primarily the argument emphasised that machinery created unemployment. The Somerset workers in 1776 asked Parliament to prohibit the spinning jenny since it threatened the livelihood of many thousands of the industrious poor.[19] The petition against the spread of scribbling engines in Yorkshire published in June 1786 claimed that 'every single machine used in scribbling' threw twelve men out of work and that 'full four thousand men are left to shift for a living how they can'.[20] The Gloucestershire scribblers claimed that scribbling engines introduced in the mid-1790s were displacing nineteen in twenty men, while the shearmen of that county in 1794 emphasised that machinery would throw countless families onto the parish.[21] This was a powerful propagandist blow. Rate-payers in the West of England in particular viewed with great alarm the poverty caused in many rural parishes by the decline of hand spinning and the general public sympathy accorded to these groups, even when they resorted to violence, was in no small way due to the rate-payers' realisation that, as in the past, the interests of the clothiers and of the community did not necessarily coincide. The woollen workers deliberately played on such suspicions and enmities, pointing out that while cost-cutting machinery was forcing up poor rates, the price of cloth had not fallen.

A further argument constantly voiced against machines was that they made inferior cloth. Scribbling engines 'tear the wool from its true staple' claimed the Gloucestershire scribblers in 1794 and the Yorkshire petitioners in 1786 had asserted that 'the injury to the Cloth is great, in so much that in Frizing, instead of leaving a nap upon the Cloth, the wool is drawn out, and the Cloth is left thread-bare'. The cloth dressers continued from 1794 to 1816 to assert that the gig mill 'injures the texture or ground of a fine cloth'. Both scribbling engines and gig mills were 'driven so violently by the impetuosity of the water' that they could not be adequately regulated. Thus cloths and yarn were stretched and strained beyond their 'true drapery'. Such faults could

---

[19] *J.H.C.*, Vol. 36, p. 7; *B.C.*, 28 Nov. 1776.
[20] Crump, *Leeds Woollen Industry*, pp. 315–16.
[21] *J.H.C.*, Vol. 49, pp. 599–600.

be temporarily disguised but would ultimately show up. Machine-made cloth was thus 'deceitfully made', contrary to many of the old statutes and the machine owners were making large short-term profits at the expense not only of the redundant labourer but also of the unwitting customer and the long-term reputation of the trade itself.[22] There was some justification for such claims. Machines could rarely perform the most skilled tasks as expertly as the skilled man. In the middle and lower quality range of cloths, however, where market growth was fastest, machines had fewer disadvantages. The clothiers for their part claimed that machinery would lead to a better product for it would ensure that standards did not fall when rushed orders were necessary.

To such arguments calling for intervention and control the innovating clothiers responded with a very different ideology. Theirs' was a philosophy which mixed boundless optimism with bottomless pessimism but which at basis was a concept of growth. In essence the innovators' premise was simple. Machines had been invented which enabled cloth to be manufactured more cheaply than before. If their respective rivals began to use them, they too must follow suit or lose all their markets. Thus the assembled clothiers of the three West of England counties declared in 1776: 'It is apprehended that unless the use of such machines be adopted in the woollen trade, the West of England will daily decline, and that the manufactory of the North will enjoy such great advantage as cannot fail to secure them preference at all markets.' In 1791 the *Gloucester Journal* noted: 'It has been found expedient to follow the example of the Northern parts of the Kingdom; who, by their ingenious machines ... [are] rendering their goods cheaper than could be afforded on this side of the country.' John Billingsley, agriculturalist and clothier, stated in 1797: 'Machinery must and will be introduced, otherwise the districts where it is not used must be sacrificed to those where it is.'[23] 'The necessity for machinery has some time existed', noted 'A Leeds Merchant' in 1803. 'It has been introduced in some parts of England; it must therefore in others.'[24] And while manufacturers sought to rally their regions with fear of relative decline – Yorkshire manufacturers were assured that machinery was well established in the West and that if it was not soon taken up in the West Riding their proportion of the trade would

[22] *J.H.C.*, Vol. 49, pp. 599–600; Crump, *Leeds Woollen Industry*, p. 315; *J.H.C.*, Vol. 58, pp. 352, 518, Vol. 60, pp. 92, 235, Vol. 71, pp. 431 *et seq.*

[23] *G.J.*, 14 Oct. 1776, 30 May 1791; J. Billingsley, *A General View of the Agriculture of the County of Somerset* (Bath, 1797), p. 161.

[24] *L.M.*, 29 Jan. 1803.

decrease, while West of England clothiers were told the same of York-shire[25] – they sought to impress all, particularly the government, that if England did not adopt woollen machinery, her foreign rivals would be quick to steal a march on her. 'If ingenuity and enterprise are to be discouraged, they will go elsewhere: other countries will take over', warned 'A Merchant'.[26] Benjamin Gott, giving evidence to a Parliamentary Committee in 1800 noted, 'the trade may be more easily removed in consequence of machinery without any great migration of people for the use of machinery facilitates the removal of any trade'.[27] John Anstie, the Wiltshire clothier, warned in 1802, 'That other nations, and more particularly France, will be disposed to avail themselves of the improvements in machinery cannot possibly be doubted.' And while 'the spirit of improvement would animate our rivals, our manufacturers, checked by injudicious restrictions, would remain in a torpid state'. Machinery, thus, had to be introduced to save the industry and therefore the livelihoods of those employed in it.[28] The *Salisbury Journal* berated the 'deluded and infatuated' workers who 'fly in the faces of their employers whenever improvements are attempted', while a writer in the *Gloucester Journal* told the workmen that they ought to be grateful to the innovators for saving the trade from ruin.[29]

However, machinery was more than a necessary insurance against imminent ruin. It also bestowed incalculable benefits. The clothiers in 1776 claimed: 'the workpeople in general will be thereby greatly benefited, the trade extended and improved, and the wages in many branches of the business increased'. A correspondent of the *Gloucester Journal* in 1791 believed that if opposition to machinery ceased and it was generally used, 'As things appear at present, there is a rational prospect that the trade will be rendered permanently flourishing.'[30] Some apologists even claimed that machinery produced no harmful effects, even of a temporary nature. The clothiers in 1776 declared 'that no mischievous consequences are likely to ensue' but agreed that 'they will be ready to discontinue the use of the machines if after a proper trial they shall be found in any degree prejudicial to the poor'. In 1791 Lord Loughborough lamented that 'unfortunate idea' that machinery

---

[25] See, for example, the Leeds cloth merchants' broadsheet, 18 Nov. 1791, reprinted in Crump, *Leeds Woollen Industry*, pp. 317–19; *S.W.J.*, 19 Aug. 1802; H.O. 42/65, Resolutions of the magistrates of Wiltshire, 24 July 1802; *L.M.*, 17 Feb. 1803.

[26] *L.M.*, 17 Feb. 1803.

[27] *The Times*, 30 April 1800.

[28] Anstie, *Observations on Machinery*, pp. 28, 32, 62–3.

[29] *S.W.J.*, 7 June 1790; *G.J.*, 22 Aug. 1791.

[30] *G.J.*, 14 Oct. 1776, 22 Aug. 1791.

harmed the poor. 'Whatever improved the manufacture must be advantageous to all . . . connected with it.' As did many others, he
pointed to the North of England where 'No persons were deprived of
employment by means of the machines, but many had found employment from them which without them they never could have had.'[31]
Henry Wansey, in one of the earliest apologias for machinery written
by a clothier, explained in 1791 why machinery could not harm the
poor. 'If there was only a certain quantity of work to do, and that being
done, a stop was to be made, the sooner that the work was done, the
worse for the labourers. But the principle of manufactures operates
differently. The more you can do well, the more you may.' The obvious
proof of this was the cotton industry, exports from which had risen ten
times. Machinery would enable woollen manufacturers to extend their
trade in the same way and 'besides, new countries are opening continually to the trade of Britain'. Thus machinery offered the prospect of
continuous growth. Wansey admitted that there was perhaps an ultimate problem that markets might become 'overstocked'. 'There is a
point somewhere beyond which things cannot grow; but it is not for
this Kingdom, under the apprehension of such an event one day or
other taking place, to neglect the present means of encreasing its
strength.'[32] Such highly optimistic claims became less prevalent in the
late 1790s after the effect of machinery, particularly on rural spinners,
had been seen. John Billingsley, though firmly convinced of the need
to mechanise, offered only conditional hope of universal prosperity.
'Whether the introduction of machinery will enable the manufacturer
to make more cloth, or whether a number of the poor must be driven to
seek subsistence by other labour may perhaps be best ascertained by
experiment.' If trade revived and sufficient wool could be obtained,
rapid growth could be achieved. But,

should the present check on the export long continue, or should it be found
that by the hands now in employ and the machinery already in use, the whole
stock of wool shall be wrought into cloth in nine or ten months of the year, the
full grown and aged labourers in this manufacture will be seriously
distressed.[33]

This was a point taken up by the woollen workers.

While earlier promises of unending prosperity gave way to more
guarded statements of optimism in the later 1790s, the West of England
clothiers generally were resolute in their resistance to any argument in

[31] *G.J.*, 14 Oct. 1776; *S.W.J.*, 15 Aug. 1791.
[32] Wansey, *Wool encouraged without exportation*, pp. 67–9; see also *G.J.*, 22 Aug. 1791.
[33] Billingsley, *General View of Somerset*, pp. 161–2.

favour of the restriction or regulation of innovation. Like Billingsley, they believed that legislative interference to regulate machinery

would be incompatible with wisdom and justice. To allow only its partial establishment would be oppressive: to admit of none would be ruinous because such machinery with its appendant branches of manufacture . . . is not only susceptible of, but . . . will shortly be in a state of migration.[34]

A similar view came from a writer from Marlborough in 1794. Restriction was inherently harmful and could only lead to the rapid migration of the clothiers and the industry.[35] Indeed, the innovators frequently threatened local paternalists that, should any attempt be made to 'interfere' with their business, they would immediately wind up their operations and move, leaving their workforce dependent upon the parish. While such warnings did little to endear the innovators to the rate-payers, they could not easily be ignored. And it is notable that as the earlier euphoric view of the benefits of machinery gave way to the more negative arguments over the dangers of failing to mechanise, such threats increased.

The case in favour of an unfettered machine economy was by no means widely accepted by the respectable classes in the West of England. In fact, the woollen workers there received powerful rhetorical support from some paternalists. Indeed, the most crushing attack on the innovating clothiers in this earlier period came in 1793 in an anonymous pamphlet addressed to 'the landholders of the county of Wilts on the alarming state of the poor'. The author, himself almost certainly a landowner, was concerned with the plight of the rural poor and the consequences of the introduction of the spinning jenny but his arguments were equally applicable to other machines and his views typified those of many rate-payers. The pamphlet pointed to the problems of unemployment caused by the jenny and stressed that these problems would grow worse as machinery came ever more widely into use unless either national or local government took immediate action to relieve the situation. The pamphleteer rejected claims that the introduction of machinery was both beneficial to the community and necessary to prevent the loss of trade to rivals. Machinery benefited no one except the clothiers. Indeed, the rest of the community paid heavily to line the clothiers' pockets. Assertions that 'the abridgement of labour' was 'a beneficial scheme' were only true if all those deprived of work were offered alternative employment but, where nineteen out of twenty displaced were forced to rely on poor

[34] *Ibid.*, p. 162.   [35] *S.W.J.*, 2 June 1794.

rates to survive, 'I must confess, it surpasses my abilities to comprehend how the public can derive any benefit from such a measure.' The
clothiers claimed machinery was essential because 'they were undersold by the clothiers in Yorkshire'. They certainly had cut their costs
considerably by machines but the cost of cloth had not fallen. 'For at
the very time the expense of manufacturing was so much lessened,
they availed themselves of a momentary rise in the price of wool and
advanced superfine cloth a shilling a yard: Nor have they again
reduced it since the value of wool has fallen.' This had been possible
because, with foreign imports banned and exports running high, 'they
had the public in their power. Never, perhaps, were the clothiers'
profits so large as when they could not afford to give the customary
wages.' Thus 'however much the public interest may be affected by
machinery, their private interest is undoubtedly advanced'.

The author, however, had no hope that government would intervene to restrict machinery. Indeed, it was not government's job to
'interfere with the jarring interests of trade'. The problem had to be
faced by local authorities. 'You can hope for relief only from your own
exertions.' He recommended the formation of combinations of
parishes to set up 'a manufactory' of their own but, recognising that
this would be condemned as too costly, suggested a cheaper alternative would be to establish an organisation to produce and market hand
spun yarn.[36] A different paternalist view came from Lord Lansdowne
in 1792. While he too rejected any governmental restriction of innovation, he believed that some action must be taken to ameliorate the
conditions of those threatened by machinery or there would be continued unrest. He wrote, 'Rather than attempt anything so arbitrary
and absurd as to stop the progress of the machinery, I am very clear
that it would be better to come to a general rise of wages, especially if
every person was compelled at the same time to belong to some
amicable society.'[37] The clothiers, firm believers in low wages, could
have found little to attract them in such a scheme. Nor were many
merchants and manufacturers swayed by the paternalist urgings of
'Looker On' whose dislike of the factory and the 'pernicious vapour of
steam engines' led him in 1803 to advocate a 'law to say no merchant
shall have a factory'. Indeed, 'A Merchant' responded that, if 'Looker
On' had a factory, 'their pernicious vapours would then lose much of
their deleterious quality'.[38]

[36] *A Letter to the Landholders of the county of Wilts.*, pp. 15, 3–5, 6–8, 9, 10–15.
[37] Cited in Mann, *Cloth Industry*, p. 133.
[38] *L.M.*, 5 Feb., 19 March 1803.

There can be little doubt that, particularly in areas in the West of England affected adversely by the jenny in the early 1790s, feelings ran high against machinery. The views of the pamphleteer in 1793 were widely shared. John Anstie wrote later that the suppression of machinery had been frequently proposed 'by persons of respectability', 'and had the opinion of the county been taken at that time, there can scarcely be a doubt but that it would have been in favour of the measure'. Indeed, even in 1803, Anstie claimed, 'there are a considerable number of persons of respectability in the three counties who ... still continue to consider the introduction of machinery into the woollen trade as unfriendly to the general interest and peculiarly injurious to the poor'.[39] 'A Merchant' likewise recalled how, when the scribbling engines were first introduced into the West Riding, 'many judicious people were caught up in the mania of decrying the machine'. The public response to the opposition of both croppers and clothiers to change in the years after 1800 indicated that here too suspicion of the innovators remained strong.[40]

The quickening pace of mechanisation and the growth of factories in the years around the turn of the century brought the issues raised over the earlier introduction of machinery back to the fore. It was, however, the decision of the West of England clothiers to petition Parliament to repeal the old regulatory code which forcibly polarised the woollen producing community in both regions. In seeking this repeal the innovators shifted the arena of the debate to Parliament, where they believed they would receive a more sympathetic hearing. They also shifted the onus of the debate onto themselves. Nonetheless, the case they presented to the Select Committees of 1803 and 1806 remained much the same as that advanced in the 1790s. The emphasis, however, was now more firmly on its negative aspects.

Above all the innovators sought to demonstrate to Parliament that the old regulatory code was both irrelevant – 'acts which nobody in the trade can or does observe' – and harmful – 'impolitic antequated shackles'. Witnesses were produced to show that much of the legislation was now inapplicable to modern cloth types and production methods. Their enforcement would in all cases occasion 'great delay and inconvenience', while in many instances they would threaten the entire trade with collapse.[41] This was particularly true of 5 & 6 Edward

---

[39] Anstie, *Observations on Machinery*, pp. 20, 7–8, 5–6.
[40] *L.M.*, 19 March 1803.
[41] T. Plomer, *The Speech of Thomas Plomer to the Committee of the House of Commons ... relating to the Woollen Trade in 1803* (Gloucester, 1804), pp. 9, 88; B.P.P., *Report from the Select Committee on the Woollen Clothiers' Petition*, (H.C.. 30), 1802/3, Vol. 5, pp. 3–10.

VI c. 22, an act for the putting down of gig mills, because, it was argued, the gig mill (which was in fact hardly used outside Gloucester-shire and the Huddersfield district) was now vital for the industry, especially for the foreign market. The old controls over stretching and straining cloths were, they claimed, obsolete. Parliament need have no fear that clothiers would over-stretch and thereby potentially damage cloths using gig mills just to obtain increased profits if these regulations were removed. Clothiers and merchants had a vested interest in main-taining the reputation of their product and would be foolish to risk this for short-term gains. Thus their self-interest matched both public and national interests. Self-regulation was the best and only effective form of control.[42]

The workers' arguments against machinery were hardly worth noticing. Thomas Plomer, the West of England repealers' counsel, told the 1803 Committee he would 'not trouble [them] on the general utility of machinery in a nation which has profited so much by it'. Machinery was 'the principal means by which we have excluded other nations from the foreign trade'. To restrict its use was madness. The workers opposed machinery because 'in the first place . . . it is machinery'. 'The manufacturers always decry them at first from the same fear of being thrown out of employ.' Machinery might create unemploy-ment, though the repealers had offered and continued to offer to find alternative work for those displaced. Even if unemployment was inevitable and not temporary, however, the alternative of restriction was far worse. Without machinery the trade would die and all work-ers, not just some, would lose their work. Thus any harm caused by the use of machinery was as nothing compared to its restriction. Repeal of vexatious controls on its use was therefore essential and imperative.[43]

The old legislative controls preventing the establishment of loom-shops and those regulating apprenticeship were likewise attacked as outmoded, allowing, as in the case of the gig mill, disgruntled workers the opportunity to prosecute employers and thereby claim large in-formants' fees. The fears that repeal would be followed by 'the uni-versal adoption of factories' were absurd. Most innovators, many disingenously, denied any intention of establishing them. The West of England clothiers, it was said, preferred domestic weaving, provided they could prevent embezzlement! The apprenticeship laws were

[42] Plomer, *Speech*, pp. 25, 26, 14–15; B.P.P., 1802–3, Vol. 7, pp. 381, 374, 334.
[43] Plomer, *Speech*, pp. 25, 39, 23, 34, 35; see also B.P.P., 1802/3, Vol. 7, p. 337; B.P.P., 1802/3, Vol. 5, pp. 10, 12; Anstie, *Observations on Machinery*, pp. 32–3.

unnecessary for trades were easily learned and, as Adam Smith had shown, unfairly restrictive of liberties. The workers only sought to preserve these statutes to safeguard their own jobs and to maintain their wage bargaining position.[44]

Thus the repealers' case demanded that the woollen trade should be freed from restriction. Parliament should 'encourage competition and not monopoly'.[45] The consequence would be the safeguarding of the trade. The alternative was its decay and destruction. Even though they themselves boasted that they had the markets of the world in their hands, the repealers' case now emphasised only dangers and disasters. The prospect of universal prosperity was a thing of the past.

Against this *laissez-faire* view of economic progress their opponents expounded a quite different economic and moral philosophy. The old case that machinery caused unemployment and impaired the quality and reputation of the cloth was reiterated but before the Select Committees and in print the woollen workers of the West of England and the master clothiers and journeymen of Yorkshire through their spokesmen developed a much wider condemnation of the unfettered introduction of machinery and the repeal of the old regulations. There were, they argued, not merely moral reasons but also sound economic and social imperatives for prohibiting the continued spread of machinery and in favour of effective and indeed tighter control. This case was put most clearly by and on behalf of the cloth dressers but it was a view widely shared by all woollen workers and by many traditionalist clothiers as the Parliamentary enquiries were to demonstrate.

The proponents of regulation denied that they opposed machinery in general. This was 'a cruel and malignant falsehood'. Like 'Looker On', a correspondent of the *Leeds Mercury*, they believed that in some cases 'Machinery may be called in as an auxiliary to human labour' in trades where 'mechanic contrivance will release [men] from occupations too servile or degrading for rational beings, or too slavish and harassing to their strength, or abridge, facilitate or expedite man's labour, still keeping him employed.' However, 'too much machinery may be applied to wool, and there is a point when it ceases to be useful and where it begins to defeat the very end for which it was adopted'.[46] The cloth workers' case assumed that 'A trade or manufacture is deemed valuable to a country in proportion to the number of hands it

---

[44] Plomer, *Speech*, pp. 40, 42, 45, 70, 71; see also *B.P.P.*, 1802/3, Vol. 5, pp. 3–4, 14; *B.P.P.*, 1802/3, Vol. 7, pp. 249–50, 262, 280, 299, 344.

[45] Plomer, *Speech*, p. 70.

[46] R. Jackson, *The Speech of Randle Jackson to the Committee of the House of Commons appointed to consider the state of the Woollen Manufacture* (1806), p. 73; *L.M.*, 5, 12 Feb. 1803.

employs.' Thus, argued Randle Jackson, the shearmen's counsel, 'The dispensing with manual labour is in itself a great and positive evil: it gives a fatal check to population and, in the language of political economy, deprives the land of a portion of its customers, a nation's best and first consideration.'[47] The extension of machinery could therefore only be justified where its advantages to the country as a whole outweighed these disadvantages. Cloth finishing machinery would, as everyone agreed, throw very large numbers of cloth dressers out of work. Such men could not, as the innovators argued, find alternative work for all other branches of the trade were fully subscribed. Thus they were doomed to the poor rates. Even this disaster might be counter-balanced if 'the improvement of the article or the saving in price be such as makes amends to the state for the numbers thrown out of work'. However, none of these criteria applied: 'the foreign market is already in our hands, the price unobjected to, and the customer satisfied . . . in such a case there is no advantage to balance its depopulating effects'. Only if foreign rivals embarked upon 'the indiscriminate application of machinery' should England follow suit. However, Jackson cited Montesquieu and de Boulainvilliers to show that their keenest rivals, the French, were sensible of the dangers of 'projects for machines' whereby 'a multitude of artizans in France [would] become useless'. Machinery could only 'lessen our home markets more than increase our foreign ones'.[48]

There was a further reason why machinery in the woollen industry should not be further extended. While advocates of mechanisation cited the growth rate of the unfettered cotton industry, the advocates of regulation urged that this was an invalid comparison. As the author of the pamphlet *Observations on Woollen Machinery* wrote, 'What might be very great improvements in some branches of trade are not so in the woollen; because it cannot be increased beyond the quantity of wool grown.' While raw cotton could 'be produced ad infinitum', supplies of wool were limited and already stretched to capacity. 'A new large mill can be much sooner erected than additional sheep reared to keep it in motion.'[49] According to John Anstie, the most persuasive pamphleteer in favour of machinery, many intelligent persons were convinced by

---

[47] *Observations on woollen machinery* (Leeds, 1803), p. 3; *Considerations upon a bill . . . for repealing . . . the whole code of laws respecting the woollen manufacture* (1803), p. 13. (While this pamphlet is anonymous, it is clear from its context, style and remarks, especially pp. 11–12, that it is Jackson's speech to the 1803 Select Committee and in reply to Plomer.)

[48] *Considerations upon a bill*, pp. 16, 38, 14, 31, 35–8, 35.

[49] *Observations on woollen machinery*, pp. 6, 12, 10, 9.

this argument, though it was in fact 'a mere vulgar error, originating at first either in ignorance or from design'. Anstie drew on customs returns to prove that imports of Spanish wool had nearly doubled from 1791 to 1799, while he cited one of Pitt's speeches in asserting that enclosures were increasing the number of domestic flocks.[50] However, not only did the master clothiers and workers view the supply of raw wool as being limited. Their whole concept of their market was that of a static one, already fully supplied. 'However powerful the machinery made use of, no more cloth could be produced – no more could be sold than is already sold.' This being so, it was clearly folly to displace men with machines only to sell the same quantity of cloths cheaper. The importing country's gain was the producer country's loss. This was the road to economic dislocation and ruin.[51] This theory of the economic value of hand labour and of selling dear was most ably expounded by 'Looker On'.

It is a well known maxim that a trade is valuable to a country in proportion to the number of hands it employs. Suppose then, that wool could be converted into cloth solely by machinery . . . it would be little better than exporting the raw material. Everyone knows that the more labour is employed on any article prior to its sale, the more generally profitable. Why then, in contradiction to this plain maxim, seek to diminish the number of people employed . . . ? or why endeavour to sell at 13s. what would bring home 18s. 6d. when in all probability all these sixpences lost to the country would not induce the sale of one yard more?[52]

This concept of a static market and of selling dear abroad was no mere ruse thought up to provide a bogus rationale for resisting machinery. It was a view which enjoyed wide currency throughout the eighteenth century and even prominent economists such as Josiah Tucker, who knew the industry well and had little patience for the woollen workers, expounded it.[53] The example of the cotton industry, from which the advocates of machinery drew countless parallels, pointing to the potentialities of ever-expanding markets if the product could be made sufficiently cheap, had, however, shown up the weakness of the old theory and was rapidly discrediting it.

[50] Anstie, *Observations on Machinery*, pp. 34–5, 37, 41, 44–7, 40.
[51] *Observations on woollen machinery*, p. 5. The style and tone of this pamphlet suggest that its author was 'Looker On', the correspondent of the *Leeds Mercury*: see below and pp. 235, 238.
[52] *L.M.*, 5, 12, Feb. 1803.
[53] For example, Tucker, *A Brief Essay*, and *Instructions for Travellers*. See also D. C. Coleman, 'Labour in the English economy of the seventeenth century', *Economic History Review*, 8 (1956), p. 281.

On similar lines the workers and master clothiers argued that England's pre-eminence in the woollen trade lay in the skill of her artisans. Defoe among others had frequently stressed this point as justification for England's higher wage costs than those of foreign rivals. However, machinery superseded this skill and thereby rendered this national asset worthless. Worse, machinery, unlike a skilled workforce, could easily be exported. Machinery 'facilitates the transferring of the woollen manufacture to other nations'. Thus foreigners would be able to compete successfully and seize our trade, leaving English workmen to starve.[54] The spokesmen for innovation rejected this, claiming that, once unfettered, constant mechanical improvement would ensure that the woollen industry would remain ahead of all rivals.

The true secret for retaining our manufactures should be sought for, not in restrictions on the use of new machines in manufactories, by which the efforts of ingenious men may be paralized . . . but in unfettered improvements, in the enlightening of the minds of the work people to discover their true interest, in the repeal of obsolete statutes wholly inapplicable to the present state of the business.[55]

It is notable, however, that in spite of such professions of faith in freeing the trade to market forces, those same innovators were ardent to uphold and augment legislation against the exportation of machinery while local newspapers highlighted the capture of foreign spies who carried plans or models of the new machinery and carried warnings to manufacturers against showing foreigners around their mills.[56]

While the innovators denounced continued regulation, the woollen workers and small clothiers saw it as both necessary and beneficial to the economy. They saw the proposed repeal merely as the aim of 'a small but affluent and powerful association of master clothiers who seek the completion of their fortunes in an utter freedom from Parliamentary restraint'. The result would be disaster. Finishing machinery, particularly the gig mill, damaged the grounds of a cloth. That was why it had been proscribed. The evidence was clear that gig milled cloths were over-strained and were in consequence thinner (and

---

[54] Jackson, *Speech*, pp. 12–19; *Considerations upon a bill*, pp. 36–7; *L.M.*, 12, 17 Feb. 1803. See also R. C. Wiles, 'The theory of wages in later English mercantilism', *Economic History Review*, 21, 1 (1968), pp. 113–26.
[55] Anstie, *Observations on Machinery*, pp. 28, 59, 62–3.
[56] See, for example, Crump, *Leeds Woollen Industry*, pp. 9–10; *G.J.*, 22 Aug. 1786; Rogers, *Wiltshire and Somerset Woollen Mills*, p. 97; Nemnich, *Neueste Reise*, pp. 218, 224–5.

admittedly softer in feel) and much less hard-wearing. Reports from many foreign markets already reflected growing complaints on these lines.[57] The gig mill owners certainly benefited in 'extra profit' from the increased length to a quite prodigious extent but ultimately the reputation of the cloth would collapse and with it the overseas markets. This would not worry the machine owners: 'long before the reputation of the fabric can become so affected as to turn the channel of trade, especially under the present circumstances of Europe . . ., these few gentlemen will have amassed princely fortunes!'.[58] For the cloth workers, however, there were no compensations. 'We, the great body of its artisans, live but by the fame of the fabric which cannot be destroyed without destroying us.' 'It is this high reputation which we are anxious to maintain.'[59] The cloth dressers poured scorn on the innovators' assertion that 'the interest of the Manufacturer' provided a 'most complete and satisfactory security against the impoverishment of the cloth'.[60] 'This is like calling upon a smuggler for his opinion of the revenue laws.' The present laws, like so many others concerned with trade, were necessary to protect the long-term interests of the economy from the short-term gains of the unscrupulous. Thus, they warned of the calamity of 'exchanging the progressive wisdom and experience of five hundred years' and risking 'the high reputation of the great staple of the country' for 'this new philosophy, this emancipation from restraint', 'which preceding ages have treated with the scorn it deserves'.[61]

The West of England woollen workers and master clothiers and journeymen of Yorkshire alike clearly expected Parliament to uphold the existing legislation or to modify it where appropriate, 'keeping in view the uniform policy of the state'. They did not necessarily intend that the existing law should be enforced to the letter. The crucial factor was how custom had interpreted the law and what boundaries of enforcement various communities accepted and felt to be right. For example, while cloth dressers, weavers and master clothiers wanted to enforce apprenticeship legislation, this did not mean they intended formal indentures for the seven years. A worker 'brought up in the trade' by his father, or by a relation, was regarded as a legal worker by the community, if more ambiguously so in law. Indeed, the weavers made it clear that they did not want the law to impinge upon such people, only on persons coming into the trade in later life without this

---

[57] *Considerations upon a bill,* pp. 3, 17, 15, 18, 41–2, 43; Jackson, *Speech,* pp. 23–4, 25, 45.
[58] *Considerations upon a bill,* pp. 40–1, 43.   [59] Jackson, *Speech,* p. 41.
[60] *Considerations upon a bill,* p. 40.   [61] Jackson, *Speech,* pp. 40, 43.

same kind of schooling in the industry. Again, while in Wiltshire and Yorkshire any use of the gig mill was seen as being strictly illegal, in Gloucestershire the gig mill was regarded as morally legal, if not in fact so, when used on coarse cloth. It had been thus used for a very long time so that custom had assimilated its presence into the work style of the community. Further, attitudes of customary legality extended beyond those machines actually banned by statute. Randle Jackson, the cloth workers' counsel, argued that while 'the shearing frames are not prohibited in the same distinct form of words' as the gig mills, 'they are prohibited in spirit and in fact'. The weavers' concern over the legislation relating to apprenticeship and loom ownership reflected this view. They were prepared to concede that aspects of the old code were in need of 'revision', provided that the 'spirit' of the code was retained.[62]

The master clothiers and workers saw continued regulation as a major social necessity. The attempt to break down the prohibitions on clothiers establishing loomshops and the move to abolish apprenticeship excited alarm and animosity. The repeal of apprenticeship was 'one of the most awful propositions ever submitted to the legislature'. Apprenticeship was a major bastion of an orderly moral society. It was foolish to see apprenticeship, as some repealers argued, as 'confined to commercial views and commercial objects'. 'It is both a moral and political institution.' It was only the innovators who sought to undermine it. 'It is a custom which has prevailed time out of mind till within these few years ... it has been relaxed, principally owing to the introduction of machinery and the factory system.' Its abolition would undermine the social fabric. Nor could such a step be justified in isolation. How could apprenticeship be abolished for skilled trades and yet be continued for haberdashers and grocers? 'If you give way in this instance', Jackson prophetically warned in 1806, 'it would be absurd to argue that the abrogation of apprenticeship will be confined to the woollen trade, and that it will not extend to all the various other branches of manufacture ... You must annihilate the system altogether.'[63] This was indeed the course which Parliament was to pursue five years after the repeal of the woollen statutes in 1809, to the anger and dismay of many other trades. To the woollen workers and

62 *Considerations upon a bill*, pp. 45–6; Jackson, *Speech*, pp. 61–3, 30; B.P.P., 1802/3, Vol. 7, pp. 40, 265, 338; B.P.P., 1806, Vol. 3, p. 342; J.H.C., Vol. 58, pp. 886–7; E. Wigley, *The Speech of E. Wigley on behalf of the Woollen Weavers of Gloucestershire to the Committee of the House of Commons appointed to consider the State of the Woollen Manufacture* (Cheltenham, 1806).
63 Jackson, *Speech*, pp. 61, 63, 62, 65.

master clothiers alike, the motivation behind this attempted repeal of apprenticeship was plain. It was to facilitate the rise of the factory system, 'a system which has been found too replete with shocking consequences to be encouraged'. Factories were 'sinks of vice and corruption' which 'deprave the morals of our labourers' and 'break up their happy domestic labouring parties'. These excesses had indeed been recognised by Parliament in enacting 42 George III c. 73. Now repealers wanted to inflict all this upon the woollen trade at the cost of the old-established and morally sustaining putting out and Domestic systems. The factory epitomised the selfish intentions of the innovators, 'this being a system which the capitalist only can embrace and which produces to him a virtual monopoly of the trade'. If allowed, it would destroy the morals of the poor in 'nurseries of vice and corruption' and see 'our valuable middle classes swept away by the monopolising power of the rich merchants'.[64]

The advocates of regulation therefore saw in the new machine economy not just technological redundancy for some but the ultimate total transformation of their industry and of society which they believed could benefit only the new industrial capitalist. They rejected the untrammelled capitalist ethic by which a manufacturer was seen to fill his own purse with the wages of machine-displaced workmen. By their unrestrained greed for increased profits, the whole community suffered. 'It is manifest that the desire for more machinery in the woollen manufactory proceeds not from public but from private advantage. It is wholly a race amongst individuals.' If the manufacturers got their way, the industry would be polarised into 'overgrown rich monopolists' and impoverished workers, with fatal results to the 'spirit, energy and patriotism' of old England. Parliament must reassert the old protective legislative code and save the woollen workers 'from falling sacrifice to the spirit of monopoly, to private cupidity in the guise of public good'.[65]

Parliament thus was urged by both sides to act against monopoly. There, however, the similarity ended. The tone and terms by which the advocates of regulation condemned monopolists conjured up the old hostility to the engrossing middleman and drew on the ethos which had informed the interventionist policy of the Book of Orders and the acts against forestallers and regraters. The innovators, however, posited monopoly in the attempts of labour groups to control

---

[64] *Considerations upon a bill*, pp. 47, 48; L.M., 12 Feb., 5 March 1803; *Observations on woollen machinery*, pp. 19, 18; B.P.P., 1806, Vol. 3, pp. 79, 107, 111, 335.

[65] *Observations on woollen machinery*, pp. 14, 22; L.M., 12 Feb. 1803.

entry into their trades and to obstruct the rise of free market forces unencumbered by such restraints. The words were the same but the meanings turned on their heads.

It is important to reiterate that in opposing this 'spirit of monopoly' the master clothiers and woollen workers were not opposing capital *per se*. They glorified the putting out and Domestic systems and believed that capital, like labour, had its rights and privileges within them which should be protected. They were at pains to differentiate the 'good, honest gentlemen', those who paid full rates and respected custom, from the rapacious innovators. Theirs was not a class analysis, nor, since many small and some quite large capitalists joined with the workers in opposing repeal, can the debate be characterised as such. The enemy was not capital but rather those capitalists who were riding roughshod over custom and rights and who were foisting change on the industry as a whole. Such men were condemned as greedy, unscrupulous and selfish, creating unnecessary competition which was forcing all employers to cut costs to stay in business. Since the proponents of custom saw the market as static and machinery as a means of cutting labour costs rather than as an engine of growth, such competition could only ruin the majority for the transitory benefit of the few. This was why workers, master clothiers and small clothiers in the West of England alike looked to Parliament to uphold the regulatory legislation. Theirs was not a concept of absolute state control. What they required, indeed what they expected, was that the state should, through its legislation, establish rules within which the game could be played. The law, they believed, should offer all protection of their rights and privileges and provide a means of remedying disputes and prohibiting 'unfair' competition. Similar views were voiced by other labour groups such as the London shipwrights.[66] The advocates of regulation believed that these legislative instruments already existed and should continue to be utilised. The innovators' desire to repeal these 'rules' they interpreted as a deliberate recipe for anarchy.

The case for regulation, order and control found little favour before either the 1803 or 1806 Commons Committees but it was the enquiry of 1806 which proved critical. From the outset it was clear that the woollen workers and master clothiers were to fight an uphill struggle. Thompson has written, 'it would be a sad understatement to say that the men's witnesses before the 1806 committee met with a frosty

---

[66] See I. Prothero, *Artisans and Politics in Early Nineteenth Century London: John Gast and his Times* (Wm Dawson, 1979), pp. 63–4, 165–6.

reception. They and their counsel were brow-beaten and threatened by the advocates of laissez-faire and the anti-Jacobin tribunes of order.'[67] The 'outrages in the West' were a constant sore point but still more was made of the aims and deeds, actual and fictional, of the Institution which increasingly took on the lurid light of a revolutionary conspiracy. Books were seized, names of executive members hunted out, reports of meetings and financial accounts pored over. Evidence concerning the harmful effects of gig mills was over-shadowed by evidence dragged from the cloth workers about their union and its activities. Tate, in particular, was subjected to a rigorous grilling. 'I do not mean to tell anything other than the truth', he exclaimed at one point. 'My character is my bread.'[68] Meanwhile, witnesses hostile to the workers were presented with loaded questions with which to concur. 'Do you believe that many very honest persons who object to these institutions on principle, thinking them both dangerous to the trade and to the government of the country, are forced into them in order to get work?' one witness was 'asked'.[69] The weavers found themselves tarred with the same brush of disorder as the shearmen, even though their counsel struggled hard to prove that they were 'unimpeached' on charges of turbulence or riot. Plomer, the West of England clothiers' counsel, even implied that the weavers had only attempted to implement the legislative code because the prosecutor received half of the penalty imposed on the convicted illegal worker or shop owner, claiming that the weavers were 'stirred on . . . with a rich prospect of reward'. Plomer also constantly made insinuations and innuendoes suggesting that the weavers' organisation was, like the Institution, essentially engaged upon illegal activities. The same attack was launched against the Clothiers' Community. E. Wigley retorted, 'Is there any more harm in the weavers of Gloucestershire associating in a body . . . than in the gentlemen who came before you in 1803 for a repeal? They also formed an association . . . Is blame to be thrown upon my clients for employing Mr. Jessop . . . and Mr. Sheppard and his friends be allowed to employ Mr. Vizard without reproach?' Yet much of the mud stuck.[70] While Jackson could argue that his clients ' must be entitled to equal credit without regard to their station in life', the Committees were inclined to heed the view aired by Plomer in 1803. He urged:

[67] Thompson, *The Making*, p. 577.
[68] *B.P.P.*, 1806, Vol. 3, p. 244.
[69] *Ibid.*, p. 185.
[70] Wigley, *Speech*; Plomer, *Speech*, pp. 21–2, 13–14.

When it is considered who are the class of persons associated, corresponding in different parts of the kingdom – their passions warmly engaged in the immediate subject of consideration – their rate of understanding and education very little able to comprehend the true interests of the trade, or their own interests – very liable to be misled by designing men – will any man tell me that it is not a serious subject of alarm to the country?[71]

With the witnesses for regulation discredited either by reason of their humble intelligence or their suspected subversiveness, and with the illustrious Sir Robert Peel expounding on the incalculable benefits to all of the factory system,[72] the Committee's mind was made up – if there had ever been any doubt as to which way they would lean. Unable to produce a collective report, they dropped the task into the lap of William Wilberforce who was happy to accept it. Mann writes that Wilberforce's conversion to the view that repeal would not harm the Domestic System was crucial.[73] If conversion it was, it was with a wholeheartedness of which an Evangelical would have been proud. The Report was a thorough-going testament to *laissez-faire* doctrine. The Report reiterated the views put forward by the manufacturers, that machinery was necessary and was making the industry expand and prosper, that foreign competition could only be kept at bay by the unhindered use of machinery and that the factories were in no way threatening the Domestic System. 'The rapid and prodigious increase' of the output of the industry the Report ascribed to

the general spirit of enterprize and industry among a free and enlightened people, left to the unrestrained exercise of their talents in the employment of a vast capital; pushing to the utmost the principle of the division of labour; calling in all the resources of scientific research and mechanical ingenuity; and finally, availing themselves of all the benefits to be derived from visiting foreign countries.

'Apprehensions entertained of factories' were 'practically erroneous'. The Report praised the Domestic System and the independent cloth-iers[74] but could see 'no solid ground for the alarm that has gone forth that the Halls should be deserted'. Nevertheless, restriction was perni-cious. The Report declaimed that 'The right of every man to employ the capital he inherits, or has acquired, according to his own discretion, without molestation or obstruction, so long as he does not infringe on

---

[71] Jackson, *Speech*, p. 4; Plomer, *Speech*, p. 13.
[72] B.P.P., 1806, Vol. 3, pp. 439–40.
[73] Mann, *Cloth Industry*, p. 149.
[74] The 'loyal and independent' master clothiers of the West Riding made up no small part of Wilberforce's electorate.

the rights or property of others' was the Englishman's birthright.[75] Not only did the Report recommend repeal of all the old legislation relating to the manufacture of cloth but it also added a long condemnation of the cloth dressers' Institution. 'Your Committee', it noted, 'need scarcely remark that such institutions are, in their ultimate tendencies, still more alarming in a political than in a commercial view.' The 'baneful effects' of such in a Sister Kingdom were clear proof.[76]

The rest of the Committee seem to have shared Wilberforce's views. 'I carried it almost finished to the committee', he wrote, 'and all of them delighted with it and most pleasingly liberal.'[77] Their Report marked the end of the real struggle. Suspension Acts delayed the inevitable until 1809, as Parliament gradually reconciled itself to the abdication of its old paternalist functions. But in 1809 the old laws were swept away and the woollen industry entered the nineteenth century. Repeal must have been a bitter pill to swallow. Since 1803, the cloth dressers complained, they had been forced into the role of 'afflicted spectators of the daily violation [of the law] by the master clothiers who have been making very large fortunes to themselves at the expense of those privileges and of that employment which Parliament has held out and guaranteed to your petitioners as the reward for long and faithful service'.[78] Now Parliament had torn away those privileges and rights and identified itself with the large manufacturers, the men of capital, the factory owners, men who were destroying old customs and community. The loss of their 'rights' in 1809 was a prelude to the more bitter crisis of 1812 in Yorkshire. The cloth workers may still have hoped that the old protective legislative code could be revived but its loss in 1809 limited their options and added a new desperation. Ned Ludd wrote to Mr Smith, Shearing Frame Holder at Hill End, York-shire, in March 1812, 'We will never lay down our Arms [till] the House of Commons passes an Act to put down all Machinery hurtful to Commonality, and repeal that to hang Frame Breakers. But We pet-ition no more, that won't do, fighting must.'[79]

---

[75] B.P.P., 1806, Vol. 3, S.C. Report, pp. 7–11, 12.

[76] *Ibid.*, p. 17.

[77] R. I. and S. Wilberforce, *The Life of William Wilberforce* (1838), Vol. III, p. 267.

[78] H.O. 42/83, shearmen's petition, 1806.

[79] H.O. 50/460, Ned Ludd to Smith, enclosed in Radcliffe to ?, 14 March 1812.

Chapter 8

Machinery, custom and class

The debate over class and class consciousness in the English Industrial Revolution has moved a long way since Engels confidently asserted, 'The history of the proletariat in England begins with the invention of the steam-engine and of machinery for working cotton.'[1] Just as our perceptions of the Industrial Revolution itself have now been stretched and expanded to include its roots early in the eighteenth century as well as the rise of the cotton factory in the 1790s, so have our notions of class formation moved away from the mechanistic equation of technology equals factory equals proletariat equals class consciousness. Both economic and social historians now recognise that technological innovation had only a limited overall impact. Its development led to key strategic changes within the economy but economic growth was as much due to a multiplication of hand workers as to machines, as much due to a proliferation of small workshops and domestic production as to large-scale factories. Industrialisation before the factory and industrialisation alongside the factory is increasingly being given its due status in understanding the process of economic transformation.[2] Industrial growth was multiform and even as late as the 1850s it was 'the juxtaposition of hand and machine labour' which characterised the economy, not machinofacture.[3]

Paralleling this widening and diffusing of our picture of the economic process of the Industrial Revolution has come an enlarged comprehension of the social and cultural impact of economic transformation. In this, paramountcy must be accorded to the work of E. P. Thompson. *The Making of the English Working Class*, first published in 1963,[4] stimulated a new approach to the study of English social

---

[1] F. Engels, *The Condition of the English Working Class in England in 1844* (1892 edn), p. 1.
[2] See, for example, Berg, Hudson and Sonenscher, eds., *Manufacture in Town and Country*, and Kriedte, Medick and Schlumbohm, *Industrialisation before Industrialisation*.
[3] R. Samuel, 'The workshop of the world: steam power and hand technology in mid-Victorian Britain', *History Workshop Journal*, 3 (1977), pp. 6–72.
[4] Thompson, *The Making*.

history and in particular to the cultural and political impact of industrial change. Thompson eschewed the notion that the Industrial Revolution's social impact was technologically and teleologically confined to the development of a factory proletariat and a new urban industrial underclass. He persuasively argued that while these groups were clearly social 'products' of industrialisation, their numbers were not large and they were strategically important only in a few areas. However, while the factory employed relatively few, the experience of intensified exploitation due to the development of a nascent industrial capitalism, of which the factory was but the tip of the iceberg, was shared by the majority of workers. Artisan, handloom weaver, miner, agricultural labourer, adult and child alike experienced the intensification of accelerating economic growth and increased subordination of labour. Each in their different trades experienced increasing and effective assaults upon, and the eventual undermining of, both custom and culture. All shared the growing burden of political repression and social control. Growing competition for work, longer hours and increased exploitation at work, decreasing autonomy over work and the destruction of old communal values characterised not just the experience of the factory worker: it was the common experience of the majority. Different groups in different trades and regions felt these pressures at different rates and times but the cumulative consequence, Thompson argued, was the generation of a common class identity, a recognition of the class-divided nature of society and the realisation of a working-class consciousness. Class consciousness, therefore, was not the simple product of economic forces nor of a new factory proletariat. It was an historical relationship which developed out of the existing social order, a social and cultural formation which evolved over time, embracing workers in most trades and in all regions.[5]

Thompson's interpretation of the making of the English working class found and continues to draw critics from both the left and right, suspicious of his emphasis upon seeing class in cultural rather than in merely discrete economic terms.[6] Nonetheless, his 'cultural marxism' has had a profound influence upon subsequent social historians. For example, Richard Price has most recently echoed this line of approach in his account of the development of class relations. Like Thompson, Price recognises class as an evolutionary relationship, criticising those who assume the existence of some notional absolute definition of class

---

[5] *Ibid.*, in particular see Preface and Postscript.
[6] See, for example, Nairn, T., 'The English working class', *New Left Review*, 24 (1964), and Donnelly, 'Ideology and early English working class history'.

consciousness. While accepting that class consciousness was a product of the Industrial Revolution, Price argues that the crucial factor in this was changing market relations, not technology or its consequent organisational transformations. 'The process of proletarianisation was not primarily a matter of subordination to a labour process that was technologically driven. Rather it was a process that occurred more in the sphere of market relations and involved increased exposure to the vagaries of market forces.' It was this rapid expansion of market demand which shattered old restraints of market regulation, broke down labour's opportunities for economic advancement, extended labour specialisation and resulted in the incursion of excess labour into an expanded labour market. Thus the Industrial Revolution saw little that was new but an intensification of pressures already in the pre-industrial economy which broke down older work customs and cultures.[7]

The shift away from a machine-dominated picture of the experience of the Industrial Revolution marks an important broadening of our understanding of the social consequences of economic change. However, we must resist entirely throwing out the baby with the bath water. The principal factor in the rapid acceleration of production in the last quarter of the eighteenth century was technological innovation. None were especially dramatic, though we have noted the considerable labour-saving capacity of the woollen textile machinery developed in this period. Certainly no industry was totally transformed by technological innovation but the machine was a major agency in the rapidly increasing pace of change and it was the dynamic which gave the impetus to those who wished to cast aside existing barriers to more wholesale industrial re-organisation. The impact of the machine upon labour can be seen in three ways. First, it directly displaced key labour groups, as for example the hand spinners, the scribblers and the cloth dressers in the woollen industry and the wool combers in the worsted trade. Secondly, its impact was experienced by a wider group at second-hand, such as by the families of those displaced or by the trades of others to which those made redundant flocked as in the case of handloom weaving. Thirdly, most remotely but most extensively, it provided a role model for other industries and trades as yet untouched directly. The machine pointed the way towards the factory and extended capitalist control over, and

---

[7] R. Price, *Labour in British Society* (Croom Helm, 1986), pp. 21–7. William Reddy makes a similar case in his highly provocative book, *The Rise of Market Culture*. See also Rule, *The Labouring Classes*, pp. 384–93.

subordination of, labour. The organisational role of the factory was certainly appreciated well before the Industrial Revolution but it was the advent of powered machinery which made the factory essential. And, once established from need, the factory system rapidly became established as a production mode to which other industrialists without the direct requirement of powered machinery began to aspire.[8] The factory, with its regularity, order, control and discipline of labour became not just a model for modern industrial efficiency but more powerfully still a metaphor for society and social relations as a whole. The fear of the factory, with its connotations of subservience and the workhouse, hung over many old handicraft groups for decades before their trades were in reality overtaken by the system itself. And if the factory was seen as a prison, it was the machine which was the treadmill, it was the machine which had crystallised the elements of subordination, discipline and production into one coherent and exploitative whole. Technological change was therefore the sharp point, the spearhead of the transformation of old industries like the woollen textile industry. This transformation may be traced back to the early decades of the eighteenth century but it was powered machinery which gave it its cutting edge, machinery which made the old system, the old ways, ultimately untenable.

This was not a sudden or rapid process. Early machinery was not very efficient, sometimes not as efficient or as cheap as hand methods. Doubtless this was a factor which led or helped persuade the employers at Shepton Mallet to abandon the attempt to use the jenny after the riots there in 1776. The culture of many gentlemen clothiers and merchants in both the West of England and the West Riding was also not immediately amenable to machine production. To the security of old methods could be added the undoubted social advantage of a merchanting lifestyle with which the risks, capital expenditure and lower social esteem accorded to those who must directly manage labour compared poorly. Thus many early innovations met not just with worker hostility but also with capitalist indifference. However, once the machine had been developed, once it was proven as a money-saver or as an accelerator of production, other capitalists were forced to follow the innovators' lead or be put out of business. The machine was thus a powerful agency coercing them to change. And, once embarked upon mechanisation, other imperatives followed: the need to subordinate and control labour, the need to break down old customs and

---

[8] As, for example, Josiah Wedgwood: see N. McKendrick, 'Josiah Wedgwood and factory discipline', *Historical Journal*, 4, 2 (1961).

work cultures. Such barriers to progress had been under siege for many decades. Machinery provided the force requisite finally to achieve the managerial breakthrough. Thus it was not just labour which was compelled to re-evaluate its attitudes and values by machinery. Capital too was compelled to accept a fundamental realignment of its self-perception and to adopt a sharper and more confrontational mode in its relationship with labour.

This raises the question, how far did the rise of the machine lead to a growing class identity? Did machinery and the factory release the 'latent' class consciousness of pre-industrial labour relations and give rise to a new awareness of economic exploitation, a new perception of a society divided horizontally on the basis of the relationship to the means of production, a new realisation of political alienation, in short a new class feeling?[9] This sort of interpretation has a long and honourable tradition dating back to men like Bronterre O'Brien and the Owenite socialists in the 1830s. With the Hammonds it entered into historical orthodoxy and its influence can still be seen in the writings of historians as diverse as Perkin and Foster. However, this line of argument has tended to be centred upon the new urban and factory workers rather than upon old pre-industrial labour groups, upon those who became components of the new machine society rather than upon those displaced or threatened by machinery.[10] What does the evidence of the introduction of machinery into the wool textile industry before 1811 indicate of the changing attitudes and economic and political perceptions of workers and small masters whose culture was deeprooted in pre-industrial modes of production?

It is clear that the introduction of machinery *per se* did not automatically lead either to resistance or economic alienation. The machine was not always seen as inherently harmful to the interests of labour. In many cases it might liberate labour, opening up new horizons of social and economic advancement. The critical determinant, as has been seen, was whether it could be accommodated within the existing structure of work without substantially altering the autonomy of labour. Thus in the West Riding preparatory machinery encountered some initial hostility but this rapidly evaporated when it became clear that it could be incorporated into the Domestic System without

---

[9] The concept of 'latent' class consciousness comes from Perkin, *The Origins of Modern English Society*, p. 26.

[10] J. Foster, *Class Struggle and the Industrial Revolution* (Weidenfeld and Nicolson, 1974), sees class consciousness in Oldham emerging through the factory spinners' trade union consciousness, not among the declining handloom weavers though they were important in early radicalism in the region.

threatening existing economic relationships. In the West of England, however, the same machinery displaced workers and initiated a continuing process of centralisation of work under the more direct control of the clothiers, a process fiercely resisted by the woollen workers. The hostility to mechanisation, therefore, was not an automatic one. Nor was it entirely implacable. Workers under threat often offered to accept a phased introduction of machinery, a gradual regulated change which might allow jobs and elements of old work practice to be retained. Such compromises were always rejected by the innovators. They recognised, some with more clarity than others, that the machine constituted a powerful weapon of control. Many were keen to make use of it as such.

Resistance to machinery, however, was informed by more than simply the fear of displacement. It drew its strength, as has been seen, from the entire woollen working community. The composition of the crowds who rioted against the jennies, scribbling engines, flying shuttle looms and gig mills, who offered widespread support to the cloth dressers both in 1802 and 1812 and who subscribed to strike funds and petitioning funds indicates a community basis for resistance rather than an occupationally specific one and a community value system which was alienated by the rise of the machine. It was because of this community-based support that resistance proved so lengthy and powerful. In what ways, therefore, did a machine economy offend this community *mentalité* and did this in consequence generate a new consciousness of class?

While, as the Select Committees of 1803 and 1806 demonstrated, the master clothiers and woollen workers had a powerful and coherent economic case against machinery, the community *mentalité* engendered by the economic and social structures of wool textile production in both the West of England and the West Riding was at base informed as much by moral imperatives as by economic ones. Capitalist work structures and relations were mediated through the powerful and restrictive matrix of custom which reinforced cultural as well as economic values. In a very positive sense here we can discern the basis of the 'moral economy of the English crowd' delineated by E. P. Thompson to describe the attitudes of eighteenth-century food rioters.[11] Historians have taken up the 'moral economy' thesis in various forms, in some cases interpreting it as a methodology in situations of conflict, in others as an anti-market philosophy and in yet others as a simple

[11] Thompson, 'The moral economy', pp. 76–136.

bargaining strategy.[12] They have, however, for the most part confined their examination to consumer protests. Yet it is clear that the values of the moral economy, namely the premium placed upon stable and regulated economic relations, the concepts of well-defined rights and parameters of autonomy, the belief in the legitimacy of actions upholding customary rights, all were forged every bit as much by these workers operating as producers rather than solely as consumers.[13] This emphasis upon consumption rather than production has had the unfortunate consequence of blinkering perceptions of the role of such a morally impelled view of economic relations and allowing some historians to set up an Aunt Sally in which the moral economy thesis is constructed as a supposedly ubiquitous value system applicable to all groups of workers at all times of hunger which is thence easily knocked down by the 'fact' that food riots, the only supposed manifestation of this moral economy, were not continuously convulsing the kingdom. Such arguments indicate a lack of contextual awareness and a naive reading of Thompson's work.[14] First, it should be obvious that a value system may indeed be widely shared without necessarily galvanising all its believers into action at all possible occasions. Not all groups of workers found themselves in a political or social context which enabled them to embark upon social protests with a reasonable expectation of success and likelihood of avoiding subsequent punishment. This is not to say, however, that these non-active groups accepted or condoned the forestalling and regrating activities of middlemen or the manipulation of market prices by cabals of wealthy farmers. Secondly, and for the purpose of this argument more importantly, the strongholds of the moral economy food rioters, the miners, the tinners, the weavers, the nailers *et al.*, were all areas of developed capitalist industry. These workers were all in clear capitalist–labour relationships, dependent upon wealthy capitalists to provide them with work and receiving their livelihood from earnings from piece work. The origins of the moral economy therefore have to be found *within* a capitalist economy, not outside or in opposition to one.

There is no evidence to suggest that food rioters were repudiating

[12] For example, see J. Stevenson, *Popular Disturbances in England, 1700–1870* (Longman, 1979), pp. 91–112; D. E. Williams, 'Morals, markets and the English crowd in 1766', *Past and Present*, 104 (1984), pp. 56–73; R. Wells, 'The revolt of the South-West, 1800–1801: a study in English popular protest', *Social History*, 6 (1977), pp. 713–44.
[13] Randall, 'The industrial moral economy', pp. 29–50.
[14] Williams, 'Morals, markets and the English crowd'. For a critique of such views see Charlesworth and Randall, 'Morals, markets and the English crowd', pp. 200–13.

the essentially capitalist structure of food marketing. Their protests were directed specifically against what they saw as 'unfair' practices within that structure whereby the owners of foodstuffs were able to utilise their economic power for their selfish interests *to the detriment* of the wider community. This concept of fairness, of justice and reasonableness, was reinforced by a customary and constitutional framework of legal imperatives. It was to these that food rioters traditionally demanded recourse or, more typically, these they attempted to implement on their own behalf in the absence of magisterial action. Food rioters did not demand popular *control* over the distribution of foodstuffs. What they sought was that the traditional model of marketing, which provisioned the needs of the local population first, should be operated transparently and fairly in the interests of all. Farmers, dealers and bakers could claim a *fair* profit but they could not be allowed to use their monopoly of a vital resource to hold a community to ransom.[15]

Likewise, these same workers can be seen holding very similar views as producers within the same sort of capitalist relations which obtained in their working lives. Custom, the workplace's equivalent to the moral economy, dictated traditional models for economic relations which were as much morally impelled as economically prescribed. Thus, in conflicts in the eighteenth century, textile workers cannot be seen as challenging a capitalist system of production. As in the market place, capitalist relations were the only relations available. Their protests and industrial actions were directed against 'abuses', against assaults upon workers' autonomy in production and against those who sought to exploit a monopoly of economic power for narrow selfish interests to the detriment of the community. The 'language' of protest confirms this. These workers condemned not employers *per se* but the 'dishonourable' men who cut wages, took on illegal workers, produced 'deceitfully made' products and sought to overturn custom. As with the moral economy, therefore, we see the attempt to ensure stable and fixed parameters which regulated the workers' relationships *within* a capitalist system of production and distribution. These parameters protected the economy, the independence and the status of the labourer and in consequence defined what was 'fair' and 'unfair'. The moral economy was an economy of free men, not slaves, but also of men who accepted a subordinate relationship within a capitalist system.[16]

---

[15] *Ibid.*, p. 207.
[16] Randall, 'The industrial moral economy', pp. 46–7.

Many aspects of this industrial moral economy may be discerned in the attitudes of skilled and organised labour groups in the nineteenth century. And later twentieth-century Britain offers us plentiful examples of workers in 'traditional' industries condemning and resisting sweeping capitalist restructuring and redefinition of industrial relations in terms of both custom and fairness. As such, this conservatism of labour groups, this attempt to ossify relatively favourable aspects of their employment into custom, can be taken as a common factor and hence dismissed. However, in eighteenth-century England both custom and the moral economy were reinforced by law. The common law, the Book of Orders and the acts against forestalling and regrating offered the food rioters a powerful sense of legitimacy in their price-fixing actions. Likewise, the many regulatory acts which governed the woollen industry gave those workers an equally strong 'legitimising notion' whenever employers sought to re-draw the boundaries of custom.

The woollen manufacturing districts of the West Riding and the West of England demonstrated clear community belief in a moral economy of productive relations in the years of the onset of the Industrial Revolution. In both regions the innovators were condemned as destroyers, their machines attacked because they were the instrument whereby the stable barriers of custom, autonomy and status were being overturned. However, while the workers of both regions could recognise the implications of a machine economy and feared them, while in both regions the arguments against machinery were couched in the rhetoric of a moral economy, there were clear differences not only in the actions taken but in the relative perceptions of the threat posed which were the consequence, in part at least, of the different organisational structures in the two regions. In the West of England machinery was introduced into an industrial structure already heavily polarised between capital and labour. It is true that in many cases the innovators were not the most prosperous gentlemen clothiers but the lesser clothiers prepared to run the risks involved in the new technologies for the opportunity of economic and social advance. These lesser clothiers were, however, accompanied by men of real substance such as John Jones of Staverton, Francis Naish of Trowbridge or Henry Wansey of Warminster. Moreover, large or small, their adoption of a mechanised economy emphasised the already wide gap between clothiers and workers, emphasising fears of a monopolistic factory system and the breakdown of the autonomy enjoyed within the putting out system. In Yorkshire, however, the men who introduced and

took up the preparatory machinery in the 1780s and 1790s were frequently the master clothiers, men who still retained roots in and
influence over the Domestic System and in the cloth halls. Incorporating these machines within the workshop economy of the master
clothiers disguised the significance of their take up and, while it is clear
that there was growing disquiet, the journeymen only slowly developed sufficient self-confidence to articulate their fears independently of their master clothier employers while the latter remained
unsure of which way to turn, half fearing the implications of the advent
of the machine age, half fearing to be left behind in its wake.

The different work structures of the West of England and West
Riding had also given rise to very different traditions of labour relations which likewise had their effect upon the behaviour of workers
in the respective regions in the years from 1776 to 1812. The West of
England's specialisation of crafts bequeathed a pattern and an experience of much more frequent industrial conflict than was found in the
West Riding. Organised and collective defence of living standards and
custom were features of the eighteenth-century experience of the
workers in the West and this willingness to resist detrimental change
was further augmented by a tradition of food rioting and other forms of
popular protest. The West Riding for the most part lacked this sort of
tradition. Thus it was that organisation only slowly emerged in the late
1790s and that the trustees of the cloth halls, the traditional spokesmen
of the master clothiers, were able to hold so significant an influence
over the cloth producers even in 1806 when it was clear that their
leadership was in many ways fundamentally opposed to the attitudes
of the majority of master clothiers and journeymen. In Yorkshire only
the cloth dressers had an established tradition of vigorous self-defence
and it is significant that it was around their struggles to resist machinery in 1812 that community support against the new system was to
coalesce.

How far did the advent of machinery undermine these value
systems and give rise to a new class feeling? In the West of England the
machine, by augmenting still further the power of the clothiers, could
reasonably be expected to have greatly increased an economic awareness of class and have given rise to increased class alienation. Many
capitalists there seemed bent upon the destruction of all the legal
bulwarks of custom. The fear of the monopolistic ambitions of such
men came over clearly in the evidence given before the Select Committees of 1803 and 1806. 'Upon them and cut them up like Chaff', read
the notice to all shearmen stuck up at Freshford in 1803, 'for they have

oppressed us long enough.'[17] While this sounds like the authentic voice of class alienation and hostility, however, it would be a misnomer to assume that a clear class identity had emerged. In fact, the very strength of the old industrial moral economy impeded recognition of the new economic relationships developing around them. Just as middlemen and factors had been condemned not for their role but for the way they fulfilled it, so were clothiers who introduced machinery condemned for their actions which violated custom, not as employers. For to have perceived all employers, all clothiers, as class enemies would have necessitated recognising the putting out system itself as a system of class conflict. The woollen workers on the contrary idealised this system and believed it to be the source of their status, independence and culture. They did not challenge the market relations of the outworking system for indeed, as Reddy notes, their 'critical social relationships were all commercial ones, all focussed on markets of one sort or another'.[18] What they challenged was not capital but the new aggressive, tradition-scorning version of capital which sought to impose an amoral vision of market relations unconstrained by any impediment. The galvanising impetus behind this vision the workers correctly identified as the machine and as machinery gradually overcame their opposition so their perceptions gradually altered. However, as long as at least some clothiers were 'content with their trade of clothing', the woollen workers were reluctant to view them as a hostile class. Men like Anstie showed that not all the leading clothiers were intent upon driving all the workers into factories. Men like Bush in Bradford on Avon, by his ostentatious refusal to join the repeal association, showed that some gentlemen clothiers of eminence were not party to the attempted destruction of the old system. It was this refusal to accept that the machine age was not just an aberration, the work of dishonourable masters who should be condemned and restrained by workers and 'good honest gentlemen' alike, which delayed recognition that their view of a stable and reciprocal economy of outworking was inevitably doomed. In Gloucestershire in particular we can see how the clothiers' adroit handling of their workforce meant that the moral economy continued to influence attitudes of weavers in the county into the 1830s. In Wiltshire, where clothiers in the eighteenth century had preferred a more confrontational style, the

---

[17] *S.W.J.*, 7 Feb. 1803.
[18] W. M. Reddy, 'The textile trade and the language of the crowd at Rouen 1752–1871', *Past and Present*, 74 (1977), pp. 73–4.

polarisation of the classes occurred rather earlier.[19] It cannot, however, be said to have occurred before the Parliamentary Select Committees of 1803 and 1806 began the process of dismantling the legislative safeguards of the workers' idealised economy.

In Yorkshire, too, the development of an economic class consciousness was a far from steady or even process. While the years from 1803 to 1806 revealed a widening gulf between capital and labour, changes were sufficiently protracted and the legacy of the old values of the Domestic System was so strong that only slowly did such a consciousness emerge. A key reason for this was the pivotal role of the master clothiers and the impact of the machine economy upon their ranks. At first most master clothiers hoped to be able to share in the early machine age. Gradually, however, there came a fracturing of their ranks, brought to a head by the West Country clothiers' petition to Parliament to repeal the old legislation. While many master clothiers were able through capital accumulation to metamorphose into manufacturers, others found themselves irresistibly forced back into the ranks of journeymen. While the majority survived in the old ways for some two decades, there was no disguising the fact that the status of the master clothier was becoming debased. Nonetheless, such recognition came but slowly. As in the West of England pretensions of status survived tenaciously in the face of reality. For the journeymen the impact was more immediate and more immediately painful. The prospect of social mobility into the ranks of the master clothiers was an important aspect of the harmonious industrial relations of the West Riding woollen industry. Machinery reduced these opportunities and meant that work had increasingly to be found in the entrepreneurs' factories rather than in the master clothiers' shops.[20] The consequence was growing frustration and bitterness. However, as long as the master clothier survived as a recognisable intermediary producer, the journeymen's sense of class feeling remained but poorly focussed.

The woollen workers in both the West of England and the West Riding therefore viewed the threat of machinery through the matrix of an ideology which was essentially conservative. It assumed a consensus of opinion about how their industry should be run which placed a major premium upon custom. For a culture which was so deeply rooted in such a belief, the transition towards a confrontational vision

---

[19] Mann, *Cloth Industry*, pp. 116–20, 240–1.
[20] See, for example, the evidence of Child and Atkinson in *B.P.P.*, 1806, Vol. 3, pp. 104, 111, 117–18.

of economic and social relations regulated only by economic might was to prove difficult.

The same was true, though to a lesser degree, for capital. In both regions the increasing delineation of 'respectable' capital from more petty-capitalists reflected not merely a growing economic gap between the entrepreneurial and the traditional but, more significantly, an emergent sense of class identity. With a growing confidence born of rising incomes and an ascendant ideology of *laissez-faire*, 'respectable' capital was radically reshaping its attitudes towards the customs of the trade and its labour relations. Nonetheless, while some like the master manufacturers of Huddersfield and Halifax were by 1803 already speaking with the authentic voice of the new industrial middle class, it was only slowly that this new language became dominant, achieved both by the gradual elimination of petty capital and by the deliberate abandonment of the trade by many old gentlemen capitalists. For capital, as for labour, values and attitudes bred up in the old ways proved difficult to shed. It was not lack of capital which held many back. It was a distate for the new order, an unwillingness to uproot a stable social consensus for an insecure scramble after augmented wealth.[21] The siren call of wholesale restructuring made acolytes of only the minority. For capital, as for labour, however, machinery was the touchstone. It could be embraced with enthusiasm or with reluctance. Once embraced, however, the machine dictated a new pattern, a new perception of economic division and class relations.

The evolution of new class attitudes was hampered not only by traditional perceptions of the role and legitimacy of capital, however. As crucial a component of the customary moral economy of both the Domestic System and the putting out system was the part ascribed to the law and to the authorities as guarantors of the parameters of custom. In the West of England in the eighteenth century the first reaction of workers threatened by assaults upon customary practice was not to embark upon collective action against the employer concerned but to appeal to the bench for advice and help. This had produced some notable successes and it was clear that while magisterial support might not always be forthcoming or helpful, the bench could prove a powerful counterweight to the clothiers. The more fruitful pattern of appeals to the bench in Gloucestershire undoubtedly was a major influence why in 1794 the scribblers and shearmen there both sought advice and help from prominent magistrates when threatened with machinery. In Wiltshire, where the bench was more

[21] See, for example, the views of 'Looker On' in his letter in *L.M.*, 12 Feb. 1803.

partisan towards the clothiers, reflecting the larger numbers of clothier magistrates active in the county, such a response proved less fruitful but, nevertheless, Wiltshire scribblers, spinners, weavers and shearmen all tried direct appeals over the heads of employers and local clothier magistrates to a wider audience of rate-payers and county magistrates with some effect. While these appeals varied both within the West of England and between the West of England and the West Riding, however, their common theme was the workers' knowledge of the legislative code which governed, if only nominally, the way the industry was run. Thus, just as the food rioters were aware of the statutes for prosecuting regraters and forestallers and expected that they would be enforced, particularly in times of dearth, so were the woollen workers and master clothiers well aware of the legislation controlling apprenticeship, limiting loom ownership and proscribing the gig mill, expecting that the local bench would carry out its constitutional duty and enforce them. Thus the moral economy of eighteenth-century workers was not a bipartite but a tripartite contract in which the state or its local officers held the role of referee, armed with the rule book provided by Parliament and the parameters laid down by custom. How did the advent of machinery lead to changes in the way the woollen workers viewed their political masters?

The experience of the years under review showed the woollen workers and master clothiers that the referee, like the innovators, was increasingly unwilling to recognise either the rules or roles of the old moral economy. While the workers expected their constitutional protection to be upheld, they found that at a local level the bench frequently sided with the factory owners while the courts, as in 1796 and 1802, were prepared to ignore ancient laws if they seemed to hamper capital. The government dispatched troops to protect the new mills and illegal machines and in 1802 sent Read to Wiltshire with instructions to break the shearmen's combination. Read's palpable disregard for the niceties or even the letter of the law cannot have improved the workers' confidence in the government's impartiality. This local experience, however, still did not prepare them for Parliament's treatment of their case. The two Select Committees' disregard for their rights, the hostility shown to them and the contempt shown for their arguments, left a legacy of deep distrust and bitterness which if anything ran even deeper in Yorkshire where the master clothiers were unaccustomed to being treated with such disdain. The failure of both local and national authorities to uphold their rights came as a body blow to the woollen workers' moral economy. How far did the experience of this apostacy by their rulers therefore lead the woollen workers to question the legitimacy of the political status quo?

Historians have frequently seen the Industrial Revolution precipitating not only increasing economic conflict between capital and labour, resulting in a growing economic awareness of class, but also as witnessing an increasing political alienation from the existing state. Nonetheless, the direct connection between industrial transformation and conflicts occasioned by mechanisation and the growth of political disaffection is rarely examined, most historians, like Perkin, seeing the development of the political manifestations of 'the birth of class' as a cumulative process, the result of a wide spectrum of changes and events.[22] The major exception to this pattern may be seen in the work of E. P. Thompson who places this issue centrally in *The Making of the English Working Class.*

Luddism plays a pivotal role in Thompson's account of the development of class relations, marking a 'watershed' in economic and political allegiances. While he recognises that the origins of Luddism are to be found in industrial grievances, technological innovation, economic depression and unemployment, 'No account of Luddism is satisfactory which is confined to a limited industrial interpretation.' 'Luddism must be seen as arising at the crisis-point in the abrogation of paternalist legislation and in the imposition of the political economy of *laissez-faire* upon, and against the will and conscience of, the working people.'[23] The preceding pages of this work have largely echoed this judgement. Thompson, however, sees Luddism going a stage further for, in their resistance to these changes, he believes the Luddites came to question the legitimacy of the entire political and social system. Threatened by the destruction of their culture and communities, assailed by repression of their trade unions, harried by more troops than Wellington had to fight the French in Spain, the Luddites took to heart the messages of the radicals and the revolutionaries and the bonds of social and political deference were for ever broken, paving the way for the absorption of a class analysis which was to characterise working-class radicalism into the Chartist period. Luddism was the point at which, Thompson claims, the Jacobin tradition of the 1790s, driven underground by Pitt's repression, rose again to the surface to effect a conjunction with popular industrial grievances and to bring about the potential for violent revolution. Thus, 'Luddism was a quasi-insurrectionary movement which continually trembled on the edge of ulterior

---

[22] Perkin, *Origins of Modern English Society*, pp. 176–217.
[23] Thompson, *The Making*, pp. 642, 594.

revolutionary objectives. This is not to say that it was a wholly conscious revolutionary movement; on the other hand it had a tendency
towards becoming such a movement and it is this tendency which is
most often understated.'[24]

Thompson's case supposes a twofold process: that machinery and
its associated changes created a growing rift between capital and
labour, between older modes and relationships of production and new
ones; and that this growing alienation allowed the radicals the opportunity to spread their ideas of political change to a widening body of
working-class opinion. Thompson's case for the politicisation of Luddism turns critically on the evidence of the Yorkshire Luddites. Here,
more clearly than in Nottinghamshire where radicalism remained low-
key in 1811–12 or in Lancashire where the links between machine
breaking and political dissent are harder to unravel, the progression
from organised industrial action to political, even revolutionary, protest may, he suggests, be discerned. This is not the place to re-open the
debate on Yorkshire Luddism[25] but it is worth investigating how far the
experiences of mechanisation in both the West Riding and the West of
England in the years before 1812 support Thompson's case.

The growing threat of a machine economy to the woollen workers'
trades in the 1790s coincided with a remarkable flowering of popular
radicalism. The French Revolution of 1789 and the writings of men like
Paine, in particular *The Rights of Man*, launched a steadily growing
assault upon the legitimacy of the British political system and laid the
foundations for a popular political agitation for democracy. A radical
presence was certainly to be found in both the West of England and the
West Riding in the decade before the Wiltshire Outrages. However, it
is by no means easy to evaluate the strength of radicalism in either
region or to ascertain the trades of the radicals themselves since the
radical tradition was at best a semi-clandestine one. Nonetheless, clear
patterns do emerge which may be related to the different structures of
work and industrial relations in the two regions.

Jacobinism was not slow to take root in the Yorkshire woollen towns
with Leeds a prominent centre. W. Hey wrote to Wilberforce from
there in 1792: 'Immense pains are now being taken to make the lower
class of people discontented and to excite rebellion. Paine's mischievous work . . . is compressed into a 6d. pamphlet and is sold and given
away in profusion . . . you may see them in the houses of our journey-

[24] *Ibid.*, p. 604.
[25] See Thompson, *The Making*, ch. 14; Thomis, *The Luddites*, particularly ch. 6; and Rule,
The Labouring Classes, ch. 14.

men cloth dressers.' Later during the year a 'quiet' loyalist mob paraded the streets and burned Paine in effigy[26] but, not long after, 'a company of poor mechanics' had formed a corresponding society and was in communication with London. 'Aristocratic Tirany and Democratic Ignorance seem to pervade the Town of Leeds', they wrote, 'to that Amazing Degree that in General we are beheld more like Monsters than friends of the People.' Times, however, were changing. 'Our numbers amount to near 200 and we constantly keep increasing.'[27] Whether any of these poor mechanics were woollen workers is not clear but it would be unreasonable to suppose none were. An old Leeds cropper, recalling this period in 1868, said he had learned his radical politics in the cropping shop.[28] Indeed, the workshop, because of its close social framework, was one of the few places where 'Aristocratic tyranny' could not easily extend. The society wrote four years later, 'We are chiefly Working Mecanicks as those tradesmen here who are friends to our cause have few of them Virtue enough to come Publickley forward as the Aristocratic influence is so great . . . that they have got Power to distress any tradesman who exposes the Villainy of a Corrupt System.'[29] A society at Halifax began corresponding with London in April 1794 after a period of 'greatest prudence and circumspection' because 'in this town . . . there are a number of men who violently oppose . . . all free discussion'. That month they held a large outdoor demonstration 'at which were many friends from Leeds, Wakefield, Huddersfield, Bradford and the adjacent neighbourhood'.[30]

The Leeds society was hard hit by the fierce repression of Jacobinism which reached its height in 1797. 'There was a good Society hear about three years since but the arbitrary proceedings of our Justices operated in so terrifying a manner on our Friends in general that their spirits have been sunk under the Standard of Moderation and the Sacred flame which had been kindled in their Breasts was almost extinguished.'[31] William Cookson and his fellow magistrates of the town were most zealous in the hunt for Jacobins. He wrote in April 1798, 'We have some very abominable wretches here, ready to disseminate and act upon the worst principles, there cannot be doubt – their caution and circumspection is now highly systematic [but] we are well

[26] Wilberforce, *Life of William Wilberforce*, Vol. II, pp. 3–5.
[27] Thompson, *The Making*, pp. 132–3.
[28] An Old Cropper, *Old Leeds, its Bygones and Celebrities* (1868), p. 4.
[29] Thompson, *The Making*, p. 194.
[30] *Ibid.*, pp. 142–3.   [31] *Ibid.*, p. 194.

willed to detect and expose them and bring them to justice if anyhow possible.'[32] The experience at Leeds was mirrored elsewhere.

Repression drove these nascent radical organisations underground just at the time when economic conditions were dramatically worsening and consequently when ideas of social rights and political liberties were more readily listened to. Increasingly after 1797 all forms of protest took on the rhetoric of political discontent.[33] This can particularly be seen in the growing politicisation of protests over the ever-rising prices of food. Thus while many handbills posted in the West Riding in 1800 and 1801 demanded 'Cheap Bread' and measures against forestallers and millers, an increasing number began to demand 'Cheap Bread and No King'. Revolutionary slogans were in some places accompanied by revolutionary plotting. In Sheffield in 1800 nightly meetings about the cost of provisions also discussed pikes and arms. Similar reports came from the woollen towns.[34] In December, 1800, Wakefield authorities were hunting the authors of various seditious handbills. By March, 1801, Halifax magistrates were writing more stridently of the 'alarming state of the manufacturing parts of this country'. Nightly meetings were frequent and at one the people were urged 'we must either rise and fight like men or pine to death like dogs'. Significantly, among the objects which that meeting's leaders blamed for the distress were not only corn jobbers and bakers but also 'worsit mills, merchant manufacturers and common slubbing billies ... and all interfering between producer and user of every article of life'.[35] While in September 1800 the populace of Leeds had threatened food riots, by March 1801 came reports of plans for a general insurrection in the town. 'There is a spirit of dissatisfaction more generally diffused than at any known period, and the coalition between Jacobinism and distress is really alarming.'[36]

Through 1801 and 1802 these nightly meetings assumed even more

---

[32] H.O. 42/43, Cookson to William Wickham, 15 April 1798.

[33] For the most detailed account of radicalism and Jacobin insurrectionary plotting in these years see R. Wells, *Insurrection: The British Experience, 1795–1803* (Alan Sutton, 1983).

[34] For revolutionary plotting in Yorkshire at this time see J. L. Baxter and F. K. Donnelly, 'The revolutionary "underground" in the West Riding: myth or reality', *Past and Present*, 64 (1974), pp. 124–32.

[35] H.O. 42/45, Rev. J. Lowe to Fitzwilliam, 5 Dec. 1800, advertisement from Wakefield, 15 Dec. 1800; H.O. 42/61, J. Busfield to Fitzwilliam, n.d., Anon. to Thomas Parker, dated 1801 (these last two letters were probably sent in March 1801).

[36] H.O. 42/51, Benjamin Gott (then Mayor) to Portland, 21 Sept. 1800; W.W.M., 7, magistrates of Leeds to Fitzwilliam, 18 March 1801; H.O. 42/53, Thomas Bancroft to King, 18 Nov. 1800.

menacing forms. An ordered discipline emerged and reports of arming and drilling on the moors increased. The United Englishmen's oath appeared throughout the North of England.[37] 'The Jacobins do not fail to avail themselves of the opportunity of working upon the feelings of the lower classes', wrote B. Frank. 'The neighbourhood of Leeds is only kept quiet and from rising in a mass by the military.'[38] A government spy who had toured the West Riding forwarded a paper entitled 'Plan for Conducting the Business'. It was a blueprint for insurrection. On the back the spy noted, 'This is the Leeds plan. Much the same at Wakefield and Sheffield.'[39]

Reports continued to flood into the Home Office of nocturnal meetings all over the woollen manufacturing area. Among them was one concerning a large meeting at Dewsbury at which usual political demands were enlarged by determinations to prevent the export of wool and to put a stop to spinning by machinery. 'The woollen manufactory of broad cloth is very dull and a great many workmen are out of employ: which circumstances added to the high price of provisions make the dangers of these meetings much more formidable.'[40] Rumours of pike-making, musket drill and clandestine meetings kept the authorities highly alarmed.[41] These meetings appear to have declined in the autumn of 1801 but revived with a vengeance in early 1802. The progress of disaffection in the area was said to be formidable.[42] A pamphlet, 'An Address to the United Britons', warning 'Tyrants tremble, the people are awake', was found near Huddersfield and later the authorities received a pamphlet sub-headed 'The Independence of Great Britain and Ireland' which was the constitution of the United Englishmen. The same document was later found on Despard's associates.[43] After the summer of 1802, however, reports of insurrectionary plotting began to decrease. In November Despard and his associates

[37] W.W.M., 9, John Gourder to Fitzwilliam, 31 March 1801.
[38] W.W.M., 11, B. Frank to B. Cooke, 9 April 1801.
[39] The plan included '1. That the whole of this business when ripe be put in execution at a certain time . . . and that a general attack be made at every place wherever societies are formed at a time which is thought proper by the heads of the societies in London.' Soldiers, their arms and ammunition were to be seized. '6. Set up your standard and secure your ground.' H.O. 42/62, Anon. to Portland, n.d. (probably June 1801).
[40] H.O. 42/62, John Walker to Addington, 13 July 1801.
[41] W.W.M., 20, W. Dawson to Fitzwilliam, 27 July 1801; H.O. 42/62, Dawson to Fitzwilliam, 31 July 1801, Fitzwilliam to Portland, 30 July 1801.
[42] H.O. 42/62, Fitzwilliam to Portland, 16 Aug. 1801; H.O. 42/65, Ralph Fletcher to Portland, 7 Jan. 1802. See also H.O. 42/65, Fletcher to Portland, 3 April 1802; W.W.M., 57, John Dixon to Fitzwilliam, 17 July 1802, Fitzwilliam to Pelham, 20 July 1802.
[43] W.W.M., 57, J. Radcliffe to Pelham (enclosure), 26 July 1802; W.W.M., 71 (i), Anon., n.d. (probably July 1802).

were arrested and the 'Constitution Society' conspiracy brought to light. 'Thereafter the "Black Lamp" appears to go out.'[44]

It is impossible to evaluate how far woollen workers made up significant numbers of the ranks of those engaged in these insurrectionary assemblies and plots, though the criticism of merchant manufacturers and slubbing billies at the Halifax meeting in March 1801, and the demands to put an end to spinning by machinery made at Dewsbury, certainly suggests an influential presence. Government and local authorities alike, however, were as much concerned at the apparent linkage between Jacobinism and trade unions, especially that of the croppers. Such reports had been periodically alarming the government since the passage of the Two Acts and the decision in 1799 to curb combinations was prompted not only by the aggressive policy of many artisan unions in maintaining their incomes in the face of wartime inflation[45] but also by growing evidence that they were being infiltrated by subversive ideas.[46] Ironically, however, the passage of the Combination Acts merely served to worsen the situation, for they sparked off a regional and inter-regional trade union tie-up of the kind the government most feared.

A general spirit of dissatisfaction [is] created in every class of artisan and mechanic by the late bill against Combinations and which I am afraid has caused more to combine than would have thought of such a measure but for the bill itself . . . it is a measure which the democrats rejoice in most extravagently and who will most assuredly strain every nerve to profit by it. I have within these last 14 days walked over 100 miles of the country and in every place found evident proof of a connected and desperate opposition being in preparation.

Thus wrote William Barlow, a government spy, from Sheffield in August 1799.[47] Opposition, centred at Manchester, Sheffield and the woollen towns, was closely co-ordinated and, it was said, of a politically as well as industrially motivated nature. Thus it was reported that

---

[44] Thompson, *The Making*, pp. 521–2.
[45] For example, in 1799 it was said that bricklayers, carpenters, cloth dressers, weavers, shoemakers, tailors and cabinet makers' labourers had all recently conducted successful strikes, by which some had managed to double their wages in four years. P.C. 1/43/A152, Observations respecting combinations.
[46] C. R. Dobson, *Masters and Journeymen: A Prehistory of Industrial Relations, 1717–1800* (Croom Helm, 1980), ch. 9, is the most recent discussion of the origins of the Combination Acts but fails to examine in any way the secret information government was receiving from spies and informants around the country. See also Thompson, *The Making*, pp. 543–5.
[47] P.C. 1/44/161, Barlow to Lord Belgrave, 8 Aug. 1799. He had, in fact, travelled from Manchester to Sheffield.

'the League . . . is under the immediate direction of republicans' who had 'so contrived to get every class of journeyman in their destructive schemes'.[48] R. Ford wrote from Manchester of this

secret combination of a very extraordinary nature and replete with very serious consequences – the bill lately passed to prevent combinations of workmen . . . is the source of this business . . . The members of this new society are exceedingly numerous. It originated at Sheffield in the Republican society there – is connected with the principal manufacturing towns of Yorkshire and to this town, Stockport and Bury.[49]

'Loyal men' were not admitted to its ranks and while the avowed aim was to petition Parliament, Ford was sure it was 'only calculated to create delay until the real grounds of universal dissatisfaction be discovered and the more minute views of the leading characters be brought to light'.[50] 'There has been more persons turned Jacobin within the little time that has elapsed since the bill was passed than for a year before.'[51]

Such reports and news of the growing size of union membership greatly alarmed both the government and local authorities. William Cookson, the mayor of Leeds whose sources were more than usually reliable, initially believed that the croppers had little to do with the nocturnal meetings and drilling on the moors. 'Very few of the cloth workers are supposed to attend those meetings. They are composed of the labouring poor of all descriptions.' Whereas the people at these nocturnal meetings sought to redress their grievances in the overthrow of Parliament, the croppers' organisation 'is directed steadily to their own immediate concern'.[52] However, he added a warning rider that there existed 'a Regulating principle, a disposition to dictate and give law to their employers, to form combinations'. A 'Secret Tribunal' of workmen existed at Leeds and other towns, he warned, which had great influence. This was probably the Institution. 'From this source it may be expected that other combinations upon a larger scale having more extensive objects will arise.'[53] A month later, he was writing, 'It may perhaps be fairly presumed that the complete power which the

[48] A delegate meeting had resolved 'that general combinations (be) so made throughout the kingdom to petition Parliament against the Bill, and to resist every attempt to enforce it, that if it be not repealed they would employ what force they have against it'. P.C. 1/44/A161, Ford to Belgrave, 8 Aug. 1799.
[49] P.C. 1/44/A161, Ford to Belgrave, Aug. 1799, from information received from Barlow. 'This town' is Manchester.
[50] P.C. 1/44/A161, Ford to Belgrave, also dated Aug. 1799.
[51] P.C. 1/44/A161, Barlow to Ford, 14 Aug. 1799.
[52] W.W.M., 79, Cookson to Fitzwilliam, 16 Aug. 1802.
[53] W.W.M., 62, Cookson to Fitzwilliam, 27 July 1802.

cloth workers have obtained over their employers may, upon similar principles, give equal ascendancy to every class of the lower orders.'[54] The Duke of Portland expressed similiar fears of the Lancashire weavers' association in August, 1799, when he noted that while it seemed they were only concerned with the strictly legal practice of petitioning Parliament 'on the subject of the manufacture in which they are engaged . . . it is manifest that if nothing injurious to the safety of Government is actually in contemplation, associations so formed contain within themselves the means of being converted at any times into a most dangerous instrument to disturb the public tranquility'.[55] Fitzwilliam, informed of 'secret meetings' in various houses in June 1802, initially conceived that they were 'only for the purpose of rising wages' and beneath magisterial interest.[56] By September, however, he had changed his mind. Letters from Cookson warning of the 'momentous shape' which combinations of all classes, particularly of shearmen, had assumed, together with news of the Gott strike, convinced him.[57] 'The temper and tone taken by some of the people employed in the woollen trade is an evil that is growing, that gives rise to many others or to many alarms.' 'I cannot help feeling a strong suspicion that all the meetings and suspicion of meetings take their rise in the combination of the very men I am now speaking about; the croppers.'[58] How deep the links between militant trade unionism and radicalism ran can only be surmised but clearly the juxtaposition of industrial and political discontents constituted a dangerous mixture. This was why the West Riding authorities, merchants and larger master clothiers grew so alarmed at the rise of the Clothiers' Community and at its presumed links with the Brief Institution. As noted above, the croppers probably did give assistance to the Clothiers' Community, particularly in its later years when it became dominated by journeymen weavers. The croppers also maintained extensive inter-union links, not merely with their fellow cloth dressers in the West of England but also with many other trades as the Institution's accounts, seized in 1806, showed.

It appears from the books that contributions have been received from all descriptions of persons in 1802 – clothiers, colliers, bricklayers, wool sorters, from the clothiers' community, joiners, sawyers, flax-dressers, shoemakers and paper makers: it also appears that to all those trades . . . money has been

54 W.W.M., 79, Cookson to Fitzwilliam, 16 Aug. 1802.
55 P.C. 1/44/A161, Portland to Bancroft, 8 Aug. 1799.
56 H.O. 42/65, Fitzwilliam to Pelham, 7 June, 28 July 1802.
57 H.O. 42/66, Cookson to Fitzwilliam, 8 Sept. 1802.
58 H.O. 42/66, Fitzwilliam to Pelham, 27, 28 Sept. 1802.

granted out of the fund; and also to the relief of the cotton spinners in Manchester.[59]

In December 1802 the authorities intercepted a letter from J.R. in Sheffield to George Palmer, the man through whom all letters were sent to the Leeds croppers, reporting on his activities among the journeymen cutlers of the town. After long talks, the cutlers had agreed that 'what we say is right and ought to be entered into by every trade'. What this was we do not know though the cutlers probably contributed towards the cloth workers' Parliamentary expenses.[60] In September 1802 Fitzwilliam was told 'There arrived here last week two delegates from Carlisle on their way to Manchester summoned by the cotton printers to agree upon certain advances in their wages.'[61] Only union business could have drawn these men so far off their route. And in March 1803 Charles Thomas, president of a trade union in Bristol, wrote offering a small remittance. 'Hope you have had liberal supplies from most towns in the kingdom.'[62] We should beware of over-emphasising such links, of painting a picture of a movement of working-class solidarity. This it was not but it is clear that even after their attempted repression, numerous inter-union linkages remained, linkages of friendship and of mutual interest. The cloth dressers' campaign to ensure the enforcement of the old restrictive legislation epitomised the struggle of all craft unions against growing industrial capital, against the new men and the new economic forces which threatened the established traditional and customary work and lifestyle of the artisan. These linkages were not overtly political but as the influential governing classes moved slowly but inexorably towards *laissez-faire*, attempts to resuscitate old industrial protective codes inevitably took on political significance.

While nightly meetings may have drawn journeymen and union links have brought weavers and croppers into contact with radical ideas, there is less evidence to suggest that master clothiers were prepared to express anti-establishment views until the later days of the Clothiers' Community though there is no doubt that many supported the campaign for peace in early 1801. However, their treatment before the 1806 Committee bitterly angered the master clothiers and their reaction was seen in the two contested county elections for Yorkshire

[59] *B.P.P.*, 1806, Vol. 3, p. 355.
[60] W.W.M., 114, J.R. to Palmer, 28 Dec. 1802.
[61] H.O. 42/66, Cookson to Fitzwilliam, 8 Sept. 1802.
[62] H.O. 42/70, Thomas to Palmer, 17 March 1803.

in 1806 and 1807. In both, they, together with the unenfranchised
journeymen weavers and croppers, especially those in Leeds, appear
to have attempted to influence the poll against Wilberforce and Lascelles, both prominent members of the 1806 Committee which recommended repeal of the restrictive, protective legislation which all
had sought to safeguard. In the 1806 contest Lascelles was unseated.
'A very unfair advantage has been taken at the expense of Mr. Lascelles
and yourself of the exasperated state of the clothiers . . . as well as of the
general class of workmen', Cookson wrote to Wilberforce. 'The clothiers who were before the committee are violent beyond all conception.'[63] In 1807 the contest was renewed and the woollen workers
campaigned actively for Lord Milton against Wilberforce and Lascelles. The old Leeds cropper recalled happily that he had 'shouted till I
was hoarse for Milton in the great contest of 1807'.[64] Wilberforce was
angry at Milton's 'mob-directing system' and lamented in early June,
'Latterly the people would not hear me and shameful treatment.'[65] In
Leeds, multitudes of the lower orders of the people assembled
together in parties during the election. 'At length this ferment broke
into acts of violence' and the mayor and many freeholders were 'assaulted and conceived themselves in danger of their lives'. The 'riot'
was quelled by troops.[66] The clothiers' and journeymen's strength and
influence, however, lay only in the large manufacturing towns and 'the
loyal and independent class of Yorkshire freeholders' saw Wilberforce
home, though Milton defeated Lascelles for the second seat.

While radicalism bit deep into the West Riding woollen district,
political discontent assumed a very much lower profile in the West of
England. Like most outworking areas, the West of England workers
were forward in their loyalism before the French Wars. Timothy Exell
believed that before 1802, 'peace and content sat upon the weaver's
brow, and his name stood enrolled amongst the loyal subjects of His
Majesty'.[67] Rioting Wiltshire weavers in 1726–7 'went about with
K.G.W. in their caps, signifying that they were King George's weavers'.[68] When the King and Queen travelled through the Wiltshire and
Somerset woollen towns in September 1789, they were met with 'the
most loyal acclamations. At Trowbridge a numerous society of weavers formed themselves in ranks to keep the crowd from pressing too

[63] *L.M.*, 7 Feb., 14 March 1801; Wilberforce, *Life of William Wilberforce*, Vol. III, p. 278.
[64] An Old Cropper, *Old Leeds*, p. 4.
[65] Wilberforce, *Life of William Wilberforce*, Vol. III, pp. 328, 331.
[66] H.O. 42/91, Richard Ramsden to Fitzwilliam, 22 May 1807.
[67] T. Exell, *A Brief History of the Weavers of the County of Gloucester* (1838), p. 6.
[68] Mann, 'Clothiers and weavers in Wiltshire', p. 69.

forward.' A display of the woollen trades at work particularly attracted the Royal couple's interest.[69]

The impact of Jacobinal ideas in the West of England woollen areas appears to have been muted. In part this can be explained by the lack of large centres of urban crafts with the strong artisan social bonds and intellectual traditions which provided the earliest strongholds of political awakening elsewhere. Nowhere in the woollen districts was there a town with even a moderately wide franchise. Calne and Westbury were pocket boroughs and although Chippenham occasionally experienced political contests, the seat was far from open. The nearest corresponding societies were established in Bristol and Tewkesbury. The city of Bath, only 10 miles from the centre of the Wiltshire and Somerset woollen area, did not lack Jacobins and the authorities harassed them throughout the 1790s.[70] How far these radicals attempted to proselytise among the woollen towns, however, is not clear. Magistrates in the woollen districts were equally zealous in their attempts to suppress sedition but in spite of a steady trickle of convictions there is little evidence of any organised radical presence. A Chippenham man was convicted of publishing a seditious paper in 1791 and there was concern in Wiltshire and Gloucestershire in 1792 that sedition was spreading among the lower orders in the manufacturing areas.[71] A Salisbury book binder was imprisoned in December 1792 for exclaiming, 'health to tom Paine and d— to the King and royal family' but the great majority there, as elsewhere, preferred to burn effigies of Paine to demonstrate their loyalty to the crown.[72] A Warminster mason was sentenced to six months' imprisonment in August 1794 for announcing his disaffection to the constitution and demanding 'guillotine reform' and the judge at the Gloucestershire assizes in 1794 warned of the dangers of sedition.[73] Magistrates in the woollen districts, however, were much more concerned at the threats of industrial rather than political unrest.

The food riots of 1795 and those of 1800 at times appeared to develop a political dimension. For example, a series of letters discovered in and

[69] *S.W.J.*, 21 Sept. 1789.
[70] *S.W.J.*, 1 Sept., 13 Oct. 1794; H.O. 42/41, Jefferys to Portland, 11 Aug. 1797; H.O. 42/47, Batchellor to Portland, 28 May 1799; H.O. 42/53, information of Wm Hunt and Thomas Allen, 11 Nov. 1800; Thompson, *The Making*, pp. 133, 142–3.
[71] *S.W.J.*, 11 April 1791; W.O. 1/1051, Bethell, Bush, Jones to Yonge, 7 Dec. 1792; *G.J.*, 24 Dec. 1792.
[72] Effigies of Paine were burned at Trowbridge, Minchinhampton, Shepton Mallet and Twerton among other places in the winter of early 1793. *S.W.J.*, 10, 24 Dec. 1792, 7, 28 Jan., 4 Feb. 1793.
[73] *S.W.J.*, 9 Aug. 1794; *G.J.*, 17 March 1794.

around Uley, Gloucestershire, in 1795 demanded cheaper bread and warned of revolution. One proclaimed, 'No King but a constitution down down down o fatall dow high caps and proud hats for ever dow down we all.' Another asserted that if food prices were not lowered, 'ye cannot but expect to loase your head'. Notices in the same hand calling a public meeting on Hampton Common on 21 September to consider the cost of food greatly alarmed the magistrates and troops were called out. About 300 people in fact assembled 'but it plainly appeared that they had no appointed leader and concerted plan, and they soon dispersed, agreeing to meet again at the same place on October 5th, and there was a second meeting in much fewer numbers'.[74] Other anonymous letters demanding cheaper bread also contained political overtones.[75] Paul believed that although 'the cry of want of bread . . . forms a body of insurgents, amongst them are mixed a number of seditious persons whose business is to excite the number to mischief, and to make them deaf to reason'.[76] How far the Jacobins in the woollen areas deliberately tried to use distress to obtain political converts, however, or how far food rioters merely added political sentiments known to frighten the authorities to their usual threatening demands, remains a matter for speculation.

The growing threat of invasion in late 1797 and 1798 increased fears of fifth columnists and encouraged magistrates to pay particular attention to the disposition of the working people. Berkeley wrote of Gloucestershire in 1798, 'the bulk of the people are religiously attached to the constitution and government . . . but a vein of bad materials runs through the lower order in the clothing part of the county which still continues to study Tom Paine with a few political clubs of the very dregs and of T. Paine's cash'.[77] The eagerness of the respectable population of the woollen districts to set up various volunteer defence forces in response to the government's appeal concerned some magistrates who feared that arms might thus get into the wrong hands. Paul urged

---

[74] A tailor from Uley, 'an obscure individual', was suspected of being the writer of the letters and notices. The magistrates had at first considered him an isolated case but after the meeting when they found 'that he had been prominently industrious to force others to assemble, his heart and intentions appeared so actively bad, and the possibility of a really dangerous meeting rendered so apparent', they decided to punish him severely. H.O. 42/36, Lloyd-Baker to Portland, Oct. 1795.

[75] See, for example, H.O. 42/50, Meyrick to Portland, 12 June 1800, enclosing a handbill found at Ramsbury, Wilts., which ran: 'Dear Brother Britons North and South younite yourselves in one body and stand true. Down with your luxzuaras Government or you starve with Hunger.'

[76] W.O. 1/1091, Paul to Sec. at War, 21 July 1795.

[77] H.O. 50/41, Berkeley to Dundas, 4 April 1798.

that such forces 'should consist of none but known and respectable householders, or persons bringing two such to answer for them'.[78] In 1803, when many such armed associations were revived, the authorities expressed the same worries.[79] While all were concerned at the potential for disorder among the woollen workers, however, fears were mainly of an industrial rather than a political nature. Paul believed, 'there is no reason to fear the political principles of the people or their readiness to act against the common enemy', but, should no enemy appear, 'the sore point of increasing machinery' might encourage some to threaten the manufacturers.[80]

As in the West Riding the years around the turn of the century saw increased radical activity and growing fears of insurrectionary plots. In a bundle of extracts from letters sent in to the Home Office concerning revolutionary societies in 1799 is one from Trowbridge, 'relative to a secret organisation'.

> The clerk of the parish . . . informed me . . . he had heard the very seditious conversation of a man whose name he does not know who affirmed that he knew two men in the neighbourhood of Bradford who were concerned in some secret association in favour of the enemies of this country – and that one of them had a book in which were enrolled all the names of a very considerable number of persons who were ready to join the French the first favourable opportunity.

Unsubstantiated as it is by any other source, this letter must be viewed sceptically, though the Home Office took it seriously enough to include it with a series of well-authenticated reports concerning suspected strongholds of the United Englishmen from other parts of the country.[81] It seems probable, however, that the speaker was referring to the Brief Institution. A firmer link came in a letter from Bradford on Avon in January 1801, concerning a conversation heard in an inn. 'A person of the name of Howard, a Master Shearman, made use of language which I shudder to commit to writing. "That he would be happy to run our Gracious Sovereign through the body, or to assist in blowing up both Houses of Parliament" and more of this execrable stuff.' The writer was especially concerned since, 'as in his line he must employ a number of hands, he may be the means of corrupting many more'. This

---

[78] H.O. 50/41, Paul to Dundas, 27 April 1798.
[79] See, for example, H.O. 50/71, Berkeley to ?, 3 Nov. 1803; H.O. 50/42, Pembroke to Dundas, 19 May 1798, enclosing 'Resolutions of a meeting of Bradford house holders, April 30, 1798'; H.O. 50/41, Austin to Berkeley, 17 March 1798.
[80] H.O. 50/41, Paul to Dundas, 27 April 1798.
[81] H.O. 42/46, extract from a letter from Trowbridge, relative to a secret association, n.d. (series covers Jan.–March 1799).

Howard was probably William Howard, a master shearman who gave evidence on behalf of the shearmen in 1806. 'I understand', the writer continued, 'there was in the same company with Howard . . . a Mr. Spenley, a notorious Jacobin, who travels in the clothing line.' Spenley 'endeavours to disseminate these detestable doctrines through the country while he is taking his orders etc., for his employer'. How far Howard was typical, or Spenley successful, we have no way of knowing, though the letter suggested that 'numbers more' could be holding 'similar conversations'.[82]

Some local magistrates and the government were certainly deeply suspicious of the linkages between the cloth dressers' union and the revolutionaries and the outrages in Wiltshire in 1802 were viewed, initially at least, as something more sinister than an industrial dispute.[83] The close links between Wiltshire and Yorkshire further worried the government. The Bradford on Avon soldier-shearman who wrote to Hobhouse in July 1802 said he had been 'informed by many that there will be a Revolution' and that if something was not done to relieve unemployment soon, things would rapidly be brought to an issue.[84] The handbill stuck up at Freshford in 1803 warned that 'if government gives the business unfavourable to the shearmen, it is the determination of the shearmen to do the business by force of arms and bid defiance to the military force',[85] while the West Riding croppers warned the Royal Exchange Insurance Company in 1805 that if Parliament did not give them their rights, 'we are determined to grant them ourselves'.[86] In January 1808, Bradford on Avon shearmen were threatening a general rising.[87] Again it is impossible to separate rhetoric from intent.

As in the West Riding, the conflict over machinery spilled over into Parliamentary politics. At the election for the two members for the borough of Chippenham in Wiltshire in the autumn of 1802, it was reported that the cry was 'Maitland and Machinery, Brooke and Liberty', though one clothier denied this, saying the cry for freedom was for a free borough, not freedom from machinery.[88] Charles Brooke was elected but subsequently unseated by a Parliamentary Select

---

[82] H.O. 42/61, Anon. to Addington, 9 Jan. 1801; *B.P.P.*, 1806, Vol. 3, pp. 303–10.
[83] See, for example, H.O. 42/65, Jones to Pelham, 27 July, Gentlemen of Melksham to Pelham, 26 July, J. Jones, Sen., to Pelham, 26 July 1802.
[84] H.O. 42/65, 'A souldier' to Hobhouse, July 1802.
[85] *S.W.J.*, 7 Feb. 1803.
[86] *B.P.P.*, 1806, Vol. 3, Report, pp. 16–17.
[87] H.O. 42/95, Jones to Hawkesbury, 31 Jan. 1808.
[88] *B.P.P.*, 1802/3, Vol. 7, p. 185.

Committee. The problem arose in part over the interpretation of the right of franchise for the borough. Brooke claimed this right rested with 'the Bailiff and Burgesses at large within the borough, paying, or liable to pay, the Poors Rates' whereas Maitland claimed only the 'Bailiff, Burgesses and Freemen being householders of and resident in the ancient Burgage Houses' were enfranchised.[89] Brooke clearly relied on this more popular franchise to secure his election, thus including in his electorate many small clothiers and master shearmen and other people who were intimately concerned with the threat of machinery. There is thus good reason to believe that the champion of borough liberties aided his popularity by declaring himself against machinery. Brooke was subsequently elected as member for Ivelchester and somewhat ineffectually espoused the woollen workers' cause in Parliament.[90]

The radical presence was thus clearly to be felt in both the West of England and the West Riding in the years up to 1802. However, it was certainly a more palpable and much more pervasive influence in Yorkshire than in the West of England where there is much less evidence of any political organisation or firm community base for radical ideas. In part we might explain this disparity by noting that, unlike the West of England woollen region where textile production predominated, the economies of the towns of the West Riding, though heavily dependent upon cloth making, were much more variegated and contained a wider range of artisan crafts and trades. However, this can hardly account in total for the difference. Both regions were experiencing the same threats to tradition and custom posed by the rise of a machine economy, both were involved in the campaign to safeguard an established way of life from the assaults of a rapacious industrial capitalism. Indeed, we might with reason have expected political alienation to have been *greater* in the West of England for here, more clearly than in Yorkshire, the local authorities had sided with the innovators, here the roots of the moral economy bit most deeply. Yet, while there is an abundance of evidence to show that radicalism in the West Riding survived the repression of the war years to blossom forth in renewed vigour once more in 1816, that in the West of England appears to have sunk into the sands. Even when popular radicalism burst its geographical and occupational banks in an extraordinary wave of growth in 1816–19, the West of England woollen districts played only a very

[89] *J.H.C.*, Vol. 58, pp. 16, 296.
[90] See *Hansard's Parliamentary Debates*, Vol. 6, pp. 349, 425; and Mann, *Cloth Industry*, p. 142.

modest part in the agitation. Indeed, it was not until the early struggles of the Chartist movement that 'the sacred flame' was fully rekindled there. Why was this the case?

One explanation may be found in the ideology of radicalism itself and its relevance to the existing values of the communities concerned. The ideology of radicalism in the 1790s and early 1800s, whether in its purest 'Jacobin' form or in the older form of the 'Norman Yoke', directed its attack upon the legitimacy of the state, against kingcraft, lordcraft and priestcraft. Government was seen as fraud and its basis was seen as resting upon robbery. Taxes and tithes were identified as the causes of popular misery and poverty. The solution to distress and hunger therefore lay in the enlightenment of the people as to their 'true' situation and in the establishment of a democratic state of independent petty-producers. Instead of appeals to some bogus 'Constitution', a fraudulent 'sepulchre of precedents' and form of 'political popery',[91] the radicals urged their listeners to slough off the dead hand of the past and to assert their native common-sense and ability to reason, thereby liberating themselves and their society from the political tutelage of a debauched aristocracy. The appeal of this rational radicalism was to the craftsman and small producer who could share its anti-statist, anti-tax and essentially egalitarian anti-aristocratic values. As Calhoun has noted, it was in many ways a reactionary radicalism, though no less dangerous to the state for that, which sought liberty from constraint for individual rights, both political and economic.[92]

The structure and *mentalité* of the West Riding woollen industry lent itself rather better to such ideas than did that of the West of England. The Domestic System's strength lay in its multiplicity of independent petty-producers and in the way in which their values, expressed in the cloth halls, the small workshops and cropping shops, were shared widely by the journeymen who worked alongside them and who had aspirations to join their ranks. Their strong sense of mutuality should not disguise the fact that they had to compete with each other in the market place on quality and price. The ethos of the Domestic System therefore reflected a society of small capitalists, conscious of personal rights and liberties and jealous of any encroachment by the large

91 T. Paine, *The Rights of Man* (1791/2; Penguin 1969 edn), p. 218. For the ideology of radicalism in the 1790s, see Thompson, *The Making*, ch. 4; Hobsbawm, *Labouring Men*, ch. 1; H. Collins, 'The London Corresponding Society', in J. Saville, ed., *Democracy and the Labour Movement* (Lawrence and Wishart, 1954).
92 C. Calhoun, *The Question of Class Struggle: Social Foundations of Popular Radicalism during the Industrial Revolution* (Blackwell, 1982), ch. 3.

merchant capitalists whose role, they believed, should be confined solely to selling and not manufacturing cloth. As property owners they felt the burden of taxes occasioned by the war against France. They saw their overseas markets dislocated. They saw the free-born English-man's vaunted civil liberties set aside in the name of national emergency. They were proud of their capacity for self-government as epitomised in the running of the cloth halls. They wanted only to be left to get on with the business they knew best, that of making and finishing cloth. The ideas of Paine could find a conducive home in a culture such as this one, especially among those small master clothiers who found their modest businesses increasingly unable to compete with those of the nascent master manufacturers and also among the journeymen weavers and croppers whose hopes of social mobility and social security were being eroded by the advent of machinery. While tribunes of the Industrial Revolution then as now trumpeted the growing freedoms made possible by economic growth, freedom increased only for some. For a large segment, perhaps the majority, of society, freedoms, economic, social and political, were reduced by the rapidly accelerating economic change which was transforming industrial and agricultural production alike. The Painite ideal of petty-producer independence reflected and ratified their view of the Domestic System, only now with the rise of mechanisation ceasing to appear secure and protected. This is not, of course, to argue that all or even most of the master clothiers, master dressers or journeymen weavers and croppers in the West Riding became radicals or held radical sympathies. Indeed, the perceived dangers of democracy were increased for those merchant and master clothier manufacturers who recognised that its consequence could be just that regulation of economic power which a popular franchise held implicit. Much was made by the burgeoning anti-radical propaganda of the supposed threat of democracy to property. However, it was its threat to the *rights* of property, rights which were now extended, released by the new ideology of *laissez-faire* from the old trammels of the duties of property, which was seen as the greater danger. It is to argue that the culture of the Domestic System was not *in itself* inimical to the ideas of Jacobinism for these ideas were at many points congruent to the community *mentalité* of the West Riding.

The same cannot be said of the West of England woollen regions. There, where the moral economy was more deeply rooted, the Jacobin emphasis upon petty-producers fitted much less easily into the culture of the woollen workers. The divorce between capital and labour was axiomatic to this culture and gave the woollen workers a strong sense of craft and class consciousness in their perceptions of their own place in society. This sense of class did not extend, however, to a hostility to that economic structure for it was the structure itself which enabled them to enjoy the status and independence they believed rightfully theirs. The bastion of these 'rights and privileges' was not, however, simply craft strength. It was the laws which regulated their trades, bolstered by custom, which these workers saw as the safeguards to their culture. Hence it was to the local and national authorities they naturally turned to uphold these safeguards whenever their economic masters chose to attempt to ride roughshod over their rights. The bench or a few sympathetic magistrates, the courts and ultimately Parliament itself were seen as having the duty to protect the woollen workers' independence. This belief in the pivotal role of the authorities in maintaining customary economic balances ill-accorded with the Jacobinal emphasis upon lack of restriction from on high and a faith in free markets. The vision of a government which governed less could appear likely to strengthen the hand of the gentlemen clothiers and innovators against their workforces. Collective security could seem therefore to be threatened by such an ideology rather than augmented by it.

The ideology of radicalism has to be examined in the cultural and customary context of the community into which it was being introduced if we are to make sense of the reception accorded to it. For the radicals had to *sell* their ideas to their prospective audience. There was nothing automatic about the acceptance of radical attitudes. The radicals needed to be able to offer not just an explanation of current ills which married with the experiences of their audience. They had also to offer a solution which would fit within the cultural heritage of that community. Here the ideas of Paine were always at a disadvantage when presented to a culture, as in the West of England, so rooted in its own view of a traditional past. Paine and his followers urged their readers and listeners to abandon the superstitions of the past, to examine their political and social situation from scratch, to apply the acid test of reason to institutions and customary relationships. In the West of England this was asking the audience to abandon the basis of their entire value system. It is little wonder that it was only among the ranks of the cloth dressers and master shearmen that we see much take-up of radicalism in the years before 1809.

It is significant that those places where Jacobinism struck deepest in the 1790s were centres of artisan production which were not dominated by large-scale capitalist employers.[93] This is not to say that such places did not contain large-scale employers or that those who joined the radical ranks did not share fears of the encroaching powers of factors, middlemen or manufacturers. They were, however, for the greatest part towns and cities where an artisanal-master worker culture was strong and deep-rooted. In those areas where industry was already dominated by large-scale 'capitalists, on the other hand, it is significant that it was not until the post-war and Chartist periods that radicalism really blossomed, if at all. This radicalism, however, was dominated by an ideology which was much more conducive to the values and cultures of these districts, namely the ideology of 'Old Corruption'. Cobbett has frequently been accused of narrowing the radical critique in his personification of Old Corruption, a view which saw the ills of the country stemming from the failure of the rulers to uphold their paternalist trust in the face of the seductive embrace of 'The Thing'. However, Cobbett, unlike Paine, did not call upon his audience to repudiate their past. Indeed, he taught them to glorify it and to use it as a benchmark against which to judge their miserable present. Cobbett did not, as White claims, 'create the myth of a Golden Age which was destroyed by the Industrial Revolution'. He simply articulated what many who heard him or read him believed: that they had indeed lost a golden age. And Cobbett offered the possibility of its revival by means of Parliamentary reform. Political reform was also on the Jacobin agenda but Cobbett's reform implied the resuscitation of all that regulatory legislation repealed during the years of war and perhaps more extensive regulation. This is why Cobbett was able to draw the weavers, the tinners and the nailers, those very groups who had formed the heartlands of the eighteenth-century moral economy, into the radical fold in a way that Paine's writings had failed to achieve. Cobbett's explanation, however, had to await the Peace before finding a national audience. In the years before 1809 the radical message struck root only in certain sorts of soil.[94]

It may well be that it was the repeal of the old legislation controlling the woollen industry which precipitated a growing sense of betrayal by government in both the West Riding and West of England and

---

[93] Manchester may be regarded as the exception to this pattern. However, the support for radicalism in Manchester in the 1790s came principally from a range of the old-established urban artisan trades, not from the new cotton workers. See Bohstedt, *Riots and Community Politics*, chs. 3, 6.
[94] For radicalism in the post-war period see Thompson, *The Making*, ch. 15; R. J. White, *Waterloo to Peterloo* (Harmondsworth, 1957; 1968 edn), p. 260.

provided that growing politicisation of the workers and small master clothiers in Yorkshire which Thompson and Dinwiddy [95] find to have accompanied and survived the Luddite disturbances. After the removal of all restrictions in 1809 and the consequent increasingly rapid spread of machinery, the identification of government with large-scale and disruptive capital could much more clearly be made. The experience of the fierce repression of Luddism in Yorkshire augmented such alienation, though, as Calhoun argues, Luddite radicalism was as much reactionary as progressive. In the West of England, however, even Parliament's abandonment of its old regulatory role did not automatically lead to an alienation of the workers from their belief in the moral economy. In particular, in Gloucestershire, where the tradition was most deep-rooted, we may see a continuing belief that the authorities would come to the aid of the increasingly distressed weavers, a belief which did not lose its appeal until 1839.

To conclude: the impact of the advent of machinery upon the economic and political perceptions of the woollen workers was complex and mixed. Machinery in the West of England polarised still further capital and labour but the values of the putting out system, the reluctance of some established gentlemen clothiers to adopt a machine economy and old attitudes towards the role of the bench all mitigated against a clearer sense of class hostility by the woollen workers towards their employers. And the ambiguous response of the local authorities likewise hindered a sense of political alienation from the state. In the West Riding the economically polarising effects of machinery were nowhere near as clearly recognised in 1802–6 since for the most part the Domestic System with its artisanal values of production had managed to absorb earlier machinery without seriously disrupting existing relationships between capital and labour. The relative weakness of large-scale capitalism as a directing agency in production facilitated the acceptance of a radical philosophy hostile to the state since the state itself could be postulated as the source of existing economic, social and political problems. In the West of England, however, the augmented strength of capitalist control, made possible by the machine, generated increasing insecurity and reinforced traditional reliance upon the authorities to act as arbiters and to protect workers' rights and

[95] Thompson, *The Making*, ch. 14; J. Dinwiddy, 'Luddism and politics in the northern counties', *Social History*, 4, 1 (1979).

privileges from rapacious employers. Their reluctance to accept that these authorities were no longer prepared to fulfil this role was in many ways extraordinary but reflects the depth of hold the old industrial moral economy retained over worker attitudes in the West.

CONCLUSION

I began this book by noting that we are often invited to derive certain 'lessons of history' from the Industrial Revolution. The study of the difficult and protracted early attempts to mechanise the English woollen industry suggests that other, perhaps less well-regarded, lessons may be drawn.

The first is the crucial need to recognise how deeply the social context of manufacturing production influences its potential for transformation. Economic historians, too ready to assume that industries are reducible to simple economic systems and structures, often ignore the obvious fact that these are also systems of human co-operation and of social as well as economic relationships. Yet if we divorce woollen cloth production from the social context of the Domestic System or the putting out system, we will be hard put to explain its tardiness, when compared to the cotton or worsted industries, in responding to the challenge of mechanisation and of the factory. Work plays a vital part in conferring social status and shaping social relations. The character of work and of work organisation give rise to social values and expectations which in turn impinge upon the development of economic relations. It is a reciprocal and symbiotic process, even if it is the economic imperatives which provide the dynamic for change. Where those economic structures had been established and stable for over a century, as was the case with the woollen industry, social systems developed in which habituation and practice became ossified and reified as custom and in which a powerful sense of community identity burgeoned. This strong sense of community, this belief in custom, can be readily discerned in both the West of England and the West Riding of Yorkshire, though in somewhat different forms in each region, shaping and determining the response to economic change in the last quarter of the eighteenth century.

Recognition of this social context of economic relationships helps explain why economic development was not a simple linear process

285

from *Kaufsystem* to *Verlagsystem* to factory system as the proto-industrialisation thesis suggests. The different structures of the West of
England and the West Riding woollen industries show this clearly, for
the generalist and non-specialising *Kaufsystem* of Yorkshire developed
a social system which made metamorphosis into the factory system
very much easier than for the advanced *Verlagsystem* of the West of
England. With all its economic advantages of capital accumulation and
a skilled, specialised and sub-divided labour force, the West of
England's social and cultural values impeded transformation so effectively that by 1830 the region was in terminal decline. In this it was
matched by those other similarly 'advantaged' textile producing
regions, East Anglia and Devonshire which likewise fell at the hurdle
marked 'Industrial Revolution'. It is inadequate to explain their failure
by reference to dearer raw materials. The West of England imported
most of the wool it used while combing wool remained plentiful in East
Anglia and Devonshire. Nor will that old chestnut, the comparative
expense of coal, really suffice. The cost of coal for power and for drying
was minimal in the total production price of a cloth. And, in any case,
the West of England and even Devonshire produced rather more
up-market products than Yorkshire which could have borne a higher
differential. Their real problems were social rather than economic, the
consequence of a society engendered by the stable and successful
organisational structures of the past, and values, shared in many cases
by both capital and labour, which were hostile or indifferent to the
need to industrialise further.

We should not over-emphasise, however, the point about the adapt-
ability of the West Riding woollen industry. As has been seen, while
the Domestic System gave rise to a rather different industrial and social
structure based around the tripartite merchant/master clothier/jour-
neyman division, producing greater opportunities for social and economic mobility than in the West Country, it engendered values,
customs and a culture which were every bit as rooted in its past as
those of the West of England putting out system. While it proved
possible to absorb some of the new technologies into the Domestic
System without radically redistributing autonomy, the threat of deregulation and of the factory was feared no less in Yorkshire than in the
West Country as the enquiry of 1806 showed.

A second 'lesson' which may be drawn from the foregoing study is
that while economic historians are busily dismantling the whole concept of an Industrial Revolution by emphasising its limited technological and organisational achievements and its very extended time scale,

we should beware of assuming that these 'truths' were self-evident to the people of the day. On the contrary, for those involved in the woollen industry, the experience of the changes wrought by the impact of mechanisation and re-organisation in the years before 1812, however limited, was traumatic and widespread. It was not only those displaced by the new technologies who felt this change, though, as we have seen, their numbers were considerable. Directly and indirectly the process of change affected and impinged upon whole communities. Relatively few forsook homes for work in the new factories. Many, however, were forced to the loom to find a livelihood. Family economies were disrupted. And over all hung the threat of wholesale restructuring. From 'a situation of comfort and independence',[1] journeymen and small masters found themselves inexorably declining into insecurity and poverty. It was not a rapid process and it was bitterly resisted and resented. But those spokesmen for the woollen workers and master clothiers who gave evidence in 1803 and 1806 could well see what fate awaited them. These opponents of change might not have realised that it was an 'Industrial Revolution' they were experiencing but they recognised that the ways and the values of the past were about to be overturned. If it proved no great shakes as an economic revolution, as a social revolution the Industrial Revolution had deep and profound consequences.

The third 'lesson' we may draw is that resistance to the machine and to the factory can no longer be dismissed simply as 'blind vandalism' or other such pejorative phrases suggestive of desperation and stupidity. Workers in the woollen industry were very clear why they did not want change and they were discriminating in the means they used to prevent it. Resistance to machinery was multiform, ranging from peaceful petitioning, appeals to the courts and negotiations to strike action, intimidation and riot. These responses were not mutually exclusive but, as has been seen, were frequently integrated and deployed as circumstances and capacities dictated. Above all, industrial violence and the industrial riot seem to me in need of rescue from the ministrations of the functionalists of the right and the Fabians of the left. Food riots have been rehabilitated and revealed as complex social events which display community values and attitudes. Industrial riots continue to languish in the doldrums. And yet, as I have argued above, the community-based riot against early preparatory machinery in many respects parallels those food riots which involved these same communities in 1766 and 1795. This should come as no surprise. The

[1] B.P.P., 1806, Vol. 3, p. 10.

base and the value systems were the same. The experience and success of the one was easily translated into the other. I have argued this case elsewhere in respect of the Gloucestershire weavers in 1756 and 1766[2] but it bears repeating. Just as food riots reveal order, discrimination and a clear moral economy, so do the community-based riots against the jenny and scribbling engine. Just as the food rioters were not prepared to allow all local food supplies to be 'transported', as they said in 1766, leaving them to starve before they acted, neither were these same people prepared to wait until jobs had been destroyed wholesale before they intervened against machinery. And just as the food market was intimately inter-connected with surrounding markets, they, as industrial producers, realised that machinery 10 miles away would soon put pressure on local employers to follow suit. We must abjure the simplistic assumption that rioters had little idea what they were doing. Cobbett warned of the foolishness of assuming that 'people are rendered stupid by remaining always in the same place'. The communities these woollen workers lived within were well informed of the state of trade over the region and had numerous mechanisms whereby action could be taken to defend themselves.

If the riot is frequently viewed as the spontaneous reaction of the unthinking, it is equally often clearly and firmly divorced from the trade union. Yet this study has shown the fallacy of such compartmentalist assumptions. The cloth dressers' battle against the gig mill and later the shearing frame reveals a response which was graduated, carefully controlled and effective, mixing all aspects of 'orthodox' trade unionism with the 'unorthodox' methods of intimidation, violence and riot. The Wiltshire Outrages clearly demonstrate that, from a powerful trade union base, the shearmen were able and prepared to fight their corner with whatever weapon proved most appropriate. I am quite sure that in 1812, as in 1802, there was no clear divide between trade unionism and Luddism. The concept of a trade split clearly between 'sensible' negotiators like Henson and 'wild' machine breakers like Mellor bears no re-semblance to the reality of the experience of eighteenth-century crafts. This tidy divorce is the product of those who view rioting as fruitless and who believe that the trade union image assiduously propagated by such as Applegarth in the mid-nineteenth century was the correct model and aspiration for 'proper' trade unions for a century before. Labour historians must break out of the shadow of

2 Randall, 'The industrial moral economy'.

this Victorian orthodoxy and address themselves, like the economic historians, to the social context of labour in the early Industrial Revolution.

With this point in mind, it is worth noting that violence in many respects proved successful. That is, it delayed the take up of machinery for some considerable time. As the wool combers found, violence could not preserve jobs indefinitely but it could provide a long period of grace. The experience of the West of England in connection with the jenny and scribbling engine showed this and the Wiltshire Outrages likewise proved effective in stemming the rush of gig mills. Thus, during the period of the suspension of the old regulatory legislation few new gig mills or shearing frames were introduced. And even when Parliament gave the innovators the green light in 1809, few clothiers other than those on the periphery of the Wiltshire cloth making districts were keen to press ahead. The memory of the outrages of 1802 lingered and helped safeguard the shearmen's position until the end of the Napoleonic Wars. The situation in Yorkshire was different. Except in Leeds, where innovators had already felt the power of the croppers, the repeal of 1809 brought a rapid take up of both gig mills and frames as the numbers destroyed in 1812 demonstrates. Increasing production helped ease the pain at first but the deepening crisis occasioned by the Orders in Council and the loss of the American market had by late 1811 produced a powder-keg in the West Riding. It needed only the fuse of direct action in Nottinghamshire for Luddism to burst forth. Yorkshire Luddism was crushed even more ferociously than the Wiltshire Outrages but it was by no means a clear failure. The machines destroyed in 1812 were not replaced for some years. Indeed, it was not until the Peace was a year old that there, as in the West of England, cloth dressing machinery made its major and decisive push. There were sporadic disturbances, firmly suppressed, and petitions to Parliament and the Prince Regent[3] but the cloth dressers' day had gone. Like the hand spinners and scribblers, they disappeared from history. But resistance had given them many extra years respite.

The resistance shown to mechanical and structural innovation was not, however, merely physical. As I have suggested, the machine and the factory represented a value system which was alien to the community culture of the woollen manufacturing districts, not merely because it offended their moral economy but because it offended their political economy as well. Armed with 'the enormous condescension

3 Randall, 'Labour and the industrial revolution', pp. 481–6; *J.H.C.*, Vol. 71, pp. 431, 517, 523; H.O. 42/152, journeymen cloth workers to Prince Regent, 30 June 1816.

of posterity', historians have ignored the possibility that resistance to change might have been informed by anything other than naked, narrow and ignorant self-interest. Maxine Berg has validly criticised them for showing little interest 'in making connections between resistance to the machine and the political and intellectual disputes over technological improvement'.[4] Only because the old corpus of regulatory legislation provided opponents of change with a potent weapon of resistance did the innovators in the woollen industry have the necessity of placing their case before Parliament for scrutiny. This, however, provided their opponents with a unique public platform from which the historian may discover their counter-economy, predicated upon regulation, protection and intervention. Yet they were surely not alone in these views? Other groups from similar circumstances, facing similar pressures, were denied such a hearing and their voices have been lost but I believe that the political and moral economies of the woollen workers were far more ubiquitous than many will concede. I would suggest that they spoke not just for the woollen trade but for many established artisan and outworking trades, for *Kaufsystem* and *Verlagsystem*, for town and country, as a sympathetic reading of the experiences of the tailors, the framework knitters and agricultural labourers in the years from 1780 to 1830 reveal. I think we may also see echoes of these views in the Chartist movement.

It was the old regulatory legislation which provided the woollen working community with its most significant source of strength in facing up to the threat of change. And ultimately it was Parliament's decision to repeal this legislation which undermined it. This decision reflected in part the triumph of the new values of political economy but it is not entirely explicable in such terms. While Parliamentary enclosure and the destruction of common rights provided the landlords with a practical example of the benefits from a deregulated economy, equally important in their abdication from the role of arbitrator was their growing insecurity and fear engendered by the rise of radicalism, trade unionism and popular protest. It was this political and social context as much as ideological conversion which persuaded them to throw away the rule book and to retain only the whistle as means of coercing popular compliance.

This is not to argue that the government was responsible for the pace of economic and social change. It has become a commonplace in the

[4] M. Berg, *The Machinery Question and the Making of Political Economy 1815–1848* (Cambridge, 1980), p. 15.

1980s to hear that government cannot create economic growth or entrepreneurship. But we should not under-estimate the capacity of government to facilitate such changes and to encourage them. The Report of the 1806 Select Committee may be seen as emblematic of this determination and led inexorably on to further divestment of responsibilities. Indeed, Parliament's decision over the woollen industry, delayed, protracted and hesitant, proved a crucial breach for labour across the economy. The oldest staple, the most hedged-around by restriction, it was the best-defended stronghold of old values. Repeal in 1809 set the way for more sweeping repeals. Jackson's prophecy in 1806 proved prescient. 'If you give way to this instance, it would be absurd to argue that the abrogation of apprenticeship will be confined to the woollen trade.' It was not. In 1813 Parliament swept away the 1563 apprenticeship legislation and the act's wage-fixing clauses followed in 1814. The specific restrictions relating to apprenticeship in the cutlery trade likewise were set aside and the last vestiges of the old controls on price-fixing in the market place went too. What Jackson referred to as 'commercial jacobinism' took and held sway.[5]

In many ways the loss of these legal rights made Luddism inevitable. To what now could recourse be made other than to force? It also made it inevitable that Yorkshire Luddism would be more single-minded, more tightly military than the Wiltshire Outrages ten years before. The Wiltshiremen fired factories with one eye on public and gentry opinion. The Yorkshire Luddites knew they were on their own, that their 'system of terror'[6] was all they had left. The loss of their rights may well have fuelled a growing acceptance of radical ideas but Luddism, by trembling 'on the edge of ulterior revolutionary objects',[7] simply confirmed the ruling class's conviction that labour needed repression, not arbitration. The resolution of the crisis in the woollen industry was thus both a product of and a shaper of a changing social and political context which accompanied economic transformation.

The need yet again to recognise the social context of economic change brings me to my final suggested 'lesson' to be learned from the study of the early Industrial Revolution in the English woollen industry. This is that it is hard to escape from one's own history. 'Men make their own history', wrote Marx, 'but they do not make it just as they please; they do not make it under circumstances chosen by

---

[5] Jackson, *Speech*, pp. 65, 39.
[6] The phrase comes from Fitzwilliam: H.O. 42/66, 27 Sept. 1802.
[7] Thompson, *The Making*, p. 604.

themselves, but under circumstances directly encountered, given and transmitted from the past.'[8] In few industries did the past transmit such powerful imperatives as in the woollen. The past had shaped a community and a culture which largely determined not just the pattern of economic change with the advent of machinery but also how that change would be interpreted and responded to by the community. This sense of community provided a powerful base from which to resist detrimental change. But, as I have noted, the cultural baggage of entrenched attitudes also proved an encumbrance, making adaptation to a changed world very difficult. It is significant that it was in those regions where industries were young and work culture had not strongly implanted itself into social culture that not only was economic transformation easiest in the Industrial Revolution but that here too we see the earliest development of newer class-based social and political attitudes. In areas such as the West of England and to a lesser extent the West Riding of Yorkshire not only was economic change slow but the social and industrial culture of the eighteenth century continued to shape attitudes long after the economic circumstances which had created them had withered away. Historians sometimes refer to the need for workers to learn 'the rules of the game' of nineteenth-century industrial relations.[9] They forget that in many areas, before workers could do this, they had to abandon the old rules of the old game first. For many this proved a very difficult and painful business. As we should be well aware, the past cannot always be so easily discarded.

[8] K. Marx, *The Eighteenth Brumaire of Louis Bonaparte*, cited in J. Elster, *Karl Marx: A Reader* (Cambridge, 1986), p. 277.

[9] Hobsbawm, *Labouring Men*, p. 345.

BIBLIOGRAPHY

PRIMARY SOURCES

A. Manuscript sources

1. London

British Library

Hardwicke MSS, Add. MSS 35, 607

Public Record Office

Courts of Assize
  Western Circuit, Process Books, ASSI. 24/
  Western Circuit, Indictments, ASSI. 25/
Home Office
  Disturbances, Correspondence, H.O. 40/
  Disturbances, Entry Books, H.O. 41/
  Domestic, George III, Correspondence, H.O. 42/
  Domestic, Entry Books, H.O. 43/
  Domestic, George IV and later, Correspondence, H.O. 44/
  Judges' Reports, H.O. 47/
  Law Officers, Reports and Correspondence, H.O. 48/
  Law Officers, Letter Books, H.O. 49/
  Military, Correspondence, H.O. 50/
  Military, Entry Books, H.O. 51/
Court of King's Bench
  Affidavits (General) K.B. 1/
  Baga de Secretis, K.B. 8/
Privy Council
  Unbound Papers, Non-Colonial, P.C. 1/
State Papers
  Domestic, Entry Books, Military, S.P. 44/
Treasury Solicitor
  Papers, T.S. 11/
War Office
  In Letters, W.O. 1/
  Out Letters, Secretary at War, W. O. 4/
  Out Letters, Marching Orders, W.O. 5/

293

Selected Unnumbered Papers, W.O. 40/

2.   Provincial repositories
     Birmingham Reference Library
Boulton and Watt MSS

     Gloucestershire Record Office
Gloucestershire Collection
Quarter Sessions
     Calendars of Prisoners, Q/S G2
     Depositions, Q/SD
     Indictments in Riot Cases, Q/SIa
     Order Books, Q/SO
     Prisoners in County Gaol, Registers, Q/GC
Deposited Collections
     Watson of Rodborough Papers, D.67
     Clifford of Frampton-on-Severn Papers, D.149
     Bathurst of Lydney Park Papers, D.421
     Blathwayt of Dyrham Papers, D.1799
     Penley, Millward and Bayley: Austin accounts, D.2078/I/Austin
     Moore and Sons: sale catalogue of goods of J. Restall, D.2080/242
     Records of Lightpill mill, Rodborough, D.2206
Parish Records
     Bisley P.47, P.47a
     Dursley P.124
     Hawkesbury P.170
     Kingswood P.193
     Minchinhampton P.217
     Stroud P.320, P.320a
     Wotton-under-Edge P.379

     Leeds City Archives
Bolland Papers, DB 69
Denison family Papers, DB 129
Papers of the Coloured Cloth Hall

     Brotherton Library, University of Leeds
Brotherton Papers
Gott family Papers
Papers of the White Cloth Hall

     Sheffield City Reference Library
Wentworth Woodhouse Manuscripts (Fitzwilliam Collection)

     Somerset Record Office
Quarter Sessions
     Calendars of Prisoners, Q/S Cal.

Rolls, Q/SR
Deposited Collections
  Lewis Papers, DD/LW
  Letter Book of James Elderton, DD/X/MSL
Parish Records
  Shepton Mallet D/P/She.

West Yorkshire Archive Service, Wakefield
Quarter Sessions Order Books, QS10
Returns of cotton and other mills, 1803, 1804, QE33

Wiltshire Archaeological and Natural History Society Library, Devizes
Calendars of Prisoners
MS diary of George Sloper
MSS Collection on the history of Warminster, compiled by H. Wansey

Wiltshire Record Office
Quarter Sessions
  Calendars of Prisoners, A2/4
  Depositions, A2/8
Deposited Collections
  Ailesbury MSS, Yeomanry and Militia Papers, W.R.O., 9
  J. and T. Clark of Trowbridge, W.R.O., 927
  Samuel Salter and Co. of Trowbridge, W.R.O., 926
  Wansey family of Warminster, W.R.O., 314
Parish Records
  Bradford on Avon W.R.O., 77
  Chippenham W.R.O., 811
  North Bradley W.R.O., 523,533
  Trowbridge W.R.O., 206, 712

3. Records in private hands
    Bath and West of England and Southern Counties Society, Bath, Archives
    Lloyd-Baker MSS (Col. A. B. Lloyd-Baker, Hardwicke Court, Gloucester)

B. Printed sources
1 Official
Calendar of Home Office Papers, 1766–1769, ed. J. Redington (1879).
The English Reports, Vol. cii, King's Bench Division, XXXI (London, 1910).
Hansard's Parliamentary Debates, Vols. 5, 6, 8.
Journal of the House of Commons, 1750–1812.
Journal of the House of Lords, 1802–12.
Statutes at Large.

2. British Parliamentary Papers
Report from the Select Committee on the Woollen Clothiers' Petition, B.P.P., 1802/3, Vol. 5 (H.C. 30).

Minutes of Evidence Taken before the Select Committee on the Woollen Clothiers' Petition, B.P.P., 1802/3, Vol. 7 (H.C. 95).

Report from the Committees on the Laws which concern the Relief and Settlement of the Poor Severally Reported in 1775–8 and 1787–8, B.P.P., 1803, Vol. 9.

Answers and Returns concerning Poor Expenses, 1804, B.P.P., 1803/4, Vol. 13 (H.C. 175).

Report of the Select Committee on the Clothworkers', Shearmen's, Weavers' and Clothiers' Petitions, B.P.P., 1805, Vol. 3 (H.C. 105).

Report of and Minutes of Evidence Taken before the Select Committee to Consider the State of the Woollen Manufacture, B.P.P., 1806, Vol. 3 (H.C. 268).

Minutes of Evidence Taken before the Select Committee on the State of the Children Employed in the Manufactories of the United Kingdom, B.P.P., 1816, Vol. 3 (H.C. 397).

Abridgment of the Abstract of the Answers and Returns Relative to the Expense of the Poor, B.P.P., 1818, Vol. 19 (H.C. 82).

Digest of Parochial Returns to the Select Committee Appointed to Inquire into the Education of the Poor, B.P.P., 1819, Vol. 9 (H.C. 224).

Report from the Select Committee on the Poor Rate Returns, B.P.P., 1825, Vol. 4 (H.C. 334).

Report from the Select Committee of the House of Lords Appointed to Take into Consideration the State of the British Wool Trade, B.P.P., 1828, Vol. 8 (H.L. 515).

Comparative Account of the Population of Great Britain in the Years 1801, 1811, 1821 and 1831, B.P.P., 1831, Vol. 18 (H.C. 348).

First Report of the Commissioners for Inquiring into the Employment of Children in Factories, B.P.P., 1833, Vol. 20 (H.C. 450).

Supplementary Report of the Factory Commissioners, 1834, Part I, B.P.P., 1834, Vol. 19 (H.C. 167).

Supplementary Report of the Factory Commissioners, 1834, Part II, B.P.P., 1834, Vol. 20 (H.C. 167).

Report from the Commissioners on the Poor Law, Appendix A, Reports from Assistant Commissioners, B.P.P., 1834, Vol. 28 (H.C. 44).

Report from the Commissioners on the Poor Law, Appendix B1, Answers to Rural Queries, B.P.P., 1834, Vol. 30 (H.C. 44).

Reports from the Assistant Handloom Weavers' Commissioners, B.P.P., 1840, Vol. 23 (H.C. 43–1).

Reports from the Assistant Handloom Weavers' Commissioners, B.P.P., 1840, Vol. 24 (H.C. 220).

Report of the Commissioners Inquiring into the Condition of the Unemployed Handloom Weavers, B.P.P., 1841, Vol. 10 (H.C. 296).

Account of the Total Population According to the Census of 1841, B.P.P., 1843, Vol. 22 (H.C. 496).

3.   Printed records

Records of the Court of the County of Wiltshire, being extracts of the Quarter Sessions Rolls of the Seventeenth Century, ed. B. H. Cunnington (Devizes, 1932).

The Trowbridge Woollen Industry as illustrated by the Stock Books of John and Thomas Clark, 1804–24, ed. R. P. Beckinsale, Wiltshire Archaeological and Natural History Society, Records Branch, Vol. VI (Devizes, 1951).
'The petitions of the weavers and clothiers of Gloucestershire in 1756', ed. W. E. Minchinton, *T.B.G.A.S.*, Vol. LXXIII, 1954 (1955).
Wiltshire Apprentices and their Masters, 1710–1760, ed. C. Dale, Wiltshire Archaeological and Natural History Society, Records Branch, Vol. XVII (Devizes, 1961).
Documents Illustrating the Wiltshire Textile Trades in the Eighteenth Century, ed. J. de L. Mann, Wiltshire Archaeological and Natural History Society, Records Branch, Vol. XIX (Devizes, 1964).
The West Riding Wool Textile Industry: A Catalogue of Business Records, ed. P. Hudson (Edington, 1975).
Early English Trade Unions, ed. A. Aspinall (1949).

4.
Newspapers and periodicals
Aris' Birmingham Gazette
Bath Chronicle
Bath Journal
Devizes Gazette
Gloucester Journal
Leeds Intelligencer
Leeds Mercury
London Gazette
Salisbury and Winchester Journal
The Times
Wiltshire Cuttings (W.A.S.L.)

Annals of Agriculture
Annual Register
The Gentleman's Magazine

5. Contemporary pamphlets and books
(Place of publication London unless otherwise stated.)
Aikin, J., *A Description of the Country from Thirty to Forty Miles round Manchester* (1795).
An Account of the Proceedings of the Merchants, Manufacturers, and others concerned in the Wool and Woollen Trade of Great Britain . . . that the laws respecting the exportation of Wool might not be altered in arranging the Union with Ireland (1800).
[Andrews, T.], *Country Commonsense, by a Gentleman of Wilts.* (1739).
Andrews, T., *Miseries of the Miserable* (1739).
Anstie, J., *A General View of the Bill for the preventing the Illicit Exportation of British Wool and live Sheep* (Bath, 1787).
Letter addressed to Edward Phillips, M.P. for the County of Somerset (1788).
A Letter to the Secretary of the Bath Agricultural Society on the subject of a premium for the Improvement of British Wool (1791).

Observations on the Importance and Necessity of Introducing Improved Machinery into the Woollen Manufactory; more particularly as it respects the interests of the Counties of Wilts., Gloucester and Somerset (1803).

Atkyns, Sir R., *The Ancient and Present State of Gloucestershire* (1712).

Bamford, S., *Passages in the Life of a Radical* (1844; 1967 edn).

Bigland, J., *A Topographical and Historical Description of the County of York* (1812).

A Bill for the better relief and employment of the poor in the County of Wilts. (1763), Wiltshire Tracts, No. 17, W.A.S.L.

Billingsley, J., *A General View of the Agriculture of the County of Somerset* (Bath, 1797).

Bodman, J., *A concise history of Trowbridge* (1814).

Brooks, R., *Observations on Milling Broad and Narrow Cloth* (1743).

Brown, R., *A General View of the Agriculture of the West Riding of Yorkshire* (Edinburgh, 1799).

The Causes of the Dearness of Provisions assigned (Gloucester, 1766).

Cincinnatus, *The Letters of Cincinnatus . . . on the Subject of the Corn Bill* (Gloucester, 1815).

Considerations upon a bill now before Parliament, for repealing (in substance) the whole code of laws respecting the woollen manufacture of Great Britain: and for dissolving the ancient system of apprenticeship (1803).

Cooke, G. A., *Topographical and Statistical Description of the County of York* (1818).

Dallaway, J., *A Scheme to make the River Stroudwater Navigable from Framiload to Wallbridge near the town of Stroud, Gloucestershire* (Gloucester, 1755).

Davies, D., *The Case of Labourers in Husbandry* (Bath, 1795).

Davis, T., *A General View of the Agriculture of the County of Wilts.* (1813).

Defoe, D., *A Tour through England and Wales* (1724–6, Everyman, 1928 edn).

Directories:

Baines, E., *Directory of Leeds* (1809, 1814).

History, Directory and Gazetteer of the County of York (Leeds, 1822).

Barfoot, P., and Wilkes, J., *Universal British Directory*, Vol. III (1793).

Binns and Brown, *A Directory for the Town of Leeds* (1800).

Gell and Bradshaw, *Directory of Gloucestershire* (1820).

Pigot and Dean, *A Commercial Directory of the West Riding* (1814–15).

Pigot's London & Provincial Directory (1822–3).

Pigot's National & Commercial Directory (1829, 1830).

A Draper of London, *The Consequences of Trade* (1740), repr. in part in *The Gentleman's Magazine*, Vol. 10.

Eden, Sir F. M., *The State of the Poor* (1797).

Gardner, E., *Reflections upon the Evill Effects of an Increasing Population and upon the Present High Price of Provisions* (Gloucester, 1800).

The Haunted Farmer or the Ghost of the Granary (Chippenham, 1800), Wiltshire Tracts, No. 7, W.A.S.L.

Haynes, J., *A View of the Present State of the Clothing Trade in England* (1706).

Jackson, R., *The Speech of Randle Jackson to the Committee of the House of Commons appointed to consider the state of the Woollen Manufacture* (1806).

Jay, W., *Memoir of the late Rev. John Clark* (1810).

Lawn, B., *The Corn Trade Investigated* (Bath, 1800).

A Letter to the Landholders of the county of Wilts. on the alarming State of the Poor (Salisbury, 1793), Wiltshire Tracts, No. 16, W.A.S.L.

Live and Let Live: a treatise on the hostile rivalships between the manufacturer and the landworker (1787).

Luccock, J., *The Nature and Properties of Wool* (Leeds, 1805).

Maitland, J., *Observations on the Impolicy of Permitting the Exportation of British Wool* (1818).

Marshall, W., *The Rural Economy of Yorkshire* (1788).

The Rural Economy of the West of England (1796).

Nemnich, P. A., *Neueste Reise durch England, Schottland und Irland* (1807).

Nield, D., *Addresses to the different classes of men in the Parish of Saddleworth, showing . . . the necessity for supporting the Plan for augmenting the price of labour in the woollen manufactory* (Leeds, 1795).

Observations on woollen machinery (Leeds, 1803).

Paine, T., *The Rights of Man* (1791/2; 1969 edn).

Partridge, W., *A Practical Treatise on Dying of Woollen Cloth and Skein Silk with the Manufacture of Broadcloth and Cassimere including the most Improved Methods in the West of England* (New York, 1823; 1975 edn).

P., G., *An Answer to the Woollen Draper's Letter on the French Treaty especially to the Woollen manufacturers* (1787).

Plomer, T., *The Speech of Thomas Plomer to the Committee of the House of Commons . . . relating to the Woollen Trade in 1803* (Gloucester, 1804).

Propositions for improving the Manufactures, Agriculture and Commerce of Great Britain (1763).

Radcliffe, W., *Origin of the new system of manufacture commonly called 'power-loom' weaving* (Stockport, 1828).

Rees, A., *The Cyclopaedia, or Universal Dictionary of Arts and Sciences*, Vol. xxxvIII (1819).

Rudder, S., *A New History of Gloucestershire* (Cirencester, 1779).

Rudge, T., *A General View of the Agriculture of Gloucestershire* (1807).

Sheffield, Lord, *Observations on the Objections made to the export of Wool from Great Britain to Ireland* (1800).

Smith, J., *Chronicon Rusticum Commerciale or Memoirs of Wool* (1747; 1757 edn).

A State of the Case, and a Narrative of Facts Relating to the late Commotions and Rising of the Weavers in the County of Gloucester (1757).

Stratford, F., *A Plan for extending the Navigation from Bath to Chippenham* (1765).

Temple, W., *The Case as it now Stands between the Clothiers, Weavers and other Manufacturers with regard to the late Riot in the County of Wilts.* (1739) [Philalethes].

A Vindication of Commerce and the Arts (1758) [I.B.].

Tucker, J., *A Brief Essay on the advantages and disadvantages which attend France and Great Britain with regard to Trade* (1753).

Instructions for Travellers (printed privately, Gloucester, 1757).

The Manifold Causes of the Increase of the Poor directly set forth (? Gloucester, 1760).

Turner, G., *A General View of the Agriculture of the County of Gloucester* (1794).

Wansey, H., *Wool encouraged without exportation, by a Wiltshire Clothier* (1791).

300   *Bibliography*

The Journal of an Excursion to the United States of America in 1794 (1796; ed. D. J. Jeremy, Philadelphia, 1970).
Thoughts on Poor Houses with a view to their General Reform (1801).
Warner, R., *Excursions from Bath* (Bath, 1801).
History of Bath (Bath, 1801).
Wigley, E., *The Speech of E. Wigley on behalf of the Woollen Weavers of Gloucestershire to the Committee of the House of Commons appointed to consider the State of the Woollen Manufacture* (Cheltenham, 1806).
Williams, A., *An Address to the woollen manufacturers of Great Britain on the Subject of the proposed exportation of wool to Ireland* (1800).
Young, A., *A Six Week Tour through the Southern Counties of England and Wales* (1769).
A Six Months Tour through the North of England (1771).

SECONDARY SOURCES
(Place of publication London unless otherwise stated.)

A.   Books

Ashton, T. S., *The Industrial Revolution 1760–1830* (1948).
Economic Fluctuations in England, 1700–1800 (Oxford, 1959).
Aspinall, A., *The Early English Trade Unions* (1949).
Atkinson, F., *Some Aspects of the Eighteenth-Century Woollen and Worsted Trade in Halifax* (Halifax, 1956).
Baddeley, W. St C., *A Cotteswold Manor – Being the History of Painswick* (Gloucester, 1907).
Baines, E., *Account of the Woollen Manufacture of England* (1858; repr. Newton Abbot, 1970).
Beresford, M. W., and Jones, G. R. J., eds., *Leeds and its Region* (Leeds, 1967).
Berg, M., *The Machinery Question and the Making of Political Economy 1815–1848* (Cambridge, 1980).
The Age of Manufactures, 1700–1820 (1985).
Berg, M., Hudson, P., and Sonenscher, M., eds., *Manufacture in Town and Country before the Factory* (Cambridge, 1983).
Bird, J. T., *History of Malmesbury* (Malmesbury, 1876).
Bischoff, J., *The Wool Question Considered* (1828).
A Comprehensive History of the Woollen and Worsted Manufacture (1842).
Blunt, J. H., *Dursley and its Neighbourhood* (Dursley, 1877).
Bohstedt, J., *Riots and Community Politics in England and Wales, 1790–1810* (Harvard, 1983).
Brewer, J., and Styles, J., *An Ungovernable People: The English and their Law in the Seventeenth and Eighteenth Centuries* (1980).
Briggs, A., *The Age of Improvement, 1783–1867* (1959).
Burnley, J., *History of Wool and Woolcombing* (1889).
Bythell, D., *The Handloom Weavers – A study in the English Cotton Industry during the Industrial Revolution* (Cambridge, 1969).
Calhoun, C., *The Question of Class Struggle: Social Foundations of Popular Radicalism during the Industrial Revolution* (Oxford, 1982).

Camidge, C. E., *A History of Wakefield* (1866).
Carter, H. B., *His Majesty's Spanish Flock* (1964).
Chapman, S. D., *The Early Factory Masters: The Transition to the Factory System in the Midlands Textile Industry* (Newton Abbot, 1967).
Charlesworth, A., *An Atlas of Rural Protest in Britain, 1548–1900* (1983).
Clapham, J. H., *The Woollen and Worsted Industries* (1907).
Cobbett, W., *Rural Rides* (1830; Harmondsworth, 1967, edn).
Cole, G. D. H., *Attempts at General Union: A Study in British Trade Union History, 1818–1834* (1953).
Cole, G. D. H., and Postgate, R., *The Common People, 1746–1946* (1938; 1949 edn).
Collier, F., *The Family Economy of the Working Classes in the Cotton Industry, 1784–1833* (1964).
Crump, W. B., *The Leeds Woollen Industry, 1780–1820* (Leeds, 1931).
Crump, W. B., and Ghorbal, G., *History of the Huddersfield Woollen Industry* (Huddersfield, 1935).
Cunningham, H., *Leisure in the Industrial Revolution* (1980).
Daniell, J. J., *The History of Warminster* (Warminster, 1879).
History of Chippenham (Chippenham, 1894).
Darvall, F. O., *Popular Disturbances and Public Order in Regency England* (Oxford, 1934).
Deane, P., and Cole, W. A., *British Economic Growth, 1688–1959* (Cambridge, 1967).
Dictionary of National Biography.
Dobson, C. R., *Masters and Journeymen: A Prehistory of Industrial Relations, 1717–1800* (1980).
Driver, C., *Tory Radical: The Life of Richard Oastler* (Oxford, 1946).
Edwards, M. M., *The Growth of the British Cotton Trade, 1780–1815* (Manchester, 1967).
Emsley, C., and Walvin, J., *Artisans, Peasants and Proletarians, 1760–1860* (1985).
Engels, F., *The Condition of the Working Class in England in 1844* (1892 edn).
Exell, T., *A Brief History of the Weavers of the County of Gloucester* (Stroud, 1838).
A Sketch of the Circumstances which providentially led to the Repeal of the Corn and Animal Food Laws (Dursley, 1847).
F., A., *History of North Bradley and Roadhill* (Trowbridge, 1881), Wiltshire Tracts, No. 62, W.A.S.L.
Facts and Reasonings Submitted by the Woollen Manufacturers of Gloucestershire in Answer to the Allegations made by the Supporters of a Bill to Regulate the Labour of Children in Mills to Show its Impolicy and Injustice (1833) [E. Sheppard].
Facts Submitted to the Sympathy of the Public to Call Attention to . . . the Distressed Weavers of Randwick (Devonport, 1832).
Finberg, H. P. R., ed., *Gloucestershire Studies* (Leicester, 1957).
Fisher, P. H., *Notes and Recollections of Stroud* (Stroud, 1871).
Foster, J., *Class Struggle and the Industrial Revolution* (1974).
Fox, H., *Quaker Homespun: The Life of Thomas Fox of Wellington, Sergemaker and Banker* (1958).

Gaskell, P., *Artisans and Machinery* (1836; repr. 1968).
George, M. D., *London Life in the Eighteenth Century* (1925; 1966 edn).
England in Transition (1931; 1953 edn).
Gilboy, E. W., *Wages in Eighteenth Century England* (Cambridge, 1934).
Gloucestershire Notes and Queries, ed. Rev. Beaver H. Blacker (1881–1904).
Graham, H., *The Annals of the Yeomanry Cavalry of Wiltshire* (Liverpool, 1886).
Gregory, D., *Regional Transformation and Industrial Revolution: A Geography of the Yorkshire Woollen Industry* (1982).
Gulvin, C., *The Tweedmakers: A History of the Scottish Fancy Woollen Industry, 1660–1914* (Newton Abbot, 1973).
Hammond, J. L. and B., *The Skilled Labourer* (1919; 1979 edn).
Hanson, T. W., *The Story of Old Halifax* (Halifax, 1920).
Harrison, J. F. C., *Robert Owen and the Owenites in Britain and America* (1969).
Harte, N. B., and Ponting, K. G., eds., *Textile History and Economic History* (Manchester, 1973).
Hartwell, R. M., *The Industrial Revolution and Economic Growth* (1971).
Hay, D., Linebaugh, P., and Thompson, E. P., *Albion's Fatal Tree* (1975).
Hayter, T., *The Army and the Crowd in Mid-Georgian England* (1978).
Heaton, H., *The Yorkshire Woollen and Worsted Industries from the Earliest Times up to the Industrial Revolution* (Oxford, 1920).
Hills, R. L., *Power in the Industrial Revolution* (Manchester, 1970).
Hirst, W., *History of the Woollen Trade for the Last Sixty Years* (Leeds, 1844).
Hobsbawm, E. J., *Labouring Men: Studies in the History of Labour* (1964; 1968 edn).
Industry and Empire (1968).
Hudson, P., *The Genesis of Industrial Capital: A Study of the West Riding Wool Textile Industry c. 1750–1850* (Cambridge, 1986).
Hunt, E. H., *British Labour History, 1815–1914* (1981).
Hunter, D. M., *The West of England Woollen Industry under Protection and Free Trade* (1910).
James, J., *History of the Worsted Manufacture in England from the Earliest Times* (1857).
Jenkins, D. T., *The West Riding Wool Textile Industry, 1750–1835: A Study of Fixed Capital Formation* (Edington, 1975).
Jenkins, D. T., and Ponting, K. G., *The British Wool Textile Industry, 1770–1914* (1982).
Jones, W. H., *Bradford-on-Avon: A History and Description* (Bradford, 1859; 1907 edn).
Joyce, P., *Work, Society and Politics: The Culture of the Factory in Later Victorian England* (1980).
Kriedte, P., Medick, H., and Schlumbohm, J., *Industrialisation before Industrialisation* (Cambridge, 1982).
Landes, D. S., *The Unbound Prometheus* (1969).
Laslett, P., *The World We Haved Lost* (1965; 1971 edn).
Lawson, J., *Letters to the Young on Progress in Pudsey in the Last Sixty Years* (Stanningley, 1887).
Lindley, E. S., *Wotton-under-Edge – Men and Affairs of a Cotswold Wool Town* (1962).

Lipson, E., *History of the Woollen and Worsted Industries* (1921).

McCulloch, J. R., ed., *Select Collection of Scarce and Valuable Tracts on Commerce* (1859).

Mann, J. de L., *The Cloth Industry in the West of England from 1640 to 1880* (Oxford, 1971).

Mantoux, P., *The Industrial Revolution in the Eighteenth Century* (1961 edn).

Mathias, P., *The First Industrial Nation: An Economic History of Britain, 1700–1914* (1969).

Mitchell, B. R., and Deane, P., *Abstract of British Historical Statistics* (Cambridge, 1962).

Moir, E., *Local Government in Gloucestershire, 1775 to 1800 – A Study of the Justices of the Peace*, Bristol and Gloucestershire Archaeological Society, Records Section, Vol. VIII (1969).

Munby, L. M., *The Luddites and Other Essays* (1971).

Musson, A. E., *British Trade Unions, 1800–1875* (1972).

Neale, R. S., *Class and Ideology in the Nineteenth Century* (1972).

An Old Cropper, *Old Leeds, its Bygones and Celebrities* (Leeds, 1868).

Parsons, E., *The Civil, Ecclesiastical, Literary, Commercial and Miscellaneous History of . . . the Manufacturing Districts of Yorkshire* (Leeds, 1834).

Peel, F., *The Risings of the Luddites, Chartists and Plug Drawers* (1880; 1968 edn).

Spen Valley: Past and Present (Heckmondwike, 1893).

Perkin, H., *The Origins of Modern English Society* (1969).

Pinchbeck, I., *Women Workers and the Industrial Revolution, 1750–1850* (1930).

Playne, A. T., *A History of the Parishes of Minchinhampton and Avening* (Gloucester, 1915).

Plummer, A., and Early, R. E., *The Blanket Makers, 1669 to 1969 – A History of Charles Early and Marriot (Witney) Ltd.* (1969).

Pollard, S., *The Genesis of Modern Management* (1965).

Ponting, K. G., *The Woollen Industry of South-west England* (Bath, 1971).

Poynter, J. R., *Society and Pauperism: English Ideas on Poor Relief, 1795–1834* (1969).

Pressnell, L. S., ed., *Studies in the Industrial Revolution* (1960).

Price, R., *Labour in British Society* (1986).

Prothero, I., *Artisans and Politics in Early Nineteenth Century London: John Gast and his Times* (1979).

Reddy, W. M., *The Rise of Market Culture: The Textile Trade and French Society, 1750–1900* (Cambridge, 1984).

Redford, A., *Labour Migration in England, 1800–1850* (Manchester, 1926; 1964 edn).

Rimmer, W. G., *Marshalls of Leeds: Flax Spinners, 1786–1886* (Cambridge, 1960).

Rogers, K. H., *Wiltshire and Somerset Woollen Mills* (Edington, 1976).

Rostow, W. W., *British Economy of the Nineteenth Century* (Oxford, 1948).

Rudd, M. A., *Historical Records of Bisley with Lypiatt, Gloucestershire* (Gloucester, 1937).

Rudé, G., *The Crowd in the French Revolution* (Oxford, 1959).

Wilkes and Liberty (Oxford 1962; 1965 edn).

The Crowd in History: A Study of Popular Disturbances in France and England, 1730–1848 (New York, 1964).

Rule, J., The Experience of Labour in Eighteenth-Century Industry (1981).
The Labouring Classes in Early Industrial England, 1750–1850 (1986).
ed., British Trade Unionism, 1750–1850: The Formative Years (1988).
Sambrook, J., William Cobbett (1973).
Shelton, W. J., English Hunger and Industrial Disturbances (1973).
Sigsworth, E. M., Black Dyke Mills (Liverpool, 1958).
Singer, C., A History of Technology (Oxford, 1957).
Smelser, N. J., Social Change in the Industrial Revolution (1959).
Stevenson, J., Popular Disturbances in England, 1700–1870 (1979).
Stevenson, J., and Quinault, R., eds., Popular Protest and Public Order (1974).
Sykes, D. F. E., The History of Huddersfield (Huddersfield, 1898).
Sykes, D. F. E., and Waller, G. H., Ben o'Bills, the Luddite (Huddersfield, ?1898).
Tann, J., Gloucestershire Woollen Mills (Newton Abbot, 1967).
The Development of the Factory (1970).
Taylor, A. J., The Standard of Living in Britain in the Industrial Revolution (1975).
Tholfsen, T. R., Working Class Radicalism in Mid-Victorian England (1976).
Thomis, M. I., The Luddites: Machine Breaking in Regency England (Newton Abbot, 1970).
The Town Labourer and the Industrial Revolution (1974).
Thompson, E. P., The Making of the English Working Class (1963; 1968 edn).
Thomson, J. K. J., Clermont-de-Lodeve, 1633–1789: Fluctuations in the Prosperity of a Languedocian Cloth-Making Town (Cambridge, 1982).
Tufnell, E. C., Character, Object and Effects of Trades' Unions (1834; repr. Manchester, 1933).
Turner, H. A., Trade Union Growth, Structure and Policy: A Comparative Study of the Cotton Unions (1962).
Ure, A., The Philosophy of Manufactures (1835; 1861 edn).
Victoria County Histories:
Gloucestershire, Vol. II (1907).
Somerset, Vol. II (1911).
Wiltshire: Vol. IV (Oxford, 1959); Vol. V (Oxford, 1957); Vol. VII (Oxford, 1953); Vol. VIII (Oxford, 1965); Vol. X (Oxford, 1975).
Wadsworth, A. P., and Mann, J. de L., The Cotton Trade and Industrial Lancashire, 1600–1780 (Manchester, 1931).
Walker, G., The Costume of Yorkshire (1814).
Webb, S. and B., The History of Trade Unionism (1920).
Wells, R., Insurrection: The British Experience, 1795–1803 (1983).
White, R. J., Waterloo to Peterloo (1957; 1968 edn).
Wilberforce, R. I. and S., The Life of William Wilberforce, Vols. II and III (1838).
Wilkinson, J., History of the Parish of Broughton Gifford, Wilts. (Devizes, 1859).
Wilson, B., Our Village (1860).
Wilson, R. G., Gentlemen Merchants: The Merchant Community in Leeds, 1700–1830 (Manchester, 1971).
Wiltshire Notes and Queries (Devizes, 1905–16).

B. **Articles**

Anderson, M., 'Sociological history and the working class family: Smelser revisited', Social History, 3 (1976).

Baxter, J. L., and Donnelly, F. K., 'The revolutionary "underground" in the West Riding: myth or reality', *Past and Present*, 64 (1974).

Behagg, C., 'Custom, class and change: the trade societies of Birmingham', *Social History*, 4, 3 (1979).

Booth, A., 'Food riots in north-west England, 1790–1801', *Past and Present*, 77 (1977).

Briggs, A., 'The language of "class" in early nineteenth century England', in A. Briggs and J. Saville, eds., *Essays in Labour History* (1960; 1967 edn).

Calhoun, C. J., 'Community: toward a variable conceptualisation for comparative research', *Social History*, 5, 1 (1980).

Chapman, S. D., 'Industrial capitalism before the industrial revolution', in N. B. Harte and K. G. Ponting, eds., *Textile History and Economic History* (Manchester, 1973).

Charlesworth, A., and Randall, A. J., 'Morals, markets and the English crowd in 1766', *Past and Present*, 114 (1987).

Church, R., and Chapman, S. D., 'Gravenor Henson and the making of the English working class', in E. L. Jones and G. E. Mingay, eds., *Land, Labour and Population in the Industrial Revolution* (1967).

Clapham, J. H., 'Industrial organisation in the woollen and worsted industries of Yorkshire', *Economic Journal*, 16 (1906).

Coates, A. W., 'Contrary moralities, plebs, paternalists and political economists', in *Past and Present*, 54 (1972).

Coleman, D. C., 'Labour in the English economy of the seventeenth century', *Economic History Review*, 8 (1956).

'Protoindustrialisation: a concept too many?', *Economic History Review*, 36, 3 (1983).

Collins, H., 'The London Corresponding Society', in J. Saville, ed., *Democracy and the Labour Movement* (1954).

Crafts, N. F. R., 'British economic growth 1700–1831: a review of the evidence', *Economic History Review*, 36, 2 (1983).

Deane, P., 'The output of the British woollen industry in the eighteenth century', *Journal of Economic History*, 17 (1957).

Dickinson, M. J., 'Fulling in the West Riding woollen cloth industry, 1689–1770', *Textile History*, 10 (1979).

Dinwiddy, J., 'The "Black Lamp" in Yorkshire, 1801–1802', *Past and Present*, 64 (1974).

'Luddism and politics in the northern counties', *Social History*, 4, 1 (1979).

Donnelly, F. K., 'Ideology and early English working class history: Edward Thompson and his critics', *Social History*, 2 (1976).

Edwards, M. M., and Lloyd-Jones, R., 'N. J. Smelser and the cotton factory family: a reassessment', in N. B. Harte and K. G. Ponting, eds., *Textile History and Economic History* (Manchester, 1973).

Flinn, M. W., 'Trends in real wages, 1750–1850', *Economic History Review*, 27 (1974).

George, M. D., 'The combination acts', *Economic History Review*, 6 (1936).

Gilboy, E. W., 'New evidence on wage assessment in the eighteenth century', *English Historical Review*, 43 (1928).

'The cost of living and real wages in eighteenth century England', *Review of Economic Statistics*, 18 (1936).

Hay, D., 'Property, authority and the criminal law', in D. Hay, P. Linebaugh and E. P. Thompson, *Albion's Fatal Tree* (1975).

Heaton, H., 'Benjamin Gott and the industrial revolution in Yorkshire', *Economic History Review*, 3 (1931).

Hobsbawm, E. J., 'The standard of living during the industrial revolution: a discussion', *Economic History Review*, 16 (1963–4).

Houston, R., and Snell, K., 'Proto-industrialisation? Cottage industry, social change and industrial revolution', *Historical Journal*, 27, 2 (1984).

Hudson, P., 'Proto-industrialisation: the case of the West Riding wool textile industry in the eighteenth and early nineteenth centuries', *History Workshop Journal*, 12 (1981).

'From manor to mill: the West Riding in transition', in M. Berg, P. Hudson and M. Sonenscher, eds., *Manufacture in Town and Country before the Factory* (Cambridge, 1983).

Hutt, W. H., 'The factory system of the early nineteenth century', in F. A. Hayek, ed., *Capitalism and the Historians* (1954).

Jones, E. L., 'The agricultural origins of industry', *Past and Present*, 40 (1968).

McKendrick, N., 'Josiah Wedgwood and factory discipline', *Historical Journal*, 4, 2 (1961).

Mann, J. de L., 'A Wiltshire family of clothiers: George and Hester Wansey, 1683–1714', *Economic History Review*, 9 (1956).

'Clothiers and weavers in Wiltshire in the eighteenth century', in L. S. Pressnell, ed., *Studies in the Industrial Revolution, Presented to T. S. Ashton* (1960).

Manuel, F. E., 'The Luddite movement in France', in *Journal of Modern History*, 10 (1938).

Marling, W. H., 'The woollen industry of Gloucestershire: a retrospect', *T.B.G.A.S.*, 36 (1913).

Medick, H., 'The proto-industrial family economy: the structural function of household and family during the transition from peasant society to industrial capitalism', *Social History*, 3 (1976).

Mendels, F. F., 'Proto-industrialisation: the first phase of the industrialisation process', *Journal of Economic History*, 32, 1 (1972).

Minchinton, W. E., 'The beginnings of trade unionism in the Gloucestershire woollen industry', in *T.B.G.A.S.*, 70 (1951).

Moir, E. A., 'The Gloucestershire Association for Parliamentary Reform', *T.B.G.A.S.*, 75 (1956).

'The gentlemen clothiers', in H. P. R. Finberg, ed., *Gloucestershire Studies* (Leicester, 1957).

Murray Brown, C. C., 'The decline and fall of the cloth trade in Dursley', in *T.B.G.A.S.*, 11 (1886–7).

Nairn, T., 'The English working class', in *New Left Review*, 24 (1964).

Oliver, W. H., 'The Consolidated Trades' Union of 1834', *Economic History Review*, 17 (1964).

Pelham, R. A., 'The application of steam power to the Wiltshire textile industry in the early nineteenth century', *Wiltshire Archaeological and Natural History Magazine*, 54 (1951).

Phelps-Brown, E. H., and Hopkins, S. V., 'Seven centuries of the prices of consumables compared with builders' wage-rates', in E. M. Carus Wilson, ed., *Essays in Economic History*, Vol. II (1962).

Pollard, S., 'Factory discipline during the Industrial Revolution', *Economic History Review*, 16 (1963–4).

Ponting, K. G., 'The structure of the Wiltshire–Somerset border woollen industry, 1816–40', in N. B. Harte and K. G. Ponting, eds., *Textile History and Economic History* (Manchester, 1973).

Randall, A. J., 'The shearmen and the Wiltshire Outrages of 1802: trade unionism and industrial violence', *Social History*, 7, 3 (1982).

'The Gloucestershire food riots of 1766', *Midland History*, 10 (1985).

'The philosophy of Luddism', *Technology and Culture*, 27, 1 (1986).

'The industrial moral economy of the Gloucestershire weavers in the eighteenth century', in J. Rule, ed., *British Trade Unionism, 1750–1850: The Formative Years* (1988).

'Work, culture and resistance to machinery in the West of England woollen industry', in P. Hudson, ed., *Regions and Industries: A Perspective on the Industrial Revolution in Britain* (Cambridge, 1989).

Reddy, W. M., 'The textile trade and the language of the crowd at Rouen, 1752–1871', *Past and Present*, 74 (1977).

'The spinning jenny in France: popular complaints and elite misconceptions on the eve of the Revolution', in *The Consortium on Revolutionary Europe, 1750–1850: Proceedings, 1981* (Athens, Georgia, U.S.A., 1981).

Rogers, K. H., 'Trowbridge clothiers and their houses, 1660–1800', in N. B. Harte and K. G. Ponting, eds., *Textile History and Economic History* (Manchester, 1973).

Rose, R. B., 'Eighteenth century price riots and public policy in England', *International Review of Social History*, 6 (1961).

Samuel, R., 'The workshop of the world: steam power and hand technology in mid-Victorian Britain', *History Workshop Journal*, 3 (1977).

Schwarz, L. D., 'The standard of living in the long run: London, 1760–1860', *Economic History Review*, 38 (1985).

Stevenson, J., 'Food riots in England, 1792–1818', in J. Stevenson and R. Quinault, eds., *Popular Protest and Public Order* (1974).

Stone, L., 'Social mobility in England, 1500–1700', *Past and Present*, 33 (1966).

Tann, J., 'The employment of power in the West of England wool textile industry, 1790–1840', in N. B. Harte and K. G. Ponting, eds., *Textile History and Economic History* (Manchester, 1973).

Thirsk, J., 'Industries in the countryside', in F. J. Fisher, ed., *Essays in the Economic and Social History of Tudor and Stuart England* (Cambridge, 1961).

'The agricultural origins of industry', *Past and Present*, 40 (1968).

Thompson, E. P., 'Time, work-discipline and industrial capitalism', *Past and Present*, 38 (1967).

'The moral economy of the English crowd in the eighteenth century', *Past and Present*, 50 (1971).

'Patrician society, plebeian culture', *Journal of Social History*, 7 (1974).
'Eighteenth-century English society: class struggle without class?', *Social History*, 3, 2 (1978).
Thomson, J. K. J., 'Variations in industrial structure in pre-industrial Languedoc', in M. Berg, P. Hudson and M. Sonenscher, eds., *Manufacture in Town and Country before the Factory* (Cambridge, 1983).
Webb, S. and B., 'The assize of bread', *Economic Journal*, 14 (1904).
Wells, R., 'The revolt of the South West, 1800–1801: a study in English popular protest', *Social History*, 6 (1977).
Wiles, R. C., 'The theory of wages in later English mercantilism', *Economic History Review*, 21, 1 (1968).
Williams, D. E.,'Morals, markets and the English crowd in 1766', *Past and Present*, 104 (1984).
Wilson, R. G., 'The supremacy of the Yorkshire cloth industry in the eighteenth century', in N. B. Harte and K. G. Ponting, eds., *Textile History and Economic History* (Manchester, 1973).

C.   Unpublished theses and manuscripts

Betteridge, A., 'A Study of Halifax administrative records 1585–1762', Ph.D. thesis, University of Leeds, 1979.
Dickinson , M. J., 'The West Riding woollen and worsted industries 1689–1770: an analysis of probate inventories and insurance policies', Ph.D. thesis, University of Nottingham, 1974.
Exelby, H. R., 'The industrial revolution in the textile industries of Wiltshire', M.A. thesis, University of Bristol, 1928.
Gulvin, C., 'The Scottish woollen industry, 1603–1914', Ph.D. thesis, University of Edinburgh, 1969.
Hartwell, R. M., 'The Yorkshire woollen and worsted industry, 1800–1850', D.Phil. thesis, University of Oxford, 1955.
Hoyle, E. A. M., 'The demographic implications of industrialisation in the textile industry of the West Riding of Yorkshire 1750–1830', B.A. dissertation, University of Cambridge, 1980.
Hudson, P., 'The genesis of industrial capital in the West Riding wool textile industry c. 1770–1850', D.Phil. thesis, University of York, 1981.
Jenkins, D. T., 'The West Riding wool textile industry, 1770–1835: a study of fixed capital formation', D.Phil. thesis, University of York, 1970.
Little, B., 'Sarum fine woollens – a story of textiles', unpublished MS in the hands of K. G. Ponting, Pasold Research Fund, 1954.
Miles, M., 'Eminent attorneys: some aspects of West Riding attorneyship, c.1750–1800', Ph.D. thesis, University of Birmingham, 1983.
Morris, J., 'The West of England woollen industry, 1750–1840', M.Sc. (Economics) thesis, University of London, 1934.
Perry, R., 'The Gloucestershire woollen industry, 1690–1914', Ph.D. (Economics) thesis, University of London, 1947.

Randall, A. J., 'Labour and the industrial revolution in the West of England woollen industry', Ph.D. thesis, University of Birmingham, 1979.

Wild, M. T., 'An historical geography of the West Yorkshire textile industries to c.1850', Ph.D. thesis, University of Birmingham, 1972.

NAME AND PLACE INDEX

Name and place index

SUBJECT INDEX

agricultural labourers, 33, 61, 68, 90, 101
agriculture: dual economy, 19, 91; links
  with woollen industry, 24–5
apprenticeship, 32, 33, 35, 88, 115, 188,
  210, 211–12, 216, 262, 291; Gott strike
  and, 147–8; weavers and, 200–4, 205,
  207; social role of, 237–8, 242–4
arson, 155, 157, 158, 159, 160, 161, 162,
  163, 164, 174, 175, 176, 179; see also
  industrial violence
artisans, 33, 69, 88, 281

Brief Institution, the: organisation and
  influence, 131–45, 173; Clothiers'
  Community and, 216–17, 219;
  radicalism and, 246, 248, 269–71, 275,
  276

carding engine, 51, 54, 59, 62, 76–8, 79,
  84; see also scribbling engine
Chartism, 263, 278, 290
class/class consciousness, 10, 40, 245,
  Chapter 8 passim; see also craft
  consciousness
cloth dressers, 18, 21–2, 28–9, 32, 40, 50,
  56, 59, 62, 64, 65, 76, 88, 96, 105,
  Chapters 4, 5 passim, 187, 217, 221,
  225, 226, 227, 230, 236, 242, 251, 258,
  261, 265, 269–71, 272, 279, 289; trade,
  18, 21–2, 88, 110–15; industrial
  relations, 18, 21–2, 40, 76, 258,
  Chapters 4, 5 passim; social mobility,
  28–9, 114; machinery and, 50, 57, 59,
  62, 65, 119–22, attitudes to, Chapter 7
  passim, response to, 105, Chapters 4, 5
  passim; wages, 57, 114–15, 157;
  petitions, 96, 124–5, 187, 225–7, 230;
  trade union organisation, 115–19,
  138–48, 217; use of courts, 128–9, 221;
  radical politics and, 265, 269–72,
  279–80; see also Brief Institution, gig
  mill, shearing frame
cloth halls, 21, 27, 63, 79, 91, 92, 247,
  258, 278–9; role, 35–8; factory system
  and, 208, 209–12, 214, 215, 216, 217

cloth halls, trustees, 258; role, 36–7;
  divisions over factory, 210–11, 214,
  215, 216, 217, 218
cloth merchants in the West Riding: role,
  21–2, 30, 37–8, 39–40; Industrial
  Revolution and, 42, 208–11, 212–13,
  214, 215, 224, 252; cloth dressers and,
  112–13, 130, 145–6
clothiers, gentlemen, in the West of
  England, 15–18, 26–35, 42, 70–1, 81,
  88, 92, 94, 109, 112–13, 151, 183, 226,
  237, 252, 257, 261–2; role, 15–16, 18;
  Industrial Revolution and, 26–7, 42,
  224–5; industrial relations, 27, 28–9, 30,
  31, 124–5, 151, 191–3, 198, 199–200,
  201, 205–6; committees of, 73, 180, 204,
  206, 222, 224, 259; combinations of,
  145–6
clothiers, master, in the West Riding,
  287; role, 18–22, 26; social mobility
  and, 28, 29–30; independence, 35–40;
  machinery and, 41–2, 70, 76, 79, 91–4,
  98, 187, 188; threat of the factory,
  207–19, 221, 224, 225, 226, 236, 242,
  258, 260, 262; radicalism and, 271–2,
  278–9
Clothiers' Community, the, 72, 216–19,
  224, 246, 270, 271
Combination Acts (1799–1800), 144, 168,
  169, 206, 268
combinations, see trade unions
combing engines, 69
Commons, House of, 205, 225–6
community: character and economy, 6–7,
  8, 33, 35; resistance to change, 44, 48,
  49, 86–93, 100, 107, 110, 119, 124, 167,
  175, 188, 219, 230, 254, 256, 257, 280,
  285, 287–8, 292
cotton industry, 13, 41, 46, 72, 78, 208,
  233, 239, 240, 249, 285
courts, prosecutions of labour, 75, 127,
  165, 171–3, 195; see also Combination
  Acts

315

Lightning Source UK Ltd.
Milton Keynes UK
UKOW03f1554201013